STRUCTURED
READING

4 EDITION

STRUCTURED READING

Lynn Quitman Troyka

Queensborough Community College,
The City University of New York

PRENTICE HALL
Upper Saddle River, New Jersey 07458

Library of Congress Cataloging-in-Publication Data

TROYKA, LYNN QUITMAN
    Structured reading / Lynn Quitman Troyka. — 4th ed.
      p. cm.
    Includes indexes.
    ISBN 0-13-030842-0
    1. College readers. I. Title.
    PE1122. T76   1995
    808'.0427—dc20   94–19881
                          CIP

Senior Acquisitions Editor: *Maggie Barbieri*
Editorial/production supervision: *Margaret Antonini*
Cover design: *DeLuca Design*
Manufacturing buyer: *Robert Anderson*

Published by Prentice Hall
A Simon & Schuster Company
Upper Saddle River, New Jersey 07458

Printed in the United States of America

10 9 8 7 6 5 4

ISBN 0-13-030842-0

PRENTICE-HALL INTERNATIONAL (UK) LIMITED, *London*
PRENTICE-HALL OF AUSTRALIA PTY. LIMITED, *Sydney*
PRENTICE-HALL CANADA INC., *Toronto*
PRENTICE-HALL HISPANOAMERICANA, S.A., *Mexico*
PRENTICE-HALL OF INDIA PRIVATE LIMITED, *New Delhi*
PRENTICE-HALL OF JAPAN, INC., *Tokyo*
SIMON & SCHUSTER ASIA PTE. LTD., *Singapore*
EDITORA PRENTICE-HALL DO BRASIL, LTDA., *Rio de Janeiro*

In memory of
Joe Schenkel,
who never lost his joy;

and

in tribute to
David Troyka,
who daily makes me rejoice.

Contents

*New for this edition

Writing: Expressing Yourself   91

PART 2 Thinking: Getting Started   93

Writing: Expressing Yourself   **263**

PART 5   Thinking: Getting Started   265

*New for this edition

APPENDIX

Preface for the Teacher

The Fourth Edition of *Structured Reading* offers a systematic, research-based approach for helping students improve their reading comprehension skills. Research in reading improvement consistently confirms that grade-point averages are raised significantly when instruction emphasizes the developmental reading skills treated in depth in this book. As in earlier editions, my teaching approach in *Structured Reading* is grounded in psycholinguistic theory, based on the principle that readers improve not by reading *about* reading, but rather by guided, hands-on experience *with* reading. That thousands of teachers throughout the United States and Canada have stayed with this text bears witness to the rapid results possible when students are given frequent chances to read and, most important, to engage in the types of analytic and critical thinking that skilled readers use naturally when they make meaning from the printed page.

Here are the major features of *Structured Reading*, along with what has been revised for this Fourth Edition:

- The opening chapter, designed to acquaint students with the reading process, includes practical advice about reading speed, vocabulary building, context clues, the SQ3R study system, and all major skills of reading analytically and critically.

- Thirty reading selections, each followed by a carefully constructed sequence of exercises, form the core of the book. Twelve reading selections are new for this edition. The mix of reading selections resulted from a long, evaluative process that sought an instructive, stimulating balance among essays, literature from books, magazines, newspapers, and textbooks in disciplines other than English.

- Structured exercises after each reading selection have been the most widely acclaimed feature of *Structured Reading* because they foster analytic and critical reasoning. They offer intensive work in reading for *literal* meaning, for *inferential* meaning, and for *critical* thinking. This developmental approach is deliberate. My teaching of basic and freshman-level college classes (and before that, high school classes) for over two decades has convinced me that effective instruction must be structured for successful accumulation of increasingly more complex skills. New exercises appear for the twelve new reading selections in this edition.

  - The exercise progression is retained from previous editions: Vocabulary; Central Theme and Main Ideas; Major Details; Inferences; Critical Thinking: Fact or Opinion (where appropriate); Critical Reading: The Writer's Craft; and Informed Opinion.

■ Answer options demand close reading and analysis. Students must marshal higher-order reasoning skills to think through the challenge of "distractors." Teachers can encourage students to build powers of concentration, persistence, and focused deliberation by urging students not only to identify correct answers but also to analyze and articulate why other choices are incorrect.

■ Clue reduction is used. Students get more guidance in finding answers early in the text, while clues are reduced later in the text—where appropriate—to help students make more independent responses.

■ Question types vary to maintain student interest and to develop student flexibility in understanding the various mental processes underlying each skill.

● Immediately following each reading selection are complete dictionary entries for the more difficult words in the selection. This unique, popular feature provides students with hands-on experience with all aspects of dictionary entries. This Fourth Edition of *Structured Reading* contains over 320 complete dictionary entries from *Webster's New World Dictionary of American English,* Third College Edition, published by Simon & Schuster.

● An appendix, "Guide to Dictionary Use," offers concise information written in plain English about how to retrieve information from dictionary entries.

● The reading selections and their exercises are divided into five parts of increasing difficulty, with shorter-to-longer selections within each part. The explanatory statements that open the "Thinking: Getting Started" sections help students become conscious of the cumulative demands on their reading comprehension and reasoning skills as they move through this text.

● Visuals, a major feature at the start of each of the five parts of *Structured Reading,* seek to stimulate students to "survey" the reading selections. The cartoons, posters, photos and ads were chosen to arouse student interest while stimulating their prediction skills.

● Ideas for writing paragraphs and essays in response to the reading selections conclude each of the five parts of the text. These optional writing prompts encourage students to express themselves and, additionally, provide a resource to teachers who wish to integrate reading and writing. ("Critical Reading: The Writer's Craft" questions in the exercise sequence have a similar purpose.)

The *Instructor's Manual* includes a chapter on instructional strategies, an analysis of *Structured Reading* as it correlates to four statewide college competency reading tests, overhead transparency masters based on material in the text, and additional vocabulary exercises for each chapter and an answer key.

ACKNOWLEDGMENTS

In working on *Structured Reading,* I am grateful especially to Professor Betty Semptner, Oscar Rose State College, for composing excellent exercises and related materials for the twelve new readings in the Fourth Edition. Her humane, wise understanding of students—along with her keen knowledge of how reading is learned—greatly enrich the pages of this book. I also heartily thank Professor Emily Gordon, Hofstra University and Queensborough Community College of The City University of New York, for helping me select the twelve new readings in the Fourth Edition—and for her indispensable work on the previous edition. I appreciate, too, the very fine additions to "Writing: Expressing Yourself" authored by Joseph W. Thweatt, Professor of English, State Technical Institute, Memphis, for the Fourth Edition. Many of Gail Benchener's noteworthy contributions to the previous edition, including the *Instructor's Manual,* have been retained.

I wish to thank the following reviewers for their helpful suggestions: Beverley J. Young, Oxnard College; Karen Houck, Bellevue Community College; Lynna Geis, Rose State College; Joseph W. Thweatt, State Technical Institute; Donna Wood, State Technical Institute; William Bean, Daytona Beach Community College; Joyce Weinsheimer, University of Minnesota; and Bertilda Garnica Henderson, Broward Community College, South Campus.

At Prentice Hall/Simon & Schuster, numerous people facilitated this book's completion. Victoria Nelson, Development Editor, lent her special brand of clarity to the evolving manuscript. Margaret Antonini, Assistant Managing Editor, steered the project with the kind of patience, energy, and solid good judgment that authors only dare imagine. A succession of talented editors oversaw the Fourth Edition: Carol Wada, formerly with Prentice Hall; Kara Hado, Assistant Editor; and Maggie Barbieri, the present Senior Acquisitions Editor. Joan Polk, Editorial Assistant, consistently helped answer the daily queries we brought her. As always, Phil Miller, President of Humanities and Social Science, and Gina Sluss, Executive Marketing Manager, lent their valuable counsel and good cheer. Tony English, new Editor-in-Chief for English, pitched in gracefully in the crucial final days.

Most of all, as in earlier editions, I thank David Troyka, my husband, for being a rigorous but gentle critic and a treasured best friend.

Lynn Quitman Troyka
New York City, 1994

STRUCTURED
READING

How to Structure Your Reading

Am I a good reader? If you have asked yourself that question and have decided that you need to improve your reading skills, this book is for you. *Structured Reading* is designed for the student who wants to learn better reading skills through guided reading and skill building. You will be able to improve your reading ability by working with material you often encounter in newspapers, magazines, books, and textbooks.

The introductory chapter which you are now reading has two purposes: first, to explain the overall plan of *Structured Reading;* and second, to give you practical advice about how to read skillfully, using *Structured Reading* for practice.

THE OVERALL PLAN OF THIS BOOK

Structured Reading is divided into five parts. Each part is organized the same way, but the parts are of increasing difficulty so that you can strengthen and expand your reading skills as you go along.

Each part starts with **visuals** such as cartoons, posters, and advertisements to get your thinking started on the subjects you will be encountering as you read. In each part there are five to seven chapters. Each chapter starts with a **reading selection** on a subject of popular interest or special importance. The selections go from shorter to longer within each part of the book, and each successive part contains selections of progressively more complex ideas and sophisticated vocabulary.

Following each reading selection are complete, up-to-date **dictionary entries** for the more difficult words in the selection. These entries are reproduced directly from *Webster's New World Dictionary of American English,* Third College Edition. As a result, you will not have to go to a separate dictionary to look up difficult words while you are reading. You will, however, get valuable experience using top-quality dictionary entries to understand and learn new words. To help you start the habit of using the dictionary as an aid to learning and to help you become familiar with using dictionary entries, *Structured Reading* includes, starting on page 357, a "Guide to Dictionary Use" and a sample dictionary page with an explanatory key. Immediately following the dictionary entries in each chapter is a **vocabulary exercise** that gives you a chance to use the words and practice your knowledge.

Each chapter also contains **structured exercises** based on the reading selection. These exercises focus on key reading skills: finding the central theme and main ideas, locating major details, extracting inferences, separating fact from opinion, recognizing features of the writer's craft, and, on

1

a more subjective level, developing informed opinions. These exercises are a major feature of *Structured Reading*. Working with them will give you repeated, guided practice in developing your reading skills so that you can read successfully on your own. All the exercises are designed to help you learn as you practice. They have been created purposely to engage you in the process of thinking through your reasoning. Therefore, using the exercises merely to catch yourself in a mistake would be a waste of an important resource in this book. **You will learn as much from exploring why you have misunderstood something as you will learn from being able to find the right answer.**

If you wish to compute your skills score and your reading rate for each chapter, you can use the "How Did You Do?" score box at the end of each chapter. The total points for each chapter add up to 100. As a result, the value given to each type of question varies slightly from chapter to chapter depending on the number of questions asked. These variations in value are purely mechanical; your goal is to try to get as high a score as possible, learning from your incorrect answers as well as your correct ones. Progress charts at the back of the book give you the chance to compute and graph your work.

Topics for writing conclude each of the five parts of *Structured Reading*, so that you can have the opportunity to express yourself in writing on subjects you encounter in the reading selections.

Now that you have read about the overall plan of *Structured Reading*, take some time to survey the book on your own. Look through the table of contents to see how the book is organized. Flip through the book slowly, exploring its structure, stopping at material that catches your eye. As you become familiar with the book's structure, you will understand better how *Structured Reading* is designed and how you can make it work for you.

HOW TO READ SKILLFULLY

Reading is not just looking at words. Reading is receiving and sorting out information from the words. How can you read skillfully? The first step is to understand the process of reading. The next step is to practice basic reading skills over and over again until they become automatic. The final step is to stay in shape by reading frequently. This chapter will introduce you to the process of reading and will tell you how to use *Structured Reading* to practice your reading skills.

Reading Speed

Your reading speed is influenced by many factors, including your skill as a reader and the difficulty of the material you are reading. Here is an explanation of key factors that affect reading speed.

- *Vocabulary.* Researchers in reading speed and comprehension have found a strong relationship between size of vocabulary and ability to comprehend what is read. Because words form ideas, a weak vocabulary can limit your ability to think about ideas, can hold back your speed, and can negatively affect your comprehension. A discussion about vocabulary later in this chapter gives specific suggestions for improving your ability to learn and remember new words. Also vocabulary exercises in this textbook will help you practice your vocabulary skills.

- *Background Knowledge of the Subject.* What you know about a subject before you meet it in print influences the way you approach reading about the topic. Skilled readers read quickly through information that confirms what they know. Skilled readers slow down to focus on new concepts. They read with flexibility, speeding up and slowing down as the material demands. You will find that *Structured Reading* offers readings on a variety of subjects. When you evaluate your reading rates and exercise scores for the readings, take into consideration how much you already know about the subject. You will probably find that on those subjects you know something about, your comprehension and speed scores are higher. Reading widely on many subjects, combined with your ongoing life experience, will help you improve your reading skills.

- *Purpose.* Whenever you approach a reading selection, you will want to have a clear idea about your purpose for reading it. Knowing your purpose will help you determine the best way to handle the material, and it will help you decide how much comprehension you need. Here are the major purposes for reading.

Casual Reading	Read to relax, to be amused. Remembering details is not crucial here.
Skimming	Read to find specific information such as facts, dates, names, or a few details.
General	Read to understand and remember general concepts and main ideas.
Study	Read to understand thoroughly and remember exactly. Often you may need to read the material more than once. Also, you may want to take notes as you read.

- *Difficulty of the material.* Your reading speed has to depend on what you are reading. Skilled readers know ahead of time what pace to set. The best way to determine the difficulty of new material is to *preview* or *preread* portions of it. For an essay or article, read the opening and closing paragraphs, where main ideas are often revealed, and then read the first lines of some of the paragraphs. For a text chapter, read the overview or first page, many of the subtitles, and the summary if

3

the author gives one. Preview the vocabulary before reading. Check the dictionary for the definitions of key difficult words. The difference between reading with previewing and without previewing is like the difference between exploring a room with all the lights on and doing so with only a flashlight. By previewing, you illuminate the contents that you will encounter; you may not note all the details, but you will likely know where most of the difficult spots occur. If you begin to read without previewing, you are enlightened only line by line, not knowing when the author sums up main points, presents important details, or uses challenging words that might cause you to stumble.

When judging your reading rate in *Structured Reading*, do not consider the time factor only. Consider the complexity of the materials, your prior knowledge of the subject matter, and your vocabulary level. Your reading rate may decrease on longer, more difficult material, or on a day when you are not up to par. Adjust your expectations accordingly, and look for an *overall* increase in your rate instead of focusing on individual reading scores.

- *The way you read.* Skilled readers look for ideas when they read, relating one to another. These readers profit from the mind's tendency to think in concepts, pulling ideas into a meaningful whole for good comprehension. Weak readers, on the other hand, read word by word, concentrating on each word as they try to piece together ideas from the reading. Such difficulty often comes from lack of confidence while reading, from vocabulary too difficult for the reader, and from poor concentration. It can often result in *regression* (the unnecessary rereading of material) and *subvocalization* (habitually repeating all the words in your head).

Breaking old habits and developing new approaches to reading take time and practice. You can apply the following three techniques to the reading selections in this text. These techniques will help you begin to establish new habits.

1. Eliminate "white space." Approximately one-third of a page of print is "margin white." Skilled readers adjust their focus on the print by indenting when they read so their field of vision does not take in the surrounding white space. Following are the first two paragraphs from the first reading in this textbook, "A Real Loss" by Fern Kupfer. Notice that lines have been drawn about five letter spaces in from each margin. Focus your eyes on these vertical lines, and let your "peripheral (surrounding) vision" take in the rest. Do not let your eyes drift over to read the material to the left and right of the vertical lines.

(1) I was sitting in back of a little girl flying as an unaccompanied minor, put on the plane by a mother who placed a Care Bear in her arms and told her to remind Daddy to call when she got to California. The girl adjusted her seat belt and sniffed back a tear, bravely setting her jaw.

> (2) As we prepared for takeoff, the man next to the girl asked her the name of her bear and nodded in approval, saying Furry was a good name for a bear. When the little girl told him she was 6 years old, the man replied that he had a daughter who was 6 years old. His daughter was missing the same teeth, in fact. He asked how much money the tooth fairy was giving out in New York these days.

To make practical use of this technique, take a minute before you read a few of the reading selections in this textbook and pencil in lines about one-half inch on each side of the print on every page. When you read, try to use these lines as boundaries. Soon you will find you have adjusted the way you approach print by avoiding the white space. Indenting saves time, and can therefore increase your speed.

2. Read by clustering ideas. Word-by-word / readers / focus / on / every / word / and / often / lose / their / train / of / thought. Efficient readers, / on the other hand, / group words / while reading / into meaningful clusters. / Because the mind / thinks in ideas, / comprehension / is usually better. / When learning this technique, you might often need to exaggerate for your eyes what you want your mind to do. To develop a new awareness about the way you approach print with this technique, take a minute before each reading and draw slash marks to separate groups of words in the first paragraphs of the selection. As you read, focus your eyes in the middle of the phrase, and try to take in every word in one glance. Then read through the paragraph and the rest of the essay with the awareness of word clusters.

3. Pace yourself through the print. One of the challenges in improving your reading speed is to find the rate that is most efficient for you. Untrained readers often try to increase their reading speed by racing through the print; then they lose the stamina necessary for concentration on long passages. Others plod along at a slow speed, trying not to miss a point, so they lose interest and drift away. Like successful long-distance runners who set a pace that allows them to endure a long race, skilled readers develop the fluid rhythm and pace appropriate to each reading task.

   One way to practice pacing while reading is to use your hand as a pacer. Your whole hand, instead of a pencil or finger, helps you focus on ideas, rather than pointing out individual words. Using either hand, begin by indenting as previously discussed, then move line by line under the print. Focus on idea clusters as you read. Speed up on familiar material, and slow down on material that is particularly difficult for you. Do not regress; that is, do not go back and reread. If you habitually regress when you read, using your hand as a pacer will help you become aware of the habit. Keep pushing on, and do not reread a paragraph until you have come to the end of the essay. Then go back and reread what you missed. You will need to practice to pace efficiently, but the key to the success of this technique is to exaggerate for the eye what you want the mind to do.

These three mechanics for developing reading speed can provide you with tools to break unhelpful habits. Use them only as transition techniques to move you into being a skilled, efficient reader.

Vocabulary

Success in college, and in certain jobs, depends heavily on knowledge of words. One of the best ways to learn new, advanced words is to discover them in your reading. As you find words you do not know—in your preview or as you read—underline, circle, or highlight them with a marking pen. When you have finished a section of your reading, go back to the words you have marked off and try to make predictions about what they mean.

An excellent way to predict a word's meaning is to think about the word in relation to nearby words. This method calls for using *context*, or the place of one element in relation to its surrounding elements. In developing your vocabulary, try to get clues from the context of surrounding material. Context clues usually occur in one of four categories.

- *A repeat context clue.* Repetition helps you figure out the meaning of a word. Writers often repeat ideas, usually in a modified form or in synonyms. Here is an example of a word defined, in easier words, by words near it in Selection 16 of this textbook "Model Minority." Use your awareness of context clues to predict the meaning of the first word in italics, based on the other words in italics.

    Since Asian cultures dictate *stoicism*, she explained, students in many cases *do not openly fight back* against harassment *or complain* about academic pressures. But though they *tend to keep their pain hidden* …

    Stoicism can be defined by the repeated descriptions of its meaning. As the dictionary entry for *stoicism* and *stoical* shows, *stoicism* has to do with "showing indifference to joy, grief, pleasure, or pain" and "calm and unflinching under suffering, bad fortunes, etc."

- *A contrast context clue.* Contrast helps you estimate the meaning of a word. Here is an example of a word defined by what it is compared with in Selection 3 of this textbook, "Tyranny of Weakness." Use your awareness of context clues to predict the meaning of the word in italics.

    She expected me to take her shopping, cook for her, stay at her house, drive her everywhere, listen to her endless complaints. I became so exhausted that it began to dawn on me that she wasn't weak and helpless, she was a *tyrant*!

Tyrant stands in contrast to *weak and helpless*. *Tyrant* points, therefore, to the concept of power and strength. As the dictionary entry for *tyrant* (in the Vocabulary List for Selection 3) shows, a *tyrant* is "an absolute ruler," and "a cruel, oppressive ruler," which stands in strong contrast to *weak and helpless*.

- *An example context clue.* Examples often help readers predict the meaning of a difficult word. Writers use examples frequently to help readers understand the specifics of what is being discussed. Here is an example of a word you can understand from the examples near it in Selection 15 of this textbook, "Escaping the Daily Grind for Life as a House Father." Use your awareness of context clues to determine the meaning of the term in italics.

  I sensed that staying home would be *therapeutic*. The chronic competitiveness and aggressiveness that had served me well as a daily journalist would subside. Something better would emerge, something less obnoxious. My ulcer would heal. (paragraph 11)

As the dictionary entry (in the Vocabulary List for Selection 15) shows, *therapeutic* means "serving to cure or heal" and "serving to preserve health." An example of being cured is a healed ulcer; an example of preserving health is becoming "less obnoxious" by reducing competitiveness and aggressiveness.

- *A definition context clue.* Among the most common context clues is definition. This occurs when an author defines a word immediately before or after it appears. The definition usually is not stated in terms of "The definition of x is x^1." Rather, the definition is embedded in the material. Here is an example of a word defined in context in Selection 27 of this textbook, "The Heart Beat." Use your awareness of context clues to predict the meaning of the word in italics.

  Coronary occlusion often results from a disease called *atherosclerosis* in which fatty substances containing large amounts of cholesterol are deposited in the walls of arteries. (paragraph 13)

Atherosclerosis is defined in the sentence itself. If you reword the sentence slightly, you can get a definition of the word: "Atherosclerosis is a disease in which fatty substances containing large amounts of cholesterol are deposited in the walls of the arteries."

    Occlusion is another difficult word appearing in the example sentence above. Here the clue is not so obvious; you have to infer the meaning from the information given about what causes it. Notice that *occlusion* occurs when fatty substances are deposited in the walls of arteries. If you remember from basic biology study that arteries need to be clear to carry blood freely, you might conclude that any fatty substance deposited in them would *block* the movement of the blood. Occlusion, in fact, means a closure or blockage of a passage.

Sometimes examining the context is not enough. Knowing word parts—prefixes, roots, and suffixes—can provide you with further clues to the meaning. About 60 percent of the English language contains Greek and Latin word parts. A knowledge of even a few of them can help you predict the meaning of unfamiliar words when they appear in context. If you knew that the prefix *oc* was a form of the Latin *ob* meaning "to or toward," *clu* was a form of *clud* or *claus* meaning "to close," and *sion* was the suffix or ending of word meaning "the quality or condition of," you might have examined the word *occlusion* as shown below.

occlusion

oc = to, towards   *clu* = to close   *sion* = the quality or condition of

Rewording the definition by beginning with the suffix, your definition of *occlusion* would be, "the quality or condition of being towards closure." Examine the context again, and you have a complete definition of this word.

How can you train yourself to remember new words? Merely looking at them and their definitions once will not help. Most forgetting takes place immediately after learning. You need, therefore, a personal method of vocabulary study that works for you. Here is a good method to try.

Choose   Choose ten words or so each week that you have found in your reading. Each word will need careful, repeated study, so do not try to master many more than ten at a time.

Display   Write each word in large letters on one side of a 3 × 5 index card. Using cards is better than learning words from a list, because you can focus on one word at a time. Your word collection is also easily portable for quick study as flash cards at various times of the day.

Below the word in small letters, tell where you found the word so that your mind will have a reference point for easy memory. Also, copy the *context* in which the word appears, the exact sentence as you found it in your reading. This gives you a model for how the word is used.

On the other side of the card, after you check the dictionary write a definition of the word in your own words. Focus on how it appears in context. If a word contains word parts, make a note of them as well.

Here is a sample card using the word *occlusion* discussed previously:

word : occlusion

source : Structured Reading, "The Heart
Beat," page 295

context : "Coronary occlusion often results
from a disease called atherosclerosis
in which fatty substances containing
large amounts of cholesterol are
deposited in the walls of the
arteries."

Side 1

definition : a blockage or closure of
an artery

Side 2

Drill	Stack your 3 x 5 cards so that you see only the sides containing the words themselves. Recall the definition of each word. Then reverse the procedure: look at the sides of the cards with the definitions, and recall the words. Practice this drill until you remember the words more and more successfully. Don't stop there, though; go on to apply your knowledge.
Apply	Work with the words. If possible, go back to the source in which you first found the new word. Observe how the word operates in context. Try to find the word in other reading material. Also, use the word when you write or talk. When you practice your learning by applying it to real situations, you will remember the material more successfully.
Teach	Teach what you have learned to someone else. Experts who have studied how people learn best always advise learners to teach. Talk with friends and family about the words you are studying. Even better, make up exercises (and their answers) like the ones in this book. Ask friends to do them. Then be ready to correct the answers and teach your "students" what they did not understand.

You can modify this method for vocabulary study in any way that works for you. For example, on each 3 x 5 card you might want to jot down an original sentence using the word. Creating your own sentence can help you remember the word, because you are creating a sentence that is meaningful to you. Also, when you drill yourself with your 3 x 5 cards, you might want to team up with a class member or a friend so that you can quiz each other. No matter what method you use for vocabulary study, make sure that it is structured. People who want to learn new words need an organized approach. You will be richly rewarded if you learn new vocabulary words, because they are basic to skillful reading.

In *Structured Reading* actual dictionary entries for many of the difficult words in the reading selections are given to you directly from *Webster's New World Dictionary of American English,* Third College Edition. Use this resource fully. Having the entries to work with gives you a good chance to get hands-on experience with a first-class dictionary, without having to look up each word. In *Structured Reading,* the "Guide to Dictionary Use" (pp. 357–365), which includes a sample page of the dictionary, will help you understand the individual elements of dictionary entries. Of course, you will likely not find a dictionary entry for every word you do not know in the reading selections. When you need to, use your complete copy of the dictionary.

Structured Reading offers you many different types of vocabulary exercises. You will find exercises that use context clues, fill-ins, multiple choices, and crossword puzzles. This variety is provided to keep your interest in vocabulary study high. An excellent way to master new words is to make up exercises of your own, imitating the kinds of exercises you find in this text. Because of the variety of vocabulary exercises, you will need to read the directions carefully. This feature gives you a chance to practice correctly following directions. Although completing vocabulary exercises can help you practice your knowledge of the word, only a structured, personal method of vocabulary study will lead you to increase your vocabulary.

Predicting

The process of *predicting* makes you an active reader. In reading, predicting means making appropriate guesses about what will come next from the information at hand. For example, when people see the words *Once upon a,* they automatically complete the phrase with the word *time.* They do this with only a fleeting glance at the word *time.* Thus, effective predicting skills can help you with your reading speed as well as with comprehension.

Predictions start when a reader sees the title of a selection. For example, in Selection 29 of this textbook the title "Magnetism" clues the reader to guess that perhaps the material will be about either (1) the scientific principle of magnetism or (2) the romantic principle of attraction between two people. Then, as soon as the reader looks beyond the title to get a general impression about what is coming next, one of these two predictions is confirmed and one is dropped. The correct prediction is next used to help the reader anticipate further as the material moves along. (Try this by turning to Selection 29 in this book.) The process of predicting is a continuous, largely automatic part of reading.

You can improve your reading skills by becoming conscious of your process of predicting and by practicing as you read. Before you start reading, *preview* or *preread* your material as discussed in the earlier section on reading speed. Then, while you are reading, pause occasionally to predict what you think will be coming next. As you move along, revise your predictions according to what you encounter. No one, not even the most skilled reader, always predicts accurately. When a prediction turns out to be wrong, skilled readers quickly revise it and move right along without worrying. The more you practice predicting, the easier and more useful it will become for you. The important idea here is that making predictions keeps your mind actively engaged in the reading process.

In *Structured Reading* the sections called "Thinking: Getting Started" which introduce each of the five parts of this textbook are designed to help you get your predicting process started as you begin to think about the subject matter in the reading selections in each part. Use the cartoons, advertisements, and posters—and the thought-provoking questions that tie each visual into a reading selection—to get ready for your reading.

The process of predicting is one of the keys to the success of the next technique explained here, SQ3R. Predicting keeps you actively involved in reading and helps you comprehend important information.

SQ3R

SQ3R stands for the words *Survey, Question, Read, Recite,* and *Review.* It is a study-reading formula to help you maximize your comprehension while minimizing your reading time. Learning how to apply SQ3R takes time, but it is worth the effort because the more you use SQ3R, the more automatic it will become. If you conscientiously apply this five-step process to the readings in this textbook, you will notice improvement in your concentration, comprehension, and reading rate. You can also apply this technique effectively to readings in your other courses. Here is a description of the SQ3R technique.

Survey	Get an overview before you start reading thoroughly. Preview by examining the title, the first and last paragraphs where general summaries are likely to appear, and subheadings. If there are visuals such as illustrations or charts, look over these as well. If there are no visuals or subheadings, as in an essay or article, read the first lines of some of the longer paragraphs to see where the author is headed. Note any difficult words for a vocabulary preview. Make predictions about the main point or thesis. Decide the best rate so you can pace yourself accordingly.

Question Turn the title and any subheadings into questions. Any new concept or idea you come across will be reinforced later when you read if you form a question about it now. Take some of the first lines of the paragraphs and form a question. If you are unsure how to begin to question, choose from the "five W's and one H" list: *who, what, when, where, why,* and *how.* Asking questions makes the reading process active rather than passive. Make predictions as you form questions about the author's main points.

Read Read thoroughly. Keep in mind your predictions and modify them if necessary. Pay close attention to key paragraphs. Move rapidly over less important material, and try not to regress. Quickly mark areas you need to return to later for careful study. If you did a good Survey and Question, you should be a good judge of the important paragraphs and should know how to adjust your pace to meet the demands of the reading. Mark any new vocabulary words you cannot determine from context. If you find you are constantly stumbling over new words, you may need to stop and do a thorough vocabulary preview before you begin again.

Recite After you have finished reading the essay or a section (about five pages) of a long chapter, tell yourself from memory the important points. Many students make the mistake of not following up on their comprehension of the material. Remember that most forgetting takes place immediately after learning. If you do not develop the habit of repeating key information, your recall will quickly fade. As you recite, note any gaps in what you remember. Then return to the Read step described above and reread the material you need to remember. When the SQ3R method is new to you, you might find that the Review step is sometimes frustrating because you do not easily recall what you have read. Do not be discouraged. Go back and reread patiently. The more you use the SQ3R method, the more your mind will develop the habit of good memory. Using the Survey step and the Question step described above are important parts of developing a good memory as you read. You can also use memory devices such as associating a new idea to one you know already or working out codes (such as "SQ3R") to give you a short way of helping your memory retain information.

Review Look over all the material again. Do not reread, but see it as a whole by noting key spots such as the title, subheadings, and important paragraphs. Highlight key areas here with a see-through marking pen. Then summarize the material by making outline notes. As you review, think back to the predictions you made as you surveyed and questioned. Were your predictions correct? If not, where and why did you guess incorrectly? Assessing your predictions and learning from your misconceptions will help you make better predictions the next time you use SQ3R.

SQ3R GUIDED PRACTICE

Here is a model of how to use SQ3R with an essay such as those in *Structured Reading*. Each step of SQ3R is explained in relation to the selection, "The Urban Spirit Has Yielded to a Siege Mentality." This guided practice is intended as an in-depth illustration of how to apply SQ3R to the readings in this textbook, as well as to the reading you encounter in all your courses.

Survey: Preview the following essay by reading the title, first and last paragraphs, and first sentence of the major paragraphs. The areas to survey have been printed in bold type for you. Try to survey in one minute or less.

The Urban Spirit Has Yielded to a Siege Mentality

Ellen Goodman

(1) **He has three keys dangling from one end of his key chain. The top one, he explains, goes into the extra safety lock. The round one turns off the burglar alarm. The bottom one opens the door. When he was a kid, he tells me, the back door of the house was always unlocked. His own kids are taught never, never, to open the door to strangers.**

(2) **She is seated next to me on the airplane.** She looks over and says I should put my gold chain in my pocketbook when I get to New York. Haven't I heard about the kids ripping necklaces off women? I take it off.

(3) **She is traveling on business again.** At the registration desk the clerk tells her that they have a new escort service. Someone is available to accompany her every time she goes to her room. Once she would have refused; now she accepts.

(4) **They are not paranoid, these people.** Nor am I. We do not cower in distant suburbs afraid to come to the city for dinner. In fact we all live in cities, and have evolved over time a certain pride in urban survival.

(5) **And yet something has changed.** Maybe it was the 13-year-old son held up on the way home from school by 17-year-old boys. Maybe it was the fourth time the car window was broken and the third time the stereo was stolen. Maybe it was the purposeful murder of John

Lennon or the random murder of Dr. Michael Halberstam. Or maybe there are simply too many incidents too close to home to brush off anymore.

(6) **But our resilience has been worn down, and so we shake our heads when we read Chief Justice Warren Burger's words to the American Bar Association:** "What people want is that crime and criminals be brought under control so that we can be safe on the streets and in our homes and for our children to be safe in schools and at play. Today that safety is very, very fragile." If Burger was out of place delivering an 11-point program as if he were an attorney general, he nevertheless clarified something that we already know: The urban spirit is turning into a fortress mentality.

(7) **The same people who talked incessantly about making a profit from their real estate now talk incessantly about protecting their real estate.** Today they improve their homes with iron bars instead of bushes. They add locks instead of shutters.

(8) **There is an edge to life, sane and sad, of self-protection.** The man who put on his necklace as a sign of free expression in the '70s takes it off for safety in the '80s. The woman who bought silver in the '50s as a tribute to financial security hides it in the '80s as a tribute to insecurity. On the street, we may fantasize a plan of self-defense. In the elevator, in the ladies' room, in the subway, an image of danger may flit across our consciousness for just a moment. We may begin almost superstitiously to avoid some place that seems dangerous to us. I have not even mentioned gun permits and California self-protection courses in the use of tear gas.

(9) **"Are we not hostages within the borders of ourselves because of alarms and locks?"** asked Burger.

(10) Yes.

(11) **It isn't just the criminal offensive that affects our lives, it is our own growing defensive. When we learn to turn on the alarm, put the jewelry in the refrigerator, push down the buttons in the car, think twice about walking down a street, our lives are diminished.**

675 words

After you survey, write your prediction of the main point of the essay:

_____

_____

Preview the vocabulary by checking in the dictionary difficult words that seem key to the meaning. List the words:

_____

_____

_____

The title of this essay has some words that may be challenging for you. If you do not know the meaning of *urban, yielded, siege,* or *mentality,* look them up in the dictionary now. When you understand the key vocabulary in the title, you will have a major way of predicting the essay's main point. Now decide the pace at which you will read the essay.

Question: The goal here is to ask questions, not answer them. You have likely noted from your survey that this essay does not have any subheadings or visuals. Form questions beginning with the title. Then form questions about first lines of some of the paragraphs that either were puzzling to you or will need clarification when you finally read the essay. Generally, forming three to five questions before you read is a good guideline. This number gives you enough information to establish a questioning stance but not overwhelm your focus on the content. Many students find that when they ask questions prior to reading, the answers seem to "jump out" from the page when they read. That is because they are providing for their minds a focus in the search for information and are approaching the reading in an active rather than passive mode. Here are some questions based on the essay. Add two of your own.

1. Why do people who live in urban areas have a siege mentality? (from title)

2. What do the man with the three keys and the women on the airplane and in the hotel all have in common? (from first four paragraphs)

3. How is our defensiveness such a problem? (from last paragraph)

4. _____

   _____

5. _____

   _____

If you have difficulty asking questions, go back to the essay and turn some of the first sentences of some of the major paragraphs into questions. Think of the "five W's and one H" as words to begin your questions: *who, what, when, where, why,* and *how.* Evaluate your questions. Will the answers to them likely reveal some of the main points, at least as far as you can tell from your survey? If not, perhaps your questions are too specific and you need to think more generally about what the author seems to be revealing from the title and major paragraphs.

Read: The "S" and "Q" steps just discussed should have taken you less than five minutes. As you get better at the preparatory techniques, you will be able to accomplish them quickly. Now you are ready to read the essay thoroughly. As you read, you build on a "prior knowledge" of the material you gained from surveying and questioning, and your mind can concentrate on filling in details.

Move rapidly through the first five paragraphs since they are mainly anecdotes. Pace with your hand if you wish. Keep a pen in hand to make a small mark at any section of the passage that you want to review later. When you find the thesis, or main point of the article, mark it in the margin as well. Put a check next to any additional difficult words you discover, but keep moving and do not let your eyes regress. Do not waste time underlining.

Recite: Review from memory what you can remember from your reading. One good way to check your understanding informally is to return to the questions from the "Q" step and answer them in your own words from memory. Try answering the questions listed on the previous page.

1. _____

2. _____

3. _____

4. _____

5. _____

If you are not sure of all of the answers, use the Review step that comes next to reread portions that you need to clarify. In the future, you may not always want to write down your questions, but you should always try to think of the answers to any you have asked when you did the Question step.

Review: This last step of SQ3R will help you pull the reading together. It will help you remember the material. This is an especially critical step when you apply SQ3R to college textbook readings and other assignments when you must be able to recall the content. As you review, look over the essay again and reread difficult sections. Find answers you could not think of during the Recite step. Note where the thesis or main point of the essay was emphasized (see paragraphs 6, 8, and 11).

Highlight specific sentences with a pen for later recall (for example, the last sentence of paragraph 6 and the last sentence of paragraph 11). For more complete recall of the important information, consider translating what you know into working outline notes.

Outlining

Outlining can be an important part of the last step of SQ3R, Review. Outlining can force you to organize the material you have just read; it is a structuring process that helps your memory retain information. Outlining is not appropriate for all reading material or in all situations, but it helps when you need to master a sizable amount of material. One useful way to outline is to divide each sheet of paper in two, as follows: from the top to the bottom draw a straight line down the sheet, with about one-third of the paper's space to the left of the vertical line and about two-thirds of the space to the right. To the right of the vertical, write your outline. To the left of the line, write key words or phrases that signal what is outlined on the right side.

When you go back later to restudy the material, first move your eye down the left side of the paper, looking at the key words and phrases to check your recall. Then, to refresh your memory, slowly read the outline on the right side, thinking about the material as you read. Then, once again move your eye down the left side of the page to see how much you can recall without looking at the right side. Doing this repeatedly will help you train your memory.

Your outline form itself depends on the material you are reading, your purpose in reading it, and how much you want to recall. If you are reading for a class or a test, your outline should include all the important main points and their supporting details. If you are reading for general recall only, your outline requires less detail.

Although you will not always outline everything you read, you might want to practice the technique so it becomes an easy way for you to make notes when thorough recall is important. Apply this technique to Selection 12, "The Urban Spirit Has Yielded to a Siege Mentality," with the idea in mind that you can use your notes in a discussion on how contemporary life has changed, in a Political Science or Sociology class. The outline has been started for you on the opposite page.

When you complete filling in the outline, you might want to compare what you have with what others in your class have done. You may find that wordings vary among different students, but be sure to check that the key ideas are the same. Be certain that the main idea (on the line that starts "Self protection") reflects clearly what the author had in mind. Be certain, also, that you have included all the supporting examples used by the author. Whenever you are not absolutely sure that you have captured the author's points, go back and reread the material.

Key Words	Outline
People defensive	People who live in urban settings are defensive.

Examples:

1. _____

_____

2. _____

_____

3. _____

_____

4. _____

_____

5. _____

_____

Resilience down   Our resilience has been worn down.

Examples:

1. Justice Burger says that people want safe streets, homes, and schools but that safety is very fragile.

2. _____

_____

3. _____

_____

Self-protection necessary but sad   Self-protection _____

Examples:

1. In the 1970's, men wore necklaces as a sign of free expression but now have to take them off for safety.

2. _____

_____

3. _____

_____

Lives diminished   Our lives are diminished when we are so defensive.
The quality of our lives is less when we are so defensive.

On, Between, and Beyond the Lines

Reading closely—the first "R" of SQ3R—demands the most practice for solid development of reading skills. Intensive practice in reading closely is provided in the structured exercises that follow each reading selection in this book. To be a skillful close reader, you need to be able to read **on** the line, **between** the lines, and **beyond** the lines.

Reading **on** the line means understanding the stated meaning of the material. Here you look for the exact, literal meaning of what is written. In *Structured Reading* three kinds of exercises have been designed especially to help you develop your ability to read on the line: "Vocabulary," "Central Theme and Main Ideas," and "Major Details."

Reading **between** the lines means understanding what is clearly implied but not stated in the material. When reading **between** the lines, look for the author's underlying attitudes which are not stated but are implied by the author's choice of words and use of evidence. In *Structured Reading* the exercises on inferences and critical reading can help you develop your ability to read between the lines.

Reading **beyond** the lines means developing informed opinions about the subject. To do this, you use what has been stated and what has been implied to come to your own conclusions. The exercises on informed opinion give you the opportunity to think about your personal point of view on many subjects. Also, the sections called "Writing: Expressing Yourself," which come at the end of each of the five parts of this book, are designed to help you further explore your personal opinions and your learning.

Every chapter of this book includes practice in reading **on, between,** and **beyond** the lines. The sequence is always the same—Vocabulary, Central Theme and Main Ideas, Major Details, Inferences, Critical Reading, and Informed Opinion. It has been said that while learning in school, "if a person cannot make a mistake, that person cannot make anything." The exercises in *Structured Reading* were created in the hope that you will use them to investigate your thinking by learning from incorrect as well as correct answers. The rest of this introductory chapter will explain how to get the most from the exercises.

Central Theme and Main Ideas

What's it all about? Your answer to this question is the central theme or main idea. In *Structured Reading* the term "central theme" refers to what an entire reading selection is about, and "main idea" refers to what a paragraph or group of paragraphs is about. The words *central* and *main* are very much alike. They stand for what is important, the key, the core, the heart of the matter. The words *theme* and *idea* are also very much alike. They stand for the thought, the thesis, the topic, or the subject.

A successful statement of a central theme or main idea is short and to the point. To get down to the central theme or main idea, try imagining this scene: A good friend who has stopped by to see you for a minute on the way to class notices that you have just finished reading something about corruption of local officials that looks especially interesting. Your friend points to the reading material and asks, "What's it about?" Now, your friend does not have time to hear all the details, nor does your friend want to hear only a word or two like "corruption." The answer you give— a summary that is neither too detailed nor too short—is the central theme or main idea. For example, you might say, "An investigation has turned up evidence that three of our local officials have been taking kickbacks on government contracts."

One warning about a summary: Attempts to be brief often end up as distortions. Statements of central themes and main ideas, therefore, need to be developed fully enough so that they are accurate.

Central themes or main ideas can be stated or implied. If the main idea is stated, you will use the reading skill of reading **on** the lines to find where the main point appears. A stated main point must contain

- the topic or subject

- the point or major concept that the author is explaining about the topic.

Main ideas often appear at the beginning of paragraphs, especially in texts, articles, and essays, but this is not always the case. The writer often places the main point at the end of a paragraph to emphasize the point, or may even put it in the middle. The following is from an essay called "Doctors Close In on the Mechanisms Behind Headaches."* Examine its main ideas and note where they appear in the paragraphs. The main ideas are shown in boldface when they are stated directly.

> **It was a headache to make history.** On April 9, 1865, Ulysses S. Grant's Union Army was chasing Robert E. Lee's Confederates across Virginia. Grant invited Lee to surrender, but the Southerner demurred. The two armies settled down near Appomattox Court House for the night.
>
> It was not an easy night for Grant. "I was suffering very severely with a sick headache," he recorded in his journal, "and stopped at a farm house on the road some distance to the rear of the main body of the army. I spent the night in bathing my feet in hot water and mustard, and putting mustard plasters on my wrists and the back of my neck, hoping to be cured by morning."
>
> At dawn the next day, Palm Sunday, Grant felt no better— until a message arrived from Lee. The Confederate general had changed his mind overnight. "When the officer reached me, I was still suffering from the sick headache," Grant wrote, "but the instant I saw the contents of the note I was cured." **Pain and nausea gone, the Union general rode off to accept Lee's surrender and end the Civil War.**

*By Edward Kiesler, Jr. From *Smithsonian* Magazine, Dec. 1987, p. 175.

In the above group of paragraphs, the opening anecdote about Ulysses S. Grant begins with a stated main idea in the first sentence. The last sentence gives the main idea again, but more fleshed out.

In the paragraph below, taken from the same essay, note that the main idea appears in the middle of the paragraph. The main point mentions the past, "the old enemy," and present scientific efforts.

> What causes headaches? And what can be done to stop them? For centuries, humans have been tussling with these questions, concocting a long and colorful history cluttered with supernatural explanations and witch doctors' remedies. **Today, thanks to an international research effort, science is beginning to close in on the old enemy.** New technology allows doctors to actually peer inside the skull and watch a headache develop, leading to a more basic understanding, which in turn could lead to surer cures.

In the following example, from an essay titled "Phenomena,"* the main idea is not directly stated. This technique is often used when a writer wishes to engage the reader's interest. Examine the details to determine the main point.

> The Northern Hemisphere is going cold and dark as the planet whirls silently toward the winter solstice, when the sun touches its lowest point in our sky. For most of us in temperate zones, the cold is uncomfortable and inconvenient, a time of struggling into overcoats and scraping ice off the windshield. But for a passionate subset of the population, a dropping thermometer means rising spirits. These are the people who come out their front doors to be slapped by an icy wind and break into broad grins, exulting to themselves: "The pond is freezing!" At night they rummage through the cellar for skates and for wooden sticks with curved blades shaped like the forceps that obstetricians use in difficult deliveries.

Main ideas, as you see, can also be implied rather than directly stated. To determine the implied main ideas, you need to read **between** the lines. From the details, examples, and illustrations given by the author, you need to draw your own conclusion about the main point. In the previous example, the author is commenting on two attitudes about very cold weather: one sees the cold as inconvenient and the other as bringing about the prospect of great fun. You can infer from the details about rummaging for skates and sticks with blades that the second attitude is held by some amateur ice hockey players.

Structured Reading provides two types of practice in finding central themes and main ideas in reading selections. First, you may be asked to select from among four choices the correct statement of a central theme or main idea. Read the choices carefully, and be ready to justify why you chose what you did and why you rejected what you did. **Reasons for not choosing can be as important as reasons for choosing.**

*By John P. Wiley, Jr. From *Smithsonian* Magazine, Dec. 1987, p. 30.

Here is an example of a **Main Idea** question:

READING SAMPLE A

Among the Pennsylvania Dutch, married couples travel in covered horse-drawn buggies. Unmarried ones drive in open carts without a roof. You guessed it: so the entire community can see that no hanky-panky is going on. On top of which, Mama sees to it that instead of hooks-and-eyes, daughter's dress is fastened with straight pins—sharp ones—placed in strategic locations. It may be a coincidence, but it is rumored any bachelor worth his salt always wears three or more Band-Aids on his pinkies.*

MAIN IDEA
Choose the best answer.

_____ 1. The main idea of this paragraph is that among the Pennsylvania Dutch
   a. unmarried couples cannot travel alone together.
   b. couples usually have long engagements.
   c. bachelors usually get stuck with straight pins when they go out on dates.
   d. the romantic morals of an unmarried couple are watched over at all times.

*From "People Are the Attraction," by Bill and Sonia Freedman. © 1976, *The Denver Post*; reprinted with permission.

answer: d

Working this type of exercise provides an extra bonus. Multiple choice tests usually contain questions similar in form to these. As you do these exercises, you will become more familiar and comfortable with the multiple choice format you will be encountering in tests.

A second type of practice in finding the central themes and main ideas is open ended. In the second half of *Structured Reading* you are asked from time to time to state a central theme or main idea in your own words. By the time you encounter this type of exercise, you will have had considerable practice with multiple choice answers, and you will be ready to try wording good summaries on your own.

Major Details

Major details support the central theme and main idea of a reading selection. Major details put the meat on the bones of a bare skeleton. Major details are often examples, facts, statistics, reasons, clarifying definitions, or quotations.

Examine the following excerpt from an essay titled "The Art of Surgery."* Note how the details are necessary to explain why the doctor has to amputate the leg of his patient.

> I invited a young diabetic woman to the operating room to amputate her leg. She could not see the great shaggy black ulcer upon her foot and ankle that threatened to encroach upon the rest of her body, for she was blind as well. There upon her foot was a Mississippi Delta brimming with corruption, sending its raw tributaries down between her toes. Gone were all the little web spaces that when fresh and whole are such a delight to loving men. She could not see her wound, but she could feel it. There is no pain like that of the bloodless limb turned rotten and festering. There is neither unguent nor anodyne to kill such a pain yet leave intact the body.
>
> For over a year, I trimmed away the putrid flesh, cleansed, anointed, and dressed the foot, staving off, delaying. Three times each week, in her darkness, she sat upon my table, rocking back and forth, holding her extended leg by the thigh, gripping it as though it were a rocket that must be steadied lest it explode and scatter her toes about the room. And I would cut away a bit here, a bit there, of the swollen blue leather that was her tissue.

In paragraphs that have a topic sentence or an implied main idea, the major details further explain the key concept the author is attempting to communicate. Examine another paragraph from the same essay. Note that the details explain the first sentence: why the doctor and the patient finally gave up trying to save her leg.

> At last we gave up, she and I. We could no longer run ahead of the gangrene. We had not the legs for it. There must be an amputation in order that she might live—and I as well. It was to heal us both that I must take up knife and saw, cut it off. And when I could feel it drop from her body to the table, see the blessed space appear between her and that leg, I too would be well.

Some paragraphs do not have a topic sentence that explains the main point, but they have the purpose of presenting major details that support a main idea given earlier or later in the essay. Note that in the first paragraph following, from the same essay, the doctor discovers something special about his patient. The main point and reason he relates the anecdote is explained later in the next paragraph.

*Richard Selzer, *Notes on the Art of Surgery.* Copyright © 1976 by Richard Selzer. Reprinted by permission of Simon & Schuster, Inc.

Now it is the day of the operation. I stand by while the anesthetist administers the drugs, watch as the tense familiar body relaxes into narcosis. I turn then to uncover the leg. There, upon her kneecap, she has drawn, blindly, upside down for me to see, a face; just a circle with two ears, two eyes, a nose, and a smiling upturned mouth. Under it she has printed SMILE, DOCTOR. Minutes later I listen to the sound of the saw, until a little crack at the end tells me it is done.

So I have learned that man is not ugly, but that he is Beauty itself. There is no other his equal. Are we not all dying, none faster or more slowly than any other? I have become receptive to the possibilities of love (for it is love, this thing that happens in the operating room), and each day I wait, trembling in the busy air. Perhaps today it will come. Perhaps today I will find it, take part in it, this love that blooms in the stoniest desert.

To understand the relationship between central themes, main ideas, and major details, think of a painting of a landscape. Imagine that it has mountains in the background and that hills, trees, a meadow, and a brook are in front of the mountains. The scene of the landscape, a view of mountain scenery, is the central theme of the painting. The main ideas are separate sections: the mountains, the hills, the trees, the meadow, and the brook. The major details reveal if the mountains are high or low. They reveal if the hills are grassy or rocky. They reveal if the trees are rich with leaves or if the branches are bare. They reveal if the meadow is green or if it is brown and dried out. They reveal if the brook is bubbling or quiet and if it is sprinkled with rocks or is clear.

To add touches of interest or to entertain, many authors use some minor details in their writing. Being able to tell the difference between a major detail and a minor detail is an important reading skill. Minor details can be interesting but are not basic to the understanding of the material being read. To remember efficiently, a reader must sort out the major details from those that are minor. Judgments about what is major and what is minor can be made only in the context of a complete reading selection.

A person's age, for example, can be a major detail if the selection is discussing the person's tragic, early death. On the other hand, the age can be a minor detail if the selection is discussing the person's thoughts on the subject of the nation's economy. Making an outline can sometimes help you figure out what is major (because it must be written on the outline) and what is minor (because it can be skipped without losing the important points).

Structured Reading provides three types of practice to help you learn to recognize major details. In the first type, you are asked to decide if a listed detail is MAJOR or MINOR. As you make each decision, be ready to defend how important that detail is **in the context of the entire reading selection.**

Here is an example of a MAJOR/MINOR exercise for **Major Details:**

READING SAMPLE B

(1) In most places tourists go to, things are the attraction—cathedrals and museums and pyramids and the like. In Pennsylvania Dutch country, it is the people. The Mennonites and Amish and Dunkers who doggedly and picturesquely manage to live 17th-century lives in the 20th century.

(2) You've seen pictures of them: bearded men in black clothes, always hatted, and regardless of what *Esquire* says, holding their trousers up with suspenders. The women are no less severely clad, usually in black, but never without a white, frilled cap on their heads. They are stern-looking, perhaps even dour, but in five minutes flat you'll find out they are the friendliest, most sincere people you have ever met.*

MAJOR DETAILS
Decide whether each detail is MAJOR or MINOR.

_____ 1. The people live as if they were in the 17th century, not the 20th century.

_____ 2. The men, who always have beards, always wear hats and black clothes.

_____ 3. The women's white caps are frilled.

*From "People Are the Attraction," by Bill and Sonia Freedman. © 1976, *The Denver Post;* reprinted with permission.

answers: (1) MAJOR; (2) MAJOR; (3) MINOR

In the second type of practice with major details, you are asked to decide if a listed detail is TRUE, FALSE, or NOT DISCUSSED. The details listed in these exercises have been chosen with care to help you sharpen your reading skills. When you have to decide if a major detail is true or false, be sure to reread carefully to make sure that you have a clear concept of what the author wrote. Close reading helps you make sure that you have not jumped to the wrong conclusions because you have read the material too quickly. When you have to decide if something was not discussed, be sure to use the extra mental discipline that it takes *not* to add material on your own. Or, sometimes the mind assumes that something has been mentioned when it has not been. This type of exercise helps you make sure that you have not misread the material and that you have not accidentally added your own material to what was written. As you answer each question, be prepared to point to the source of each of your decisions.

Here is an example of a TRUE/FALSE/NOT DISCUSSED exercise for **Major Details:**

(See READING SAMPLE B)

MAJOR DETAILS
Decide whether each detail is true (T), false (F), or not discussed (ND).

_____ 1. Pennsylvania Dutch country is located in Lancaster County, Pennsylvania.

_____ 2. The Pennsylvania Dutch consist of Mennonites, Amish, and Dunkers.

_____ 3. The women do not wear severe clothes.

_____ 4. The men look stern but they are friendly.

answers: (1) ND; (2) T; (3) F; (4) T

The third type of practice with major details asks you to FILL IN the missing words in a statement. Doing this helps you to retrieve accurate information as you refer to the reading selection. As you do the fill-ins, be prepared to point to the material that led you to complete the statements the way that you did. When you check your answers, consider a close synonym of the answer given to be correct.

A very effective way to develop confidence in your ability to find major details is to write exercises like the ones in *Structured Reading*. Doing this puts you in the role of a teacher, which is an excellent way to learn. Ask friends to work your exercises. Then be prepared to check the answers and explain them.

Tables, graphs, and figures usually illustrate major details in a reading selection. This is true especially in textbooks. For example, look at Selections 27, 28, and 29 in this textbook. Important information is provided in each visual display. These visual displays might appear to be complicated at first, but digging into a table or graph and forcing yourself to figure it out gives you valuable help in understanding the major details of a reading selection. Read the title of the table or graph first. Next, read the caption, if any. Then, read the labels. Try to pull together all the information to get the point. Do not give up if you do not understand the material at first. Skill in reading tables and graphs takes practice, but once you catch on, you will find the next time easier. Work with the tables and graphs that accompany some of the reading selections in *Structured Reading*, and then apply the skills you have developed to other materials.

Here is an example of a FILL-IN exercise for **Major Details:**

READING SAMPLE C

(1) It's a dream come true for anyone who has wished for his or her own horse. The U.S. Department of the Interior's Bureau of Land Management is giving away thousands of wild mustangs and hundreds of wild burros under its new "Adopt a Horse" program.

(2) Why the gift? The government can no longer care for the growing numbers of wild horses currently grazing on federal lands in the West. To control the horse population and maintain enough land for them to feed on, the Bureau began offering many of the horses for adoption last spring—and any U.S. resident can apply to be a "foster parent."

(3) It's not necessary to own a ranch or acres of land to be eligible to adopt a horse. "We have no set formula of requirements—a healthy acre is better than a large tract of barren land," explains Nancy Manzi, head of the program. "What *is* important, is that the applicant is able to accept responsibility for the horse's care throughout its lifetime." To qualify, you must own—or have access to—adequate shelter and pasture or boarding facilities for the animal. Although the horse is initially free, you must be willing to handle food and medical bills. According to the Bureau, costs for feeding alone can run to about $600 a year.*

MAJOR DETAILS
Fill in the word that correctly completes each statement.

1. The "Adopt a _____ Program" has been organized by the Bureau of Land Management of the U.S. Department of the Interior.

2. The government can no longer care for the _____ horses.

3. To qualify, you do not have to own a _____

4. It costs about _____ dollars a year to feed a horse.

*From "Look, A Gift Horse," by Janet Chan. © 1976, *McCall's*, October 1976.

answers: (1) Horse; (2) wild; (3) ranch; (4) 600

Inferences

To read **between** the lines, a reader needs to be able to make inferences. Making inferences means keeping the following questions in mind: What does the author assume that I know already, even before I start to read a selection? What information or conclusions does the author expect me to fill in as I read along? A skillful reader thinks about what is not stated and looks for what is implied. To make inferences, take your hints from what is stated and then go on to fill in the gaps.

Three useful strategies to help you make valid inferences when you are reading are

- understanding clearly the facts and stated main ideas

- examining the author's attitude about the subject

- drawing a logical conclusion about what *is not* stated from information that *is* stated.

Understanding the Facts and Main Ideas

To make valid inferences, you must have a clear understanding of exactly what the author has stated. Many incorrect conclusions are drawn in all types of communication, including that between readers and authors, because only part of the information given has been understood. You cannot read **between** the lines until you have first read efficiently **on** the lines.

A skilled reader makes inferences based on his or her fund of prior knowledge. For example, if an author mentions a famous person without pausing to give any details about that person, the author assumes that the reader knows about the person. If the reader lacks that information, he or she has to look up the person's name and find out enough information to make the reading understandable.

Examining the Author's Attitude

An author's attitude toward a subject also affects the inferences that a reader makes. Skilled readers always think about an author's purpose. The purpose of most textbook authors is to *inform* the reader, primarily relating facts and verifiable information. Such reading does not contain personal opinion or emotional language. On the other hand, writers of essays, editorials, and articles may have other purposes than only to inform the reader. These writers may want to *persuade* the reader to accept their point of view on a subject.

Skilled readers need to examine an author's background by reading between the lines to consider how that background colors what the author has written. For example, if a writer seeks to persuade readers that women in prison should keep their newborn babies with them instead of the infants being placed in foster care, readers want—before making up their minds—to think through the expertise and/or bias of the author. Sometimes background information does not reveal itself by what the writer says or implies. In such cases, readers need either to do research about the writer or to settle for little background information.

Even when the author's background can be extracted from what is written, readers rarely arrive easily at judgments. And often those judgments can only be tentative. For example, if the writer about the newborn babies of imprisoned women is herself in such a situation, the woman certainly can draw on the authority of her experience. Readers would have to read between the lines to decide whether the woman brings a uniquely valuable perspective to the issue or, conversely, is too close to the situation to mount a sound argument. Suppose, however, that the writer is a child-care professional, such as a teacher or a child psychiatrist. Readers then would have to decide whether that professional has sufficient knowledge and experience to marshall convincing evidence and opinions. What would further complicate matters for readers would be a case in which the writer is both an imprisoned woman and a former highly respected teacher—a woman who killed her lover in a jealous rage. (Try an analysis yourself by considering the author's attitude in Selection 22, "The Babies of Bedford.")

Drawing a Logical Conclusion

After you have understood the author's subject and have determined the author's purpose, you are ready to draw some conclusions based on what you know. Many different inferences can be drawn from readings. After you have made inferences, you should be able to defend them. If you cannot find main points or facts in the article to support your conclusions, your inference likely is invalid. *Structured Reading* provides practice in drawing inferences from reading. Reading between the lines demands thought. When you do the Inference exercises, read the answer choices carefully and be ready to defend your reasons for choosing or not choosing each option.

Making valid inferences is a critical skill in becoming an efficient reader. Often, the basic understanding of the main point of a piece depends on your ability to make good inferences. In Selection 24 in this text, "How to Stay Alive," the author begins his piece this way:

> Once upon a time there was a man named Snadley Klabberhorn who was the healthiest man in the whole wide world.
>
> Snadley wasn't always the healthiest man in the whole wide world. When he was young, Snadley smoked what he

wanted, drank what he wanted, ate what he wanted, and exercised only with young ladies in bed.

The opening storybook phrase, "Once upon a time . . .," the unusual name "Snadley Klabberhorn," and the exaggerated statement that he was the "healthiest man in the whole world" imply that the author is probably not writing a serious article on staying alive. Your reading of the opening should signal to you that you will have to **read between the lines** to get his true meaning. If your prior knowledge about the author, Art Hoppe, is that he writes humorous satire, poking fun at the ills and whims of human life, you will have a further clue about the spirit of the essay.

Sometimes authors develop an essay so that a literal reading of its content actually does not make sense at all. It is not until the reader draws inferences that the reading has meaning. Read paragraphs 1, 2, 4, 7, and 10 from Selection 6 in this textbook, "The Girl with the Large Eyes." Then apply the three strategies just discussed for drawing correct inferences. First, here are the *stated facts and main points.*

1. An unmarried girl with beautiful eyes lives in an African village.

2. The village is suffering from a drought and the day is spent looking for water.

3. A fish talks to the girl and brings her water.

4. The fish embraces the girl and they are married.

The *author's attitude* seems to be positive about the relationship between the girl and the fish. Both are described in positive terms. Next you must draw a *logical conclusion*. There is a basic problem, though, in the logic of the story. Fish do not talk, and people and fish do not embrace and marry. One inference that may be drawn is that the author is using the girl and fish to stand for something other than what they really are. Perhaps the relationship between the two represents relationships that are usually not culturally acceptable. The logic of that inference holds up in light of the fact that the relatives of the girl were so upset when they found out about the relationship.

Be sure to read the whole story to analyze fully the main point the author wants to deliver. As you read, be alert for additional inferences the author wants you to make.

Although the necessity of making inferences from what you read may not always be as obvious as in the "The Girl with the Large Eyes," reading **between the lines** always demands thought. *Structured Reading* provides practice in making inferences from the reading selections.

Here is an example of an **Inference** question:

(See READING SAMPLE B)

INFERENCES
Choose the best answer.

_____ 1. *Read paragraph 2 again.* The authors refer to *Esquire* because *Esquire* is a well-known magazine that often includes articles about
    a. the Pennsylvania Dutch.
    b. the legal profession.
    c. men's modern fashions and lifestyles.
    d. unusual types of men and women.

answer: c

Critical Reading

Critical reading is another way to read **between** the lines. Reading critically means analyzing how an author develops ideas in a particular writing. There are many aspects to critical reading. Two presented in this text are determining fact and opinion, and recognizing how the craft of the writer influences the reader.

Facts and opinions usually are used by a writer to support the main ideas of a piece of writing. *Facts* are statements that can be verified. There are three tests you can apply to a statement to see if it qualifies as a fact:

- *Experiment.* For example: "During rest, the heart beats about 70 times per minute." [From "The Heart Beat," paragraph 8]

- *Research.* For example: "There is no agreed total for the number of languages spoken in the world today. Most reference books give a figure of 4,000 to 5,000, but estimates have varied from 3,000 to 10,000." [From "How Many Languages?" paragraph 1]

- *Observation.* For example: "I remember when Jesse's head reached my belt line." [From "A License to Drive," paragraph 10]

If a statement does not pass one of these three tests, chances are good that the statement is an opinion rather than a fact. *Opinions* are statements of personal beliefs that are open to debate. Opinions often contain abstract ideas, information that cannot be verified, or emotionally charged words.

Sometimes an opinion can be written so that it appears to be a fact. This is especially true when someone is quoted. For example, an author might quote a horse owner as follows: "Having a healthy horse to ride, work, show, or even keep as a pet is a rare privilege." This is the speaker's opinion, one that would be shared by some people but not likely by all. A quotation does not make a statement a fact. The content of the quotation must be factual. You are dealing with a fact, however, when the horse owner says, "It costs me about $600 a year to feed my horse."

Structured Reading provides practice in distinguishing between facts and opinions. (When a reading selection in this book is all factual, such as material from some textbooks, or is totally fiction or personal opinion, a FACT OR OPINION exercise is not included.)

Here is an example of a FACT OR OPINION question for **Critical Reading:**

(See READING SAMPLE B)

CRITICAL READING: FACT OR OPINION
Decide whether each statement is FACT or OPINION.

_____ 1. *From paragraph 1:* In Pennsylvania Dutch country, [live] Mennonites, Amish, and Dunkers.

_____ 2. *From paragraph 2:* The men hold their trousers up with suspenders.

_____ 3. *From paragraph 2:* They are the friendliest, most sincere people you have ever met.

answers: (1)FACT; (2) FACT; (3) OPINION

The writing craft of the writer often influences the reader. A skilled reader stays aware of how the author gets and holds the reader's attention. Furthermore, appreciating the art of the writer can add to the reader's enjoyment. What images does the author use? What techniques of good writing does the author employ? *Structured Reading* provides exercises that direct your attention to the writer's craft of each reading selection.

Here are the opening lines of Selection 21, "A License to Drive." Why does the article begin with an incident in the life of the author's son?

I was speaking with my son Jesse over the telephone. He's 15 and lives with his mother and her new husband 120 miles north, in the Catskills. It was Friday evening. I asked him what he'd done that afternoon.

Gone into Kingston, he told me, to see a movie. Gone with his friend Eric.

Kingston is 25 miles away.

I was startled: he had never before left his home in a car driven by one of his own friends.

I was also frightened.

When the author writes, "I was also frightened," he likely intends to heighten your anticipation about what will come next. Why was he afraid? Is there a problem with his son? Did he lose someone in a car accident recently? Doesn't he trust his son? Or is the author only having a hard time adjusting to the fact that his son is growing up? Appreciation of a writer's craft usually comes upon *rereading* a selection. WRITER'S CRAFT questions in *Structured Reading* are best answered after you have finished a selection and can reread it.

Here is an example of a WRITER'S CRAFT question for **Critical Reading** based on the opening lines of Selection 21:

CRITICAL READING: THE WRITER'S CRAFT
Choose the best answer.

_____ 1. The author begins his essay with an incident in his son's life and his reaction to it. How does this beginning contribute to the impact of the article?

    a. It reveals the author's mounting anger at being bothered by his son, and thereby it creates tension.

    b. It states the main point of the article so that the material will be clear to the reader.

    c. It engages the reader's interest by revealing the father's strong reactions to a relatively common boyhood event.

    d. It creates a mood of disillusionment about fatherhood that the reader can anticipate will be explained later.

answer: c

Informed Opinion

When you offer an informed opinion, it's your turn. What do *you* think? Based on what you have read, based on your previous experience, based on your best reasoning, what is your opinion? An opinion that is informed is an educated opinion, one formed on the basis of knowledge and thought.

Structured Reading provides many opportunities for you to express your informed opinion. Two open-ended questions follow each reading selection. Here no answer is right or wrong, but you should be ready to defend your point of view if others challenge it. The more informed your opinion, the less likely that it will be argued down by others.

You can also express yourself on the subjects in the reading selections by using the sections, "Writing: Expressing Yourself," which conclude each of the five parts of *Structured Reading*. The suggestions for paragraphs and essays provide a chance for you to write or discuss ideas so that you can practice your skills in shaping informed opinions.

A FINAL WORD

Developing reading skill takes time. Be patient with yourself. The first steps are the slowest. Stick with your determination to improve your reading skills, and do not be discouraged when you miss a word or get wrong answers. Use all parts of *Structured Reading* to the fullest. Becoming skillful in reading demands the same patience and repetition that learning a sport or musical instrument demands. With steady application, and with stubborn determination, you will soon be able to say, "Yes, I am a good reader."

To help you reach your goal, apply the reading strategies discussed in this chapter.

- *Strategy 1:* Read widely to increase your vocabulary and enlarge your knowledge base. Reading widely will help you bring prior knowledge to whatever you read.

- *Strategy 2:* Improve the way you read. Preview to determine purpose and to assess the difficulty of the material. Cluster ideas when you read. Pace through the print and eliminate unnecessary regressions.

- *Strategy 3:* Use context clues and word parts to help you determine the meaning of words. Develop a personal vocabulary card collection for daily study of new words you come across in your reading. Sharpen and use your dictionary skills.

- *Strategy 4:* Approach your reading tasks actively rather than passively. Make predictions as you read.

- *Strategy 5:* Apply SQ3R (Survey, Question, Read, Recite, Review) to your reading when you want to have good comprehension of content. Make outline notes that work for you.

- *Strategy 6:* When you read, determine the main ideas and supporting details by identifying the topic, the main point the author is making about the topic, and details which further explain it. Do not concentrate on unnecessary information that does not explain the main point.

- *Strategy 7:* Look beyond what the author says and read between the lines. Draw inferences first by understanding the main points and then by examining the author's attitude about them. Check to see if your conclusions are logical and can be supported by specific points from the reading.

- *Strategy 8:* Analyze how an author develops his or her themes by critically examining the facts and opinions. If a statement cannot be verified by experiment, research, or observation, it is likely an opinion. Examine the writer's craft by looking at the style and techniques used to influence the reader.

- *Strategy 9:* Make an informed opinion about what you read. Be sure you can back up your answer with specifics from the reading.

- *Strategy 10:* Sharpen your skills by writing on the same subjects you read about. Use the knowledge you have gained from the readings as a base from which to write.

- *Strategy 11:* Be patient with yourself. If you apply the techniques explained in this chapter—the thirty reading selections and related questions offer you lots of opportunity to practice—you will improve your skills.

Thinking:
Getting Started

Reading is an active process. During reading, your eyes and brain interact with the words on a page. This process of reading works most efficiently if you are conscious of how it operates. In addition to using your eyes, you need also to use your mind's "prior knowledge." This prior knowledge is what you know *before* you start reading; it provides a foundation for adding new knowledge to your fund of information. Learning happens when you associate new knowledge with prior knowledge.

Reading needs the active participation of your mind. The more your mind is "ready" to read actively when you start to look at a printed page, the more you will get out of your reading. Just as computers must "power up" before they begin to process information, your brain needs to "power up" before it starts to read. The next three pages of visual material are offered to help you start thinking about your prior knowledge on the subjects in the reading selections in Part 1 of this book.

Look closely and you can see the scars.

There are no bruises. And no broken bones. She seems the picture of the perfect child. But if you look closely you can see how rejection, fear and constant humiliation have left scars that have tragically affected her childhood.

So now only a shattered spirit remains. And the light of laughter has gone out. Remember that words hit as hard as a fist. So watch what you say. You don't have to lift a hand to hurt your child.

Take time out. Don't take it out on your kid.

 Write: National Committee for Prevention of Child Abuse, Box 2866E, Chicago, Illinois 60690

What are the major benefits of wide circulation of warnings about child abuse?
(See "A Real Loss.")

How can school teachers help children overcome the abuse of prejudice?
(See "I Became Her Target.")

Is the small U.S. farm worth saving? (See "The Death of a Farm.")

When does a gentle voice imply a loud shout? (See "Tyranny of Weakness.")

More on next page . . .

AMERICA'S ENERGY IS MINDPOWER

Never before has this nation
had a greater need for educated minds...
to help solve problems of energy,
the economy, equal rights,
employment, and the environment.
Higher education must be a higher priority
because educated people solve problems.
Support our colleges and universities!

Reprinted with permission of the Council for Advancement and Support of Education.

*Why do so many people assume
that if a person has a physical
handicap, that person also has
a handicapped mind?
(See "Darkness at Noon.")*

*Although many
marriages today end
in divorce, many do
not, and the couple
stays deeply in love.
What makes some love
so strong that it lasts
forever? (See "The
Girl with the Large
Eyes.")*

"*And so they were married and lived together
happily for quite some time.*"

Drawing by Donald Reilly, © 1972. The New Yorker Magazine, Inc.

A Real Loss

Fern Kupfer

(1) I was sitting in back of a little girl flying as an unaccompanied minor, put on the plane by a mother who placed a Care Bear in her arms and told her to remind Daddy to call when she got to California. The girl adjusted her seat belt and sniffed back a tear, bravely setting her jaw.

(2) As we prepared for takeoff, the man next to the girl asked her the name of her bear and nodded in approval, saying Furry was a good name for a bear. When the little girl told him she was 6 years old, the man replied that he had a daughter who was 6 years old. His daughter was missing the same teeth, in fact. He asked how much money the tooth fairy was giving out in New York these days.

(3) By the time we were in the air, the man and the little girl were playing tic-tac-toe, and she revealed to him the names of her favorite friends. Somewhere over Ohio, I fell asleep, awakened by my mother instinct when I heard a child announce that she had to go to the bathroom.

(4) "It's in the back, right?" I heard the girl say to the man. She looked tentative. The flight attendants were busy collecting lunch trays.

(5) "Do you want me to take you there?" the man asked, standing.

(6) At once my antennae were up and, leaning into the aisle, I craned my neck, practically knocking heads with the woman in the seat across from me. For one moment our eyes locked. She had been listening, too, and both of us had the same idea. Would this man go into the bathroom with the child? I held my breath as he held open the bathroom door. Suddenly, he became transformed in my eyes—the dark business suit looked sinister, the friendly smile really a lure to something evil.

(7) Then the man showed the little girl how the lock worked and waited outside the door. The woman and I sighed in relief. She said, "Well, you can't be too careful these days."

(8) I've thought about that man on the plane since then, and the image of him and the little girl always leaves an empty sorrow. I know that a new heightened consciousness about child molestation is in itself a good thing. I know that sexual abuse of children is awful, and that we must guard against it. But it saddened me that I looked at someone who understood a child's fear and saw a child molester.

From *Newsday* Magazine, Sept. 27, 1987. Reprinted with permission of the author.

(9) These are trying times for men. We women say how we want men to be sensitive and nurturing, to be caring and affectionate. But my sense is that now these qualities cannot be readily displayed without arousing suspicion. Perhaps there is some sort of ironic retribution for all those years of accepting the male stereotypes. But there is a real loss here for us all when we must always be wary of the kindness of strangers.

498 words

Vocabulary List

Here are some of the more difficult words in "A Real Loss."

antennae
(paragraph 6)

an·ten·na (an ten′ə) *n.* ⟦L, earlier *antenna*, sail yard⟧ **1** *pl.* **-nae** (-ē) or **-nas** either of a pair of movable, jointed sense organs on the head of most arthropods, as insects, crabs, or lobsters; feeler **2** *pl.* **-nas** *Radio, TV* an arrangement of wires, metal rods, etc. used in sending and receiving electromagnetic waves; aerial

craned
(paragraph 6)

crane (krān) *n.* ⟦ME < OE *cran*: akin to Du *kraan*, Ger *kranich* < IE *gr-on* < base *ger-*: see CROW[1]⟧ **1** *pl.* **cranes** or **crane** *a)* any of a family (Gruidae) of usually large gruiform wading birds with very long legs and neck, and a long, straight bill *b)* popularly, any of various unrelated birds, as herons and storks **2** any of various machines for lifting or moving heavy weights by means of a movable projecting arm or a horizontal beam traveling on an overhead support **3** any device with a swinging arm fixed on a vertical axis /a fireplace *crane* is used for holding a kettle/ —*vt., vi.* **craned, cran′ing 1** to raise or move with a crane **2** to stretch (the neck) as a crane does, as in straining to see over something

WHOOPING CRANE   CRAWLER CRANE

heightened
(paragraph 8)

height·en (hīt″n) *vt., vi.* ⟦< HEIGHT + -EN⟧ **1** to bring or come to a high or higher position; raise or rise **2** to make or become larger, greater, stronger, brighter, etc.; increase; intensify —*SYN.* INTENSIFY —**height′en·er** *n.*

ironic
(paragraph 9)

i·ron·ic (ī rän′ik) *adj.* **1** meaning the contrary of what is expressed **2** using, or given to the use of, irony **3** having the quality of irony; directly opposite to what is or might be expected Also **i·ron′i·cal** — **i·ron′i·cal·ly** *adv.*

i·ron·y[1] (ī′rə nē, ī′ər nē) *n., pl.* **-nies** ⟦Fr *ironie* < L *ironia* < Gr *eirōneia* < *eirōn*, dissembler in speech < *eirein*, to speak < IE base *wer-*, to speak > WORD⟧ **1** *a)* a method of humorous or subtly sarcastic expression in which the intended meaning of the words is the direct opposite of their usual sense /the *irony* of calling a stupid plan "clever"/ *b)* an instance of this **2** the contrast, as in a play, between what a character thinks the truth is, as revealed in a speech or action, and what an audience or reader knows the truth to be: often **dramatic irony 3** a combination of circumstances or a result that is the opposite of what is or might be expected or considered appropriate /an *irony* that the firehouse burned/ **4** *a)* a cool, detached attitude of mind, characterized by recognition of the incongruities and complexities of experience *b)* the expression of such an attitude in a literary work **5** the feigning of ignorance in argument: often **Socratic irony** (after Socrates' use in Plato's *Dialogues*) — *SYN.* WIT[1]

Vocabulary List

molestation
(paragraph 8)

mo·lest (mə lest′, mō-) *vt.* ⟦ME *molesten* < OFr *molester* < L *molestare* < *molestus*, troublesome < *moles*, a burden: see MOLE³⟧ **1** to annoy, interfere with, or meddle with so as to trouble or harm, or with intent to trouble or harm ☆**2** to make improper advances to, esp. of a sexual nature **3** to assault or attack (esp. a child) sexually —**mo·les·ta·tion** (mō′les tā′shən; *also* mäl′əs-) *n.* —**mo·lest′er** *n.*

nurturing
(paragraph 9)

nur·ture (nur′chər) *n.* ⟦ME < OFr *norreture* < LL *nutritura*, pp. of L *nutrire*, to nourish: see NURSE⟧ **1** anything that nourishes; food; nutriment **2** the act or process of raising or promoting the development of; training, educating, fostering, etc.: also **nur′tur·ance 3** all the environmental factors, collectively, to which one is subjected from conception onward, as, distinguished from one's nature or heredity —*vt.* **-tured, -tur·ing 1** to feed or nourish **2** *a)* to promote the development of *b)* to raise by educating, training, etc. —**nur′tur·ant** or **nur′tur·al** *adj.* —**nur′tur·er** *n.*

retribution
(paragraph 9)

ret·ri·bu·tion (re′trə byōō′shən) *n.* ⟦ME *retribucioun* < OFr *retribution* < LL(Ec) *retributio* < L *retributus*, pp. of *retribuere*, to repay < *re-*, back + *tribuere*, to pay: see TRIBUTE⟧ punishment for evil done or reward for good done; requital —**re·trib′u·tive** (ri trib′yoo tiv) or **re·trib′u·to′ry** (-tôr′ē) *adj.* —**re·trib′u·tive·ly** *adv.*

sinister
(paragraph 6)

sin·is·ter (sin′is tər) *adj.* ⟦ME *sinistre* < L *sinister*, left-hand, or unlucky (side), orig. lucky (side) < IE base **sene-*, to prepare, achieve > Sans *sántyān*, more favorable: early Roman augurs faced south, with the east (lucky side) to the left, but the Greeks (followed by later Romans) faced north⟧ **1** *a)* orig., on, to, or toward the left-hand side; left *b) Heraldry* on the left side of a shield (the right as seen by the viewer) (opposed to DEXTER) **2** threatening harm, evil, or misfortune; ominous; portentous *[sinister* storm clouds*]* **3** wicked, evil, or dishonest, esp. in some dark, mysterious way *[a sinister plot]* **4** most unfavorable or unfortunate; disastrous *[met a sinister fate]* —**sin′is·ter·ly** *adv.* —**sin′is·ter·ness** *n.*
SYN.—**sinister,** in this connection, applies to that which can be interpreted as presaging imminent danger or evil *[a sinister* smile*]*; **baleful** refers to that which is inevitably deadly, destructive, pernicious, etc. *[a baleful* influence*]*; **malign** is applied to that which is regarded as having an inherent tendency toward evil or destruction *[a malign* doctrine*]*

tentative
(paragraph 4)

ten·ta·tive (ten′tə tiv) *adj.* ⟦LL *tentativus* < pp. of L *tentare*, to touch, try: see TENT²⟧ **1** made, done, proposed, etc. experimentally or provisionally; not definite or final *[tentative* plans, a *tentative* explanation*]* **2** indicating timidity, hesitancy, or uncertainty *[a tentative* caress*]* —**ten′ta·tive·ly** *adv.* —**ten′ta·tive·ness** *n.*

transformed
(paragraph 6)

trans·form (*for v.* trans fôrm′; *for n.* trans′fôrm′) *vt.* ⟦ME *transformen* < L *transformare* < *trans-*, TRANS- + *formare*, to form < *forma*, FORM⟧ **1** to change the form or outward appearance of **2** to change the condition, nature, or function of; convert **3** to change the personality or character of **4** *Elec.* to change (a voltage or current value) by use of a transformer **5** *Linguis.* to change by means of a syntactic transformational rule **6** *Math.* to change (an algebraic expression or equation) to a different form having the same value **7** *Physics* to change (one form of energy) into another —*vi.* [Rare] to be or become transformed —*n. Math.* the process or result of a mathematical transformation —**trans·form′a·ble** *adj.* —**trans·form′a·tive** *adj.*
SYN.—**transform,** the broadest in scope of these terms, implies a change either in external form or in inner nature, in function, etc. *[she was transformed* into a happy girl*]*; **transmute,** from its earlier use in alchemy, suggests a change in basic nature that seems almost miraculous *[transmuted* from a shy youth into a sophisticated man about town*]*; **convert** implies a change in details so as to be suitable for a new use *[to convert* an attic into an apartment*]*; **metamorphose** suggests a startling change produced as if by magic *[a tadpole is metamorphosed* into a frog*]*; **transfigure** implies a change in outward appearance which seems to exalt or glorify *[his whole being was transfigured* by love*]* See also CHANGE

wary
(paragraph 9)

war·y (wer′ē) *adj.* **war′i·er, war′i·est** ⟦< WARE² + -Y²⟧ **1** cautious; on one's guard **2** characterized by caution *[a wary* look*]* —**SYN.** CAREFUL —**wary of** careful of

1A VOCABULARY

From the context of "A Real Loss," explain the meaning of each of the vocabulary words shown in boldface below.

1. *From paragraph 4:* She looked **tentative.**

   _____

   _____

   _____

   _____

2. *From paragraph 6:* At once my **antennae** were up and, leaning into the aisle, I **craned** my neck.

   _____

   _____

   _____

   _____

3. *From paragraph 6:* Suddenly, he became **transformed** in my eyes—the dark business suit looked **sinister.**

   _____

   _____

   _____

   _____

4. *From paragraph 8:* I know that a new **heightened** consciousness about child **molestation** is in itself a good thing.

   _____

   _____

   _____

   _____

Name   Date

5. *From paragraph 9:* We women say how we want men to be sensitive and **nurturing.**

_____

_____

6. *From paragraph 9:* Perhaps there is some sort of **ironic retribution** for all those years of accepting the male stereotypes.

_____

_____

_____

_____

7. *From paragraph 9:* But there is a real loss here for us all when we must always be **wary** of the kindness of strangers.

_____

_____

1B   CENTRAL THEME AND MAIN IDEAS

Choose the best answer.

_____ 1. What is the central theme of "A Real Loss"?
   a. These are trying times for men because all the media attention on child molestation has made even their simple kindnesses toward children appear to be evil.
   b. The author felt sorry for the little girl who had to fly from New York to California by herself, but at the same time the author admired the child's bravery.
   c. Child molesters can find victims everywhere, even on airplanes, so all travelers should be suspicious of anyone who is kind to children flying alone.
   d. Because of her increased awareness that some people are child molesters, the author now realizes that she has become suspicious of people who are kind to children they do not know.

Name   Date

_____ 2. What is the main idea of paragraph 6?
   a. Airplane passengers often listen to other people's conversations and exchange glances about what is said.
   b. Becoming suspicious, the author leaned far into the aisle and nearly bumped heads with another watchful woman.
   c. As she waited to see what the man would do, he suddenly changed in her eyes into an evil person.
   d. The man opened the bathroom door for the little girl as the author held her breath.

1C MAJOR DETAILS

Decide whether each detail is MAJOR or MINOR.

_____ 1. The author was sitting in back of a little girl who was flying alone.

_____ 2. The little girl's mother placed a Care Bear in the girl's arms.

_____ 3. The little girl was going to California.

_____ 4. The little girl knew how to adjust her seat belt.

_____ 5. The bear's name was Furry.

_____ 6. Both the girl and the man's daughter were six years old.

_____ 7. The little girl announced that she had to go to the bathroom.

_____ 8. At that moment, the flight attendants were busy collecting lunch trays, so the man offered to take the girl to the bathroom.

_____ 9. The man showed the girl how the lock worked, and then he waited for her outside the door.

_____ 10. The other woman sighed in relief.

_____ 11. The author's image of the man and the little girl on the plane left her with a feeling of loss.

_____ 12. A new heightened consciousness about child molestation is in itself a good thing.

Name   Date

ID INFERENCES

Choose the best answer.

_____ 1. *Read paragraph 1 again.* Why did the little girl's mother tell her to remind Daddy to call?
   a. The mother did not want to spend the money to call California herself.
   b. The mother wanted to know that the girl had arrived safely after the long trip.
   c. The father was not considerate of the woman's feelings, so he had to be reminded to call.
   d. The mother wanted to know that the girl's father was in good health.

_____ 2. *Read paragraph 2 again.* Why did the man say Furry was a good name?
   a. He had once had a bear named Furry.
   b. He wanted to make the little girl settle down so that she would not bother him and he could rest or read quietly.
   c. He wanted to make her feel comfortable and secure.
   d. The bear was very fluffy, and so Furry seemed an appropriate name.

_____ 3. *Read paragraph 3 again.* Why did the little girl's announcement that she had to go to the bathroom wake up the author?
   a. The child was speaking very loudly and moving around in her seat, indicating that she was very uncomfortable.
   b. The author was afraid the little girl might have an accident unless someone took her to the bathroom right away.
   c. As a mother, the author thought she should be the one asked to take the little girl to the bathroom if the flight attendants were busy.
   d. As a mother, the author was used to listening—even in her sleep—for children's calls for help.

_____ 4. *Read paragraph 7 again.* By saying "Well, you can't be too careful these days" the woman was communicating that she was
   a. annoyed at the flight attendants for being too busy to take the little girl to the bathroom.
   b. angry that the little girl had asked the man for help instead of turning to a nearby woman.
   c. slightly embarrassed that she had worried about what the man might do to the little girl.
   d. somewhat worried that the girl was too little to learn how to use the bathroom lock.

Name   Date

_____ 5. *Read paragraphs 8 and 9 again.* What does the author mean when she says "there is a real loss here for us all when we must always be wary of the kindness of strangers"?

  a. Constant suspicion is a poisonous feeling, preventing people from enjoying some of the pleasanter moments in life, such as watching a man being kind to a child.

  b. Because rarely is there a way of telling who might be evil, people stop talking to strangers and miss chances to make friends.

  c. Years ago, fewer child molesters existed, so children's lives were safer, and their parents had peace of mind that now has been lost.

  d. Because people today are constantly on the lookout for child molesters, nice people like the author are afraid to be kind to strangers' children for fear of being suspected of molestation.

_____ 6. The word *loss* used in the title refers to the

  a. author's loss of trust of adults who are kind to children.

  b. little girl's having to leave her mother behind.

  c. negative effect on children when divorced parents live long distances apart.

  d. man's missing his own little girl who was also six years old.

1E CRITICAL READING: FACT OR OPINION

Decide whether each statement, even if it quotes someone, contains a FACT or OPINION.

_____ 1. *From paragraph 1:* The girl adjusted her seat belt and sniffed back a tear.

_____ 2. *From paragraph 2:* He asked her how much money the tooth fairy was giving out in New York these days.

_____ 3. *From paragraph 3:* She revealed to him the names of her favorite friends.

_____ 4. *From paragraph 4:* She looked tentative.

_____ 5. *From paragraph 6:* He became transformed in my eyes.

_____ 6. *From paragraph 6:* The dark business suit looked sinister.

_____ 7. *From paragraph 7:* The woman and I sighed in relief.

Name   Date

_____ 8. *From paragraph 7:* "You can't be too careful these days."

_____ 9. *From paragraph 8:* A new heightened consciousness about child molestation is in itself a good thing.

_____ 10. *From paragraph 9:* These are trying times for men.

1F CRITICAL READING: THE WRITER'S CRAFT

Choose the best answer.

_____ 1. To get the reader's attention, the author opens with
    a. a brief anecdote.
    b. a description.
    c. a startling fact.
    d. a quotation.

_____ 2. *Read paragraph 2 again.* To show how the man gains the little girl's trust, the author describes how he
    a. tells the girl jokes.
    b. asks the girl questions about herself.
    c. shows her pictures of his own daughter.
    d. talks to her stuffed bear.

_____ 3. *Read paragraphs 4 and 5 again.* The author uses dialogue here
    a. to show she has a detailed, reliable memory of the event.
    b. to highlight that this was the most important part of the conversation.
    c. to demonstrate how to write direct dialogue.
    d. because every story should have at least one passage of direct dialogue.

_____ 4. *Read paragraph 9 again.* The author concludes her essay with
    a. a dramatic call to action.
    b. a forecast of the future.
    c. an evaluation of the situation.
    d. a final example of the problem.

49

Name   Date

1G INFORMED OPINION

1. *Read paragraph 9 again.* Do you think we must always be wary of strangers? Explain your answer, using specific examples.

2. To avoid molesters and other people who might harm them, children are usually taught not to trust strangers. How should this be done so that children do not grow up always to be fearful of other people?

How Did You Do?   1   A Real Loss

SKILL (number of items)	Number Correct		Points for Each		Score
Vocabulary (11)	_____	×	2	=	_____
Central Theme and Main Ideas (2)	_____	×	6	=	_____
Major Details (12)	_____	×	3	=	_____
Inferences (6)	_____	×	2	=	_____
Critical Reading: Fact or Opinion (10)	_____	×	1	=	_____
Critical Reading: The Writer's Craft (4)	_____	×	2	=	_____

(Possible Total: 100) *Total* _____

SPEED

Reading Time: _____ Reading Rate (page 348): _____ Words Per Minute

Name   Date

The Death of a Farm

Amy Jo Keifer

(1) I am a farmer's daughter. I am also a 4-H member, breeder and showman of sheep and showman of cattle. My family's farm is dying and I have watched it, and my family, suffer.

(2) Our eastern Pennsylvania farm is a mere 60 acres. The green rolling hills and forested land are worth a minimum of $300,000 to developers, but no longer provide my family with the means to survive. It's a condition called asset rich and cash poor, and it's a hard way of life.

(3) My grandfather bought our farm when he and my grandmother were first married. He raised dairy cattle and harvested the land full time for more than 20 years. When he died, my father took over and changed the farm to beef cattle, horses and pigs, and kept the crops. But it wasn't enough to provide for a young family, so he took on a full time job, too.

(4) I can remember, when I was young, sitting on the fence with my sister and picking out a name for each calf. My sister's favorite cow was named Flower, and so we named her calves Buttercup, Daisy, Rose and Violet. Flower was the leader of a herd of more than 20. The only cattle left on our farm are my younger sister's and brother's 4-H projects.

(5) I can remember a huge tractor-trailer backed into the loading chute of our barn on days when more than 200 pigs had to be taken to market. That was before the prices went down and my father let the barn go empty rather than take on more debt.

(6) I can remember my father riding on the tractor, larger than life, bailing hay or planting corn. When prices started dropping, we began to rent some land to other farmers, so they could harvest from it. But prices have dropped so low this year there are no takers. The land will go unused; the tractor and the equipment have long since been sold off.

(7) I don't remember the horses. I've seen a few pictures in which my father, slim and dark, is holding his newborn daughter on horseback amid a small herd. And I've heard stories of his delivering hay to farms all over the state, but I can't ever remember his loading up a truck to do it.

(8) Piece by piece, our farm has deteriorated. We started breeding sheep and now have about 25 head, but they yield little revenue. My mother, who works as a registered nurse, once said something that will remain with me forever: "Your father works full time to support the farm. I work full time to support the family."

(9) I've seen movies like "The River" and "Places in the Heart." They tell the real struggle. But people can leave a movie theater, and

there's a happy ending for them. There aren't many happy endings in a real farmer's life. I was reared hearing that hard work paid off, while seeing that it didn't. My younger brother would like to take over the farm some day, but I'm not sure it will hold on much longer. Its final breath is near.

(527 words)

Vocabulary List

Here are some of the more difficult words in "Death of a Farm."

amid
(paragraph 7)

a|mid (ə mid') *prep.* ‖ ME *amidde* < *on middan* < *on*, at + *middan*, middle ‖ in the middle of; among

asset
(paragraph 2)

as·set (as'et) *n.* ‖ earlier *assets* < Anglo-Fr *assetz* (in legal phrase *aver assetz*, to have enough) < OFr *assez*, enough < VL *ad satis*, sufficient < L *ad*, to + *satis*, enough: see SAD ‖ 1 anything owned that has exchange value 2 a valuable or desirable thing to have *[charm is your chief asset]* 3 *[pl.] Accounting* all the entries on a balance sheet showing the entire resources of a person or business, tangible and intangible, including accounts and notes receivable, cash, inventory, equipment, real estate, goodwill, etc. 4 *[pl.] Law a)* property, as of a business, a bankrupt, etc. *b)* the property of a deceased person available to his or her estate for the payment of debts and legacies

chute
(paragraph 5)

☆chute¹ (sho͞ot) *n.* ‖ Fr, a fall < OFr *cheute* < *cheoite*, pp. of *cheoir*, to fall < L *cadere*: see CASE¹ ‖ 1 *a)* a waterfall *b)* rapids in a river 2 an inclined or vertical trough or passage down which something may be slid or dropped *[laundry chute]* 3 a steep slide, as for tobogganing

debt
(paragraph 5)

debt (det) *n.* ‖ altered (after L) < ME & OFr *dette* < L *debitum*, neut. pp. of *debere*, to owe < *de-*, from + *habere*, to have: see HABIT ‖ 1 something owed by one person to another or others 2 an obligation or liability to pay or return something 3 the condition of owing *[to be in debt]* 4 *Theol.* a sin

deteriorated
(paragraph 8)

de·te|ri|o·rate (dē tir'ē ə rāt', di-) *vt., vi.* -rat|ed, -rat'ing ‖ < LL *deterioratus*, pp. of *deteriorare*, to make worse < L *deterior*, worse, inferior < *deter*, below < *de-*, from + *-ter*, compar. suffix ‖ to make or become worse; lower in quality or value; depreciate —de·te'ri|o·ra'tion *n.*

harvested
(paragraph 3)

har·vest (här'vist) *n.* ‖ ME *hervest* < OE *hærfest*, akin to Ger *herbst* (OHG *herbist*) < IE *(s)kerp-* < base *(s)ker-*, to cut > SHEAR, SHORT, L *caro*, flesh, *cernere* & Gr *krinein*, to separate, *karpos*, fruit: basic sense "time of cutting" ‖ 1 the time of the year when matured grain, fruit, vegetables, etc. are reaped and gathered in 2 a season's yield of grain, fruit, etc. when gathered in or ready to be gathered in; crop 3 the gathering in of a crop 4 the outcome or consequence of any effort or series of events *[the tyrant's harvest of hate]* —*vt., vi.* 1 to gather in (a crop, etc.) 2 to gather the crop from (a field) 3 to catch, shoot, trap, etc. (fish or game), often for commercial purposes 4 to get (something) as the result of an action or effort —har'vest·a|ble *adj.*

reared
(paragraph 9)

rear² (rir) *vt.* ⟦ME *reren* < OE *ræran,* caus. of *risan,* to RISE⟧ **1** to put upright; elevate **2** to build; erect **3** to grow or breed (animals or plants) **4** to bring up by educating, nurturing, training, etc.; raise *[to rear a child]* —*vi.* **1** to rise or stand on the hind legs, as a horse **2** to rise (*up*), as in anger **3** to rise high, as a mountain peak —*SYN.* LIFT

registered
(paragraph 8)

reg·is·tered (-tərd) *adj.* officially recorded or enrolled; specif., *a)* designating bonds, etc. having the owner's name listed in a register *b)* designating a dog, horse, cow or bull, etc. having its ancestry recorded and authenticated by a breeders' association established to promote the breed *c)* legally certified or authenticated

☆**registered nurse** a nurse who, after completing extensive training and passing a State examination, is qualified to perform complete nursing services

revenue
(paragraph 8)

rev·e|nue (rev′ə n$\overline{oo}$′, -ny$\overline{oo}$′) *n.* ⟦ME < MFr < fem. pp. of *revenir,* to return, come back < *re-,* back + *venir* < L *venire,* to COME⟧ **1** the return from property or investment; income **2** *a)* an item or source of income *b)* [*pl.*] items or amounts of income collectively, as of a nation **3** the income from taxes, licenses, etc., as of a city, state, or nation **4** the governmental service that collects certain taxes

2A   VOCABULARY

Choose the best answer.

_____ 1. All of the following would be **assets** except
   a. lakefront property.
   b. a charming personality.
   c. partnership in a bankrupt company.
   d. inherited government stocks and bonds.

_____ 2. A **chute** would probably be used by a housewife to
   a. refinish all the kitchen cabinets.
   b. send laundry to the basement.
   c. plant summer vegetables in the garden.
   d. cultivate her lawn and gardens.

_____ 3. When the farmer **harvested** his crop, he
   a. gathered in all of his vegetables.
   b. made certain the crop had enough water.
   c. planted row upon row of corn.
   d. used fertilizer to grow large fruits.

_____ 4. A **registered** dental assistant would probably
   a. work only in an approved hospital setting.
   b. have been admitted previously to dental school.
   c. be required to work before taking an examination.
   d. have had the appropriate training and passed an examination.

Name   Date

_____ 5. If the city's **revenue** fell, the city would
    a. need to rebuild the town hall.
    b. probably share its wealth with the citizens.
    c. find good reason to lower taxes.
    d. have trouble paying all of its bills.

_____ 6. If Frank sat **amid** the scholars, he
    a. was probably in the middle of the group.
    b. knew more than the rest of the members.
    c. was probably the youngest member.
    d. quit school at a very early age.

_____ 7. A person in **debt** would probably
    a. be able to pay his bills monthly.
    b. have money to loan to his friends.
    c. owe money to his bank.
    d. qualify for a low-interest loan.

_____ 8. A child **reared** by strict parents would
    a. be in trouble with the law.
    b. be educated or trained to be obedient.
    c. be placed with lenient foster parents.
    d. become an expert on raising children.

_____ 9. As the farm **deteriorated,** the farmer
    a. was able to complete his plowing.
    b. had no equipment left to use.
    c. felt that it was time to pay off old loans.
    d. planned his crops for next season.

2B   CENTRAL THEME AND MAIN IDEAS
Choose the best answer.

_____ 1. The central theme of "The Death of a Farm" is the author's
    a. knowledge of raising livestock and crops.
    b. attempt to explain the painful death of her family's farm.
    c. desire to remember the good times on the farm.
    d. effort to justify her father's failure on the farm.

Name   Date

_____ 2. The main idea of paragraph 2 is that
     a. developers would pay more for the farm than it is worth.
     b. if the land were producing more crops, it would be worth much more.
     c. it seems to be a contradiction that the land itself is an asset and worth money even though it is not producing enough crops to make money.
     d. housing developers would make the land worth more if it were sold to them to build houses.

_____ 3. The main idea of paragraph 9 is that
     a. movies tell the real story about farm life.
     b. the author's brother will own the farm some day.
     c. in real life hard work doesn't always pay off.
     d. the author's brother would make a success of the farm.

2C MAJOR DETAILS

Number the following details from the story according to the order in which they occurred in the author's life. Number the events from 1 to 9, with 1 next to the event that happened first.

_____ As a newborn, the author rode horseback with her father amid their small herd.

_____ The author's younger brother would like to take over the farm some day.

_____ The author's father took on a full-time job in addition to operating the farm.

_____ The author's grandfather bought a 60-acre farm in order to raise dairy cattle and crops.

_____ Besides farming the land, the author's father decided to raise beef cattle, horses, and pigs.

_____ When they were children, the author and her sister named the cows.

_____ The farm might not last long enough to pass on to a new generation.

_____ The author's father started breeding sheep.

_____ The author's father inherited the farm.

2D INFERENCES

Decide whether each statement below can be inferred (YES) or cannot be inferred (NO) from the reading selection.

_____ 1. The author is proud of her farm heritage.

_____ 2. The author's father was not a careful money manager.

_____ 3. The author's father would have had to borrow money in order to keep raising pigs.

_____ 4. The author's mother is resentful of having to work to support the family.

_____ 5. The statement by the author's mother ("Your father works full time to support the farm. I work full time to support the family.") greatly influenced the author's feelings about farm life.

_____ 6. Things have been bad on the farm for most of the author's life.

_____ 7. The author is bitter about the death of the farm because she can remember the better days.

_____ 8. The author is confused by the sentiment that hard work pays off when she can see that it doesn't.

2E CRITICAL READING: FACT OR OPINION

Decide whether each statement contains a FACT or OPINION.

_____ 1. From paragraph 2: It's a hard way of life.

_____ 2. From paragraph 3: It wasn't enough to provide for a young family, so he took on a full-time job.

_____ 3. From paragraph 4: My sister's favorite cow was named Flower.

_____ 4. From paragraph 8: [The sheep] yield little revenue.

_____ 5. From paragraph 9: There aren't many happy endings in a real farmer's life.

_____ 6. From paragraph 9: Its final breath is near.

Name   Date

2F CRITICAL READING: THE WRITER'S CRAFT

Choose the best answer.

_____ 1. The use of expressions such as "the farm is dying" in paragraph 1 and "its final breath is near" in paragraph 9 serve to
   a. give the farm human qualities that the reader can relate to.
   b. gain sympathy from the reader.
   c. show that the author is too involved with the farm.
   d. prove that the author's father let the farm go.

_____ 2. The author begins paragraph 4, 5, and 6 with the same three words. What are they?

_____

_____ 3. The author repeats these words in order to
   a. demonstrate the author's ability to remember exact details.
   b. emphasize the solemn quality of the author's remembrances.
   c. impress the reader with her knowledge of farm life.
   d. stress the importance of being able to remember.

_____ 4. Although the land is worth $300,000 to housing developers, it does not make enough money as farmland to keep animal, crops, and family going. The author uses this as an example of
   a. logic.
   b. irony.
   c. fantasy.
   d. unity.

2G INFORMED OPINION

1. In paragraph 1, the author talks of her family's suffering. Besides lack of money, what else may be causing the family to suffer during this period when the farm is dying? Use specific examples to explain your opinion.

2. If farm life is as much at risk as "The Death of a Farm" indicates, should the U.S. government step in and give special help to ailing farmers? Explain the reasons for your position, using specific examples.

57

How Did You Do?   **2** Death of a Farm

SKILL *(number of items)*	Number Correct	Points for Each		Score
Vocabulary (9)	_____	×	2	= _____
Central Theme and Main Ideas (3)	_____	×	4	= _____
Major Details (9)	_____	×	2	= _____
Inferences (8)	_____	×	4	= _____
Critical Reading: Fact or Opinion (6)	_____	×	2	= _____
Critical Reading: The Writer's Craft (4)	_____	×	2	= _____

(Possible Total: 100) *Total* _____

SPEED

Reading Time: _____ Reading Rate (page 348): _____ Words Per Minute

Name   Date

Selection 3

Tyranny of Weakness

Eda LeShan

(1) If I were to ask you who are the most aggressive people you know, chances are you would describe someone who tells other people what to do, bosses people around, has a great deal of energy—a forceful personality.

(2) Wrong! The most aggressive, the strongest people we know are the weak ones. They are people who want someone else to take care of them and have somehow managed to convince those around them that they are too sick, too weak, too helpless, too incompetent to do anything for themselves. They are not really sick or helpless at all, but they have found a way to control the world that is fool-proof.

(3) I suppose it begins in childhood when a child realizes that helplessness is a way of controlling parents and teachers and other kids. And anyone who chooses such techniques may very well believe they really are unable to function.

(4) I recall a time when I had been on a book publicity tour for 10 days and came home to face preparing Thanksgiving dinner for 14 people. I asked a friend who did not work if she could bring a salad and she said she was too tired. Or there is a man who was sure he wanted a quiet, shy helpless wife because his mother had been aggressive, competent and somewhat overpowering. So he has spent his life taking care of a wife who "gets sick" at every family crisis and takes to her own bed if a child gets sick, if the family has to move, if her husband is in a car accident.

(5) Often people who have been strong and competent become helpless after some major emotional trauma. A friend told me, "I have a full-time job and three school-age kids, and when my father died, my mother, who had always been a competent person, suddenly turned into an infant. She expected me to take her shopping, cook for her, stay at her house, drive her everywhere, listen to her endless complaints. I became so exhausted that it began to dawn on me that she wasn't weak and helpless, she was a tyrant!

(6) Weakness and helplessness can be a form of aggression. But its origins may start with feelings of incompetence, fear, lack of self-esteem.

(7) When we meet with the tyranny of weakness, we need to help the person discover strengths, ways of accepting the challenges of life.

(8) One husband, married 40 years, told me "I don't know what happened, except I finally realized my wife had made me her slave—not by yelling at me or ordering me around, but by appearing to be helpless. I was getting a few aches and pains of my own, I guess, and it wasn't fun anymore feeling I was 'The Big Man' who could do everything. Finally, one day when she told me to mop the kitchen floor because she needed to take a nap, I said, 'Do it yourself or leave it dirty!' I thought she'd faint

From *New York Newsday*, January 19, 1991. Copyrighted by Edna LeShan, 1991. Reprinted by permission of Rosenstone/Wender, New York.

from the shock, but it did her a world of good. I seemed to break a pattern that was bad for both of us."

(9) It's a very good idea to keep in mind that it is not only the strong who push us around, but very often it is the person who appears to be weak and helpless.

(563 words)

Vocabulary List

Here are some of the more difficult words in "Tyranny of Weakness."

aggressive
(paragraph 1)

ag·gres·sive (ə gres'iv) *adj.* **1** aggressing or inclined to aggress; starting fights or quarrels **2** ready or willing to take issue or engage in direct action; militant **3** full of enterprise and initiative; bold and active; pushing **4** *Psychiatry* of or involving aggression —**ag·gres'sive·ly** *adv.* —**ag·gres'sive·ness** *n.* —**ag·gres·siv·i·ty** (ag'res iv'ə tē, ag'res-; ə gres'-) *n.*
SYN.—**aggressive** implies a bold and energetic pursuit of one's ends, connoting, in derogatory usage, a ruthless desire to dominate and, in a favorable sense, enterprise or initiative; **militant** implies a vigorous, unrelenting espousal of a cause, movement, etc. and rarely suggests the furthering of one's own ends; **assertive** emphasizes self-confidence and a persistent determination to express oneself or one's opinions; **pushing** is applied derogatorily to a forwardness of personality that manifests itself in officiousness or rudeness

competent
(paragraph 4)

com·pe·tent (-tənt) *adj.* ⟦ME < OFr < L *competens*, prp. of *competere*: see COMPETE⟧ **1** well qualified; capable; fit *[a competent doctor]* **2** sufficient; adequate *[a competent understanding of law]* **3** permissible or properly belonging: with *to* **4** *Law* legally qualified, authorized, or fit —*SYN.* ABLE —**com'pe·tent·ly** *adv.*

incompetent
(paragraph 2)

in·com·pe·tent (in käm'pə tənt) *adj.* ⟦Fr *incompétent* < LL *incompetens*: see IN-² & COMPETENT⟧ **1** without adequate ability, knowledge, fitness, etc.; failing to meet requirements; incapable; unskillful **2** not legally qualified **3** lacking strength and sufficient flexibility to transmit pressure, thus breaking or flowing under stress: said of rock structures —*n.* an incompetent person; esp., one who is mentally deficient —**in·com'pe·tence** or **in·com'pe·ten·cy** *n.* —**in·com'pe·tent·ly** *adv.*

personality
(paragraph 1)

per·son·al·i·ty (pur'sə nal'ə tē) *n., pl.* **-ties** ⟦ME *personalite* < LL *personalitas* < *personalis*, personal⟧ **1** the quality or fact of being a person **2** the quality or fact of being a particular person; personal identity; individuality **3** *a*) habitual patterns and qualities of behavior of any individual as expressed by physical and mental activities and attitudes; distinctive individual qualities *b*) the complex of qualities and characteristics seen as being distinctive to a group, nation, place, etc. **4** *a*) the sum of such qualities seen as being capable of making, or likely to make, a favorable impression on other people *b*) [Colloq.] personal attractiveness; engaging manner or qualities **5** a person; esp., a notable person; personage **6** [*pl.*] remarks, usually of an offensive or disparaging nature, aimed at or referring to a person —*SYN.* DISPOSITION

self-esteem
(paragraph 6)

self-es·teem (-e stēm') *n.* **1** belief in oneself; self-respect **2** undue pride in oneself; conceit —*SYN.* PRIDE

techniques
(paragraph 3)

tech·nique (tek nēk') *n.* ⟦Fr < Gr *technikos*: see TECHNIC⟧ **1** the method of procedure (with reference to practical or formal details), or way of using basic skills, in rendering an artistic work or carrying out a scientific or mechanical operation **2** the degree of expertness in following this *[a pianist with good technique but poor expression]* **3** any method or manner of accomplishing something

trauma
(paragraph 5)

trau·ma (trô'mə; *also* trä'-, trou'-) *n., pl.* **-mas** or **-ma·ta** (-mə tə) ⟦ModL < Gr *trauma* (gen. *traumatos*): for IE base see THROE⟧ **1** *Med.* a bodily injury, wound, or shock **2** *Psychiatry* a painful emotional experience, or shock, often producing a lasting psychic effect and, sometimes, a neurosis —**trau·mat·ic** (trô mat'ik; *also* trə-, trä-, trou-) *adj.* —**trau·mat'i·cal·ly** *adv.*

tyrant
(paragraph 5)

ty·rant (tī'rənt) *n.* ⟦ME *tirant* < OFr *tiran, tirant* (with *-t* after ending *-ant* of prp.) < L *tyrannus* < Gr *tyrannos*⟧ **1** an absolute ruler; specif., in ancient Greece, etc., one who seized sovereignty illegally; usurper **2** a cruel, oppressive ruler; despot **3** any person who exercises authority in an oppressive manner; cruel master **4** a tyrannical influence

3A VOCABULARY

Using the vocabulary words listed on page 60, fill in the blanks.

1. _____ employees will earn not only a bonus but also praise from their employers.

2. The president of the company, while appearing to be a _____ , was actually loved by his employees.

3. Research shows that _____ behavior in a younger child is often learned from an older sibling.

4. A _____ disorder should be diagnosed and treated by a trained professional.

5. Art students study various artists and their _____ in order to develop their own styles.

6. The teacher was judged to be highly _____ when her students failed to learn to read.

7. Constant criticism by a spouse is likely to damage one's _____.

8. The parents went into shock after the _____ of seeing their only child struck by a car.

3B CENTRAL THEME AND MAIN IDEAS

Choose the best answer.

_____ 1. What is the central theme of "Tyranny of Weakness"?
   a. The strongest people we know are often those who appear weak and helpless.
   b. Children should always give in to the demands of parents.
   c. A wife should be able to expect household help from her husband when she is tired.
   d. Weak people often take advantage of their good-natured friends.

_____ 2. What is the main idea of paragraph 5?
   a. Mothers should help adult daughters who have full-time jobs and children of their own.
   b. The roles of parent and child may be reversed as the parent ages.
   c. Often an emotional trauma will turn a strong individual into a helpless one.
   d. Medical studies claim that women who lose their husbands are no longer able to take care of themselves.

Name   Date

_____ 3. What is the main idea of paragraph 8?
   a. After 40 years of marriage, a husband should willingly help his wife.
   b. It is never too late in a marriage to reverse an undesirable behavior pattern.
   c. After many years of marriage, a husband will become tired of being "The Big Man."
   d. Unwillingness by a husband to help his wife may signal the beginning of the end of the marriage.

3C   MAJOR DETAILS
Decide whether each detail is MAJOR or MINOR.

_____ 1. Children learn early in life that helplessness can be a controlling technique.

_____ 2. The author's friend was too tired to bring a salad for Thanksgiving dinner.

_____ 3. A man who marries a woman opposite in personality to his mother is trading one set of problems for another.

_____ 4. The intent of the incompetent individual is often to control family and friends.

_____ 5. Sudden helplessness in a healthy, competent individual may have been triggered by an emotional trauma.

_____ 6. A person may display aggressive behavior because of feelings of low self-esteem or even fear.

3D   INFERENCES
Decide whether each statement below can be inferred (YES) or cannot be inferred (NO) from the story.

_____ 1. Aggressive behavior is bad manners.

_____ 2. People who appear to be incompetent and helpless may actually be very controlling.

_____ 3. A friend who will not help cook Thanksgiving dinner is not a true friend.

Name   Date

_____ 4. An only child will feel more responsibility toward a weak, help-less parent than toward a competent one.

_____ 5. Refusing to cooperate with a spouse's helpless behavior will "cure" the spouse.

_____ 6. A man should marry a woman whose personality is the opposite of his mother's personality.

_____ 7. A person who has behaved in a certain way toward a spouse for many years will not be able to change.

3E CRITICAL READING: FACT OR OPINION

Decide whether each statement, even if it quotes someone, contains a FACT or OPINION.

_____ 1. *From paragraph 2:* The most aggressive, the strongest people we know are the weak ones.

_____ 2. *From paragraph 3:* I suppose it begins in childhood when a child realizes that helplessness is a way of controlling parents.

_____ 3. *From paragraph 4:* The man wanted a quiet, shy, helpless wife because his mother had been aggressive and overpowering.

_____ 4. *From paragraph 4:* She said she was too tired.

_____ 5. *From paragraph 5:* A competent mother will turn into a weak, helpless widow.

_____ 6. *From paragraph 8:* "It seemed to break a pattern that was bad for both of us."

3F CRITICAL READING: THE WRITER'S CRAFT

Choose the best answer.

_____ 1. The title of the selection suggests
   a. a contradiction of descriptions.
   b. a war between weak individuals.
   c. a conflict between weak and strong men.
   d. a relationship between like personalities.

_____ 2. To make her point, the author uses all of these techniques **except**
   a. definitions of key terms.
   b. personal experience.
   c. research studies by experts.
   d. anecdotes.

Name   Date

_____ 3. The author's tone in this essay is
   a. serious.
   b. sarcastic.
   c. alarmed.
   d. suspicious.

_____ 4. The author's own attitude toward weak people who seek to manipulate others might best be described as
   a. resigned.
   b. merciless.
   c. compassionate.
   d. pessimistic.

3G   INFORMED OPINION

1. Is the widowed mother described in paragraph 5 entitled to the "services" she expects from her daughter? Why or why not?

2. Describe someone you know personally or have observed in the television or motion picture media who tyrannizes in the way described in the essay.

How Did You Do?			**3** Tyranny of Weakness	
SKILL (number of items)	Number Correct	Points for Each		Score
Vocabulary (8)	_____	× 2	=	_____
Central Theme and Main Ideas (3)	_____	× 4	=	_____
Major Details (6)	_____	× 4	=	_____
Inferences (7)	_____	× 4	=	_____
Critical Reading: Fact or Opinion (6)	_____	× 2	=	_____
Critical Reading: The Writer's Craft (4)	_____	× 2	=	_____
	(Possible Total: 100) *Total*			_____

SPEED

Reading Time: _____ Reading Rate (page 348): _____ Words Per Minute

Name   Date

Darkness at Noon

Harold Krents

(1) Blind from birth, I have never had the opportunity to see myself and have been completely dependent on the image I create in the eye of the observer. To date it has not been narcissistic.

(2) There are those who assume that since I can't see, I obviously also cannot hear. Very often people will converse with me at the top of their lungs, enunciating each word very carefully. Conversely, people will also often whisper, assuming that since my eyes don't work, my ears don't either. For example, when I go to the airport and ask the ticket agent for assistance to the plane, he or she will invariably pick up the phone, call a ground hostess and whisper, "Hi, Jane, we've got a 76 here." I have concluded that the word "blind" is not used for one of two reasons: Either they fear that if the dread word is spoken, the ticket agent's retina will immediately detach, or they are reluctant to inform me of my condition of which I may not have been previously aware.

(3) On the other hand, others know that of course I can hear, but believe that I can't talk. Often, therefore, when my wife and I go out to dinner, a waiter or waitress will ask Kit if *"he* would like a drink" to which I respond that "indeed *he* would." This point was graphically driven home to me while we were in England. I had been given a year's leave of absence from my Washington law firm to study for a diploma-in-law degree at Oxford University. During the year I became ill and was hospitalized. Immediately after admission, I was wheeled down to the X-ray room. Just at the door sat an elderly woman—elderly I would judge from the sound of her voice. "What is his name?" the woman asked the orderly who had been wheeling me.

"What's your name?" the orderly repeated to me.

"Harold Krents," I replied.

"Harold Krents," he repeated.

"When was he born?"

"When were you born?"

"November 5, 1944," I responded

"November 5, 1944," the orderly intoned.

(4) This procedure continued for approximately five minutes at which point even my saint-like disposition deserted me. "Look," I finally blurted out, "this is absolutely ridiculous. Okay, granted I can't see, but it's got to have become pretty clear to both of you that I don't need an interpreter."

"He says he doesn't need an interpreter," the orderly reported to the woman.

(5) The toughest misconception of all is the view that because I can't see, I can't work. I was turned down by over forty law firms because of my blindness, even though my qualifications included a cum laude degree from Harvard College and a good ranking in my Harvard Law School class. The attempt to find employment, the continuous frustration of being told that it was impossible for a blind person to practice law, the rejection letters, not based on my lack of ability but rather on my disability, will always remain one of the most disillusioning experiences of my life.

(6) Fortunately, this view of limitation and exclusion is beginning to change. On April 16, 1976, the Department of Labor issued regulations that mandate equal-employment opportunities for the handicapped. By and large, the business community's response to offering employment to the disabled has been enthusiastic.

(7) I therefore look forward to the day, with the expectation that it is certain to come, when employers will view their handicapped workers as a little child did me years ago when my family still lived in Scarsdale. I was playing basketball with my father in our backyard according to procedures we had developed. My father would stand beneath the hoop, shout, and I would shoot over his head at the basket attached to the garage. Our next-door neighbor, aged five, wandered over into our yard with a playmate. "He's blind," our neighbor whispered to her friend in a voice that could be heard distinctly by Dad and me. Dad shot and missed; I did the same. Dad hit the rim: I missed entirely; Dad shot and missed the garage entirely. "Which one is blind?" whispered back the little friend.

(8) I would hope that in the near future when a plant manager is touring the factory with the foreman and comes upon a handicapped and nonhandicapped person working together, his comment after watching them work will be, "Which one is disabled?"

775 words

Here are some of the more difficult words in "Darkness at Noon."

disillusioning
(paragraph 5)

dis·il·lu·sion (dis'i loo'zhən) *vt.* **1** to free from illusion or false ideas; disenchant **2** to take away the ideals or idealism of and make disappointed, bitter, etc. —*n.* DISILLUSIONMENT

enunciating
(paragraph 2)

e|nun·ci·ate (ē nun'sē āt', i-; *also,* -shē-) *vt.* -at|ed, -at'ing [< L *enuntiatus,* pp. of *enuntiare* < e-, out + *nuntiare,* to announce < *nuntius,* a messenger] **1** to state definitely; express in a systematic way [*to enunciate* a theory] **2** to announce; proclaim **3** to pro-

exclusion
(paragraph 6)

ex·clude (eks klood', ik sklood') *vt.* -clud|ed, -clud'ing [ME *excluden* < L *excludere* < ex-, out + *claudere,* CLOSE³] **1** to refuse to admit, consider, include, etc.; shut out; keep from entering, happening, or being; reject; bar **2** to put out; force out; expel —ex·clud'-a|ble *adj.* —ex·clud'er *n.*
SYN.—exclude implies a keeping out or prohibiting of that which is not yet in [*to exclude* someone from membership]; **debar** connotes the existence of some barrier, as legal authority or force, which excludes someone from a privilege, right, etc. [*to debar* certain groups from voting]; **disbar** refers only to the expulsion of a lawyer from the group of those who are permitted to practice law; **eliminate** implies the removal of that which is already in, usually connoting its undesirability or irrelevance [*to eliminate* waste products]; **suspend** refers to the removal, usually temporary, of someone from some organization, institution, etc., as for the infraction of some rule [*to suspend* a student from school] —*ANT.* admit, include

ex·clu·sion (eks kloo'zhən, ik skloo'-) *n.* [ME *exclusioun* < L *exclusio* < pp. of *excludere*] **1** an excluding or being excluded **2** a thing excluded —to the exclusion of so as to keep out, bar, etc. — ex·clu·sion·ar|y *adj.*

intoned
(paragraph 3)

in·tone (in tōn') *vt.* -toned', -ton'ing [ME *entonen* < OFr *entoner* < ML *intonare:* IN-¹ & TONE] **1** to utter or recite in a singing tone or in prolonged monotones; chant **2** to give a particular intonation to **3** to sing or recite the opening phrase of (a chant, canticle, etc.) —*vi.* to speak or recite in a singing tone or in prolonged monotones; chant —in·ton'er *n.*

invariably
(paragraph 2)

in·vari·a|ble (in ver'ē ə bəl) *adj.* [ML *invariabilis*] not variable; not changing; constant; uniform —*n.* an invariable quantity; constant — in·var|i·a|bil'i|ty or in·var|i·a|ble·ness *n.* —in·var|i·a|bly *adv.*

mandate
(paragraph 6)

man·date (man'dāt') *n.* [L *mandatum,* neut. pp. of *mandare,* lit., to put into one's hand, command, entrust < *manus,* a hand + pp. of *dare,* to give: see MANUAL & DATE¹] **1** an authoritative order or command, esp. a written one **2** [Historical] *a)* a commission from the League of Nations to a country to administer some region, colony, etc. *b)* the area so administered: cf. TRUSTEESHIP (sense 2), TRUST TERRITORY **3** the wishes of constituents expressed to a representative, legislature, etc., as through an election and regarded as an order **4** *Law a)* an order from a higher court or official to a lower one: a **mandate on remission** is a mandate from an appellate court to the lower court, communicating its decision in a case appealed *b)* in English law, a bailment of personal property with no consideration *c)* in Roman law, a commission or contract by which a person undertakes to do something for another, without recompense but with indemnity against loss *d)* any contract of agency —*vt.* -dat|ed, -dat'ing to assign (a region, etc.) as a mandate —man·da'tor *n.*

misconception
(paragraph 5)

mis·con·ceive (mis'kən sēv') *vt., vi.* -ceived', -ceiv'ing to conceive wrongly; interpret incorrectly; misunderstand —mis'con·cep'tion (-sep'shən) *n.*

narcissistic
(paragraph 1)

nar·cis·sism (när'sə siz'əm; *chiefly Brit,* när sis'iz'am) *n.* [Ger *Narzissismus* (< *Narziss,* NARCISSUS) + -ismus, -ISM] **1** self-love; excessive interest in one's own appearance, comfort, importance, abilities, etc. **2** *Psychoanalysis* arrest at or regression to the first stage of libidinal development, in which the self is an object of erotic pleasure Also nar'cism —nar'cis·sist *n., adj.* —nar·cis·sis'tic *adj.*

retina
(paragraph 2)

reti·na (ret"n ə) *n., pl.* -nas or -nae' (-ē') [ML, prob. < L *rete* (gen. *retis*), net < IE base *ere-, loose, separate > Gr *erēmos,* solitary, Lith *rētis,* sieve & (prob.) L *rarus,* rare] the innermost coat lining the interior of the eyeball, containing various layers of photoreceptive cells that are directly connected to the brain by means of the optic nerve: see EYE, illus.

4A VOCABULARY

Using the dictionary entries on page 67, fill in the blanks.

1. The rear part of the eyeball that is sensitive to light is called the

    _____ .

2. In the United States the _____ of any person from employment because of his race, color, or sex is both illegal and immoral.

3. It is _____ when we discover that a public official has used his or her office to force people to pay bribes.

4. The diplomat spoke precisely, carefully _____ each word clearly for his audience.

5. Some people are so self-centered and convinced of their own

    importance that they can easily be labeled "_____ ."

6. The restaurant owners decided to _____ all smokers from the main dining room.

7. The higher court issued a _____ which reversed the lower court's ruling concerning discrimination.

8. A person with employable skills will _____ have better job opportunities than will a person without such skills.

9. An adult can _____ a child very quickly if that adult sets a bad example by breaking the law or by being cruel to people.

10. At the funeral the minister _____ special passages from the Bible.

11. The tenant was acting under the serious _____ that he could continue to occupy his apartment without paying rent.

Name   Date

4B   CENTRAL THEME AND MAIN IDEAS
Choose the best answer.

_____ 1. What is the central theme of "Darkness at Noon"?
   a. The author leads a very fulfilling life as a lawyer and hus-band.
   b. Blind people often have difficulty finding jobs because employers prefer to hire sighted people.
   c. Handicapped people need to organize and campaign for bet-ter laws to protect them.
   d. People often assume that because blind people cannot see, they cannot hear, learn, or work.

_____ 2. What is the main idea of paragraph 2?
   a. It is generally assumed that people who cannot see cannot hear.
   b. The way that many people behave in the presence of the blind can be described as downright "silly."
   c. Some people think that it is improper to use the word "blind" in the presence of blind people.
   d. Airline personnel use the number "76" to refer to blind peo-ple.

_____ 3. What is the main idea of paragraph 5?
   a. The worst frustration for the author was when 40 or more law firms refused to hire him because he was blind.
   b. Many employers think that if a lawyer cannot see, he or she cannot work.
   c. The author got his undergraduate degree from Harvard University and his law degree from Harvard Law School.
   d. The rejection letters sent to the author were disillusioning.

4C   MAJOR DETAILS
Decide whether each detail is MAJOR or MINOR.

_____ 1. The author has been blind from birth.

_____ 2. People often shout at blind people and pronounce every word with great care.

_____ 3. Airline personnel use a code to refer to blind people.

_____ 4. The author goes out to dinner with his wife Kit.

_____ 5. If a blind person and a sighted person are together, other people will usually communicate with them by talking with the sighted person.

Name   Date

_____ 6. The author was given a year's leave of absence from his Washington law firm to study for a diploma-in-law degree at Oxford University.

_____ 7. The author had to be hospitalized while he was studying in England.

_____ 8. In 1976 the Department of Labor issued regulations that require equal employment opportunities for the handicapped.

_____ 9. On the whole, the business community's response to offering employment of the handicapped has been enthusiastic.

_____ 10. The author and his father played basketball in the backyard using a special system they had worked out.

_____ 11. The author's father shot for the basket and missed completely.

_____ 12. The neighbor's friend was not sure if the author or his father was blind.

4D INFERENCES

Decide whether each statement below can be inferred (YES) or cannot be inferred (NO) from the reading selection.

_____ 1. The title of the essay suggests that it is sighted people, not blind people, who cannot "see."

_____ 2. The author feels that he is greatly admired by people who meet him.

_____ 3. The author feels that he can make his point more effectively with humor than with a stern lecture.

_____ 4. The author often eats in restaurants with his wife Kit.

_____ 5. The author was highly entertained by the conversation in the hospital between the elderly lady and the orderly.

_____ 6. The author got good grades at Harvard Law School because he was given special privileges reserved for blind students.

_____ 7. The April 10, 1976, Department of Labor regulations were enacted because the author had complained publicly about the discrimination he experienced while looking for a job.

_____ 8. The author's father was a much better basketball player than was the author.

Name   Date

4E   CRITICAL READING: FACT OR OPINION

Decide whether each statement contains a FACT or OPINION.

_____ 1. *From paragraph 1:* Blind from birth, I have never had the opportunity to see myself.

_____ 2. *From paragraph 2:* They fear that if the dread word is spoken, the ticket agent's retina will immediately detach.

_____ 3. *From paragraph 3:* I had been given a year's leave of absence from my Washington law firm to study for a diploma-in-law at Oxford University.

_____ 4. *From paragraph 5:* I was turned down by over forty law firms because of my blindness.

_____ 5. *From paragraph 6:* By and large, the business community's response to offering employment to the disabled has been enthusiastic.

_____ 6. *From paragraph 7:* Dad shot [the basketball] and missed the garage entirely.

4F   CRITICAL READING: THE WRITER'S CRAFT

Choose the best answer.

_____ 1. The author shows the connections between each of his ideas with all of these words *except*
   a. to date   (paragraph 1)
   b. obviously   (2)
   c. also   (2)
   d. conversely   (2)
   e. for example   (2)
   f. on the other hand (3)
   g. therefore   (3)
   h. finally   (4)

_____ 2. In paragraph 3, rather than telling what happened in his own words, the author uses dialogue. He does this for all of these reasons *except*
   a. to help the reader experience the situation.
   b. to illustrate exactly how foolishly the people behaved.
   c. to impress the reader with his ability to recall the exact words in a conversation.
   d. to dramatize the frustration he felt.

Name   Date

71

_____ 3. The last sentence of paragraph 4 is an example of
   a. irony.   (definition on page 162)
   b. calamity.   (definition on page 113)
   c. coherence.   (definition on page 276)

4G   INFORMED OPINION

1. Would you avoid using a particular lawyer if he or she were blind? Explain.

2. Why is it that some people are not sure how to behave when they are with physically handicapped people?

How Did You Do?   **4** Darkness at Noon

SKILL (number of items)	Number Correct	Points for Each	Score
Vocabulary (11)	_____ ×	3	= _____
Central Theme and Main Ideas (3)	_____ ×	4	= _____
Major Details (12)	_____ ×	2	= _____
Inferences (8)	_____ ×	2	= _____
Critical Reading: Fact or Opinion (6)	_____ ×	2	= _____
Critical Reading: The Writer's Craft (3)	_____ ×	1	= _____

(Possible Total: 100) *Total* _____

SPEED

Reading Time: _____ Reading Rate (page 348): _____ Words Per Minute

Name   Date

Selection 5

I Became Her Target

Roger Wilkins

(1) My favorite teacher's name was "Deadeye" Bean. Her real name was Dorothy. She taught American history to eighth graders in the junior high section of Creston, the high school that served the north end of Grand Rapids, Michigan. It was the fall of 1944. Franklin D. Roosevelt was president; American troops were battling their way across France; Joe DiMaggio was still in the service; the Montgomery bus boycott was more than a decade away, and I was a 12-year-old black newcomer in a school that was otherwise all white.

(2) My mother, who had been a widow in New York, had married my stepfather, a Grand Rapids physician, the year before, and he had bought the best house he could afford for his new family. The problem for our new neighbors was that their neighborhood had previously been pristine (in their terms) and they were ignorant about black people. The prevailing wisdom in the neighborhood was that we were spoiling it and that we ought to go back where we belonged (or alternatively, ought not intrude where we were not wanted). There was a lot of angry talk among the adults, but nothing much came of it.

(3) But some of the kids, those first few weeks, were quite nasty. They threw stones at me, chased me home when I was on foot and spat on my bike seat when I was in class. For a time, I was a pretty lonely, friendless and sometimes frightened kid. I was just transplanted from Harlem, and here in Grand Rapids, the dominant culture was speaking to me insistently. I can see now that those youngsters were bullying and culturally disadvantaged. I knew then that they were bigoted, but the culture spoke to me more powerfully than my mind and I felt ashamed for being different—a nonstandard person.

(4) I now know that Dorothy Bean understood most of that and deplored it. So things began to change when I walked into her classroom. She was a pleasant-looking single woman, who looked old and wrinkled to me at the time, but who was probably about 40. Whereas my other teachers approached the problem of easing in their new black pupil by ignoring him for the first few weeks, Miss Bean went right at me. On the morning after having read our first assignment, she asked me the first question. I later came to know that in Grand Rapids, she was viewed as a very liberal person who believed, among other things, that Negroes were equal.

From *Newsday* Magazine, Sept. 6, 1987. Reprinted with permission of the author.

(5) I gulped and answered her question and the follow-up. They weren't brilliant answers, but they did establish the facts that I had read the assignment and that I could speak English. Later in the hour, when one of my classmates had bungled an answer, Miss Bean came back to me with a question that required me to clean up the girl's mess and established me as a smart person.

(6) Thus, the teacher began to give me human dimensions, though not perfect ones for an eighth grader. It was somewhat better to be an incipient teacher's pet than merely a dark presence in the back of the room onto whose silent form my classmates could fit all the stereotypes they carried in their heads.

(7) A few days later, Miss Bean became the first teacher ever to require me to think. She asked my opinion about something Jefferson had done. In those days, all my opinions were derivative. I was for Roosevelt because my parents were and I was for the Yankees because my older buddy from Harlem was a Yankee fan. Besides, we didn't have opinions about historical figures like Jefferson. Like our high school building or old Mayor Welch, he just was.

(8) After I had stared at her for a few seconds, she said: "Well, should he have bought Louisiana or not?"

(9) "I guess so," I replied tentatively.

(10) "Why?" she shot back.

(11) Why! What kind of question was that, I groused silently. But I ventured an answer. Day after day, she kept doing that to me, and my answers became stronger and more confident. She was the first teacher to give me the sense that thinking was part of education and that I could form opinions that had some value.

(12) Her final service to me came on a day when my mind was wandering and I was idly digging my pencil into the writing surface on the arm of my chair. Miss Bean impulsively threw a hunk of gum eraser at me. By amazing chance, it hit my hand and sent the pencil flying. She gasped, and I crept mortified after my pencil as the class roared. That was the ice breaker. Afterward, kids came up to me to laugh about "Old Deadeye Bean." The incident became a legend, and I, a part of that story, became a person to talk to. So that's how I became just another kid in school and Dorothy Bean became "Old Dead-Eye."

800 words

Here are some of the more difficult words in "I Became Her Target."

bigoted
(paragraph 3)

big|ot (big′ət) *n.* [Fr < OFr, a term of insult used of Normans, apparently a Norman oath < ? ME *bi god*, by God] 1 a person who holds blindly and intolerantly to a particular creed, opinion, etc. 2 a narrow-minded person —*SYN.* ZEALOT —big′ot|ed *adj.* —big′ot·ed|ly *adv.*

boycott
(paragraph 1)

boy·cott (boi′kät′) *vt.* [after Capt. C. C. *Boycott*, land agent ostracized by his neighbors during the Land League agitation in Ireland in 1880] 1 to join together in refusing to deal with, so as to punish, coerce, etc. 2 to refuse to buy, sell, or use *[to boycott* a newspaper*]* —☆*n.* an act or instance of boycotting

Deadeye
(paragraph 1)

dead·eye (-ī′) *n.* 1 a round, flat block of wood with three holes in it for a lanyard, used in pairs on a sailing ship to hold the shrouds and stays taut 2 [Slang] an accurate marksman

derivative
(paragraph 7)

de·riv|a·tive (də riv′ə tiv) *adj.* [ME *derivatif* < LL *derivativus* < L *derivatus*, pp. of *derivare*: see fol.] 1 derived 2 using or taken from other sources; not original 3 of derivation —*n.* 1 something derived 2 *Chem.* a substance derived from, or of such composition and properties that it may be considered as derived from, another substance by chemical change, esp. by the substitution of one or more elements or radicals 3 *Linguis.* a word formed from another or others by derivation 4 *Math.* the limiting value of a rate of change of a function with respect to a variable; the instantaneous rate of change, or slope, of a function (Ex.: the derivative of y with respect to x, often written dy/dx, is 3 when $y = 3x$) —de·riv′|a·tive|ly *adv.*

de·rive (di riv′) *vt.* -rived′, -riv′ing [ME *deriven* < OFr *deriver* < L *derivare*, to divert, orig., to turn a stream from its channel < *de-*, from + *rivus*, a stream: see RIVAL] 1 to get or receive (something) *from* a source 2 to get by reasoning; deduce or infer 3 to trace from or to a source; show the derivation of 4 *Chem.* to obtain or produce (a compound) from another compound by replacing one element with one or more other elements —*vi.* to come (*from*); be derived; originate —*SYN.* RISE —de·riv′a|ble *adj.* —de·riv′|er *n.*

dominant
(paragraph 3)

dom|i·nant (däm′ə nənt) *adj.* [L *dominans*, prp. of *dominari*: see fol.] 1 exercising authority or influence; dominating; ruling; prevailing 2 *Genetics* designating or relating to that one of any pair of allelic hereditary factors which, when both are present in the germ plasm, dominates over the other and appears in the organism: opposed to RECESSIVE: see MENDEL'S LAWS 3 *Music* of or based upon the fifth tone of a diatonic scale —*n.* 1 *Ecol.* that species of plant or animal most numerous in a community or exercising control over the other organisms by its influence upon the environment 2 *Genetics* a dominant character or factor 3 *Music* the fifth note of a diatonic scale —dom′i·nantly *adv.*
SYN.—**dominant** refers to that which dominates or controls, or has the greatest effect *[dominant* characteristics in genetics*]*; **predominant** refers to that which is at the moment uppermost in importance or influence *[the predominant* reason for his refusal*]*; **paramount** is applied to that which ranks first in importance, authority, etc. *[of paramount* interest to me*]*; **preeminent** implies prominence because of surpassing excellence *[the preeminent* writer of his time*]*; **preponderant** implies superiority in amount, weight, power, importance, etc. *[the preponderant* religion of a country*]*

groused
(paragraph 11)

grouse (grous) *vi.* **groused, grous'ing** [orig. Brit army slang < ?]
[Colloq.] to complain; grumble —*n.* [Colloq.] a complaint —
grous'er *n.*

incipient
(paragraph 6)

in·cip·i·ent (in sip′ē ent) *adj.* [L *incipiens*, prp. of *incipere*, to begin,
lit., take up < *in-*, in, on + *capere*, to take: see HAVE] in the first
stage of existence; just beginning to exist or to come to notice [an
incipient illness] —**in·cip′i·ence** or **in·cip′i·en·cy** *n.* —**in·cip′i·ent·ly**
adv.

insistently
(paragraph 3)

in·sist (in sist′) *vi.* [MFr *insister* < L *insistere*, to stand on, pursue
diligently, persist < *in-*, in, on + *sistere*, to stand, redupl. of *stare*,
STAND] to take and maintain a stand or make a firm demand: often
with *on* or *upon* —*vt.* **1** to demand strongly **2** to declare firmly or
persistently —**in·sist′er** *n.* —**in·sist′ing·ly** *adv.*

in·sist·ent (-tənt) *adj.* [L *insistens*] **1** insisting or demanding; persistent in demands or assertions **2** compelling the attention [an
insistent rhythm] —**in·sist′ent·ly** *adv.*

mortified
(paragraph 12)

mor·ti·fy (môrt′ə fī′) *vt.* **-fied′, -fy′ing** [ME *mortifien* < OFr *mortifier*
< LL(Ec) *mortificare*, to kill, destroy < L *mors*, death (see MORTAL)
+ *facere*, to make, DO¹] **1** to punish (one's body) or control (one's
physical desires and passions) by self-denial, fasting, etc., as a means
of religious or ascetic discipline **2** to cause to feel shame, humiliation, chagrin, etc.; injure the pride or self-respect of **3** [Now Rare]
to cause (body tissue) to decay or become gangrenous **4** to destroy
the vitality or vigor of —*vi.* **1** to practice MORTIFICATION (sense 1a)
2 [Now Rare] to decay or become gangrenous —**mor′ti·fi′er** *n.*

pristine
(paragraph 2)

pris·tine (pris′tēn′, -tin; pris tēn′; *chiefly Brit* pris′tīn′) *adj.* [L *pris-
tinus*, former < OL *pri*, before: see prec.] **1** characteristic of the
earliest, or an earlier, period or condition; original **2** still pure
uncorrupted; unspoiled [*pristine* beauty] —**pris′tine·ly** *adv.*

ventured
(paragraph 11)

ven·ture (ven′chər) *n.* [ME, aphetic for *aventure*: see ADVENTURE] **1**
a risky or dangerous undertaking; esp., a business enterprise in
which there is danger of loss as well as chance for profit **2** something on which a risk is taken, as the merchandise in a commercial
enterprise or a stake in gambling **3** chance; fortune: now only in **at a
venture** by mere chance, at random —*vt.* **-tured, -tur·ing 1** to
expose to danger or risk [to *venture* one's life] **2** to expose (money,
merchandise, etc.) to chance of loss **3** to undertake the risk of; brave
[to *venture* a storm] **4** to express at the risk of criticism, objection,
denial, etc. [to *venture* an opinion] —*vi.* to do or go at some risk —
ven′tur·er *n.*

5A VOCABULARY

From the context of "I Became Her Target," explain the meaning of each of the vocabulary words shown in boldface below.

1. *From paragraph 1:* My favorite teacher's name was **"Deadeye"** Bean.

   _____

   _____

2. *From paragraph 1:* The Montgomery bus **boycott** was more than a decade away, and I was a 12-year-old black newcomer in a school that was otherwise all white.

   _____

   _____

3. *From paragraph 2:* The problem for our new neighbors was that their neighborhood had previously been **pristine.**

   _____

   _____

4. *From paragraph 3:* I was just transplanted from Harlem, and here in Grand Rapids, the **dominant** culture was speaking to me **insistently.**

   _____

   _____

   _____

   _____

5. *From paragraph 3:* I knew then that they were **bigoted.**

   _____

   _____

6. *From paragraph 6:* It was somewhat better to be an **incipient** teacher's pet than merely a dark presence in the back of the room.

   _____

   _____

7. *From paragraph 7:* In those days, all my opinions were **derivative.**

   _____

   _____

Name   Date

8. *From paragraph 11:* What kind of question was that, I **groused** silently. But I **ventured** an answer.

_____

_____

_____

_____

9. *From paragraph 12:* I crept **mortified** after my pencil as the class roared.

_____

_____

5B   CENTRAL THEME AND MAIN IDEAS

Choose the best answer.

_____ 1. What is the central theme of "I Became Her Target"?
   a. Roger Wilkins' teacher did not like him and asked him trick questions because he was black and she was a racist.
   b. Roger Wilkins' classmates had been raised by their parents to be racists, and until they were forced to be nice to Wilkins they had no idea what black people were really like.
   c. Roger Wilkins' teacher helped him realize his worth and get the respect of the other students by challenging him to show his intelligence and answer hard questions.
   d. Roger Wilkins' classmates became his friends once they realized that he and they shared a dislike of their American history teacher.

_____ 2. What is the main idea of paragraph 7?
   a. Roger Wilkins did not like being called upon to answer hard questions.
   b. Roger Wilkins did not know anything about President Jefferson.
   c. All of Roger Wilkins' opinions were derived from his parents or friends.
   d. Roger Wilkins was not used to being asked to think and form his own opinions.

Name   Date

_____ 3. What is the main idea of paragraph 12?
  a. Miss Bean helped Roger Wilkins gain his classmates' acceptance by throwing an eraser at him when his attention wandered.
  b. Miss Bean always looked for opportunities to embarrass her students by throwing erasers at them.
  c. Miss Bean had only pretended to be interested in Roger Wilkins' education, but she was a racist underneath.
  d. Roger Wilkins was accepted by his classmates only after he mortified Miss Bean in front of them.

5C MAJOR DETAILS

Decide whether each detail is true (T), or false (F), or not discussed (ND).

_____ 1. Roger Wilkins' favorite teacher was Dorothy Bean.

_____ 2. He was in her eighth grade American history class in 1944.

_____ 3. Before Wilkins, no black student had ever attended Creston High School in Grand Rapids, Michigan.

_____ 4. Wilkins' mother met his stepfather in New York.

_____ 5. The adults in Wilkins' new neighborhood threw stones at his house because they wanted his family to move away.

_____ 6. Miss Bean asked Roger Wilkins the very first question on the very first assignment.

_____ 7. Dorothy Bean was viewed as a very liberal person, who believed, among other things, that blacks were equal to whites.

_____ 8. Roger Wilkins had never been to Harlem.

_____ 9. Miss Bean kept asking Roger Wilkins questions day after day until his answers became increasingly confident.

_____ 10. It was the tradition at Creston High School to give teachers nicknames.

Name   Date

5D INFERENCES

Choose the best answer.

_____ 1. *Read paragraphs 1, 2, and 4 again.* Why does the author change from using the word "black" in these paragraphs to using the word "Negroes" in the last sentence of paragraph 4?

a. By using the word "Negroes," the author shows that he is prejudiced against his own black people.

b. The preferred, formal term for blacks was "Negroes" in 1944, and the author wants to recreate that time for the reader.

c. The author assumes that the words "Negroes" and "blacks" are interchangeable, although today the preferred term is "blacks."

d. The author prefers the word "Negroes," even though in 1987, when he wrote this essay, the preferred word was "blacks."

_____ 2. *Read paragraph 3 again.* What is the author implying when he calls the white students "culturally disadvantaged," a term that is usually applied to undereducated minority people?

a. The author is not aware of how the term is usually used.

b. The author is implying that the students at Creston High School had not gotten a good education and had not developed good study habits.

c. The author is trying to be polite by using a nice word for "stupid."

d. The author is being mildly sarcastic, applying a term to these students that they or their parents might have applied to him.

_____ 3. *Read paragraph 6 again.* Why did Roger Wilkins feel "it was somewhat better to be an incipient teacher's pet than merely a dark presence in the back of the room"?

a. He preferred being liked by the teacher to being liked by no one at all.

b. He felt that being teacher's pet might result in his getting special privileges or a higher grade.

c. He did not like the other students and did not care what they thought of him.

d. He did not like sitting in the back of the room, and he hoped that Miss Bean would change his seat.

Name   Date

5E CRITICAL READING: THE WRITER'S CRAFT

Choose the best answer.

_____ 1. The author gives Dorothy Bean's nickname in paragraph 1 in order to
   a. immediately arouse the reader's curiosity.
   b. add to the list of historic facts.
   c. give an anecdote.
   d. make a comparison.

_____ 2. *Read paragraphs 8 to 10 again.* The author includes this dialogue for all of the following reasons *except* it
   a. was typical of his early questioning by Miss Bean.
   b. shows how she tried to embarrass him in front of the other students.
   c. demonstrates Miss Bean's personality as a teacher.
   d. shows how Miss Bean forced him to think.

_____ 3. *Read paragraph 10 again.* If the phrase "shot back" were replaced by the word "asked," Miss Bean's response would seem *less*
   a. cruel.
   b. humble.
   c. dramatic.
   d. professional.

_____ 4. *Read paragraph 12 again.* This anecdote accomplishes all of the following *except* to
   a. explain how Dorothy Bean earned her nickname.
   b. show that Miss Bean was a tough disciplinarian.
   c. tell how the other students came to accept the author by identifying with his embarrassment.
   d. demonstrate that the author felt comfortable with Miss Bean.

5F INFORMED OPINION

1. A new student in any established class often has a hard time fitting in. What role do you think teachers in high school and college should take in helping new students to adjust? Using specific examples, explain your point of view.

2. Suppose the "best house" you could "afford" (paragraph 2) were in a neighborhood where people of your race, religion, or ethnic background are not wanted. Would you move into that neighborhood? Explain your point of view fully.

Name   Date

How Did You Do?   **5 I Became Her Target**

SKILL (number of items)	Number Correct		Points for Each		Score
Vocabulary (11)	_____	×	3	=	_____
Central Theme and Main Ideas (3)	_____	×	4	=	_____
Major Details (10)	_____	×	4	=	_____
Inferences (3)	_____	×	1	=	_____
Critical Reading: The Writer's Craft (4)	_____	×	3	=	_____

(Possible Total: 100) *Total* _____

SPEED

Reading Time: _____ Reading Rate (page 348): _____ Words Per Minute

Name   Date

The Girl with the Large Eyes

Julius Lester

(1) Many years ago in a village in Africa, there lived a girl with large eyes. She had the most beautiful eyes of any girl in the village, and whenever one of the young men looked at her as she passed through the marketplace, her gaze was almost more than he could bear.

(2) The summer she was to marry, a drought came upon the region. No rain had fallen for months, and the crops died, the earth changed to dust, and the wells and rivers turned to mudholes. The people grew hungry, and when a man's mind can see nothing except his hunger, he cannot think of marriage, not even to such a one as the girl with the large eyes.

(3) She had little time to think of the wedding that would have been had there been no drought. She had little time to daydream of the hours of happiness she would have been sharing with her new husband. Indeed, she had little time at all, for it was her job each day to find water for her family. That was not easy. She spent the morning going up and down the river bank, scooping what little water she could from the mudholes until she had a pitcher full.

(4) One morning, she walked back and forth along the river bank for a long while, but could find no water. Suddenly, a fish surfaced from the mud and said to her, "Give me your pitcher and I will fill it with water."

(5) She was surprised to hear the fish talk, and a little frightened, but she had found no water that morning, so she handed him the pitcher, and he filled it with cold, clear water.

(6) Everyone was surprised when she brought home a pitcher of such clear water, and they wanted to know where she had found it. She smiled with her large eyes, but she said nothing.

(7) The next day she returned to the same place, called the fish, and again he filled her pitcher with cold, clear water. Each day thereafter she returned, and soon she found herself becoming fond of the fish. His skin was the colors of the rainbow and as smooth as the sky on a clear day. His voice was soft and gentle like the cool, clear water he put in her pitcher. And on the seventh day, she let the fish embrace her, and she became his wife.

(8) Her family was quite happy to get the water each day, but they were still very curious to know from where she was getting it. Each day

From *Black Folktales* by Julius Lester. Published by the Richard W. Baron Publishing Co., Inc. Reprinted by permission.

they asked her many questions, but she only smiled at them with her large eyes and said nothing.

(9) The girl's father was a witch doctor, and he feared that the girl had taken up with evil spirits. One day he changed the girl's brother into a fly and told him to sit in the pitcher and find out from where she was getting the water. When she got to the secret place, the brother listened to the girl and the fish and watched them embrace, and he flew quickly home to tell his father what he had heard and seen. When the parents learned that their daughter had married a fish, they were greatly embarrassed and ashamed. If the young men of the village found out, none of them would ever marry her. And if the village found out, the family would be forced to leave in disgrace.

(10) The next morning, the father ordered the girl to stay at home, and the brother took him to the secret place beside the river. They called to the fish, and, when he came up, they killed him and took him home. They flung the fish at the girl's feet and said, "We have brought your husband to you."

(11) The girl looked at them and at the fish beside her feet, his skin growing dull and cloudy, his colors fading. And her eyes filled with tears.

(12) She picked up the fish and walked to the river, wondering what was to become of the child she was carrying inside her. If her parents had killed her husband, would they not kill her child when it was born?

(13) She walked for many miles, carrying her husband in her arms, until she came to a place where the waters were flowing. She knew that suffering could only be cured by medicine or patience. If neither of those relieved it, suffering would always yield to death.

(14) Calling her husband's name, she waded into the water until it flowed above her head. But as she died, she gave birth to many children, and they still float on the rivers to this day as water lilies.

850 words

Here are some of the more difficult words in "The Girl with the Large Eyes."

drought
(paragraph 2)

drought (drout) *n.* ⟦ME < OE *drugoth*, dryness < *drugian*, to dry up; akin to *dryge*, DRY⟧ **1** a prolonged period of dry weather; lack of rain **2** a prolonged or serious shortage or deficiency **3** [Archaic] thirst — **drought′y, drought′i·er, drought′i·est,** *adj.*

fond
(paragraph 7)

fond[1] (fänd) *adj.* ⟦ME, contr. of *fonned*, foolish, pp. of *fonnen*, to be foolish⟧ **1** [Now Rare] foolish, esp. foolishly naive, credulous, or hopeful **2** tender and affectionate; loving; sometimes, affectionate in a foolish or overly indulgent way; doting **3** cherished with great or unreasoning affection; doted on *[a fond hope]* —**fond of** having a liking for

gaze
(paragraph 1)

gaze (gāz) *vi.* **gazed, gaz′ing** ⟦ME *gazen* < Scand, as in Norw & Swed dial. *gasa*, to stare < ON *gas*, GOOSE⟧ to look intently and steadily; stare, as in wonder or expectancy —*n.* a steady look —**gaz′-er** *n.*

scooping
(paragraph 3)

scoop (skoōp) *n.* ⟦ME *scope* < MDu *schope*, bailing vessel, *schoppe*, a shovel, akin to Ger *schöpfen*, to dip out, create⟧ **1** any of various utensils shaped like a small shovel or a ladle; specif., *a)* a kitchen utensil used to take up sugar, flour, etc. *b)* a small utensil with a round bowl, for dishing up ice cream, mashed potatoes, etc. *c)* a small, spoonlike surgical instrument **2** the deep shovel of a dredge or steam shovel, which takes up sand, dirt, etc. **3** the act or motion of taking up with or as with a scoop **4** the amount taken up at one time by a scoop **5** a hollowed-out place ☆**6** [Colloq.] *a)* the publication or broadcast of a news item before a competitor; beat *b)* such a news item *c)* current, esp. confidential, information —*adj.* designating a rounded, somewhat low neckline in a dress, etc. —*vt.* **1** to take up or out with or as with a scoop **2** to empty by bailing **3** to dig (*out*); hollow (*out*) **4** to make by digging out **5** to gather (*in* or *up*) as if with a scoop ☆**6** [Colloq.] to publish or broadcast a news item before (a competitor) —**scoop′er** *n.*

surfaced
(paragraph 4)

sur·face (sur′fis) *n.* ⟦Fr < *sur-* (see SUR-[1]) + *fqce*, FACE, based on L *superficies*⟧ **1** *a)* the outer face, or exterior, of an object *b)* any of the faces of a solid *c)* the area or extent of such a face **2** superficial features, as of a personality; outward appearance **3** AIRFOIL **4** *Geom.* an extent or magnitude having length and breadth, but no thickness —*adj.* **1** of, on, or at the surface **2** intended to function or be carried on land or sea, rather than in the air or under water *[surface forces, surface mail]* **3** merely apparent; external; superficial —*vt.* **-faced, -fac·ing 1** to treat the surface of, esp. so as to make smooth or level **2** to give a surface to, as in paving **3** to bring to the surface; esp., to bring (a submarine) to the surface of the water —*vi.* **1** to work at or near the surface, as in mining **2** to rise to the surface of the water **3** to become known, esp. after being concealed —**sur′-facer** *n.*

6A   VOCABULARY

From the context of "The Girl with the Large Eyes," explain the meaning of each of the vocabulary words shown in boldface below.

1. *From paragraph 1:* . . . and whenever one of the young men looked at her as she passed through the marketplace, her **gaze** was almost more than he could bear.

   _____

   _____

   _____

2. *From paragraph 2:* The summer she was to marry, a **drought** came upon the region.

   _____

   _____

   _____

3. *From paragraph 3:* She spent the morning going up and down the river bank, **scooping** what little water she could from the mudholes until she had a pitcher full.

   _____

   _____

   _____

4. *From paragraph 4:* A fish **surfaced** from the mud and said to her . . .

   _____

   _____

   _____

5. *From paragraph 7:* Each day thereafter she returned, and soon she found herself becoming **fond** of the fish.

   _____

   _____

   _____

Name _____ Date _____

6B CENTRAL THEME AND MAIN IMAGES

Choose the best answer.

_____ 1. "The Girl with the Large Eyes" is a story about
   a. a beautiful girl who feels that the purpose of her life is to give birth to water lilies.
   b. a beautiful girl who falls in love with and marries a fish.
   c. a father and son who want to protect the beautiful girl from disgracing herself in the village.
   d. a fish that falls in love with and marries the most beautiful girl in the village.

_____ 2. What is the moral of the underlying central theme of "The Girl with the Large Eyes"?
   a. Love is blind.
   b. Humans and fish have a right to marry each other.
   c. Families have to protect their reputations.
   d. Prejudice in all forms is destructive and cruel.

_____ 3. The unexpected main image of paragraph 4 is
   a. the girl's walking on the river bank.
   b. a fish that surfaced from the mud.
   c. a fish that could talk.
   d. the fish's offer to fill the pitcher.

_____ 4. The main image in paragraph 7 is of
   a. the girl and the fish falling in love.
   b. the girl who is calling to the fish.
   c. the girl who is returning every day to see the fish.
   d. the fish's smooth colorful skin and gentle voice.

_____ 5. The main image in paragraphs 10 and 11 is of
   a. the brother and father going to the secret place at the river.
   b. the fish's skin growing dull and cloudy.
   c. the brutal murder of the fish followed by the girl's grief.
   d. the father's ordering the girl to stay at home.

_____ 6. The unexpected main image in paragraph 12 is
   a. the girl's picking up the dead fish.
   b. the girl's being pregnant.
   c. the girl's walking to the river.
   d. the girl's knowing that her parents killed her husband.

87

Name   Date

6C MAJOR DETAILS

Fill in the word or words that correctly complete each statement.

1. The girl with the large eyes was the most _____ girl in the village.

2. Because of the terrible drought, the girl had to spend her time _____ for water.

3. One day a _____ offered to bring her water.

4. On the _____ day, the girl let the fish embrace her, and she became his_____.

5. The girl's witch-doctor father turned her _____ into a _____ so he could discover where the girl got the water.

6. The father and brother _____ the fish and _____ it at the girl's feet.

7. The girl was pregnant and was afraid her parents would kill the _____ when they found out.

8. The girl knew that suffering could usually be cured by medicine or _____ rather than death.

9. The grief stricken girl carried her dead husband to the river and waded into it until it _____ above her head.

10. As she died, she gave birth to many children which to this day float on rivers as _____ .

Name   Date

6D INFERENCES

Choose the best answer.

_____ 1. *Read paragraphs 6 and 8 again.* The girl did not tell her family about the fish because she
   a. knew the fish did not want her to say anything.
   b. knew they would not approve.
   c. was saving the news for a surprise.
   d. was embarrassed that she loved a fish.

_____ 2. The creation of the water lilies at the end of the story implies that
   a. water lilies are part human and part fish.
   b. the deaths of the girl and the fish had a purpose.
   c. people should feel sad when they see water lilies.
   d. the result of true love is beauty.

6E CRITICAL READING: THE WRITER'S CRAFT

Choose the best answer.

_____ 1. "The Girl with the Large Eyes" is a folktale, which is a story handed down orally among the common people. The purpose of this folktale is to
   a. teach the history of an African tribe.
   b. warn people not to trust fish.
   c. explain the effects of a drought.
   d. illustrate the destructive power of prejudice.

_____ 2. The word "embrace" in paragraph 7 means to
   a. kiss.
   b. hug.
   c. make love with.
   d. become close friends with.

_____ 3. If the word "flung" in paragraph 10 were replaced by the word "placed," what feelings would be missing?
   a. love and concern
   b. anger and triumph
   c. embarrassment and fear
   d. tenderness and disappointment

Name   Date

_____ 4. Water appears often in this folktale. Water appears in connection with all these *except*
   a. the fish's voice.
   b. the girl's tears.
   c. the drought.
   d. the girl's death.

6F   INFORMED OPINION

1. Was the father justified in spying on his daughter? Explain.

2. *Read paragraph 13 again.* Does suffering that cannot be cured by medicine or patience *always* yield to death? Explain.

How Did You Do?   6 The Girl with the Large Eyes

SKILL (number of items)	Number Correct		Points for Each		Score
Vocabulary (5)	_____	×	4	=	_____
Central Theme and Main Ideas (6)	_____	×	6	=	_____
Major Details* (13)	_____	×	2	=	_____
Inferences (2)	_____	×	3	=	_____
Critical Reading: The Writer's Craft (4)	_____	×	3	=	_____

(Possible Total: 100) *Total* _____

SPEED

Reading Time: _____ Reading Rate (page 348): _____ Words Per Minute

*Questions 4, 5, and 6 in this exercise call for two separate answers each. In computing your score, count each separate answer toward your number correct.

Writing:
Expressing Yourself

What are *your* ideas on the subjects that you have read about in Part 1 of this book? Now is *your* chance to express your ideas in writing.

Below are some topics to write about. You are not expected to write on all of them, of course. Just select what appeals to you. Or, feel free to make up your own topics. Most important, try to find a subject that moves you to want to express yourself in writing.

All of the topics below relate in some way to the reading selections in Part 1 of this book. Some of the topics have been touched on already in the opening section of Part 1, "Thinking: Getting Started," page 37, or in the Informed Opinion questions that followed each of the reading selections in Part 1. Others of these topics are introduced here for the first time.

The topics below give you a choice among various kinds of writing. You can write a **narrative** that will tell your reader an interesting story. You can write a **description** that will give your reader a vivid picture of the image you have in mind. You can write a **report** that will give your reader important information about a subject, process, or event. You can write an **argument** to try to persuade your reader to agree with you. Differences among these kinds of writing are not always clear-cut, and so you can feel free to use any **combination** that works for you. As you write, see if you can make use of the new vocabulary words that you have been studying in Part 1.

IDEAS FOR PARAGRAPHS

1. Why do some people consider it "unmanly" when men are kind, considerate, and wholesomely affectionate toward children?

2. Do you believe that "hard work pays off"? Cite a specific example to prove your point of view.

3. "The most aggressive, the strongest people we know are the weak ones" ("Tyranny of Weakness," paragraph 2). Explain what you think is meant by this statement.

4. Do you know someone who uses helplessness as a means to control family members, co-workers, or friends? Describe some specific techniques this person uses to control others.

5. How do you think physically handicapped people feel when they have to be with people who "can't see the person behind the handicap"? Using specific examples, explain your ideas fully.

6. Should parents try to stop their children from marrying someone the parents do not like? Using specific examples, explain your point of view.

IDEAS FOR ESSAYS

1. Traditionally, American society has not encouraged men to be especially affectionate, even toward their own children. But attitudes seem to be changing. Discuss the benefits for men, for women, and for children when men are free to express wholesome affection.

2. Imagine that you own 60 acres of farm land worth $300,000. Because the land does not make enough money as farm land to keep animals, crops, and family going, you have to sell the land. What would you do with $300,000? Be specific as to the ways you would use the money.

3. The traditional view of a marriage is that housework is a woman's job. Do you think a husband should be expected to help with household chores, such as cooking and cleaning? Explain your point of view.

4. How do you feel about yourself? Is your self-esteem high or low? Using specific examples, describe several incidents that have influenced the way you perceive yourself.

5. In recent years our society has started to pay more attention to the needs of people who are physically handicapped. Do you think that society is doing enough? Using specific examples, explain your point of view.

6. Discuss a teacher or other adult who had a big impact on you when you were growing up. Using specific details and examples, describe the ways in which he or she affected you.

7. Should two people from very different backgrounds marry? Using specific examples, explain your point of view.

Thinking:
Getting Started

Using your prior knowledge of a subject helps you efficiently read and remember new material on that subject. Skilled readers approach reading with a confident attitude. They believe they usually know something—even a little bit, no matter how remote—about almost any subject they encounter. That little bit of prior knowledge becomes the foundation upon which they build a larger bank of learned information.

Before you start to dive into a reading, think about the subject about which you are going to read and try to recall what you know about the subject. Use the next three pages of visuals and accompanying questions to start becoming conscious of your prior knowledge about the subjects in the reading selections in Part 2 of this book. As you finish interacting with each separate visual, turn to its related reading selection and use the technique of *survey*, explained on page 11 and illustrated in the "SQ3R Guided Practice" that starts on page 11.

What sorts of events can happen in people's lives that drastically alter the way they look at the world? (See "Summer.")

TIME, 150 Years of Photo Journalism, Fall 1989, p. 61. Civil Rights - Birmingham 1963. Photo © Charles Moore/Black Star.

This photograph was taken in Birmingham, Alabama, in 1963. What kinds of national and international leaders does it take to end terrible violations of human rights and personal dignity? (See "Coretta King: A Woman of Courage.")

What accounts for people's preferences for what they eat and how they eat?
(See "You Are How You Eat.")

Which side do you think will prevail in everyday life?
(See "Flour Children.")

More on next page . . .

"And now, for all of you out there who are in love, or if you've ever been in love, or if you think you'll be in love someday, or even if you only think you might like to be in love someday, this song is for you."

Drawing by B. Grace. © 1982 The New Yorker Magazine, Inc.

How might feelings of love between a man and a woman be so intense as to bring harm to them and their friends?
(See "Deer Hunter and Corn Maiden.")

Selection 7

Summer

Jonathan Schwartz

(1) I am running down an alley with a stolen avocado, having climbed over a white brick fence and into the forbidden back yard of a carefully manicured estate at the corner of El Dorado and Crescent Drive in Beverly Hills, California. I have snatched a rock-hard Fuerte avocado from one of the three avocado trees near the fence. I have been told that many ferocious dogs patrol the grounds; they are killers, these dogs. I am defying them. They are nowhere to be found, except in my mind, and I'm out and gone and in the alley with their growls directing my imagination. I am running with fear and exhilaration, beginning a period of summer.

(2) Emerging from the shield of the alley I cut out into the open. Summer is about running, and I am running, protected by distance from the dogs. At the corner of Crescent Drive and Lomitas I spot Bobby Tornitzer on a bike. I shout *"Tornitzer!"* He turns his head. His bike wobbles. An automobile moving rapidly catches Tornitzer's back wheel. Tornitzer is thrown high into the air and onto the concrete sidewalk of Crescent Drive. The driver, a woman with gray hair, swirls from the car hysterically and hovers noisily over Tornitzer, who will not survive the accident. I hold the avocado to my chest and stand, frozen, across the street. I am shivering in the heat, and sink to my knees. It is approximately 3:30 in the afternoon. It is June 21, 1946. In seven days I will be 8 years old.

215 words

Vocabulary List

Here are some of the more difficult words in "Summer."

avocado
(paragraph 1)

☆av|o·ca|do (av′ə kä′dō, ä′və-) *n., pl.* -dos [altered (infl. by earlier Sp *avocado,* now *abogado,* advocate) < MexSp *aguacate* < Nahuatl *a:wakaʌ,* avocado, lit., testicle; so named from its shape] **1** a widespread, thick-skinned, pear-shaped tropical fruit, yellowish green to purplish black, with a single large seed and yellow, buttery flesh, used in salads; alligator pear **2** the tree (*Persea americana*) of the laurel family, that it grows on **3** a yellowish-green color

defying
(paragraph 1)

de|fy (dē fī′, di-; *also, for n.,* dē′fī) *vt.* -fied′, -fy′ing [ME *defien* < OFr *defier,* to distrust, repudiate, defy < LL **disfidare* < *dis-,* from + **fidare,* to trust < *fidus,* faithful: see FAITH] **1** to resist or oppose boldly or openly **2** to resist completely in a baffling way [the puzzle *defied* solution] **3** to dare (someone) to do or prove something **4** [Archaic] to challenge (someone) to fight —*n., pl.* -fies a defiance or challenge

estate
(paragraph 1)

es·tate (e stāt′, i-) *n.* [ME & OFr *estat,* STATE] **1** a) state or condition [to restore the theater to its former *estate*] b) a condition or stage of life [to come to man's *estate*] c) status or rank **2** [Historical] esp. in feudal times, any of the three social classes having specific political powers: the first estate was the Lords Spiritual (clergy), the second estate the Lords Temporal (nobility), and the third estate the Commons (bourgeoisie): see also FOURTH ESTATE **3** property; possessions; capital; fortune **4** the assets and liabilities of a dead or bankrupt person **5** landed property; individually owned piece of land containing a residence, esp. one that is large and maintained by great wealth **6** [Brit.] DEVELOPMENT (sense 4) **7** [Archaic] display of wealth; pomp **8** *Law* a) the degree, nature, extent, and quality of interest or ownership that one has in land or other property b) all the property, real or personal, owned by one

exhilaration
(paragraph 1)

ex·hil|a·rate (eg zil′ə rāt′, ig-) *vt.* -rat|ed, -rat′ing [< L *exhilaratus,* pp. of *exhilarare,* to gladden < *ex-,* intens. + *hilarare,* to gladden < *hilaris,* glad: see HILARIOUS] **1** to make cheerful, merry, or lively **2** to invigorate or stimulate —*SYN.* ANIMATE —ex·hil′a·ra|tive *adj.*

ex·hil|a·ra·tion (eg zil′ə rā′shən, ig-) *n.* [LL *exhilaratio*] **1** the act of exhilarating **2** an exhilarated condition or feeling; liveliness; high spirits; stimulation

ferocious
(paragraph 1)

fe·ro·cious (fə rō′shəs) *adj.* [< L *ferox* (gen. *ferocis*), wild, untamed < *ferus,* FIERCE + base akin to *oculus,* EYE + -OUS] **1** fierce; savage; violently cruel **2** [Colloq.] very great [a *ferocious* appetite] —fe·ro′·cious|ly *adv.* —fe·ro′cious·ness *n.*

hovers
(paragraph 2)

hov|er (huv′ər, *also* häv′-) *vi.* [ME *hoveren,* freq. of *hoven,* to stay (suspended)] **1** to stay suspended or flutter in the air near one place **2** to linger or wait close by, esp. in an overprotective, insistent, or anxious way **3** to be in an uncertain condition; waver (*between*) —*n.* the act of hovering —hov′|er·er *n.*

hysterically
(paragraph 2)

hys·ter|i·cal (hi ster′i kəl) *adj.* [HYSTERIC + -AL] **1** of or characteristic of hysteria **2** a) like or suggestive of hysteria; emotionally uncontrolled and wild b) extremely comical **3** having or subject to hysteria —hys·ter′|i·ca|ly *adv.*

manicured
(paragraph 1)

man|i·cure (man′i kyoor) *n.* [Fr < L *manus,* a hand + *cura,* care: see CURE] the care of the hands; esp., a trimming, polishing, etc. of the fingernails —*vt.* -cured′, -cur′ing **1** a) to trim, polish, etc. (the fingernails) b) to give a manicure to **2** [Colloq.] to trim, clip, etc. meticulously [to *manicure* a lawn]

7A VOCABULARY

Match eight of the imaginary quotations with a vocabulary word listed on page 98. Write "none" for the two extra quotations.

1. "If you walk too near that savage animal, it will attack you."

1. _____

2. "Look at those neatly trimmed bushes and that beautifully edged lawn."

2. _____

3. "Mr. Lloyd Dexter lives in a huge house surrounded by acres of woods."

3. _____

4. "Sometimes my doctor prescribes pain killers for my headaches."

4. _____

5. "The young parents ran to the lifeguard in a panic when they thought their child might be drowning."

5. _____

6. "While the eggs are beginning to hatch, the bird is fluttering protectively over its nest."

6. _____

7. "I think skydivers sometimes think they can ignore the laws of gravity."

7. _____

8. "Wow! That ice cold shower certainly gives me a feeling of high spirits."

8. _____

9. "What do you call that pear-shaped, yellowish-green fruit on the table?"

9. _____

10. "No person should drive while under the influence of alcohol or drugs."

10. _____

7B   MAIN IDEA AND IMAGES
Choose the best answer.

_____ 1. Another title for this story could be
  a. June 21, 1946.
  b. Killer Dogs.
  c. My Eighth Birthday.
  d. The Alley.

_____ 2. The main image in paragraph 1 is of a young boy
  a. climbing a white brick fence.
  b. snatching avocados.
  c. running with fear and exhilaration.
  d. defying ferocious dogs.

_____ 3. The main image in paragraph 2 is of
  a. Tornitzer riding his bike.
  b. the playful, then horrified boy.
  c. the 7-year-old emerging from the alley.
  d. the hysteria of the woman driver

7C   MAJOR DETAILS
Decide whether each detail is MAJOR or MINOR.

_____ 1. The 7-year-old was running from imagined ferocious dogs.

_____ 2. The stolen avocado was still hard.

_____ 3. The avocado tree was on an estate.

_____ 4. The 7-year-old froze in horror when he saw the accident.

_____ 5. Bobby Tornitzer was riding his bike.

_____ 6. A car hit Tornitzer's bike.

_____ 7. Tornitzer was going to die.

_____ 8. A woman was driving the car.

_____ 9. The street was called Crescent Drive.

Name   Date

7D INFERENCES

Decide whether each statement below can be inferred (YES) or cannot be inferred (NO) from the story.

_____ 1. Climbing over other people's fences is against the law.

_____ 2. This experience probably left a deep emotional scar on the 7-year-old.

_____ 3. The 7-year-old was being punished for stealing an avocado.

_____ 4. Seven-year-old children are destructive.

_____ 5. A single moment can drastically alter lives.

_____ 6. The 7-year-old hated Tornitzer.

_____ 7. Women are poor drivers.

_____ 8. The driver was drunk.

_____ 9. Tornitzer had recently arrived in America, and so he did not understand English very well.

_____ 10. Tornitzer was also 7 years old.

7E CRITICAL READING: THE WRITER'S CRAFT

Choose the best answer.

_____ 1. The story starts with the feeling of _____ and

ends with a feeling of _____ .
   a. joyful action . . . horrified inaction
   b. running . . . standing
   c. being alone . . . being with others
   d. being out in the open . . . shivering in the heat

_____ 2. The fact that Tornitzer will die is stated in paragraph 2 at the end of a long sentence that describes the upset car driver. The author writes this way because he wants to
   a. hint that Tornitzer is the driver's son.
   b. force the reader to concentrate on the effect of the accident on the 7-year-old.
   c. convey the casual suddenness of the accident.
   d. scare the reader into realizing the importance of bicycle safety.

_____ 3. The word "swirls" (line 17) implies
   a. a storm.
   b. curiosity.
   c. panic.
   d. calm.

_____ 4. The phrase "hovers noisily" (line 18) conveys the image of someone who is
   a. sick.
   b. panicked.
   c. worried.
   d. happy.

_____ 5. The phrase "shivering in the heat" (line 20) dramatically
   describes shock through
   a. the use of minute detail.
   b. the unexpected combination of hot and cold.
   c. its implied reference to the word "frozen."
   d. the contrast of death and play.

7F   INFORMED OPINION

1. Describe how you felt after reading "Summer."

2. The story "Summer" tells much in a few words. Do you think its short-
   ness gives the story extra impact? Explain.

How Did You Do?   **7** Summer

SKILL (number of items)	Number Correct	Points for Each	Score
Vocabulary (10)	_____ ×	3	= _____
Main Ideas and Images (3)	_____ ×	6	= _____
Major Details (9)	_____ ×	3	= _____
Inferences (10)	_____ ×	2	= _____
Critical Reading: The Writer's Craft (5)	_____ ×	1	= _____

(Possible Total: 100) _Total_ _____

SPEED

Reading Time: _____ Reading Rate (page 348): _____ Words Per Minute

Name   Date

Coretta King: A Woman of Courage

Paula Taylor

(1) Over the years Coretta's courage was tested time and again. Once she got a phone call telling her Martin had been rushed to the hospital in New York. A mentally disturbed woman had stabbed him in the chest with a letter opener. Three hours of surgery were needed to remove the weapon. Afterwards doctors told Coretta that its point had been touching Martin's heart. If he had panicked and moved suddenly or even sneezed, he would have died instantly. Even after the successful surgery, he remained on the critical list for several days.

(2) Though terribly worried, Coretta remained calm. When Martin began to recover, she took his place at meetings and gave speeches from his notes. Many people credit her with holding the (civil rights) movement together during this critical time.

(3) Shortly before Dexter was born, Coretta again feared for her husband's life. He was arrested for leading a sit-in at a lunch counter in Atlanta. For this minor offense, the judge handed down a harsh sentence of 6 months hard labor at the State Penitentiary. Coretta was terribly upset. The penitentiary was 300 miles from the Kings' home in Atlanta. Pregnant and with 2 small children, she could rarely make the 8-hour trip to visit her husband. She knew how black prisoners were treated in southern jails. Martin might be beaten—or worse.

(4) Before lawyers had time to appeal the judge's decision, Martin was roughly dragged from his Atlanta jail cell. He was chained and handcuffed. In the middle of the night, he was taken to the penitentiary. When Coretta heard what had happened, she was distraught. Just as she was about to give up hope, the telephone rang. "Just a moment, Mrs. King," the long-distance operator said, "Senator John F. Kennedy wants to speak to you." "How are you, Mrs. King?" a warm voice inquired. After chatting a few minutes about her family and the new baby they were expecting, Senator Kennedy told Coretta he was concerned about Martin's arrest. "Let me know if there's anything I can do to help," he told her. The next day, Martin was released.

(5) Two years later, Coretta had another talk with John Kennedy. By then he was President. Martin had been jailed in Birmingham. Coretta was not allowed to see or even phone him. Fearing the worst, she called the White House. Once again, Kennedy came to the rescue, and Martin was freed.

(6) Through all the dark moments of her life, Coretta never doubted that the cause to which she and Martin had dedicated their lives was

From *Coretta Scott King: A Woman of Peace,* by Paula Taylor. Reprinted with permission of Creative Education, Inc.

right. Even on April 4, 1968, when she faced the supreme test—the death of her husband—her faith never wavered. She had suffered much. A lesser woman might have withdrawn from the world in grief. Coretta did not.

(7) The day after Martin was shot, Coretta made an eloquent statement to the press. She said that both she and Martin had accepted the fact that his life might suddenly be cut short. They both felt it wasn't how long one lived that was important, but how well. Martin Luther King had given his life trying to help people find a better way to solve their problems than by hatred and violence. Coretta urged those who had loved and admired her husband to help carry on the work he had begun.

(8) The day before his funeral, Coretta took Martin's place in the march he was to lead in Memphis. From all over the country thousands of people came to march with her. Thousands more stood along the route in silent tribute to the memory of their leader and the bravery of his widow.

(9) Coretta's faith carried her heroically through the ordeal of Martin's funeral. Throughout the long hours of speeches and television coverage, she never broke down. All who saw her marveled at her serenity and inner strength.

640 words

Here are some of the more difficult words in "Coretta King: A Woman of Courage."

critical
(paragraph 1)

crit·i·cal (krit′i kəl) *adj.* **1** tending to find fault; censorious **2** characterized by careful analysis and judgment *[a* sound *critical* estimate of the problem] **3** of critics or criticism **4** of or forming a crisis or turning point; decisive **5** dangerous or risky; causing anxiety *[a critical* situation in international relations] **6** of the crisis of a disease **7** designating or of important products or raw materials subject to increased production and restricted distribution under strict control, as in wartime **8** *a)* designating or of a point at which a change in character, property, or condition is effected *b)* designating or of the point at which a nuclear chain reaction becomes self-sustaining —**crit′i·cal·ly** *adv.* —**crit′i·cal′i·ty** (-kal′ə tē) or **crit′i·cal·ness** *n.* **SYN.**—**critical,** in its strictest use, implies an attempt at objective judging so as to determine both merits and faults *[a critical* review], but it often (and **hypercritical,** always) connotes emphasis on the faults or shortcomings; **faultfinding** implies a habitual or unreasonable emphasis on faults or

distraught
(paragraph 4)

dis·traught (di strôt′) *adj.* [ME, var. of DISTRAIT] **1** extremely troubled; mentally confused; distracted; harassed **2** driven mad; crazed —**SYN.** ABSENT-MINDED

eloquent
(paragraph 7)

el·o·quent (el′ə kwənt) *adj.* [ME & OFr < L *eloquens,* prp. of *eloqui,* to speak out, utter < *e-,* out + *loqui,* to speak] **1** having, or characterized by, eloquence; fluent, forceful, and persuasive **2** vividly expressive *[an eloquent* sigh] —**el′o·quent·ly** *adv.*

ordeal
(paragraph 9)

or·deal (ôr dēl′, ôr′dēl′) *n.* [ME *ordal* < OE, akin to Ger *urteil,* judgment < WGmc **uzdailjo-,* what is dealt out < **uzdailjan,* to deal out, allot, adjudge < **uz-,* out + **dailjan* < **dails,* a part, share] **1** an ancient method of trial in which the accused was exposed to physical dangers, from which he was supposed to be divinely protected if he was innocent **2** any difficult, painful, or trying experience; severe trial

serenity
(paragraph 9)

se·rene (sə rēn′) *adj.* [L *serenus* < IE **ksero-,* dry (> Gr *xēros,* dry, OHG *serawēn,* to dry out) < base **ksā-,* to burn] **1** clear; bright; unclouded *[a serene* sky] **2** not disturbed or troubled; calm, peaceful, tranquil, etc. **3** [S-] exalted; high-ranking: used in certain royal titles *[his Serene* Highness] —*n.* [Old Poet.] a serene expanse, as of sky or water —**SYN.** CALM —**se·rene′ly** *adv.* —**se·rene′ness** *n.*

se·ren·i·ty (sə ren′ə tē) *n., pl.* **-ties** [Fr *sérénité* < L *serenitas*] **1** the quality or state of being serene; calmness; tranquillity **2** [S-] a royal title of honor: preceded by *Your* or by *His* or *Her* —**SYN.** EQUANIMITY

wavered
(paragraph 6)

wa·ver (wā′vər) *vi.* [ME *waveren,* freq. of *waven,* to WAVE] **1** to swing or sway to and fro; flutter **2** to show doubt or indecision; find it hard, or be unable, to decide; vacillate **3** to become unsteady; begin to give way; falter **4** to tremble; quaver: said of the voice, etc. **5** to vary in brightness; flicker: said of light **6** to fluctuate **7** to totter —*n.* the act of wavering, trembling, vacillating, etc. —**wa′-ver·er** *n.* —**wa′ver·ing·ly** *adv.*

8A VOCABULARY

Choose the best answer.

_____ 1. An **eloquent** person is one who
    a. likes to argue.
    b. speaks persuasively.
    c. feels superior.
    d. is highly educated.

_____ 2. Something labeled **critical** can be described as
    a. being very valuable or rare.
    b. appearing to be ugly or offensive.
    c. being in a state of crisis or danger.
    d. pleasing or uplifting to look at.

_____ 3. A person possessing **serenity** could be described as
    a. prepared to commit suicide.
    b. having great physical or spiritual beauty.
    c. having an untroubled and peaceful nature.
    d. expecting to be treated like royalty.

_____ 4. An **ordeal** is a
    a. strict order or command.
    b. person with orderly habits.
    c. criminal act without a motive.
    d. trying or painful event.

_____ 5. A person who is **distraught** is
    a. extremely upset or worried.
    b. overcome with anger and frustration.
    c. extremely distrustful and suspicious.
    d. feeling foolish for having been tricked.

_____ 6. If your faith in something **wavered,** it would have
    a. remained steady or unchanged.
    b. become doubtful or undecided.
    c. completely collapsed.
    d. demonstrated your good judgment.

_____ 7. Someone who is **serene**
    a. is calm and quiet.
    b. has royal blood.
    c. is attractive.
    d. has a bright personality.

Name   Date

8B CENTRAL THEME AND MAIN IDEAS

Choose the best answer.

_____ 1. What is the central theme of "Coretta King: A Woman of Courage"?
   a. Coretta King rushed to her husband's bedside when he was stabbed by a mentally disturbed woman.
   b. Coretta King showed great inner strength and courage in her devotion to her husband and the civil rights movement.
   c. Martin Luther King was made to suffer great dangers and many injustices for the civil rights movement and finally he gave his life for the cause.
   d. The true leader of the civil rights movement during Martin Luther King's lifetime was Coretta King.

_____ 2. What is the main idea of paragraph 3?
   a. Coretta King feared for her husband's life when he was in the Georgia State Penitentiary.
   b. Martin Luther King received a harsh prison sentence for a minor offense.
   c. Coretta King was pregnant when Martin was in the Georgia State Penitentiary.
   d. Coretta King knew that black prisoners were treated especially poorly in southern prisons.

_____ 3. What is the main idea of paragraph 4?
   a. Martin was given a temporary release from the penitentiary to visit Coretta when their baby was born.
   b. Coretta was deeply upset and gave up hope when she heard that Martin had been taken to the penitentiary in the middle of the night.
   c. Coretta chatted with Senator Kennedy about her family and the new baby that she was expecting.
   d. Martin was released from the penitentiary after Senator Kennedy called Coretta to discuss his concern for Martin's welfare.

_____ 4. What is the main idea of paragraph 7?
   a. Coretta's statement was angry.
   b. Coretta's statement was inspiring.
   c. Coretta's statement was short.
   d. Coretta's statement was confusing.

Name   Date

8C MAJOR DETAILS

Fill in the word or words that correctly complete each statement.

1. When Martin was stabbed, the knife was so close to his

   _____ that he would have _____ if he
   had sneezed or moved suddenly.

2. Coretta was given credit for holding the civil rights

   _____ together while Martin recovered.

3. Martin was sentenced to _____ months' hard labor

   for leading a _____ at a _____

   _____ in Atlanta.

4. In southern jails, black prisoners were often _____ ,
   or worse.

5. After Martin was _____ , handcuffed, and taken to

   the penitentiary, Senator _____ telephoned

   Coretta to say that he was worried about _____ .

6. Martin died on _____ .

7. After the assassination, Coretta said that she and Martin had

   realized that his _____ might be cut short.

8. Coretta urged people to carry on Martin's _____ .

9. The day before Martin's _____ , Coretta led a march

   in _____ , and _____ of people came to
   pay tribute to Martin.

10. Throughout the ordeal of Martin's _____ , Coretta
    showed great inner strength.

8D INFERENCES

Choose the best answer.

_____ 1. *Read paragraph 3 again.* Coretta knew that black prisoners were poorly treated in southern jails because
   a. black prisoners usually complained more than white prisoners about poor food and health care in prison.
   b. the guards resented the civil rights movement and took out their anger on black prisoners.
   c. Coretta had been in jail and therefore knew that black prisoners were mistreated.
   d. the South had a long history of mistreatment of blacks both in and out of prison.

_____ 2. *Read paragraph 4 again.* Coretta was about to give up hope because she felt that
   a. the lawyers were not very capable and therefore were unable to help Martin.
   b. the lawyers were secretly plotting with the judge to make sure that Martin was kept in jail.
   c. after the rough treatment given Martin in the Atlanta jail, there was almost no hope he could survive the even tougher world of the penitentiary.
   d. she would not be allowed to visit Martin while he was in the penitentiary.

_____ 3. *Read paragraph 5 again.* President Kennedy was able to get Martin released from the Birmingham jail because
   a. the warden was repaying Kennedy for past favors.
   b. he promised the Birmingham authorities that Martin, upon release, would end his activities in the civil rights movement.
   c. a person occupying high public office can usually bring pressure to bear on local officials who impose overly harsh prison sentences.
   d. the Birmingham officials realized that they had been unfair in jailing Martin.

_____ 4. *Read paragraph 8 again.* The main reason that Coretta took Martin's place was because she wanted
   a. to show her children that she was brave.
   b. to step into Martin's shoes immediately so that she could become the new leader of the civil rights movement.
   c. to give people who could not attend Martin's funeral a chance to see her.
   d. to inspire people not to be afraid and to continue the work that Martin had begun.

Name   Date

8E CRITICAL READING: THE WRITER'S CRAFT

Choose the best answer.

_____ 1. The author presents her details organized according to
   a. their chronological order.
   b. order of location.
   c. the most to the least important.
   d. the least to the most important.

_____ 2. The author refers to Coretta King and to Martin Luther King by their first names. She does this because
   a. she does not really respect them.
   b. she wants to save space.
   c. she was a good personal friend of theirs.
   d. she wants her readers to feel close to them.

8F INFORMED OPINION

1. *Read paragraph 3 again.* Do you think that six months at hard labor for leading a sit-in at a lunch counter was a harsh sentence? Explain.

2. Why do most people find it inspiring and comforting to observe Coretta King's "inner strength and serenity"?

How Did You Do?   8 Coretta King: A Woman of Courage

SKILL (number of items)	Number Correct	Points for Each	Score
Vocabulary (7)	_____ ×	3	= _____
Central Theme and Main Ideas (4)	_____ ×	4	= _____
Major Details* (17)	_____ ×	3	= _____
Inferences (4)	_____ ×	2	= _____
Critical Reading: The Writer's Craft (2)	_____ ×	2	= _____

(Possible Total: 100) *Total* _____

SPEED

Reading Time: _____ Reading Rate (page 349): _____ Words Per Minute

*Question 1 in this exercise calls for two separate answers. Questions 3, 5, and 9 call for three separate answers each. In computing your score, count each separate answer toward your number correct.

Name   Date

You Are How You Eat

Enid Nemy

(1) There's nothing peculiar about a person walking along a Manhattan street, or any other street for that matter, eating an ice cream cone. It's the approach that's sometimes a little strange—ice-cream-cone-eating is not a cut-and-dried, standardized, routine matter. It is an accomplishment with infinite variety, ranging from methodical and workmanlike procedures to methods that are visions of delicacy and grace. The infinite variety displayed in eating ice cream isn't by any means unique; it applies to all kinds of food. The fact is that although a lot of research has been done on what people eat and where they eat it, serious studies on the way food is eaten have been sadly neglected.

(2) Back to ice cream, as an example. If five people leave an ice cream store with cones, five different methods of eating will likely be on view. There are people who stick out their tongues on top of a scoop, but don't actually eat the ice cream. They push it down into the cone—push, push, push—then take an intermission to circle the perimeter, lapping up possible drips. After this, it's again back to pushing the ice cream farther into the cone. When the ice cream has virtually disappeared into the crackly cone, they begin eating. These people obviously don't live for the moment; they plan for the future, even if the future is only two minutes away. Gobble up all the ice cream on top and be left with a hollow cone? Forget it. Better to forgo immediate temptation and then enjoy the cone right to the end.

(3) On the other hand, there are the "now" types who take great gobby bites of the ice cream. Eventually, of course, they get down to an empty cone, which they might eat and, then again, they might throw away (if the latter, one wonders why they don't buy cups rather than cones, but no point in asking).

(4) The most irritating of all ice cream eaters are the elegant creatures who manage to devour a whole cone with delicate little nibbles and no dribble. The thermometer might soar, the pavement might melt, but their ice cream stays as firm and as rounded as it was in the scoop. No drips, no minor calamities—and it's absolutely not fair, but what can you do about it?

(5) Some of the strangest ice cream fans can be seen devouring sundaes and banana splits. They are known as "layer by layer" types. First they eat the nuts and coconut and whatever else is sprinkled on top. Then they eat the sauce; then the banana, and finally the ice cream, flavor by

flavor. Some might feel that they are eating ingredients and not a sundae or a split, but what do they care?

(6) As for chocolate eaters, there are three main varieties, at least among those who like the small individual chocolates. A certain percentage pop the whole chocolate into their mouths, crunch once or twice and down it goes. Others pop the whole chocolate into their mouths and let it slowly melt. A smaller number hold the chocolate in hand while taking dainty little bites.

(7) Peanuts and popcorn are a completely different matter. Of course, there are always one or two souls who actually pick up single peanuts and popcorn kernels, but the usual procedure is to scoop up a handful. But even these can be subdivided into those who feed them in one at a time and those who sort of throw the handful into the open mouth, then keep on throwing in handfuls until the plate, bag or box is empty. The feeders-in-one-at-a-time are, needless to say, a rare breed with such iron discipline that they probably exercise every morning and love it.

(8) Candies like M&M's are treated by most people in much the same way as peanuts or popcorn. But there are exceptions, among them those who don't start eating until they have separated the colors. Then they eat one color at a time, or one of each color in rotation. Honestly.

(9) A sandwich cookie is a sandwich cookie, and you take bites of it, and so what? So what if you're the kind who doesn't take bites until it's pulled apart into two sections. And if you're this kind of person, and an amazing number are, the likelihood is that the plain part will be eaten first, and the one with icing saved for last. Watch Oreo eaters.

(10) A woman who seems quite normal in other respects said that although she considers her eating habits quite run-of-the-mill, she has been told that they are, in fact, peculiar. "If I have meat or chicken and a couple of vegetables on a plate, I go absolutely crazy if they don't come out even," she said. "I like to take a piece of meat and a little bit of each vegetable together. If, as I'm eating, I end up with no meat and a lot of broccoli, or no potatoes and a piece of chicken, it drives me mad."

(11) A man listening to all this rolled his eyes in disbelief. Peculiar is putting it mildly, he said. He would never eat like that. How does he eat? "One thing at a time," he said. "First I eat the meat, then one of the vegetables, then the other. How else would you eat?"

894 words

Here are some of the more difficult words in "You Are How You Eat."

calamities
(paragraph 4)

ca·lam·i·ty (-tē) *n., pl.* -ties [MFr *calamité* < L *calamitas*: see CLAS-TIC] **1** deep trouble or misery **2** any extreme misfortune bringing great loss and sorrow; disaster —*SYN.* DISASTER

devour
(paragraph 4)

de·vour (di vour') *vt.* [ME *devouren* < OFr *devorer* < L *devorare* < *de-*, intens. + *vorare*, to swallow whole: see VORACIOUS] **1** to eat or eat up hungrily, greedily, or voraciously **2** to consume or destroy with devastating force **3** to take in greedily with the eyes, ears, or mind [the child *devours* fairy tales] **4** to absorb completely; engross [*devoured* by curiosity] **5** to swallow up; engulf —de·vour'er *n.*

forgo
(paragraph 2)

for·go (fôr gō') *vt.* -went', -gone', -go'ing [ME *forgon* < OE *forgan*: see FOR- & GO²] **1** orig., *a*) to go past *b*) to overlook; neglect **2** to do without; abstain from; give up —*SYN.* RELINQUISH —for·go'er *n.*

infinite
(paragraph 1)

in·fi·nite (in'fə nit) *adj.* [ME < L *infinitus*: see IN-² & FINITE] **1** lacking limits or bounds; extending beyond measure or comprehension: without beginning or end; endless **2** very great; vast; immense **3** *a*) *Math.* indefinitely large; greater than any finite number however large *b*) capable of being put into one-to-one correspondence with a part of itself [*infinite* set] —*n.* something infinite, as space or time —the Infinite (Being) God —in'fi·nite·ly *adv.* —in'fi·nite·ness *n.*

methodical
(paragraph 1)

me·thod·i·cal (mə thäd'i kəl) *adj.* [< LL *methodicus* < Gr *methodikos* + -AL] characterized by method; orderly; systematic Also me·thod'ic —me·thod'i·cal·ly *adv.* —me·thod'i·cal·ness *n.*

perimeter
(paragraph 2)

pe·rim·e·ter (pə rim'ə tər) *n.* [L *perimetros* < Gr < *peri-*, around + *metron*, MEASURE] **1** the outer boundary of a figure or area **2** the total length of this **3** an optical instrument for testing the scope of vision and the visual powers of various parts of the retina **4** *Mil.* a boundary strip where defenses are set up —*SYN.* CIRCUMFERENCE

rotation
(paragraph 8)

ro·ta·tion (rō tā'shən) *n.* [L *rotatio*] **1** a rotating or being rotated **2** the spinning motion around the axis of a celestial body: cf. REVOLUTION (sense 1a) **3** regular and recurring succession of changes [a *rotation* of duties] ★**4** a form of the game of pool in which the balls must be pocketed in the order of their numbers —ro·ta'tion·al *adj.*

standardized
(paragraph 1)

stand·ard·ize (stan'dər diz') *vt.* -ized', -iz'ing **1** to make standard or uniform; cause to be without variations or irregularities **2** to compare with, test by, or adjust to a standard —stand'ard·i·za'tion *n.* —stand'ard·iz'er *n.*

unique
(paragraph 1)

u·nique (yōō nēk') *adj.* [Fr < L *unicus*, single < *unus*, ONE] **1** one and only; single; sole [a *unique* specimen] **2** having no like or equal; unparalleled [a *unique* achievement] **3** highly unusual, extraordinary, rare, etc.: a common usage still objected to by some —u·nique'-ly *adv.* —u·nique'ness *n.*

9A VOCABULARY

Choose the best answer.

_____ 1. Something that is **standardized** is
   a. irregular.
   b. controlled by the government.
   c. open to personal interpretation.
   d. without variations.

_____ 2. If you were to **forgo** something you desired, you would
   a. do without it, at least for a while.
   b. go ahead and try to get it.
   c. force yourself to save for it.
   d. borrow or rent it.

_____ 3. If a number is **infinite,** it
   a. cannot be divided evenly.
   b. has a negative value.
   c. extends beyond measure.
   d. is limited in size.

_____ 4. **Calamities** are also known as
   a. ex-Californians.
   b. telephone keypads.
   c. disasters.
   d. squid, cooked Italian style.

_____ 5. To be **methodical** is to be
   a. careless.
   b. systematic.
   c. open-minded.
   d. a member of the Methodist Church.

_____ 6. When people speak in **rotation,** they
   a. ramble and change the topic frequently.
   b. take turns talking in regular and recurring order.
   c. deliver memorized speeches.
   d. participate in public speaking contests.

_____ 7. The **perimeter** of an object is its
   a. outer boundary.
   b. surface area.
   c. approximate volume.
   d. texture.

_____ 8. To **devour** something is to
   a. travel around it.
   b. swallow it without chewing.
   c. leave it unopened.
   d. eat it hungrily.

_____ 9. A **unique** experience is
   a. usual and ordinary.
   b. old-fashioned.
   c. rare or one of a kind.
   d. something one does by oneself.

9B   CENTRAL THEME AND MAIN IDEAS

Choose the answer.

_____ 1. What is the central theme of "You Are How You Eat"?
   a. People eat ice cream and other foods in an infinite variety of ways.
   b. Ice cream can be eaten in five different ways.
   c. Scientific studies of how people eat are needed, but unfortunately they have not been done.
   d. People with peculiar ways of eating ice cream or other foods may be entirely normal in other respects.

_____ 2. What is the main idea of paragraph 4?
   a. People should not eat ice cream during hot weather.
   b. People who eat ice cream cones slowly without dripping, even when the thermometer soars, irritate the author.
   c. People who can eat ice cream without dripping are irritating when they brag about it.
   d. When people eat ice cream cones properly, the ice cream remains as firm and rounded as it was in the scoop.

_____ 3. What is the main idea of paragraph 9?
   a. All sandwich cookies are alike.
   b. The easiest sandwich cookies to eat are Oreos.
   c. Nutritionists claim that the proper way to eat a sandwich cookie is to split it in half and then eat one half at a time.
   d. A surprising number of people eat sandwich cookies by pulling the cookie apart and eating the plain side first.

Name   Date

9C MAJOR DETAILS

Fill in the word or words that correctly complete each statement.

1. It is not strange to see a person walking along a _____

   eating an _____ _____ cone.

2. Some people use their tongues to _____ the ice

   cream deep into the _____ .

3. Many people fight the _____ to eat all the ice cream
   immediately.

4. People who throw away their empty ice cream cones should consider

   buying ice cream _____ instead of cones.

5. People who eat sundaes in layers are eating separate

   _____ , not sundaes.

6. There are _____ main varieties of people who eat

   small individual _____ .

7. Most people eat peanuts and popcorn by the _____ .

8. People who eat peanuts and popcorn one piece at a time have iron

   _____ .

9. Some people eat M&M's one _____ at a time; others go

   from color to color in _____ .

10. When given a plate of meat and vegetables, some people like to
    eat little bits of each food together, and others prefer to finish one

    _____ at a time.

Name   Date

9D INFERENCES

Choose the best answer.

_____ 1. *Read the title again.* What does the title mean?
   a. What people eat shows how they were raised.
   b. How people eat can provide clues to their temperaments or personalities.
   c. Your health and sense of well-being are strongly affected by what you eat and how you eat it.
   d. Proper eating manners are essential for people who want to make a good impression on others.

_____ 2. *Read paragraph 7 again.* Why does the author say that people who eat peanuts and popcorn one piece at a time "probably exercise every morning"?
   a. People who exercise regularly are usually trying to lose weight, so they eat small amounts of food.
   b. People who exercise and people who eat one peanut at a time are alike in not being able to have fun and enjoy life.
   c. People who limit their intake of high-calorie foods and who exercise regularly are alike in having much self-discipline.
   d. People who exercise think that eating one peanut or piece of popcorn at a time will strengthen their jaw and facial muscles.

_____ 3. *Read paragraph 8 again.* Why do some people eat all M&M's of one color before starting another, while other people eat the colors in strict rotation?
   a. They believe they will digest the M&M's better if they follow one of these routines.
   b. The coating on some colors of M&M's melts faster than does the coating on others.
   c. They like to be able to structure even small aspects of their lives.
   d. As they eat the M&M's they like to count the number of each color in each package.

9E CRITICAL READING: THE WRITER'S CRAFT

Choose the best answer.

_____ 1. The author states her central theme only in
   a. the title and last paragraph.
   b. the title and first paragraph.
   c. the first and last paragraphs.
   d. the title.

117

_____ 2. To support her central theme, the author uses
   a. observations and statistics.
   b. observations, questions, quotations.
   c. questions and quotations.
   d. statistics, questions, quotations.

_____ 3. Which of these words is *not* used by the author to show connections among ideas?
   a. "after this"   (paragraph 2)
   b. "on the other hand"   (paragraph 3)
   c. "eventually"   (paragraph 3)
   d. "then again"   (paragraph 3)
   e. "first"   (paragraph 5)
   f. "then"   (paragraph 5)
   g. "finally"   (paragraph 5)
   h. "of course"   (paragraph 7)
   i. "among"   (paragraph 8)

9F   INFORMED OPINION

1. Do you think that the way a person eats reveals his or her personality? Using specific examples, explain your answer.

2. Food is a central part of many official holidays, many types of family celebrations, many religious practices, and many other occasions. Other than to satisfy hunger, why do you think food is such a central part of most human cultures? Using specific examples, explain your answer.

How Did You Do?   9 You Are How You Eat

SKILL (number of items)	Number Correct		Points for Each		Score
Vocabulary (9)	_____	×	1	=	_____
Central Theme and Main Ideas (3)	_____	×	5	=	_____
Major Details* (14)	_____	×	5	=	_____
Inferences (3)	_____	×	1	=	_____
Critical Reading: The Writer's Craft (3)	_____	×	1	=	_____

(Possible Total: 100) Total _____

SPEED

Reading Time: _____ Reading Rate (page 349): _____ Words Per Minute

*Questions 1, 2, 6, and 9 in this exercise call for two separate answers. In computing your score, count each separate answer toward your number correct.

Name   Date

Flour Children

Lexine Alpert

(1) "Hey, Mister V., what are you doing dressed like that?" says a student as he enters the classroom at San Francisco's Mission High School. "I'm getting ready to deliver your baby," replies the sex education teacher, in surgical greens from cap to booties. "Do you have to take this thing so seriously?" asks another, laughing nervously as she watches her teacher bring out rubber gloves. "Yes, babies are a serious matter," he answers. As the students settle into their seats, Robert Valverde, who has been teaching sex education for four years—and "delivering babies" for three—raises his voice to convene the class.

(2) "Welcome to the nursery," he announces. "Please don't breathe on the babies. I just brought them from the hospital." The students' giggles quickly change to moans as Valverde delivers a "baby"—a five-pound sack of flour—to each student. "You must treat your baby as if it were real twenty-four hours a day for the next three weeks," he says. "It must be brought to every class. You cannot put the baby in your locker or your backpack. It must be carried like a baby, lovingly, and carefully in your arms. Students with jobs or other activities must find babysitters." To make sure the baby is being cared for at night and on weekends, Valverde calls his students at random. "If the baby is lost or broken, you must call a funeral parlor and find what it would cost to have a funeral," he says. The consequence is a new, heavier baby—a ten-pound flour sack.

(3) Valverde came up with the flour baby idea after hearing that some sex education classes assign students the care of an egg; he decided to try something more realistic. "A flour sack is heavier and more cumbersome—more like a real baby," Valverde says. To heighten the realism, he has the students dress their five-pound sacks in babies' clothes, complete with diaper, blanket, and bottle.

(4) "The primary goal is to teach responsibility," says Valverde. "I want those who can't do it to see that they can't, and to acknowledge that the students who can are doing someting that is very difficult and embarrassing." After 36 classes and more than a thousand students, Valverde's project seems to be having the effect he wants. "I look at all the circumstantial evidence—the kids are talking to their parents in ways they never have before, and for the first time in their lives, they are forced to respond to an external environment. They have to fill out forms every day saying where they'll be that night and who's taking care of the baby. If their plans

change I make them call me and say who's with the baby. They're forced to confront people's comments about their babies."

(5) Lupe Tiernan, vice-principal of the predominantly Hispanic and Asian inner-city high school, believes Valverde's class has helped to maintain the low number of teenage pregnancies at her school. "His students learn that having a baby is a novelty that wears off very quickly, and by three weeks, they no longer want any part of it," she says.

(6) At the beginning of the assignment, some students' parental instincts emerge right away. During the first week, sophomore Cylenna Terry took the rules so seriously that she was kicked out of her English class for refusing to take the baby off her lap and place it on the floor as instructed. "I said, 'No way am I putting my baby on the floor.' " Others, especially the boys, learn early that they can't cope with their new role. "I just couldn't carry the baby around," says Enrique Alday, 15. "At my age it was too embarrassing so I just threw it in my locker." He failed the class.

(7) By the second week, much of the novelty has worn off and the students begin to feel the babies are intruding on their lives. "Why does it have to be so heavy?" Cylenna Terry grumbles. "It's raining out—how am I supposed to carry this baby and open up my umbrella at the same time?" She has noticed other changes as well. "There's no way a boy is even going to look at me when I have this in my arms. No guys want to be involved with a girl who has a baby—they just stay clear."

(8) Rommel Perez misses baseball practice because he can't find a babysitter. Duane Broussard, who has helped care for his one-year-old nephew who lives in his household, learns new respect for how hard his mother and sister work at childcare. "At least this baby doesn't wake me in the middle of the night," he says. Maria Salinis says, "My boyfriend was always complaining about the sack and was feeling embarrassed about having it around. I told him, 'Imagine if it was a real baby.' It made us ask important questions of one another that we had never before considered."

(9) On the last day of the assignment, the temporary parents come to class dragging their feet. Valverde calls the students one by one to the front of the room to turn in their babies. Most, their paper skin now fragile from wear, are returned neatly swaddled in a clean blanket. But others have ended up broken and lying in the bottom of a trash bin; a half-dozen students wound up with ten-pound babies. The students' consensus is that babies have no place in their young lives. "I know that if I had a baby it would mess up my future and hold me down," says Broussard. "At this time in my life I don't want anything to hold me down." "After this class, I don't want to have a baby. I couldn't handle it," says 15-year-old Erla Garcia. "It was only a sack of flour that didn't cry or scream, didn't need to be fed or put to sleep, and I still couldn't wait to get rid of it."

(1004 words)

Name   Date

Here are some of the more difficult words in "Flour Children."

circumstantial
(paragraph 4)

cir·cum·stan·tial (sur'kəm stan'shəl) *adj.* 1 having to do with, or depending on, circumstances 2 not of primary importance; incidental 3 full or complete in detail 4 full of pomp or display; ceremonial —cir'cum·stan'tial·ly *adv.*

confront
(paragraph 4)

con·front (kən frunt') *vt.* 〚Fr *confronter* < ML *confrontare* < L *com-*, together + *frons*, forehead: see FRONT〛 1 to face; stand or meet face to face 2 to face or oppose boldly, defiantly, or antagonistically 3 to bring face to face (*with*) /to *confront* one with the facts/ 4 to set side by side to compare —con·fron·ta·tion (kän'frən tā'shən) or con·front'al *n.* —con'fron·ta'tion·al *adj.*

consensus
(paragraph 9)

con·sen·sus (kən sen'səs) *n.* 〚L < pp. of *consentire*: see fol.〛 1 an opinion held by all or most 2 general agreement, esp. in opinion

consequence
(paragraph 2)

con·se·quence (kän'si kwens', -kwəns) *n.* 〚OFr < L *consequentia* < *consequens*, prp. of *consequi*, to follow after < *com-*, with + *sequi*, to follow: see SEQUENT〛 1 a result of an action, process, etc.; outcome; effect 2 a logical result or conclusion; inference 3 the relation of effect to cause 4 importance as a cause or influence /a matter of slight *consequence*/ 5 importance in rank; influence /a person of *consequence*/ —SYN. EFFECT, IMPORTANCE —in consequence (of) as a result (of) —take the consequences to accept the results of one's actions

convene
(paragraph 1)

con·vene (kən vēn') *vi.* -vened', -ven'ing 〚ME *convenen* < OFr *convenir* < L *convenire* < *com-*, together + *venire*, to COME〛 to meet together; assemble, esp. for a common purpose —*vt.* 1 to cause to assemble, or meet together 2 to summon before a court of law —SYN. CALL —con·ven'er *n.*

cumbersome
(paragraph 3)

cum·ber·some (kum'bər səm) *adj.* hard to handle or deal with as because of size, weight, or many parts; burdensome; unwieldy; clumsy —SYN. HEAVY —cum'ber·some·ly *adv.* —cum'ber·some·ness *n.*

instincts
(paragraph 6)

in·stinct (*for n.* in'stiŋkt'; *for adj.* in stiŋkt', in'stiŋkt') *n.* 〚< L *instinctus*, pp. of *instinguere*, to impel, instigate < *in-*, in + *stinguere*, to prick: for IE base see STICK〛 1 (an) inborn tendency to behave in a way characteristic of a species; natural, unlearned, predictable response to stimuli /suckling is an *instinct* in mammals/ 2 a natural or acquired tendency, aptitude, or talent; bent; knack; gift /an *instinct* for doing the right thing/ 3 *Psychoanalysis* a primal psychic force or drive, as fear, love, or anger; specif., in Freudian analysis, either the life instinct (Eros) or the death instinct (Thanatos) —*adj.* filled or charged (*with*) /a look *instinct* with pity/ —in·stinc·tu·al (in stiŋk'chōō əl) *adj.*

intruding
(paragraph 7)

in·trude (in trōōd') *vt.* -trud'ed, -trud'ing 〚L *intrudere* < *in-*, in + *trudere*, to thrust, push: see THREAT〛 1 to push or force (something *in* or *upon*) 2 to force (oneself or one's thoughts) upon others without being asked or welcomed 3 *Geol.* to force (liquid magma, etc.) into or between solid rocks —*vi.* to intrude oneself —in·trud'er *n.* SYN.—intrude implies the forcing of oneself or something upon another without invitation, permission, or welcome /to *intrude* upon another's privacy/; obtrude connotes even more strongly the distractive nature or the undesirability of the invasion /side issues keep *obtruding*/; interlope implies an intrusion upon the rights or privileges of another to the disadvantage or harm of the latter /the *interloping* merchants have ruined our trade/; butt in (or into) (at BUTT²) is a slang term implying intrusion in a meddling or officious way /stop *butting into* my business/ See also TRESPASS

novelty
(paragraph 5)

nov·el·ty (näv'əl tē) *n., pl.* -ties 〚ME *novelte* < OFr *noveleté* < LL *novellitas*〛 1 the quality of being novel; newness; freshness 2 something new, fresh, or unusual; change; innovation 3 a small, often cheap, cleverly made article, usually for play or adornment: *usually used in pl.*

predominantly
(paragraph 5)

pre·dom·i·nant (prē däm'ə nənt, pri-) *adj.* 〚Fr *prédominant* < ML *predominans*, prp. of *predominari*: see PRE- & DOMINANT〛 1 having ascendancy, authority, or dominating influence over others; superior 2 most frequent, noticeable, etc.; prevailing; preponderant —SYN. DOMINANT —pre·dom'i·nance, *pl.* -cies, or pre·dom'i·nan·cy *n.* —pre·dom'i·nant·ly *adv.*

swaddled
(paragraph 9)

swad·dle (swäd''l) *vt.* -dled, -dling 〚ME *swathlen*, prob. altered (infl. by *swathen*, to SWATHE¹) < *swethlen* < OE *swethel*, swaddling band, akin to *swathian*, to SWATHE¹〛 1 to wrap (a newborn baby) in long, narrow bands of cloth, as was formerly the custom 2 to bind in or as in bandages; swathe —*n.* 〚ME *swathil* < OE *swethel*: see the *v.*〛 a cloth or bandage used for swaddling

10A   VOCABULARY

Using the vocabulary words on page 121, fill in this crossword puzzle.

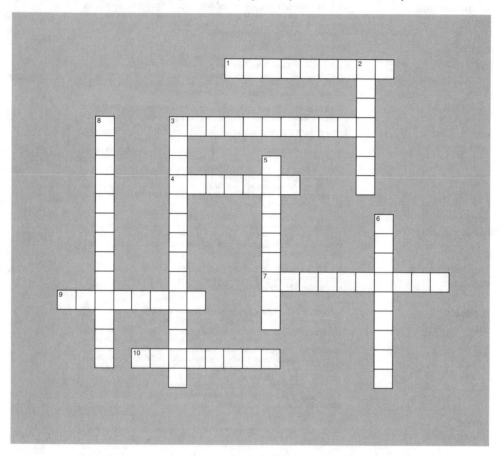

Across

1. forcing oneself on others
3. the logical result of an action
4. to call together
7. difficult to handle; heavy
9. to face or meet face to face
10. wrapped in long pieces of cloth

Down

2. something unusual
3. full or complete in detail
5. natural talents
6. opinion held by most people
8. most noticeably

Name   Date

10B   CENTRAL THEME AND MAIN IDEAS

Choose the best answer.

_____ 1. What is the central theme of "Flour Children"?
   a. Mr. Valverde hopes to teach students the responsibility involved in having children.
   b. Students learn that taking care of a baby is a 24-hour-a-day job.
   c. Students learn that babies may cause them to miss out on planned events in their lives.
   d. High school girls learn that boys are not interested in girls who have babies.

_____ 2. What is the main idea of paragraph 2?
   a. Mr. Valverde intends to check up on his students to make sure they take the project seriously.
   b. Failure to take good care of the baby will result in a new, heavier baby.
   c. The flour babies must be treated as if they were real babies.
   d. Students do not take their flour babies seriously.

_____ 3. What is the main idea of paragraph 8?
   a. Students often missed after-school activities in order to care for their "babies."
   b. Students learn that they probably don't want to have babies.
   c. Many students were embarrassed at having to care for a flour baby.
   d. The flour babies affected students' lives in different ways.

10C   MAJOR DETAILS

Decide whether each detail is true (T), false (F), or not discussed (ND).

_____ 1. Mr. Valverde takes his job teaching sex education very seriously.

_____ 2. For the first time students are not forced to respond to an external environment.

_____ 3. Flour sacks instead of eggs are used because they more nearly resemble caring for an infant.

_____ 4. San Francisco's Mission High School Board requires this course of all students.

_____ 5. The students' parents have agreed to participate in the flour babies' care.

123

_____ 6. Students were concerned about the embarrassment of carrying a flour baby.

_____ 7. To make the babies seem more real, students must equip them with clothes, diapers, and bottles.

_____ 8. Students who communicate with their parents do well as flour baby parents.

10D INFERENCES

Choose the best answer.

_____ 1. *Read paragraph 6 again.* By refusing to put her flour sack on the floor during English, Cylenna Terry is showing that
   a. she is afraid any damage would result in getting a larger baby.
   b. she has accepted the responsibility of a baby.
   c. she knows someone would tell Mr. Valverde.
   d. she is too embarrassed to let anyone see it on the floor.

_____ 2. *Read paragraph 9 again.* "The temporary parents came to class dragging their feet" indicates that they were
   a. tired of playing this game.
   b. anxious to find out if they had passed.
   c. certain they did not want to have real babies.
   d. hesitant to part with their babies after all.

10E CRITICAL READING: FACT OR OPINION

Decide whether each statement, even if it quotes someone, contains a FACT or an OPINION.

_____ 1. *From paragraph 1:* "Yes, babies are a serious matter."

_____ 2. *From paragraph 4:* "The primary goal is to teach responsibility."

_____ 3. *From paragraph 5:* The class has helped to maintain the low number of teen pregnancies at the school.

_____ 4. *From paragraph 6:* "At my age, it was too embarrassing."

_____ 5. *From paragraph 7:* "No guys wanted to be involved with a girl who has a baby."

_____ 6. *From paragraph 9:* . . . Babies have no place in their young lives.

Name   Date

10F CRITICAL READING: THE WRITER'S CRAFT

Choose the best answer.

_____ 1. The author begins "Flour Children" with
   a. a satirical monologue.
   b. a comparison.
   c. a dramatic scene.
   d. contrasting opinions.

_____ 2. To hold the reader's interest, the author
   a. alternates her opinions with those of the students.
   b. describes different student experiences.
   c. avoids the use of too many details.
   d. quotes authorities who are experts in the field of parenthood.

_____ 3. In paragraphs 6–10, the author quotes the students in their own words instead of just describing what each did. She does this to
   a. demonstrate the regional accents used by various characters.
   b. keep the story as entertaining as possible.
   c. make the story seem vivid and real.
   d. create a suspenseful atmosphere.

_____ 4. *Read paragraph 9 again.* If the expression "their paper skin now fragile from wear" were replaced by "their packaging torn," the revised passage would
   a. lose the connection with human babies.
   b. be much more dramatic.
   c. provide greater clarity.
   d. better illustrate the careless treatment of the flour sacks.

10G INFORMED OPINION

1. Was Mr. Valverde justified in requiring his students to account for their flour sacks 24 hours a day? Using specific examples, explain your position.

2. From a parent's point of view, do you think sex education and parenthood classes should be taught in the public schools? Explain your point of view.

Name   Date

How Did You Do?   **11** Flour Children

SKILL *(number of items)*	Number Correct		Points for Each		Score
Vocabulary (11)	_____	×	2	=	_____
Central Theme and Main Ideas (3)	_____	×	4	=	_____
Major Details (8)	_____	×	4	=	_____
Inferences (2)	_____	×	4	=	_____
Critical Reading: Fact or Opinion (6)	_____	×	3	=	_____
Critical Reading: The Writer's Craft (4)	_____	×	2	=	_____

(Possible Total: 100) *Total* _____

SPEED

Reading Time: _____ Reading Rate (page 349): _____ Words Per Minute

Name   Date

Deer Hunter and White Corn Maiden

Translated from the Tewa* by Alfonso Ortiz

(1) Long ago in the ancient home of the San Juan people, in a village whose ruins can be seen across the river from present-day San Juan, lived two magically gifted young people. The youth was called Deer Hunter because even as a boy, he was the only one who never returned empty-handed from the hunt. The girl, whose name was White Corn Maiden, made the finest pottery, and embroidered clothing with the most beautiful designs, of any woman in the village. These two were the handsomest couple in the village, and it was no surprise to their parents that they always sought one another's company. Seeing that they were favored by the gods, the villagers assumed that they were destined to marry.

(2) And in time they did, and contrary to their elders' expectations, they began to spend even more time with one another. White Corn Maiden began to ignore her pottery making and embroidery, while Deer Hunter gave up hunting, at a time when he could have saved many of his people from hunger. They even began to forget their religious obligations. At the request of the pair's worried parents, the tribal elders called a council. This young couple was ignoring all the traditions by which the tribe had lived and prospered, and the people feared that angry gods might bring famine, flood, sickness, or some other disaster upon the village.

(3) But Deer Hunter and White Corn Maiden ignored the council's pleas and drew closer together, swearing that nothing would ever part them. A sense of doom pervaded the village, even though it was late spring and all nature had unfolded in new life.

(4) Then suddenly White Corn Maiden became ill, and within three days she died. Deer Hunter's grief had no bounds. He refused to speak or eat, preferring to keep watch beside his wife's body until she was buried early the next day.

(5) For four days after death, every soul wanders in and around its village and seeks forgiveness from those whom it may have wronged in life. It is a time of unease for the living, since the soul may appear in the form of a wind, a disembodied voice, a dream, or even in human shape. To prevent such a visitation, the villagers go to the dead person before burial and utter a soft prayer of forgiveness. And on the fourth day after death, the relatives gather to perform a ceremony releasing the soul into the spirit world, from which it will never return.

---

*One of the seven North American Indian groups living in the New Mexico and Arizona region of the southwest United States.

(6) But Deer Hunter was unable to accept his wife's death. Knowing that he might see her during the four-day interlude, he began to wander around the edge of the village. Soon he drifted farther out into the fields, and it was here at sundown of the fourth day, even while his relatives were gathering for the ceremony of release, that he spotted a small fire near a clump of bushes.

(7) Deer Hunter drew closer and found his wife, as beautiful as she was in life and dressed in all her finery, combing her long hair with a cactus brush in preparation for the last journey. He fell weeping at her feet, imploring her not to leave but to return with him to the village before the releasing rite was consummated. White Corn Maiden begged her husband to let her go, because she no longer belonged to the world of the living. Her return would anger the spirits, she said, and anyhow, soon she would no longer be beautiful, and Deer Hunter would shun her.

(8) He brushed her pleas aside by pledging his undying love and promising that he would let nothing part them. Eventually she relented, saying that she would hold him to his promise. They entered the village just as the relatives were marching to the shrine with the food offering that would release the soul of White Corn Maiden. They were horrified when they saw her, and again they and the village elders begged Deer Hunter to let her go. He ignored them, and an air of grim expectancy settled over the village.

(9) The couple returned to their home, but before many days had passed, Deer Hunter noticed that his wife was beginning to have an unpleasant odor. Then he saw that her beautiful face had grown ashen and her skin dry. At first he only turned his back on her as they slept. Later he began to sit up on the roof all night, but White Corn Maiden always joined him. In time the villagers became used to the sight of Deer Hunter racing among the houses and through the fields with White Corn Maiden, now not much more than skin and bones, in hot pursuit.

(10) Things continued in this way, until one misty morning a tall and imposing figure appeared in the small dance court at the center of the village. He was dressed in spotless white buckskin robes and carried the biggest bow anyone had ever seen. On his back was slung a great quiver with the two largest arrows anyone had ever seen. He remained standing at the center of the village and called, in a voice that carried into every home, for Deer Hunter and White Corn Maiden. Such was its authority that the couple stepped forward meekly and stood facing him.

(11) The awe-inspiring figure told the couple that he had been sent from the spirit world because they, Deer Hunter and White Corn Maiden, had violated their people's traditions and angered the spirits; that because they had been so selfish, they had brought grief and near-disaster to the village. "Since you insist on being together," he said, "you shall have your wish. You will chase one another forever across the sky, as visible

reminders that your people must live according to tradition if they are to survive." With this he set Deer Hunter on one arrow and shot him low into the western sky. Putting White Corn Maiden on the other arrow, he placed her just behind her husband.

(12) That evening the villagers saw two new stars in the west. The first, large and very bright, began to move east across the heavens. The second, a smaller, flickering star, followed close behind. So it is to this day, according to the Tewa; the brighter one is Deer Hunter, placed there in the prime of his life. The dimmer star is White Corn Maiden, set there after she had died; yet she will forever chase her husband across the heavens.

(1103 words)

Here are some of the more difficult words in "Deer Hunter and White Corn Maiden."

ashen
(paragraph 9)

ash|en¹ (ash′ən) *adj.* **1** of ashes **2** like ashes, esp. in color; pale; pallid —*SYN.* PALE¹

buckskin
(paragraph 10)

buck·skin (buk′skin′) *n.* **1** the skin of a buck **2** a soft, usually napped, yellowish-gray leather made from the skins of deer or sheep ☆**3** a yellowish-gray horse **4** [*pl.*] clothes or shoes made of buckskin ☆**5** [*often* B-] an American backwoodsman of earlier times —*adj.* made of buckskin

consummated
(paragraph 7)

con·sum·mate (kən sum′it, kän′sə mit; *for v.* kän′sə māt′) *adj.* [L *consummatus,* pp. of *consummare,* to sum up, finish < *com*-, together + *summa,* SUM] **1** complete or perfect in every way; supreme [*consummate* happiness] **2** very skillful; highly expert [a *consummate* liar] —*vt.* -mat|ed, -mat′ing [ME *consummaten*] **1** to bring to completion or fulfillment; finish; accomplish **2** to make (a marriage) actual by sexual intercourse —**con·sum′mate|ly** *adv.* —**con·sum·ma·tive** (kän′sə māt′iv, kən sum′ə tiv′) or **con·sum′ma·to′ry** (-ə tôr′ē) *adj.* —**con′sum·ma′tor** *n.*

disembodied
(paragraph 5)

dis·em·bod|y (dis′im bäd′ē, dis′im bäd′ē) *vt.* -bod′ied, -bod′y·ing to free from bodily existence; make incorporeal —**dis′em·bod′ied** *adj.* —**dis′em·bod′i·ment** *n.*

embroidered
(paragraph 1)

em·broi·der (em broi′dər, im-) *vt.* [ME *embrouderen* < OFr *embroder:* see EN-¹ & BROIDER] **1** to ornament (fabric) with a design in needlework **2** to make (a design, etc.) on fabric with needlework **3** to embellish (an account or report); add fanciful details to; exaggerate —*vi.* **1** to do embroidery **2** to exaggerate —**em·broi′der|er** *n.*

famine
(paragraph 2)

fam·ine (fam′in) *n.* [ME < OFr < VL *famina < L fames,* hunger < IE base *dhē*-, to wither away > DAZE] **1** an acute and general shortage of food, or a period of this **2** any acute shortage **3** [Archaic] starvation

Vocabulary List

finery
(paragraph 7)

fin·er·y[1] (fīn'ər ē) *n., pl.* **-er·ies** showy, gay, elaborate decoration, esp. clothes, jewelry, etc.

imploring
(paragraph 7)

im·plore (im plôr') *vt.* **-plored', -plor'ing** [L *implorare*, to beseech, entreat < *in-*, intens. + *plorare*, to cry out, weep] **1** to ask or beg earnestly for; beseech **2** to ask or beg (a person) to do something; entreat —*SYN.* BEG —**im·plor'ing·ly** *adv.*

imposing
(paragraph 10)

im·pos·ing (im pō'ziŋ) *adj.* making a strong impression because of great size, strength, dignity, etc.; impressive —*SYN.* GRAND —**im·pos'ing·ly** *adv.*

interlude
(paragraph 6)

in·ter·lude (in'tər lōōd') *n.* [ME *enterlude* < OFr *entrelude* < ML *interludium* < L *inter*, between + *ludus*, play: see LUDICROUS] **1** a short, humorous play formerly presented between the parts of a miracle play or morality play **2** a short play of a sort popular in the Tudor period, either farcical or moralistic in tone and with a plot typically derived from French farce or the morality play **3** any performance between the acts of a play **4** instrumental music played between the parts of a song, liturgy, play, etc. **5** *a)* anything that fills time between two events *b)* intervening time or, rarely, space

obligations
(paragraph 2)

ob·li·ga·tion (äb'lə gā'shən) *n.* [ME *obligacioun* < OFr *obligation* < L *obligatio*] **1** an obligating or being obligated **2** a binding contract, promise, moral responsibility, etc. **3** a duty imposed legally or socially; thing that one is bound to do by contract, promise, moral responsibility, etc. **4** the binding power of a contract, promise, etc. **5** *a)* the condition or fact of being indebted to another for a favor or service received *b)* a favor or service **6** *Law a)* an agreement or duty by which one person (the *obligor*) is legally bound to make payment or perform services for the benefit of another (the *obligee*) *b)* the bond, contract, or other document setting forth the terms of this agreement —**ob'li·ga'tion·al** *adj.*

pervaded
(paragraph 3)

per·vade (pər vād') *vt.* **-vad'ed, -vad'ing** [L *pervadere* < *per*, through + *vadere*, to go: see EVADE] **1** [Now Rare] to pass through; spread or be diffused throughout **2** to be prevalent throughout —**per·va'sion** (-vā'zhən) *n.*

prospered
(paragraph 2)

pros·per (präs'pər) *vi.* [ME *prosperen* < MFr *prosperer* < L *prosperare*, to cause to prosper < *prosperus*, favorable < *prospere*, fortunately < *pro spere* < *pro*, according to (see PRO-²) + stem of *spes*, hope < IE base *spēi-*, to flourish, succeed > SPEED] to succeed, thrive, grow, etc. in a vigorous way —*vt.* [Archaic] to cause to prosper

quiver
(paragraph 10)

quiv·er[2] (kwiv'ər) *n.* [ME *quyuere* < OFr *coivre* < Gmc *kukur* (> OE *cocer*, quiver, sheath, Ger *köcher*, quiver), prob. a loanword from the Huns] **1** a case for holding arrows **2** the arrows in it

11A VOCABULARY

Choose the best answer.

_____ 1. If the business **prospered**, it would probably
   a. cause a decline in the gross national product.
   b. hire more employees at a variety of locations.
   c. close offices and factories at some rural locations.
   d. hire a new manager to oversee labor negotiations.

_____ 2. A person whose face looks **ashen** is probably
   a. sick.
   b. sunburned.
   c. afraid.
   d. very pale.

_____ 3. A country is experiencing a **famine** when
   a. more food is exported than imported.
   b. its citizens sell all they can produce.
   c. its people have a severe shortage of food.
   d. there is abundance of produce.

_____ 4. A musical **interlude** often occurs
   a. before the actors go on stage.
   b. between the acts of a play.
   c. before the play begins.
   d. between the main characters.

_____ 5. An **embroidered** blouse would
   a. be made in Mexico.
   b. have designs painted on it.
   c. be made of all one color.
   d. have needlework decoration.

_____ 6. An **obligation** to a friend is
   a. a promise or responsibility.
   b. not to be taken seriously.
   c. repayment for a loan.
   d. a threat of future harm.

_____ 7. **Imploring** your teacher for a good grade probably means
   a. you are willing to beg or plead for it.
   b. you anticipate doing well on the examination.
   c. the teacher would take pity and give you extra credit.
   d. you would like to schedule a make-up test.

Name   Date

_____ 8. **Buckskin** can best be described as
   a. soft fabric used for children's clothes.
   b. colorful, woven material.
   c. beaded and decorated fabric.
   d. leather made from deer or sheep.

_____ 9. A **quiver** is a necessary item for
   a. a fisherman
   b. an athlete.
   c. a hunter.
   d. a teacher.

_____ 10. **Finery** as used in this story means
   a. clothes from a factory.
   b. formal men's wear.
   c. fancy, decorated clothes.
   d. traditional clothing.

_____ 11. A **disembodied** voice would
   a. be deep and quiet.
   b. not come from within a body.
   c. be in one's imagination.
   d. come from a wounded child.

_____ 12. The word **pervade** is closest in meaning to
   a. widespread.
   b. a derivative.
   c. nearly complete.
   d. punctual.

_____ 13. An **imposing** politician is likely to
   a. spread lies.
   b. not be reelected.
   c. be influential.
   d. be very impressive.

_____ 14. If the ceremony wasn't **consummated,** it wasn't
   a. legitimate.
   b. completed.
   c. unusual.
   d. politically correct.

Name   Date

11B   CENTRAL THEME AND MAIN IDEAS

Choose the best answer.

_____ 1. "Deer Hunter and White Corn Maiden" is a folktale handed down orally by the Tewa Indians of the New Mexico and Arizona region of the southwest United States. Its purpose as a folktale is to
   a. warn young couples of the perils of romantic love.
   b. sympathize with one spouse's inability to accept the other's death.
   c. relate the story of an ill-fated young couple who ignored their elders' warnings.
   d. teach the importance of following and obeying traditions and religious obligations.

_____ 2. "Deer Hunter and White Corn Maiden" is a story about
   a. a young couple whose love for each other leads them to make foolish choices.
   b. a young maiden who refuses to let her husband go, even in death.
   c. a young husband who defies the gods to keep his wife with him.
   d. a young couple who are punished for putting their love above their people's welfare and beliefs.

_____ 3. The main event in paragraph 2 is that
   a. the villagers became afraid that the spirits would be angry.
   b. White Corn Maiden began to ignore her pottery and embroidery.
   c. the young couple's parents became increasingly worried.
   d. the young couple began to ignore their duties to their community.

_____ 4. The unexpected main action in paragraph 7 is that
   a. Deer Hunter begged White Corn Maiden to stay.
   b. White Corn Maiden appeared to Deer Hunter.
   c. White Corn Maiden was concerned that the spirits would be angry.
   d. White Corn Maiden feared Deer Hunter would shun her.

_____ 5. The moral of "Deer Hunter and White Corn Maiden" is that
   a. death cannot separate lovers.
   b. people risk disaster if they choose to anger the gods.
   c. people must live according to tradition if they are to survive.
   d. religious obligations are an important part of one's heritage.

11C MAJOR DETAILS

Number the following details from the story according to the order in which they occurred. Number the details from 1 to 10, with 1 next to the detail that happened first.

_____ One morning an imposing figure from the spirit world appeared and called for White Corn Maiden and Deer Hunter to approach.

_____ White Corn Maiden died one day, but Deer Hunter was unable to accept his wife's death.

_____ As time went on, Deer Hunter tried more and more frequently to get away from White Corn Maiden, but she continued to pursue him.

_____ White Corn Maiden pleaded with Deer Hunter to let her go, knowing that soon she would no longer be beautiful.

_____ Two gifted and handsome young people in the village seemed destined to marry.

_____ To this day, the first new star moving east across the heavens is Deer Hunter; the small star chasing after is White Corn Maiden.

_____ The young couple in time began to ignore their religious obligations.

_____ Since the couple insisted on being together always, the spirit would make a visible reminder that young people must live according to tradition.

_____ As time passed, her body began to decay.

_____ The villagers feared that because the couple was neglecting their roles in the community, the angry gods would bring disaster upon the villagers.

11D INFERENCES

Choose the best answer.

_____ 1. *Read paragraph 2 again.* It was contrary to their elders' expectations for the young couple to spend so much time together. This would imply
   a. that the elders resented the amount of time the young couple spent together.
   b. that they feared the young couple would grow tired of each other and not stay together.
   c. that the elders were alarmed that this togetherness would cause jealousy among other couples in their village.
   d. that love and marriage in the Tewa culture were placed in a larger framework of individual duties and responsibilities.

Name   Date

_____ 2. *Read paragraphs 11–12 again.* From the Tewa point of view, the creation of the new stars in the heavens implies that
   a. the elders are capable of using magic.
   b. drastic events may befall those who choose to defy religious and social custom.
   c. even grief and near disaster may result in lasting beauty.
   d. one should not placate the gods.

_____ 3. *Read paragraph 8 again.* The villagers were horrified when Deer Hunter brought White Corn Maiden back after she had died because
   a. they knew her soul had already been released by the ceremony.
   b. they knew it was a violation of the natural order to bring a person back from the dead.
   c. they knew White Corn Maiden wanted to pass on to the spirit world.
   d. they feared White Corn Maiden would put a curse on them.

11E   CRITICAL READING: THE WRITER'S CRAFT
Choose the best answer.

_____ 1. The mood intended to be evoked in the reader (or the listener) in paragraph 2 is one of
   a. fear.
   b. disgust.
   c. annoyance.
   d. sadness.

_____ 2. The fact that White Corn Maiden dies is stated in paragraph 4. The author, however, uses a variety of vivid physical details to suggest that even though her spirit lives, her body is indeed losing its beauty. List two of those details.

   _____

   _____

_____ 3. *Read paragraphs 11–12 again.* The mood at the end of this tale changes to one of
   a. sadness.
   b. lightheartedness.
   c. solemnity.
   d. forgiveness.

Name   Date

_____ 4. The Tewa people would recognize the two new stars in the sky called Deer Hunter and White Corn Maiden. Linking a story with familiar objects in the natural world is a popular way to

a. make it easier for children to remember the important details.

b. increase the story's believability.

c. relate it to a child's fairy tale.

d. expand the moral values taught in the folktale.

11F INFORMED OPINION

1. Read paragraph 9 again. Was Deer Hunter justified in turning from White Corn Maiden after pleading with her to stay with him and pledging his undying love? Explain.

2. Do you believe that observing traditional rules and obligations is more important than following personal feelings? Using specific examples, explain your point of view.

How Did You Do? 11 Deer Hunter and White Corn Maiden

SKILL (number of items)	Number Correct		Points for Each		Score
Vocabulary (14)	_____	×	2	=	_____
Central Theme and Main Ideas (5)	_____	×	5	=	_____
Major Details (10)	_____	×	3	=	_____
Inferences (3)	_____	×	3	=	_____
Critical Reading: The Writer's Craft (4)	_____	×	2	=	_____

(Possible Total: 100) *Total* _____

SPEED

Reading Time: _____ Reading Rate (page 349): _____ Words Per Minute

Name   Date

Writing: Expressing Yourself

What are *your* ideas on the subjects that you have read about in Part 2 of this book? Now is *your* chance to express your ideas in writing.

Below are some topics to write about. You are not expected to write on all of them, of course. Just select what appeals to you. Or feel free to make up your own topics. Most important, try to find a subject that moves you to want to express yourself in writing.

All of the topics below relate in some way to the reading selections in Part 2 of this book. Some of the topics have been touched on already in the opening section of Part 2, "Thinking: Getting Started," page 93, or in the Informed Opinion questions that followed each of the reading selections in Part 2. Others of these topics are introduced here for the first time.

The topics below give you a choice among various kinds of writing. You can write a **narrative** that will tell your reader an interesting story. You can write a **description** that will give your reader a vivid picture of the image you have in mind. You can write a **report** that will give your reader important information about a subject, process, or event. You can write an **argument** to try to persuade your reader to agree with you. Differences among these kinds of writing are not always clear-cut, and so you can feel free to use any **combination** that works for you. As you write, see if you can make use of the new vocabulary words that you have been studying in Part 2.

IDEAS FOR PARAGRAPHS

1. In your opinion, what motivated John F. Kennedy to help Martin Luther King as he did? (See "Coretta King: A Woman of Courage.") Explain your reasons fully.

2. Many people have one set of table manners for eating with family and another set for more formal situations. What is your opinion of having dual standards? Explain your point of view.

3. If you were a high school student and had the option to register for a sex education class that required students to care for flour sack babies (see "Flour Children"), would you enroll? Give specific reasons for your position.

4. Most families have meaningful traditions, especially at holidays or

special occasions. Is there a tradition that you participate in with your family? Explain what that tradition is, what it involves, and what it means to you.

IDEAS FOR ESSAYS

1. Was there a dramatic event, good or bad, in your childhood that you will never forget? Describe and discuss its effect on you.

2. Make up a continuation for the story "Summer." You can cover the next few hours, the next few days, the rest of the summer, or whatever amount of time you wish.

3. Martin Luther King made a profound impact on history as well as on the personal lives of many people. Write a research report about Martin Luther King in which you discuss that profound impact. Use specific examples to illustrate your point.

4. The civil rights movement has had a profound effect on American society. Write a research report in which you discuss how American society has changed as a result of the civil rights movement.

5. Describing the way people eat ice cream, chocolate, peanuts, popcorn, and Oreos is only a beginning (see "You Are How You Eat"). Select another popular food and spend some time observing people eating it. Then write a description of the different ways that people eat that food, and offer your speculations about what the different ways reveal about the people.

6. You may be a single parent, or you may know who someone is. Discuss several problems and difficulties a single parent faces.

7. In recent years our society has taken two viewpoints about pregnancy: pro-life and pro-choice. Using specific reasons, argue for either one or both sides.

8. Have you ever experienced the loss of a loved one? Explain in detail how the death affected you.

9. Have you ever been so in love with someone that you made some foolish choices? Using specific examples, explain what you did.

10. Have you ever unwisely ignored someone's advice in order to pursue your heart's desire, only later to realize the wisdom of the advice? If so, state specifically your desire, the advice given, and the unfortunate results.

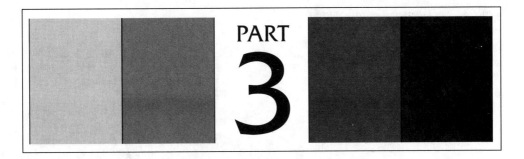

Thinking:
Getting Started

As you get ready to read, remain conscious of the fact that your mind must participate actively during reading. Use the visuals and accompanying questions on the next three pages to begin engaging with the topics in Part 3 of this book. Turn also to each reading selection in Part 3 and *survey* it by looking at its title and its first and last paragraphs. Predict what the selection will be about. Your prediction might be off the mark—especially until you get more experienced at making predictions. Still, making a prediction focuses your mind usefully on what you will be reading.

After you *survey*, ask *questions*. This technique is explained on page 12 and illustrated in the "SQ3R Guided Practice" that starts on page 11. You need only ask the questions, not answer them. Later, when you read with questions in mind, the answers will often seem to "jump out" from the page as you come across them. The purpose of asking questions, then, is to gear up your mind so that it actively confronts new information.

What are the various ways that the young and the elderly can communicate? (See "Village English in Rural Alaska.")

Why does it take leadership and people's determination to protect the equal rights that all Americans are born with? (See "Coretta King: A Woman of Courage.")

In what ways are twins born equal to each other, and in what ways do they differ? (See "Genes and Behavior: A Twin Legacy.")

WE NEED BULLETS LIKE WE NEED A HOLE IN THE HEAD.

BAN BULLETS FOR HAND GUNS

What does the expression "like a hole in the head" mean? What are some arguments for and against gun control laws? Do you think that banning bullets would solve the problem of gun abuse?
(See "Richard Cory, All Over Again.")

In what specific ways can parents share in both the joys and the responsibilities of raising children? (See "Escaping the Daily Grind for Life as a House Husband.")

More on next page . . .

Photo by Charles Duprez/Brown Brothers, Sterling, PA.

What challenges, good and bad, must immigrants to a new country face? (See "Model Minority.")

Copyright Stuart Franklin/Magnum Photos, Inc.

What can be the results of an ordinary person doing something extraordinary? (See "A New Dawn.")

Village English in Rural Alaska

Hannah Paniyavluk Loon

Hannah Paniyavluk Loon's first language is Inupiaq, which she grew up speaking in Selawik, an outlying village in Northwest Arctic Alaska. A mother of five, today Hannah lives in Kotzebue, this remote region's trade and transportation hub, where she works for her Native regional corporation. In her job, people often call on her to translate and interpret Inupiaq and English. She wrote this essay as a student, for Chukchi News and Information Service, an award-winning publication project that operates from Chukchi College, a branch campus in Kotzebue of the University of Alaska.

(1) Village English, a common form of speech in Alaskan villages, is a variety of non-standard English, which educators call a "local English." Here in northwest Alaska, village English is spoken in most of the communities.

(2) Before western contact, the people spoke the *Inupiaq* (Eskimo) language in this region. But when the early explorers arrived, they not only brought goods to trade, but they came with their language as well. The English language then took hold among the *Inupiat*.

(3) After contact, the early missionaries and teachers fanned out through this region. The *naluagmiu* (white man) established schools and churches with whatever materials were available, and in doing so created permanent villages. Until then, clans of people had lived spread throughout the region at their winter or summer camps.

(4) Unfortunately, when the *Inupiat* were taught English in the new schools, they got punished for speaking their original Native language. As a result, the *Inupiat* learned English with much difficulty.

(5) Today, English is the predominant language in their region, yet *Inupiaq* still is spoken by a majority of older people. It is rare to hear a child speak fluent *Inupiaq* today. A few people in their 20's and 30's speak some *Inupiaq*, but mainly English or village English. Today, it is common to hear people speaking a blend of English and *Inupiaq*. If they are not fluent in *Inupiaq*, they tend to mix English with incomplete *Inupiaq* words or vice versa. In northwest Alaska, people have gotten used to blending the two languages for intergroup communication and have adapted to speaking village English.

(6) For instance, in the office environment, I speak standard English to non-Natives every day, yet I run into situations where I have difficulty explaining typical Native processes, such as how to make a half-dried salmon. Also, I can carry on a conversation in *Inupiaq*, especially if I'm comfortable talking to a

Reprinted with permission of the author and the Chukchi News and Information Service at the University of Alaska in Kutzebue.

person. Yet, if I were to explain the process of making a half-dried salmon to a tough guy like Charles Bronson, you would see my mouth open without a single word coming out!

(7) In any case, I can explain or describe a situation to any local person in three different languages: English, village English, and *Inupiaq*. I am likely to speak *Inupiaq* to an elder because it is necessary, but I will use village English if someone asks me, for instance, "When you come?" I can quickly switch between village English and standard English. To compare the two languages, in English, a person might say, "I have not eaten yet," whereas in village English, one would say, "I never eat yet." Speakers of village English tend to communicate indirectly rather than directly. For instance, one would say, "Just try taste it," rather than the command, "Taste it." I do not use proper English with those who speak to me in village English because it may intimidate them or make them feel uncomfortable. For those of us who speak village English, it is best to speak this language only to those who understand it.

(8) Village English exists in me and in many people who live in the communities in northwest Alaska. Because of my *Inupiaq* background, I must admit English is hard to master in speeches and on paper.

(9) Although village English may sound "funny"—meaning "bad"—to English instructors, it has its own beauty to my ears. There's no such thing as "correct" village English. I structure my sentences any way I desire. Rules don't limit village English as long as the listener understands.

(10) Village English is truly a spoken language. It is a form of communication used by the *Inupiat* people of this region, young and old. The *Inupiat* generally enjoy the humorous side of life, so they speak village English with a sense of humor. Village English is infectious once you've spent time in the village.

(643 words)

Vocabulary List

Here are some of the more difficult words in "Village English in Rural Alaska."

adapted
(paragraph 5)

a|dapt (ə dapt′) *vt.* [Fr *adapter* < L *adaptare* < *ad-*, to + *aptare*, to fit: see APT] 1 to make fit or suitable by changing or adjusting 2 to adjust (oneself) to new or changed circumstances —*vi.* to adjust oneself
SYN.—**adapt** implies a modifying so as to suit new conditions and suggests flexibility *[to adapt oneself to a new environment]*; **adjust** describes the bringing of things into proper relation through the use of skill or judgment *[to adjust brakes, to adjust differences]*; **accommodate** implies a subordinating of one thing to the needs of another and suggests concession or compromise *[he accommodated his walk to the halting steps of his friend]*; **conform** means to bring or act in harmony with some standard pattern, principle, etc. *[to conform to specifications]*

clans
(paragraph 3)

clan (klan) *n.* ‖ Gael & Ir *clann, cland*, offspring, tribe < L *planta*, offshoot: see PLANT ‖ 1 an early form of social group, as in the Scottish Highlands, composed of several families claiming descent from a common ancestor, bearing the same family name, and following the same chieftain 2 in certain primitive societies, a tribal division, usually exogamous, of matrilineal or patrilineal descent from a common ancestor 3 a group of people with interests in common; clique; set 4 [Colloq.] FAMILY (sense 3)

fluent
(paragraph 5)

flu·ent (flōō′ənt) *adj.* ⟦L *fluens* (gen. *fluentis*), prp. of *fluere,* to flow: see FLUCTUATE⟧ **1** flowing or moving smoothly and easily *[fluent verse]* **2** able to write or speak easily, smoothly, and expressively *[fluent* in French*]* —**flu′ent·ly** *adv.*

humorous
(paragraph 10)

hu·mor·ous (hyōō′mər əs; *also* yōō′-) *adj.* ⟦HUMOR + -OUS; sense 2 < Fr *humoreux* (< L), sense 3 < L *humorosus*⟧ **1** having or expressing humor; funny; amusing; comical **2** [Archaic] whimsical; capricious **3** [Obs.] *a*) moist *b*) humoral —*SYN.* WITTY —**hu′mor·ous·ly** *adv.*

infectious
(paragraph 10)

in·fec·tion (in fek′shən) *n.* ⟦ME *infeccioun* < OFr *infection* < LL *infectio*⟧ **1** an infecting; specif., *a*) the act of causing to become diseased *b*) the act of affecting with one's feelings or beliefs **2** the fact or state of being infected, esp. by the presence in the body of bacteria, protozoans, viruses, or other parasites **3** something that results from infecting or being infected; specif., *a*) a disease resulting from INFECTION (sense 2) *b*) a feeling, belief, influence, etc. transmitted from one person to another **4** anything that infects
in·fec·tious (in fek′shəs) *adj.* **1** likely to cause infection; containing disease-producing organisms or matter **2** designating a disease that can be communicated by INFECTION (sense 2) **3** tending to spread or to affect others; catching *[an infectious* laugh*]* **4** [Obs.] infected with disease —**in·fec′tious·ly** *adv.* —**in·fec′tious·ness** *n.*

Intergroup
(paragraph 5)

in·ter·group (in′tər grōōp′) *adj.* between, among, or involving different social, ethnic, or racial groups

intimidate
(paragraph 7)

in·tim·i·date (in tim′ə dāt′) *vt.* **-dat′ed, -dat′ing** ⟦< ML *intimidatus,* pp. of *intimidare,* to make afraid < L *in-,* in + *timidus,* afraid, TIMID⟧ **1** to make timid; make afraid; daunt **2** to force or deter with threats or violence; cow —**in·tim′i·da′tion** *n.* —**in·tim′i·da′tor** *n.*

missionaries
(paragraph 3)

mis·sion (mish′ən) *n.* ⟦L *missio,* a sending, sending away < *missus,* pp. of *mittere,* to send < IE base **smeit-,* to throw > Avestan *hamista-,* cast down⟧ **1** a sending out or being sent out with authority to perform a special service; specif., *a*) the sending out of persons by a religious organization to preach, teach, and convert *b*) the sending out of persons to a foreign government to conduct negotiations *c*) the work done by such persons **2** *a*) a group of persons sent by a religious body to spread its religion, esp. in a foreign land *b*) its organization, headquarters, or place of residency *c*) [pl.] organized missionary work **3** a group of persons sent to a foreign government to conduct negotiations; diplomatic delegation; embassy **4** a group of technicians, specialists, etc. sent to a foreign country **5** the special duty or function for which someone is sent as a messenger or representative; errand **6** the special task or purpose for which a person is apparently destined in life; calling **7** any charitable, educational, or religious organization for helping persons in need **8** a series of special religious services designed to increase faith or bring about conversion **9** a district without a church of its own, served by a nearby church ✩**10** *Mil.* a specific combat operation assigned to an individual or unit; esp., a single combat flight by an airplane or group of airplanes —*adj.* **1** of a mission or missions ✩**2** of or in the style of the early Spanish missions in the SW U.S.; specif., designating a type of heavy, dark furniture with simple, square lines —*vt.* **1** to send on a mission **2** to establish a religious mission in (district) or among (a people)
mis·sion·ar·y (-er′ē) *adj.* ⟦ModL (Ec) *missionarius*⟧ of or characteristic of missions or missionaries, esp. religious ones —*n., pl.* **-ar′ies** a person sent on a mission, esp. on a religious mission: also **mis′sion·er** (-ər)

salmon
(paragraph 6)

salm·on (sam′ən) *n., pl.* **-on** or **-ons** ⟦ME *salmoun* < MFr < OFr *saumon* < L *salmo* (gen. *salmonis*) < ?⟧ **1** any of various salmonoid fishes (family Salmonidae); specif., any of several species of game and food fishes (genera *Oncorhynchus* and *Salmo*) of the Northern Hemisphere, with silver scales and flesh that is yellowish pink to pale red when cooked: they live in salt water and spawn in fresh water, though some species are landlocked in lakes **2** yellowish pink or pale red: also **salmon pink**

145

12A VOCABULARY

From the context of "Village English in Rural Alaska," explain the meaning of each of the vocabulary words shown in boldface below.

1. *From paragraph 3:* After contact, the early **missionaries** and teachers fanned out through this region.

   _____

   _____

2. *From paragraph 3:* Until then, **clans** of people had lived spread throughout the region . . .

   _____

   _____

3. *From paragraph 5:* If they are not **fluent** in *Inupiaq*, they tend to mix English . . .

   _____

   _____

4. *From paragraph 5:* In northwest Alaska, people have gotten used to blending the two languages for intergroup communication and have **adapted** to speaking village English.

   _____

   _____

5. *From paragraph 6:* . . . where I have difficulty explaining typical Native processes, such as how to make a half-dried **salmon**.

   _____

   _____

6. *From paragraph 7:* I do not use proper English with those who speak to me in village English because it may **intimidate** them or make them feel uncomfortable.

   _____

   _____

Name   Date

7. *From paragraph 10:* The *Inupiat* generally enjoy the **humorous** side of life . . .

_____

_____

8. *From paragraph 10:* Village English is **infectious**. . . .

_____

_____

12B   CENTRAL THEME AND MAIN IDEAS

Choose the best answer.

_____ 1. What is the central theme of "Village English in Rural Alaska"?
   a. The author enjoys her ability to communicate in English, *Inupiaq*, and a mixture of the two known as village English.
   b. Village English should be spoken only within the confines of the villages.
   c. The white man was the first to introduce village English in northwest Alaska.
   d. An educated Eskimo can speak English, *Inupiaq*, and village English.

2. In your own words, give the main idea of paragraph 5.

_____

_____

_____

_____ 3. What is the main idea of paragraph 9?
   a. There should be a uniform pattern in village English.
   b. If the village English sounds funny, it is probably grammatically incorrect.
   c. Village English follows strict grammatical guidelines.
   d. Village English is "correct" as long as communication takes place.

_____   _____
           Name   Date

12C MAJOR DETAILS

Decide whether each detail is MAJOR or MINOR.

_____ 1. The English language took hold among the *Inupiat*.

_____ 2. The *Inupiat* were punished in school for speaking their native language.

_____ 3. The author would be left speechless if she tried to explain the process of making a half-dried salmon to Charles Bronson.

_____ 4. When early explorers arrived in northwest Alaska, they brought a new language to the *Inupiat*.

_____ 5. Villages were created around the early schools and churches.

_____ 6. Those people who know only a little *Inupiaq* mix it with English in order to be understood.

_____ 7. The author can speak English, *Inupiaq*, or village English, depending on the situation.

_____ 8. The author will usually answer in the language in which she is addressed.

_____ 9. There is no such thing as "correct" village English.

_____ 10. The *Inupiat* generally enjoy the humorous side of life.

12D INFERENCES

Decide whether each statement below can be inferred (YES) or cannot be inferred (NO) from the reading selection.

_____ 1. Less of the *Inupiaq* language is being passed on from one generation to the next today.

_____ 2. The author is able to speak other languages in addition to English, village English, and *Inupiaq*.

_____ 3. The author is more skilled in conversing in English than in *Inupiaq*.

_____ 4. The author appears resentful of the white settlers who forced English on the *Inupiat*.

_____ 5. Speaking village English to a person from another part of the world would make the author appear ignorant or uneducated.

_____ 6. Village English is a written as well as spoken means of communication.

Name   Date

_____ 7. A newcomer to a village would probably be able to pick up the village English if he or she were familiar with *Inupiaq*.

_____ 8. The early missionaries and teachers made no attempt to learn the *Inupiaq* language.

12E CRITICAL READING: FACT OR OPINION

Decide whether each statement, even if it quotes someone, contains a FACT or OPINION.

_____ 1. The *Inupiat* were punished for speaking their own language in the new schools.

_____ 2. English is the predominant language in northwest Alaska today.

_____ 3. It is rare to hear a child speak fluent *Inupiaq* today.

_____ 4. It [village English] has its own beauty.

_____ 5. The *Inupiat* speak village English with a sense of humor.

_____ 6. Village English is infectious.

_____ 7. Village English is truly a spoken language.

12F CRITICAL READING: THE WRITER'S CRAFT

Choose the best answer.

_____ 1. Defining key terms at the beginning of an essay is a writer's device that

   a. provides the reader with information needed to understand the essay.
   b. creates suspense about the outcome of the essay.
   c. illustrates the importance of those terms to the overall essay.
   d. contrasts the important vocabulary words with those of less importance.

_____ 2. To support her central theme, the author uses

   a. personal observations and statistics.
   b. questions, answers, and quotations.
   c. personal experience and historical fact.
   d. statistics and professional opinions.

Name   Date

_____ 3. The author shows connections between her ideas with all of these words *except*

a. before	(paragraph 2)
b. but	(2)
c. not only . . . but	(2)
d. until then	(3)
e. as a result	(4)
f. yet	(5)
g. for instance	(6)
h. such as	(6)
i. also	(6)

12G INFORMED OPINION

1. If English is the official language of Alaska today, should village English also be an acceptable form of communication? Be specific in explaining your point of view.

2. Read paragraph 5 again. Should the village elders be encouraged and trained to pass on *Inupiaq* to the younger generations? Why or why not?

How Did You Do?   **12** Village English in Rural Alaska

SKILL (number of items)	Number Correct		Points for Each		Score
Vocabulary (8)	_____	×	2	=	_____
Central Theme and Main Ideas (3)	_____	×	4	=	_____
Major Details (10)	_____	×	2	=	_____
Inferences (8)	_____	×	2	=	_____
Critical Reading: Fact or Opinion (7)	_____	×	3	=	_____
Critical Reading: The Writer's Craft (3)	_____	×	3	=	_____

(Possible Total: 100) *Total* _____

SPEED

Reading Time: _____ Reading Rate (page 349): _____ Words Per Minute

Name   Date

Selection 13

Genes and Behavior: A Twin Legacy

Constance Holden

(1) Biology may not be destiny, but genes apparently have a far greater influence on human behavior than is commonly thought. Similarities ranging from phobias to hobbies to bodily gestures are being found in pairs of twins separated at birth. Many of these behaviors are "things you would never think of looking at if you were going to study the genetics of behavior," says psychologist Thomas J. Bouchard, Jr., director of the Minnesota Center for Twin and Adoption Research at the University of Minnesota.

(2) Bouchard reports that so far, exhaustive psychological tests and questionnaires have been completed with approximately 50 pairs of identical twins reared apart, 25 pairs of fraternal twins reared apart and comparison groups of twins reared together. "We were amazed at the similarity in posture and expressive style," says Bouchard. "It's probably the feature of the study that's grabbed us the most." Twins tend to have similar mannerisms, gestures, speed and tempo in talking, habits, and jokes.

(3) Many of the twins dressed in similar fashion—one male pair who had never previously met arrived in England sporting identical beards, haircuts, wire-rimmed glasses and shirts. (Their photo shows them both with thumbs hooked into their pants tops.) One pair had practically the same items in their toilet cases, including the same brand of cologne and a Swedish brand of toothpaste.

(4) Although many of the separated pairs had differing types of jobs and educational levels, the investigators are finding repeated similarities in hobbies and interests—one pair were both volunteer firefighters, one pair were deputy sheriffs, a male pair had similar workshops in their basements and a female pair had strikingly similar kitchen arrangements. In one case, two women from different social classes, one of whom was a pharmacological technician and the other a bookkeeper and a high school dropout, had results on their vocational-interest tests that were "remarkably similar."

(5) Bouchard doesn't have enough information on abnormal behavior or psychopathology to make generalizations, but he has found repeated similarities. One pair of women were both very superstitious; another pair would burst into tears at the drop of a hat, and questioning revealed that both had done so since childhood. "They were on a talk show together and both started crying in response to one of the ques-

tions," says Bouchard. A third pair had the same fears and phobias. Both were afraid of water and had adopted the same coping strategy: backing into the ocean up to their knees. Bouchard took them to a shopping center one day, driving up a long, winding parking ramp to let them off. He later learned that they were both so frightened by the drive they sat on a bench for two hours to collect themselves.

(6) The most striking example of common psychopathology, however, came from a pair of fraternal twins reared apart. One had been reared by his own (poor) family; the other had been adopted into a "good solid upper-middle-class family." Both are now considered to be antisocial personalities, suffering from lack of impulse control, and both have criminal histories. Although fraternal twins share, on average, 50 percent of their genes, Bouchard suggests that the overlap is probably considerably more with this pair.

(7) Another eerie congruence that occurred in the absence of identical genes was observed in the case of two identical-twin women reared apart. Each has a son who has won a statewide mathematics contest, one in Wyoming, one in Texas.

(8) Personality similarities between the identical twins reared apart are almost as pervasive as they are with identical twins reared together, according to the results of a test developed by University of Minnesota psychologist Auke Tellegen. His personality questionnaire contains scales such as "social closeness," "harm avoidance" and "well-being." The researchers were especially surprised to find that "traditionalism"—a trait implying conservatism and respect for authority—can be inherited. In fact, says Bouchard, his and other studies have found about 11 personality traits that appear to have significant genetic input.

(9) Overall, the emerging findings of the Minnesota study constitute a powerful rebuttal to those who maintain that environmental influences are the primary shaping forces of personality. The textbooks are going to have to be rewritten, Bouchard predicts.

694 words

Vocabulary List

Here are some of the more difficult words in "Genes and Behavior: A Twin Legacy."

congruence
(paragraph 7)

con·gru·ence (käŋ'grōō əns, kän'-) *n.* [ME < L *congruentia*: see fol.] **1** the state or quality of being in agreement; correspondence; harmony **2** *Geom.* the property of a plane or solid figure that makes it able to coincide with another plane or solid figure after a rigid transformation **3** *Math.* the relation between two integers each of which, when divided by a third (called the *modulus*), leaves the same remainder Also con'gru·en|cy

conservatism
(paragraph 8)

con·serv|a·tism (kən sur'və tiz'əm) *n.* the principles and practices of a conservative person or party; tendency to oppose change in institutions and methods con·ser|va·tive (kən sur′və tiv) *adj.* [OFr *conservatif* < LL *conservativus*] **1** conserving or tending to conserve; preservative **2** tending to preserve established traditions or institutions or to resist or oppose any changes in these [*conservative* politics, *conservative* art] **3** of or characteristic of a conservative **4** [C-] designating or of the major political party of Great Britain or the similar one in Canada that is characterized by conservative positions on social and economic issues **5** [C-] designating or of a movement in Judaism that accepts moderate adaptation of religious ritual and traditional forms to the framework of modern life ☆**6** moderate; cautious; safe [a *conservative* estimate] —*n.* **1** [Archaic] a preservative **2** a conservative person **3** [C-] a member of the Conservative Party of Great Britain or of the Progressive Conservative Party of Canada — con·serv′|a·tive|ly *adv.* —con·serv′a·tive·ness *n.*

destiny
(paragraph 1)

des·ti|ny (des′tə nē) *n.*, *pl.* **-nies** [ME *destine* < OFr *destinee*, fem. pp. of *destiner*: see DESTINE] **1** the seemingly inevitable or necessary succession of events **2** what will necessarily happen to any person or thing; (one's) fate **3** that which determines events: said of either a supernatural agency or necessity —*SYN.* FATE

fraternal twins
(paragraph 2)

fra·ter·nal (frə turn′əl) *adj.* [ME < ML *fraternalis* < L *fraternus*, brotherly < *frater*, BROTHER] **1** of or characteristic of a brother or brothers; brotherly **2** of or like a fraternal order or a fraternity **3** designating twins, of either the same or different sexes, developed from separately fertilized ova and thus having hereditary characteristics not necessarily the same: cf. IDENTICAL (sense 3) —fra·ter′nal·ism *n.* —fra·ter′nal|ly *adv.*

genes
(paragraph 1)

☆**gene** (jēn) *n.* [< Ger *gen*, short for *pangen* (< *pan-*, PAN- + *-gen*, -GEN, after PANGENESIS)] *Genetics* any of the units occurring at specific points on the chromosomes, by which hereditary characters are transmitted and determined: each is regarded as a particular state of organization of the chromatin in the chromosome, consisting primarily of DNA and protein: see DOMINANT, RECESSIVE, MENDEL'S LAWS

genetics
(paragraph 1)

ge·net·ics (jə net′iks) *n.pl.* [GENET(IC) + -ICS] [*with sing. v.*] **1** the branch of biology that deals with heredity and variation in similar or related animals and plants **2** the genetic features or constitution of an individual, group, or kind

Identical twins
(paragraph 2)

i|den·ti·cal (ī den′ti kəl; ī-, ə-) *adj.* [IDENTIC + -AL] **1** the very same **2** exactly alike or equal: often followed by *with* or *to* **3** designating twins, always of the same sex, developed from a single fertilized ovum and very much alike in physical appearance: cf. FRATERNAL (sense 3) —*SYN.* SAME —i|den′ti·cal|ly *adv.*

pervasive
(paragraph 8)

per·va·sive (pər vā′siv) *adj.* tending to pervade or spread throughout —per·va′sive|ly *adv.* —per·va′sive·ness *n.*

phoblas
(paragraph 1)

pho·bi|a (fō′bē ə, fō′byə) *n.* [ModL < Gr *phobos*, fear: see -PHOBE] an irrational, excessive, and persistent fear of some particular thing or situation —pho′bic *adj.*

psychopathology
(paragraph 5)

psy|cho·pa·thol·o|gy (sī′kō pə thäl′ə jē) *n.* [PSYCHO- + PATHOLOGY] **1** the science dealing with the causes and development of mental disorders **2** psychological malfunctioning, as in a mental disorder — psy′cho·path′o·log′|i·cal (-path′ə läj′i kəl) *adj.* —psy′cho·pa·thol′o·gist *n.*

rebuttal
(paragraph 9)

re·but (ri but′) *vt.* **-but′ted**, **-but′ting** [ME *rebuten* < Anglo-Fr *reboter* < OFr *rebuter* < *re-*, back + *buter*, to thrust, push: see BUTT²] **1** to contradict, refute, or oppose, esp. in a formal manner by argument, proof, etc., as in a debate **2** [Obs.] to force back; repel —*vi.* to provide opposing arguments —*SYN.* DISPROVE —re·but′ta|ble *adj.*

re·but·tal (-but′'l) *n.* a rebutting, esp. in law

vocational
(paragraph 4)

vo·ca·tion|al (-shə nəl) *adj.* **1** of a vocation, trade, occupation, etc. ☆**2** designating or of education, training, a school, etc. intended to prepare one for an occupation, sometimes specif. in a trade —vo·ca′tion·al·ism *n.* —vo·ca′tion·al|ly *adv.*

153

13A VOCABULARY

Using the vocabulary words listed on pages 152–153, fill in the blanks.

1. Police statistics show that there is _____ between the amount of drug use and the number of burglaries in any neighborhood.

2. Specific areas of the brain control specific behaviors, and as scientists' knowledge of such connections improves, methods may be developed to repair damaged or misformed parts of the brain

   and cure some kinds of _____ .

3. Although some people believe that fate controls their lives, polls indicate that on the average, Americans believe that they control

   their own _____ .

4. _____ is the study of heredity in animals and plants,

   including how _____ transmit various characteristics.

5. Students who plan to learn a trade choose to attend a

   _____ school.

6. People with excessive and persistent fears ought to seek professional

   counseling before _____ destroy their lives.

7. Expressions based on sports are _____ in our society; even people who have never seen a basketball game may speak of being "fouled" by an unfair competitor.

8. Most people think of twins as looking absolutely alike; actually, such

   complete resemblance is typical only of _____

   _____ , and _____ often look very different from one another.

9. The _____ of candidates who call for a return to the "good old days" is appealing to voters who are uncomfortable with rapid progress.

10. The band members compiled a list of songs with social messages as a

    _____ to charges that rock music encourages irresponsible behavior.

Name   Date

13B   CENTRAL THEME AND MAIN IDEAS

Choose the best answer.

_____ 1. What is the central theme of "Genes and Behavior: A Twin Legacy"?
   a. Extensive psychological tests and questionnaires have been completed by numbers of identical and fraternal twins.
   b. Carefully controlled studies show that many identical as well as fraternal twins, even when they are reared apart, tend to dress in similar fashion.
   c. Studies of twins, both identical and fraternal, provide evidence for the theory that genes have a greater influence on human behavior than is commonly thought.
   d. Thorough research about both identical and fraternal twins reveals that even if they are raised apart, they generally share the same phobias, hobbies, and gestures.

_____ 2. What is the main idea of paragraph 2?
   a. Bouchard has studied fraternal and identical twins, some reared apart and some reared together.
   b. Bouchard has studied only identical twins, some reared apart and some together.
   c. Bouchard has studied only fraternal twins, some reared apart and some together.
   d. Bouchard has studied fraternal and identical twins, all of whom were raised apart.

_____ 3. What is the main idea of paragraph 5?
   a. Research shows that abnormal behavior in separated, identical twins is rare.
   b. Studies reveal that female identical twins are more likely than male identical twins to develop fears and phobias.
   c. Fear of long, winding ramps seem to be genetically determined, according to the research of Dr. Bouchard.
   d. Researchers have not found enough examples of abnormal behavior in separated identical twins to be certain that a pattern exists.

13C   MAJOR DETAILS

Decide whether each detail is true (T), false (F), or not discussed (ND).

_____ 1. Thomas J. Bouchard is the director of the Minnesota Center for Twin and Adoption Research.

_____ 2. The behavior of separated twins is being compared with the behavior of a group of 25 pairs of twins raised together.

Name   Date

_____ 3. Even though many of the separated twins have different jobs, they often share the same hobbies and interests.

_____ 4. One pair of identical twins who burst into tears easily both cried when asked to appear on a talk show.

_____ 5. Twins who are afraid of water are usually also afraid of the dark and of animals.

_____ 6. One set of separated fraternal twins both had antisocial personalities and grew up to be criminals.

_____ 7. A woman's twin sons won mathematics competitions in Wyoming and Texas.

_____ 8. Social closeness is essential for happiness in humans.

_____ 9. Environmental influences are the most important shapers of personality.

_____ 10. Genes determine almost all personality traits.

13D   INFERENCES

Choose the best answer.

_____ 1. *Read paragraph 1 again.* What does the author mean by "Biology may not be destiny"?
a. Most psychologists believe that biology controls people's destinies.
b. Most psychologists believe that biology does not control people's destinies.
c. The debate over whether biology or environment controls people's destinies has been going on for a long time.
d. The author is not sure whether biology is destiny, so she is showing that she does not support the conclusions of Bouchard's study.

_____ 2. *Read paragraph 1 again.* Why does Bouchard say these behaviors are "things you would never think of looking at if you were going to study the genetics of behavior"?
a. These behaviors seemed too unimportant for scientists to observe.
b. These behaviors seemed too intimate to allow scientists to observe them.
c. Psychologists assumed these relatively external characteristics could not be biologically based.
d. Psychologists assumed that the causes of these behaviors were too complicated for current methods of observation.

Name   Date

_____ 3. *Read paragraph 5 again.* Why does Bouchard need more information before he can make generalizations?

a. He has not yet found a strong pattern of particular kinds of abnormal behavior among separated identical twins.

b. The government says researchers must have ten examples before they can make a generalization about a psychological issue.

c. He is afraid of being sued if he makes a statement that might later be shown to be inaccurate.

d. He does not want to embarrass the people in the small group he has studied, and so he is looking for additional, anonymous twins to study.

13E   CRITICAL READING: THE WRITER'S CRAFT

Choose the best answer.

_____ 1. To make her point, the author uses all of these devices *except*

a. quotations from experts.

b. detailed examples.

c. anecdotes.

d. definitions of key terms.

_____ 2. The author shows connections between her ideas with all of these words *except*

a. but   (paragraph 1)

b. so far   (2)

c. in one case   (4)

d. but   (5)

e. one . . . another (5)

f. however   (6)

g. one . . . the other (6)

h. in fact   (8)

i. overall   (9)

_____ 3. The author ends her essay with

a. a quotation from the Minnesota study.

b. a summary

c. a detailed analysis of an opposing opinion.

d. reference to an authority.

Name   Date

13F INFORMED OPINION

1. Should parents of twins encourage them to dress and act differently or alike? Using specific examples, explain your point of view.

2. *Read paragraphs 8 and 9 again.* If personality traits are inherited, what is the role of parents in forming their children's characters? Using specific examples, explain your answer.

How Did You Do? 13 Genes and Behavior: A Twin Legacy

SKILL (number of items)	Number Correct		Points for Each		Score
Vocabulary* (12)	_____	×	3	=	_____
Central Theme and Main Ideas (3)	_____	×	5	=	_____
Major Details (10)	_____	×	4	=	_____
Inferences (3)	_____	×	2	=	_____
Critical Reading: The Writer's Craft (3)	_____	×	1	=	_____

(Possible Total: 100) *Total* _____

SPEED

Reading Time: _____ Reading Rate (page 349): _____ Words Per Minute

*Questions 4 and 8 in this exercise call for two separate answers each. In computing your score, count each separate answer toward your number correct.

Name   Date

Richard Cory, All Over Again

Roy Meador

(1) The same as the rest of us, my friend wanted to be somebody. To make his mark in the world. To have his life count. At the end, he did make his mark in headlines: *Deaths Called Murder-Suicide. Son Finds Bodies.*

(2) Carl L. Stinedurf was a good friend. We often lunched together, and our conversations ranged from politics to literature. Carl enjoyed ideas. He knew how to laugh. Face-to-face, most people used his middle name, Larry. But the waitress called him "Frank" because he preferred Sinatra's old records to new stuff. Carl often talked enthusiastically about his family, his son at the university, his daughter in high school. He mentioned his wife, Norma, with special pride. In her 30's, with his help she had finished college and begun teaching. Carl was delighted with his family's accomplishments. But underneath, well-masked, there must have been agonizing terror. Carl carried his pain in silence.

(3) My friend worked as an estimator and customer representative for a large printing firm. He was gentle, always soft-spoken, exceptionally conscientious. When I gave him work to do for my company, I knew it would be finished with care.

(4) Carl tended toward the liberal. He thought more of people than of profits. He deplored cruelty. I considered him one of those who patiently keep what we call civilization humming along after its fashion.

(5) There was just one anomaly I never understood. Carl's hobby was guns. He kept a loaded .38 in his bedroom. There were handguns and rifles throughout his home. Carl used them for target shooting and hunting. A fellow hunter said Carl was an expert marksman, that when he fired at game he made certain of his shot so the animal wouldn't suffer.

(6) I couldn't appreciate the gun side of my friend's character. I guess I had seen too much of the gun religion in the Korean war. Carl and I disagreed about guns. He would vote for George McGovern and simultaneously support every argument of the National Rifle Association and the gun lobbies. Yet because he was a peaceful, compassionate man, I considered him one of those who could be trusted to own and use guns responsibly.

(7) I saw Carl on that last Friday afternoon. We talked about a printing job. He was cheerful, and I think he was already on the other side of his decision. He finished his work that day like someone going on vacation. Like someone not expecting to return on Monday.

(8) We had a relaxed talk. Later I learned of the misery he had concealed. "He saw customers and kept control," his employer told me. "When the customer left, he often went in the restroom and vomited. Family trouble."

(9) The virus of restlessness. Norma, after 23 years, with a new career and new friends, wanted to leave. She needed to seek that popular, elusive goal, "more out of life." But Carl was an old-fashioned man captive in a time of new fashions. He couldn't handle this threat to the family. He sought medical advice, but every answer seemed to require letting Norma go, with the frail hope she might come back. Carl couldn't live with the uncertainty.

(10) It rained that Friday night. Carl went home and in their bedroom he put two bullets through his wife's head, one through his own. He used a .357 magnum handgun. One of Carl's friends told me this proved it was carefully planned. The .357 magnum meant Carl didn't want Norma to suffer. That friend and others were reluctant to credit guns as factors in the event. "Guns are simply tidier than axes," said one. But Carl was a sensitive, orderly man. I doubt he could ever have done the job with less efficient, messier weapons. It had to be over in a moment. So he used the mercy weapon, the no-pain gun, the .357 magnum. It was handy in a house of guns.

(11) Endless postmortems began among those who knew Carl and Norma. Why in his torment couldn't he wait? Why couldn't he give time a chance? Why?

(12) No one I listened to blamed the guns, questioned their proximity, their easy availability. It will probably be a long time before Carl's small estate is settled for the son who found the bodies, for the daughter in high school. I suppose his guns eventually will be sold and redistributed, including the .357 magnum. Guns are made from enduring metal. They outlive their owners. They go on about their business.

(13) News accounts carried the standard facts: Description of Carl's hobby. His age, 39. The comment of a neighbor that Carl and Norma were "very nice." Details of the funeral. There was no indication whether or not gun clubs and the National Rifle Association sent flowers, or assistance for the survivors.

(14) The irony department: Carl learned enthusiasm for guns as an adult. His teacher later abandoned guns in favor of photography.

(15) I'll miss Carl very much. His last day was Edwin Arlington Robinson's poem translated into tragic fact. "And Richard Cory, one calm summer night,/Went home and put a bullet through his head." Richard Cory wasn't the sort to use an ice pick. The same with Carl. Only a gun.

(16) Damn those guns.

950 words

Richard Cory

EDWIN ARLINGTON ROBINSON

Whenever Richard Cory went down town,
We people on the pavement looked at him:
He was a gentleman from sole to crown,
Clean favored, and imperially slim.

And he was always quietly arrayed,
And he was always human when he talked;
But still he fluttered pulses when he said,
"Good-morning," and he glittered when he walked.

And he was rich—yes, richer than a king—
And admirably schooled in every grace:
In fine,* we thought that he was everything
To make us wish that we were in his place.

So on we worked, and waited for the light,
And went without the meat, and cursed the bread;
And Richard Cory, one calm summer night,
Went home and put a bullet through his head.

*In short

Vocabulary List

Here are some of the more difficult words in "Richard Cory, All Over Again."

agonizing
(paragraph 2)

ag·o·nize (ag′ə nīz′) *vi.* -nized′, -niz′ing [LL *agonizare* < Gr *agōnizesthai*, to contend for a prize < *agōn*, AGON] 1 to make convulsive efforts; struggle 2 to be in agony or great pain; feel anguish —*vt.* to cause great pain to; torture —ag′o·niz′ing *adj.* —ag′o·niz′ing·ly *adv.*

anomaly
(paragraph 5)

a·nom·a·ly (ə näm′ə lē) *n., pl.* -lies [L *anomalia* < Gr *anōmalia*, inequality: see ANOMALOUS] 1 departure from the regular arrangement, general rule, or usual method; abnormality 2 anything anomalous 3 *Astron.* a measurement used for any orbiting body, as a planet's angular distance around its orbit from its perihelion, taken as if viewed from the sun

compassionate
(paragraph 6)

com·pas·sion·ate (-it; *for v.*, -āt′) *adj.* feeling or showing compassion; sympathizing deeply; pitying —*vt.* -at′ed, -at′ing to pity — *SYN.* TENDER¹ —com·pas′sion·ate·ly *adv.*

conscientious
(paragraph 3)

con·sci·en·tious (kän′shē en′shəs) *adj.* [Fr *conscientieux* < ML *conscientiosus:* see CONSCIENCE & -OUS] 1 governed by, or made or done according to, what one knows is right; scrupulous; honest 2 showing care and precision; painstaking —con′sci·en′tious·ly *adv.* —con′sci·en′tious·ness *n.*

deplored
(paragraph 4)

de·plore (dē plôr′, di-) *vt.* -plored′, -plor′ing [Fr *déplorer* < L *deplorare* < *de-*, intens. + *plorare*, to weep] 1 to be regretful or sorry about; lament 2 to regard as unfortunate or wretched 3 to condemn as wrong; disapprove of —de·plor′er *n.*

elusive
(paragraph 9)

e·lu·sive (ē lōō′siv, i-) *adj.* [< L *elusus* (see ELUSION) + -IVE] 1 tending to elude 2 hard to grasp or retain mentally; baffling Also [Rare] e·lu′so·ry (-sə rē) —e·lu′sive·ly *adv.* —e·lu′sive·ness *n.*

irony
(paragraph 14)

i·ro·ny¹ (ī′rə nē, ī′ər nē) *n., pl.* -nies [Fr *ironie* < L *ironia* < Gr *eirōneia* < *eirōn*, dissembler in speech < *eirein*, to speak < IE base *wer-*, to speak > WORD] 1 a) a method of humorous or subtly sarcastic expression in which the intended meaning of the words is the direct opposite of their usual sense [the *irony* of calling a stupid plan "clever"] b) an instance of this 2 the contrast, as in a play, between what a character thinks the truth is, as revealed in a speech or action, and what an audience or reader knows the truth to be: often **dramatic irony** 3 a combination of circumstances or a result that is the opposite of what is or might be expected or considered appropriate [an *irony* that the firehouse burned] 4 a) a cool, detached attitude of mind, characterized by recognition of the incongruities and complexities of experience b) the expression of such an attitude in a literary work 5 the feigning of ignorance in argument: often **Socratic irony** (after Socrates' use in Plato's *Dialogues*) — *SYN.* WIT¹

lobbies
(paragraph 6)

lob|by (läb'ē) *n., pl.* **-bies** ⟦LL *lobia:* see LODGE⟧ **1** a hall or large anteroom, as a waiting room or vestibule of an apartment house, hotel, theater, etc. **2** a large hall adjacent to the assembly hall of a legislature and open to the public ☆**3** a group of lobbyists representing the same special interest *[the oil lobby]* —☆*vi.* **-bied, -by·ing 1** to act as a lobbyist **2** to attempt to influence in favor of something: often with *for* —☆*vt.* **1** to attempt to influence (a public official) by acting as a lobbyist **2** to attempt to influence the passage of (a measure) by acting as a lobbyist

☆**lob·by·ist** (-ist) *n.* a person, acting for a special interest group, who tries to influence the introduction of or voting on legislation or the decisions of government administrators —**lob'by·ism** *n.*

postmortems
(paragraph 11)

post-mor|tem (pōst'môr'təm) *adj.* ⟦L, lit., after death⟧ **1** happening, done, or made after death **2** having to do with a post-mortem examination —*n.* **1** *short for* POST-MORTEM EXAMINATION **2** a detailed examination or evaluation of some event just ended

proximity
(paragraph 12)

prox·im·i|ty (präks im'ə tē) *n.* ⟦MFr *proximité* < L *proximitas* < *proximus:* see PROXIMATE⟧ the state or quality of being near; nearness in space, time, etc.

14A VOCABULARY

From the context of "Richard Cory, All Over Again," explain the meaning of each of the vocabulary words shown in boldface below.

1. *From paragraph 2:* But underneath, well-masked, there must have been **agonizing** terror.

_____

_____

2. *From paragraph 3:* He was gentle, always soft-spoken, exceptionally **conscientious.**

_____

_____

3. *From paragraph 4:* He **deplored** cruelty.

_____

_____

163

4. *From paragraph 5:* There was just one **anomaly** I never understood. Carl's hobby was guns.

_____

_____

5. *From paragraph 6:* He would vote for George McGovern and simultaneously support every argument of the National Rifle Association and the gun **lobbies.**

_____

_____

6. *From paragraph 6:* Yet because he was a peaceful, **compassionate** man, I considered him one of those who could be trusted to own and use guns responsibly.

_____

_____

7. *From paragraph 9:* She needed to seek that popular, **elusive** goal, "more out of life."

_____

_____

8. *From paragraph 11:* Endless **postmortems** began among those who knew Carl and Norma.

_____

_____

9. *From paragraph 12:* No one I listened to blamed the guns, questioned their **proximity,** their easy availability.

_____

_____

10. *From paragraph 14:* The **irony** department: Carl learned enthusiasm for guns as an adult. His teacher later abandoned guns in favor of photography.

_____

_____

14B CENTRAL THEME AND MAIN IMAGES

Follow the directions for each item below.

1. There are two central themes in "Richard Cory, All Over Again." One central theme is about Carl L. Stinedurf. The second central theme is about guns. Explain each central theme.

   a. *About Carl L. Stinedurf:* _____

   _____

   _____

   b. *About guns:* _____

   _____

   _____

2. In Edwin Arlington Robinson's poem "Richard Cory," there are two images. One image is a picture of Richard Cory. The second image is a picture of the people telling the story. Describe each image.

   a. *Of Richard Cory:* _____

   _____

   _____

   b. *Of the people telling the story:* _____

   _____

   _____

14C MAJOR DETAILS

Decide whether each detail is MAJOR or MINOR.

_____ 1. Carl L. Stinedurf was a good friend of Roy Meador.

_____ 2. The waitress called Carl "Frank."

_____ 3. Carl often talked enthusiastically about his family.

_____ 4. Carl's wife, Norma, had recently finished college and had begun to teach.

_____ 5. Underneath Carl's delight, there must have been a well-masked agonizing terror.

_____ 6. Carl worked as a printing estimator and a customer representative.

_____ 7. Carl was gentle, soft-spoken, and hated cruelty.

_____ 8. Carl's hobby was guns.

_____ 9. The .38 that Carl kept in his bedroom was loaded.

_____ 10. Norma, after 23 years of marriage, wanted to leave Carl.

_____ 11. Carl went home and put two bullets through his wife's head and one through his own.

_____ 12. Roy Meador feels that Carl would not have been able to kill if he had had to use a messy weapon such as an ice pick.

_____ 13. Roy Meador did not know if gun clubs and the National Rifle Association sent flowers to the funeral.

14D INFERENCES

Choose the best answer.

_____ 1. *Read paragraph 6 again.* George McGovern, the 1972 Democratic presidential candidate, ran against Richard Nixon. McGovern's liberal views included being in favor of strong gun-control legislation. Why did Carl vote for McGovern?
   a. Carl was a liberal.
   b. Carl was anti-Nixon.
   c. Carl was influenced by Roy Meador.
   d. Carl wanted to impress his wife.

_____ 2. *Read paragraph 7 again.* Carl was cheerful on that last Friday afternoon because he
   a. was looking forward to a weekend with his guns.
   b. enjoyed his lunches with Roy.
   c. had made up his mind and the uncertainty was now over.
   d. was going to see his beloved wife soon.

_____ 3. *Read paragraph 10 again.* The .357 magnum is considered "the mercy weapon, the no-pain gun" because
   a. it is very well made.
   b. it wounds but does not kill.
   c. it is not a real gun.
   d. it kills instantly.

Name   Date

_____ 4. *Read paragraph 13 again.* The gun clubs or the National Rifle Association might have sent flowers or assistance for the survivors because
   a. they had a humane concern for the survivors of people killed by guns or rifles.
   b. they hoped to receive contributions from the survivors and their friends to help support their efforts to get gun control laws passed.
   c. they wanted to lessen the chance that the survivors and the media would start another outcry for gun control laws.
   d. Carl was an active member of their groups, and they wanted to pay their respects.

14E   CRITICAL READING: THE WRITER'S CRAFT

Choose the best answer.

_____ 1. In paragraph 9 the image "virus of restlessness" is contained in the words
   a. "Carl was an old-fashioned man."
   b. ". . . to seek that popular, elusive goal, 'more out of life.' "
   c. ". . . this threat to the family."
   d. "He sought medical advice."

_____ 2. In paragraph 15 the author quotes from Edwin Arlington Robinson's poem "Richard Cory," because Roy Meador wants to
   a. show he knows how to translate.
   b. urge people to improve themselves by reading poetry.
   c. describe how much he liked Carl.
   d. illustrate that themes recur often, in life as well as in literature.

_____ 3. *Read the poem again.* Why does Roy Meador call his essay "Richard Cory, All Over Again"?
   a. Both Richard and Carl were wealthy.
   b. Both Richard and Carl were married.
   c. Both Richard and Carl were envied by everyone.
   d. Both Richard and Carl, though seemingly happy, committed suicide.

_____ 4. Why does the author of the poem wait until his last two lines to reveal what happened to Richard Cory?
   a. He probably could not have worked out his end-of-line rhymes any other way.
   b. He wanted to dramatize the suddenness of the suicide.
   c. He wanted to write about Richard Cory's life, not his death.
   d. He did not want to horrify his readers with too many details about the death.

Name   Date

14F INFORMED OPINION

1. In your opinion, if guns had not been available to Carl, would he have killed his wife and committed suicide? Explain.

2. *Read paragraphs 8 and 9 again.* What is your opinion of Norma's wanting to leave her husband so that she could get "more out of life"? Explain.

How Did You Do?   **14** Richard Cory, All Over Again

SKILL (number of items)	Number Correct		Points for Each		Score
Vocabulary (10)	_____	×	2	=	_____
Central Theme and Main Images* (4)	_____	×	5	=	_____
Major Details (13)	_____	×	4	=	_____
Inferences (4)	_____	×	1	=	_____
Critical Reading: The Writer's Craft (4)	_____	×	1	=	_____

(Possible Total: 100) *Total* _____

SPEED

Reading Time: _____ Reading Rate (page 349): _____ Words Per Minute

*Both questions in this exercise call for two separate answers each. In computing your score, count each separate answer toward your number correct.

Name   Date

Escaping the Daily Grind for Life as a House Father

Rick Greenberg

(1) "You on vacation?" my neighbor asked.

(2) My 15-month-old son and I were passing her yard on our daily hike through the neighborhood. It was a weekday afternoon and I was the only working-age male in sight.

(3) "I'm uh . . . working out of my house now," I told her.

(4) Thus was born my favorite euphemism for house fatherhood, one of those new lifestyle occupations that is never merely mentioned. Explained, yes. Defended. Even rhapsodized about. I was tongue-tied then, but no longer. People are curious and I've learned to oblige.

(5) I joined up earlier this year when I quit my job—a dead-end, ulcer-producing affair that had dragged on interminably. I left to be with my son until something better came along. And if nothing did, I'd be with him indefinitely.

(6) This was no simple transition. I had never known a house father, never met one. I'd only read about them. They were another news magazine trend. Being a traditionalist, I never dreamed I'd take the plunge.

(7) But as the job got worse, I gave it serious thought. And more thought. And in the end, I still felt ambivalent. This was a radical change that seemed to carry as many drawbacks as benefits. My dislike for work finally pushed me over the edge. That, and the fact that we had enough money to get by.

(8) Escaping the treadmill was a bold stroke. I had shattered my lethargy and stopped whining, and for that I was proud.

(9) Some friends said they were envious. Of course they weren't quitting one job without one waiting—the ultimate in middle-class taboos. That ran through my mind as I triumphantly, and without notice, tossed the letter of resignation on my boss's desk. Then I walked away wobbly-kneed.

(10) The initial trauma of quitting, however, was mitigated by my eagerness to raise our son. Mine was the classic father's lament: I felt excluded. I had become "the man who got home after dark," that other person besides Mama. It hurt when I couldn't quiet his crying.

(11) I sensed that staying home would be therapeutic. The chronic competitiveness and aggressiveness that had served me well as a daily journalist would subside. Something better would emerge, something less obnoxious. My ulcer would heal. Instead of beating deadlines, I'd

be doing something important for a change. This was heresy coming from a newspaper gypsy, but it rang true.

(12) There was unease, too. I'd be adrift, stripped of the home-office-home routine that had defined my existence for more than a decade. No more earning a living. No benchmarks. Time would be seamless. Would Friday afternoons feel the same?

(13) The newness of it was scary.

(14) Until my resignation, my wife and I typified today's baby-boomer couples, the want-it-all generation. We had two salaries, a full-time nanny and guilt pangs over practicing parenthood by proxy.

(15) Now, my wife brings home the paychecks, the office problems and thanks for good work on the domestic front. With me at home, her work hours are more flexible. Nanny-less, I change diapers, prepare meals and do all the rest. And I wonder what comes next.

(16) What if I don't find another job? My field is tight. At 34, I'm not getting any more marketable and being out of work doesn't help.

(17) As my father asked incredulously: "Is this going to be what you do?"

(18) Perhaps. I don't know. I wonder myself. It's even more baffling to my father, the veteran of a long and traditional 9-to-5 career. For most of it, my mother stayed home. My father doesn't believe in trends. All he knows is that his only son—with whom he shares so many traits—has violated the natural order of men providing and women raising children. In his view, I've shown weakness and immaturity by succumbing to a bad job.

(19) But he's trying to understand, and I think he will.

(20) I'm trying to understand it myself. House fatherhood has been humbling, rewarding and unnerving.

(21) "It's different," I tell friends. "Different."

(22) Imagine never having to leave home for the office in the morning. That's how different. No dress-up, no commute. Just tumble out of bed and you're there. House fathering is not for claustrophobics.

(23) I find myself enjoying early morning shopping. My son and I arrive right after the supermarket opens. The place is almost empty. For the next hour we glide dreamily, cruising the aisles to a Muzak accompaniment. This is my idyll. My son likes it, too; he's fascinated by the spectacle.

(24) Housekeeping still doesn't seem like work, and that's by design. I've mastered the art of doing just enough chores to get by. This leaves me enough free time. Time to read and write and daydream. Time with my son. Time to think about the structure.

(25) So much time, and so little traditional structure, that the days sometimes blur together. I remember on Sunday nights literally dreading the approaching work week, the grind. Today, the close of the weekend still triggers a shiver of apprehension; I now face the prospect of a week without tangible accomplishments, a void.

(26) On our hikes to the playground, I can feel my old identity fading. All around are people with a mission, a sense of purpose. Workers.

And then, there's the rest of us—the stroller and backpack contingent. The moms, the nannies, and me. I wonder if I've crossed over a line never to return.

(27) Still, the ulcer seems to be healing. I take pride in laying out a good dinner for the family and in pampering my wife after a tough day at the office. I love reading to my son. Running errands isn't even so bad. A lot of what had been drudgery or trivia is taking on new meaning; maybe I'm mellowing.

(28) Which is ironic. To be a truly committed and effective at-home parent, there must be this chance—a softening, a contentment with small pleasures, the outwardly mundane. This is a time of reduced demands and lowered expectations. Progress is gradual, often agonizingly so. Patience is essential. Ambition and competitiveness are anathema. Yet eliminating these last two qualities—losing the edge—could ruin my chances of resurrecting my career. I can't have it both ways.

(29) The conflict has yet to be resolved. And it won't be unless I make a firm commitment and choose one lifestyle over the other. I'm not yet ready for that decision.

(30) In the meantime, a wonderful change is taking place in our home. Amid all the uncertainties, my son and I have gotten to know each other. He can't put a phrase together, but he confides in me. It can be nothing more than a grin or a devilish look. He tries new words on me, new shtick. We roll around a lot; we crack each other up. I'm no longer the third wheel, the man who gets home after dark. Now, I'm as much a part of his life as his mother is. I, too, can stop his crying. So far, that has made the experiment worthwhile.

(1197 words)

Here are some of the more difficult words in "Escaping the Daily Grind for Life as a House Father."

ambivalent
(paragraph 7)

am·biv·a·lence (am biv'ə ləns) *n.* ⟦AMBI- + VALENCE⟧ simultaneous conflicting feelings toward a person or thing, as love and hate Also [Chiefly Brit.] **am·biv'a·len·cy** —**am·biv'a·lent** *adj.* —**am·biv'a·lent·ly** *adv.*

anathema
(paragraph 28)

a·nath·e·ma (ə nath'ə mə) *n., pl.* **-mas** ⟦LL(Ec) < Gr, thing devoted to evil; previously, anything devoted < *anatithenai*, to dedicate < *ana-*, up + *tithenai*, to place: see DO¹⟧ **1** a thing or person accursed or damned **2** a thing or person greatly detested **3** *a*) a solemn ecclesiastical condemnation of a teaching judged to be gravely opposed to accepted church doctrine, or of the originators or supporters of such a teaching *b*) the excommunication often accompanying or following this condemnation —*adj.* **1** greatly detested **2** viewed as accursed or damned **3** subjected to an ecclesiastical anathema

claustrophobics
(paragraph 22)

claus·tro·pho·bia (klôs'trə fō'bē ə) *n.* ⟦< L *claustrum* (see CLOISTER) + -PHOBIA⟧ an abnormal fear of being in an enclosed or confined place —**claus'tro·pho'bic** *adj.*

Vocabulary List

Vocabulary List

contingent
(paragraph 26)

con·tin·gent (kən tin′jənt) *adj.* ⟦L *contingens*, prp. of *contingere*, to touch: see CONTACT⟧ **1** [Obs.] touching; tangential **2** that may or may not happen; possible **3** happening by chance; accidental; fortuitous **4** unpredictable because dependent on chance **5** dependent (*on* or *upon* something uncertain); conditional **6** *Logic* true only under certain conditions or in certain contexts; not always or necessarily true **7** *Philos.* not subject to determinism; free —*n.* **1** an accidental or chance happening **2** a share or quota, as of troops, laborers, delegates, etc. **3** a group forming part of a larger group — **con·tin′gent·ly** *adv.*

euphemism
(paragraph 4)

eu·phe·mism (yo͞o′fə miz′əm) *n.* ⟦Gr *euphēmismos* < *euphēmizein*, to use words of good omen < *euphēmos*, of good sound or omen < *eu-* (see EU-) + *phēmē*, voice < *phanai*, to say: see BAN¹⟧ **1** the use of a word or phrase that is less expressive or direct but considered less distasteful, less offensive, etc. than another **2** a word or phrase so substituted (Ex.: *remains* for *corpse*) —**eu′phe·mist** *n.* — **eu′phe·mis′tic** or **eu′phe·mis′ti·cal** *adj.* —**eu′phe·mis′ti·cal·ly** *adv.*

heresy
(paragraph 11)

her·e·sy (her′i sē) *n., pl.* **-sies** ⟦ME *heresie* < OFr < L *haeresis*, school of thought, sect, in LL(Ec), heresy < Gr *hairesis*, a taking, selection, school, sect, in LGr(Ec), heresy < *hairein*, to take⟧ **1** *a*) a religious belief opposed to the orthodox doctrines of a church; esp., such a belief specifically denounced by the church *b*) the rejection of a belief that is a part of church dogma **2** any opinion (in philosophy, politics, etc.) opposed to official or established views or doctrines **3** the holding of any such belief or opinion

idyll
(paragraph 23)

i·dyll or **i·dyl** (id′′l; *Brit* id′′l) *n.* ⟦L *idyllium* < Gr *eidyllion*, dim. of *eidos*, a form, figure, image: see -OID⟧ **1** a short poem or prose work describing a simple, peaceful scene of rural or pastoral life **2** a scene or incident suitable for such a work **3** a narrative poem somewhat like a short epic [Tennyson's "*Idylls* of the King"] **4** *Music* a simple, pastoral composition

lethargy
(paragraph 8)

leth·ar·gy (leth′ər jē) *n., pl.* **-gies** ⟦ME *litarge* < OFr < LL *lethargia* < Gr *lēthargia* < *lēthargos*, forgetful < *lēthē* (see LETHE) + *argos*, idle < *a-*, not + *ergon*, WORK⟧ **1** a condition of abnormal drowsiness or torpor **2** a great lack of energy; sluggishness, dullness, apathy, etc.

mitigated
(paragraph 8)

mit·i·gate (mit′ə gāt′) *vt., vi.* **-gat′ed, -gat′ing** ⟦ME *mitigaten* < L *mitigatus*, pp. of *mitigare*, to make mild, soft, or tender < *mitis*, soft (see MIGNON) + *agere*, to drive: see ACT⟧ **1** to make or become milder, less severe, less rigorous, or less painful; moderate **2** [< confusion with MILITATE] to operate or work (*against*): generally considered a loose or erroneous usage —*SYN.* RELIEVE —**mit′i·ga·ble** (-i gə bəl) *adj.* —**mit′i·ga′tion** *n.* —**mit′i·ga·tive** *adj.* —**mit′i·ga·tor** *n.* —**mit′i·ga·to′ry** (-gə tôr′ē) *adj.*

mundane
(paragraph 28)

mun·dane (mun′dān′, mun dān′) *adj.* ⟦LME *mondeyne* < OFr *mondain* < LL *mundanus* < L *mundus*, world (in LL(Ec), the secular world, as opposed to the church)⟧ **1** of the world; esp., worldly, as distinguished from heavenly, spiritual, etc. **2** commonplace, everyday, ordinary, etc. —*SYN.* EARTHLY —**mun′dane·ly** *adv.*

proxy
(paragraph 14)

prox·y (präks′ē) *n., pl.* **prox′ies** ⟦ME *prokecie*, contr. < *procuracie*, the function of a procurator, ult. < L *procuratio*⟧ **1** the agency or function of a deputy **2** the authority to act for another **3** a document empowering a person to act for another, as in voting at a stockholders' meeting **4** a person empowered to act for another — *SYN.* AGENT

rhapsodized
(paragraph 4)

rhap·so·dize (-dīz′) *vi.* **-dized′, -diz′ing 1** to speak or write in an extravagantly enthusiastic manner **2** to recite or write rhapsodies —*vt.* to recite or utter as a rhapsody
rhap·so·dy (rap′sə dē) *n., pl.* **-dies** ⟦Fr *r(h)apsodie* < L *rhapsodia* < Gr *rhapsōidia* < *rhapsōidos*, one who strings songs together, reciter of epic poetry < *rhaptein*, to stitch together (< IE *werp-, *wrep-*, extension of base *wer-*, to turn, bend > WORM, WRAP, RAVEL) + *ōidē*, song: see ODE⟧ **1** in ancient Greece, a part of an epic poem suitable for a single recitation **2** any ecstatic or extravagantly enthusiastic utterance in speech or writing **3** great delight; ecstasy **4** [Obs.] a miscellany **5** *Music* an instrumental composition of free, irregular form, suggesting improvisation

schtick
(paragraph 30)

☆**shtick** (shtik) *n.* ⟦< E Yidd *shtik*, pl., pranks, interpreted as sing. < *shtik*, lit., piece < MHG *stücke*⟧ [Slang] **1** a comic scene or piece of business, as in a vaudeville act **2** an attention-getting device **3** a special trait, talent, etc.

taboos
(paragraph 9)

ta·boo (tə boõ′, ta-) *n.* [< a Polynesian language: cf. Tongan, Samoan, Maori, etc. *tapu*] **1** *a)* among some Polynesian peoples, a sacred prohibition put upon certain people, things, or acts which makes them untouchable, unmentionable, etc. *b)* the highly developed system or practice of such prohibitions **2** *a)* any social prohibition or restriction that results from convention or tradition *b) Linguis.* the substitution of one word or phrase for another because of such restriction —*adj.* **1** sacred and prohibited by taboo **2** restricted by taboo: said of people **3** prohibited or forbidden by tradition, convention, etc. —*vt.* **1** to put under taboo **2** to prohibit or forbid because of tradition, convention, etc.

therapeutic
(paragraph 11)

ther|a·peu·tic (ther′ə pyoōt′ik) *adj.* [ModL *therapeuticus* < Gr *therapeutikos* < *therapeutēs*, attendant, servant, one who treats medically < *therapeuein*, to nurse, treat medically] **1** *a)* serving to cure or heal; curative *b)* serving to preserve health *[therapeutic abortion]* **2** of therapeutics Also **ther|a·peu′ti·cal** —**ther|a·peu′ti·ca‖y** *adv.*

Vocabulary List

15A   VOCABULARY

From the context of "Escaping the Daily Grind for Life as a House Father," explain the meaning of each of the vocabulary words shown in boldface below.

1. *From paragraph 4:* Thus was born my favorite **euphemism** for house fatherhood . . .

   _____

   _____

2. *From paragraph 4:* Explained, yes. Defended. Even **rhapsodized** about.

   _____

   _____

3. *From paragraph 7:* And in the end, I still felt **ambivalent**.

   _____

   _____

4. *From paragraph 8:* I had shattered my **lethargy** and stopped whining, and for that I was proud.

   _____

   _____

5. *From paragraph 9:* . . . the ultimate in middle-class **taboos**.

   _____

   _____

6. *From paragraph 10:* The initial trauma of quitting, however, was **mitigated** by my eagerness to raise our son.

   _____

   _____

173

7. *From paragraph 11:* I sensed that staying home would be **therapeutic**.

_____

_____

8. *From paragraph 11:* This was **heresy** . . .

_____

_____

9. *From paragraph 14:* We had two salaries, a full-time nanny and guilt pangs over practicing parenthood by **proxy**.

_____

_____

10. *From paragraph 22:* House fathering is not for **claustrophobics**.

_____

_____

11. *From paragraph 23*: This is my **idyll**.

_____

_____

12. *From paragraph 26:* . . . the stroller and backpack **contingent**.

_____

_____

13. *From paragraph 28:* . . . a softening, a contentment with small pleasures, the outwardly **mundane**.

_____

_____

14. *From paragraph 28:* Ambition and competitiveness are **anathema**.

_____

_____

15. *From paragraph 30:* He tries new words on me, new **schtick**.

_____

_____

Name   Date

15B CENTRAL THEME AND MAIN IDEAS

Choose the best answer.

_____ 1. What is the central theme of "Escaping the Daily Grind for Life as a House Father"?
   a. More fathers should quit work to take care of their children.
   b. One man finds that raising a child can be as fulfilling an occupation as a traditional career.
   c. The author discovers that he is better at being a house father than at being a journalist.
   d. House fathering is a new occupation for fathers suffering from stress and job burnout.

2. In your own words, give the main idea of paragraph 18.

   _____

   _____

3. In your own words, give the main idea of paragraph 28.

   _____

   _____

_____ 4. What is the main idea of paragraph 30?
   a. The author and his son enjoy spending quality time with each other.
   b. Radical lifestyle change is often beneficial for parents experiencing child-rearing stress.
   c. Children adapt well to changes in their lifestyles.
   d. The author has succeeded in getting to know his son as well as his mother does.

15C MAJOR DETAILS

Decide whether each detail is MAJOR or MINOR.

_____ 1. Some friends were envious about the author's lifestyle change.

_____ 2. The author was willing to be with his son until a better job came along, or indefinitely.

Name   Date

_____ 3. Because of his intense dislike of his job, the author felt that staying home with his son would be therapeutic.

_____ 4. The author usually got home from work too late to spend much time with his son.

_____ 5. The author and his wife had a nanny.

_____ 6. The author felt excluded from the child-raising process.

_____ 7. The author takes his son grocery shopping.

_____ 8. The author was a daily journalist.

_____ 9. Now the author can stop his son's crying, too.

15D   INFERENCES

Choose the right answer.

_____ 1. *Read paragraph 4 again.* The author was tongue-tied because
   a. he thought his neighbor was too nosy.
   b. he was embarrassed to admit his new lifestyle.
   c. he didn't want to explain in front of his son.
   d. he thought his wife should explain the situation.

_____ 2. *Read paragraph 9 again.* Why did the author walk away from his boss's desk with wobbly knees?
   a. He was worried about his boss's reaction.
   b. He was shy about quitting his job.
   c. He was nervous about quitting his job.
   d. He didn't think he would be good at house fathering.

_____ 3. *Read paragraph 10 again.* Why does the author describe himself as "the man who got home after dark"?
   a. The author is making a sarcastic reference to the time he returns home from work.
   b. The author prefers not to use his real name in the article.
   c. Because of the author's work schedule, the son does not know his father nearly as well as he knows his mother.
   d. The author is making a social remark about the long hours he works.

_____ 4. *Read paragraph 15 again.* The author's remark "And I wonder what comes next" suggests that he
   a. is hesitant about the change in his domestic responsibilities.
   b. is eager for the challenge of new experiences.
   c. resents the lowered expectations of house fathering.
   d. doesn't feel confident about the future.

Name   Date

_____ 5. *Read paragraph 22 again.* House fathering is not for claustrophobics because claustrophobics
   a. would find staying at home every day too confining.
   b. enjoy working in small, confined areas.
   c. need to go to work every day in order to feel productive.
   d. feel the need to work with many people in a controlled setting.

_____ 6. *Read paragraph 26 again.* "And then there's the rest of us" implies that the author
   a. is longing for his old job and sense of identity.
   b. views child care as a pastime requiring few skills or expertise.
   c. now identifies with a group of people who are not qualified for any other occupation.
   d. sees himself as part of a group having no particular mission or sense of purpose.

15E CRITICAL READING: FACT OR OPINION

Decide if each statement, even if it quotes someone, contains a FACT or OPINION.

_____ 1. *From paragraph 7:* This was a radical change that seemed to carry as many drawbacks as benefits.

_____ 2. *From paragraph 9:* Some friends said they were envious.

_____ 3. *From paragraph 10:* It hurt when I couldn't quiet his crying.

_____ 4. *From paragraph 15:* With me at home, her work hours are more flexible.

_____ 5. *From paragraph 11:* Something better would emerge, something less obnoxious.

15F CRITICAL READING: THE WRITER'S CRAFT

Choose the best answer.

_____ 1. The use of short sentences and often one-sentence paragraphs is customary in newspaper reporting. The presence of that style in this selection indicates that the author
   a. is concerned with the difficulty level of the selection.
   b. is unfamiliar with a more sophisticated method of composition.
   c. is writing as he has been trained to do as a daily journalist.
   d. is writing in a style indicative of his subject matter.

Name   Date

_____ 2. The author's tone in paragraph 30 is
   a. proud and optimistic.
   b. conceited yet enthusiastic.
   c. bewildered but hopeful.
   d. exasperated but fascinated.

15G   INFORMED OPINION

1. Many couples are shedding traditional husband and wife roles. How do you think this change affects the children in a family? Use specific examples to explain your point of view.

2. Read paragraphs 17 and 18 again. How would you justify to such a person a man's decision to quit a traditional job to become a house father? Use specific examples to explain your reasons fully.

How Did You Do?   **15** Escaping the Daily Grind for Life as a House Father

SKILL (number of items)	Number Correct	Points for Each	Score
Vocabulary (15)	_____ ×	2	= _____
Central Theme and Main Ideas (4)	_____ ×	4	= _____
Major Details (9)	_____ ×	2	= _____
Inferences (6)	_____ ×	3	= _____
Critical Reading: Fact or Opinion (5)	_____ ×	2	= _____
Critical Reading: The Writer's Craft (2)	_____ ×	4	= _____

(Possible Total: 100) *Total* _____

SPEED

Reading Time: _____ Reading Rate (page 350): _____ Words Per Minute

Name   Date

Model Minority

Felicia R. Lee

(1) Zhe Zeng, an 18-year-old junior at Seward Park High School in lower Manhattan, translates the term "model minority" to mean that Asian-Americans are terrific in math and science. Mr. Zeng is terrific in math and science, but he insists that his life is no model for anyone.

(2) "My parents give a lot of pressure on me," said Mr. Zeng, who recently came to New York from Canton with his parents and older brother. He has found it hard to learn English and make friends at the large, fast-paced school. And since he is the only family member who speaks English, he is responsible for paying bills and handling the family's interactions with the English-speaking world.

(3) "They work hard for me," he said, "so I have to work hard for them."

(4) As New York's Asian population swells, and with many of the new immigrants coming from poorer, less-educated families, more and more Asian students are stumbling under the burden of earlier emigrés' success—the myth of the model minority, the docile whiz kid with one foot already in the Ivy League. Even as they face the cultural dislocations shared by all immigrants, they must struggle with the inflated expectations of teachers and parents and resentment from some non-Asian classmates.

(5) Some students, like Mr. Zeng, do seem to fit the academic stereotype. Many others are simply average students with average problems. But, in the view of educators and a recent Board of Education report, all are more or less victims of myth.

(6) "We have a significant population of Chinese kids who are not doing well," said Archer W. Dong, principal of Dr. Sun Yat Sen Junior High School near Chinatown, which is 83 percent Chinese. "But I still deal with educators who tell me how great the Asian kids are. It puts an extra burden on the kid who just wants to be a normal kid."

(7) **The Dropout Rate Rises** Perhaps the starkest evidence of the pressures these students face is the dropout rate among Asian-American students, which has risen to 15.2 percent, from 12.6 percent, in just one year, though it remains well below the 30 percent rate for the entire school system. In all, there are about 68,000 Asians in the city's school system. In all, there are about 68,000 Asians in the city's schools, a little more than 7 percent of the student population.

(8) Behind these figures, the Board of Education panel said, lies a contrary mechanism of assured success and frequent failure. While teachers expect tal-

ent in math and science, they often overlook quiet Asian-American students who are in trouble academically.

(9) The report also said that Asian students frequently face hostility from non-Asians who resent their perceived success. And though New York's Asian population is overwhelmingly Chinese, this resentment is fed by a feeling in society that the Japanese are usurping American's position as a world economic power. Some educators said that because they are often smaller and quieter, Asian students seem to be easy targets for harassment.

(10) Teresa Ying Hsu, executive director of an advocacy group called Asian-American Communications and a member of the board panel, described what she called a typical exchange at a New York City school. One student might say, "You think you're so smart," she said, then "someone would hit a kid from behind and they would turn around and everyone would laugh."

(11) Since Asian cultures dictate stoicism, she explained, students in many cases do not openly fight back against harassment or complain about academic pressures. But though they tend to keep their pain hidden, she said, it often is expressed in ailments like headaches or stomach troubles.

(12) **"Acutely Sensitive"** "We have a group of youngsters who are immigrants who are acutely sensitive to things other students take in stride, like a door slamming in their face," said John Rodgers, principal of Norman Thomas High School in Manhattan.

(13) Norman Thomas, whose student body is about 3 percent Asian, had two recent incidents in which Chinese students were attacked by non-Asian students. The attackers were suspended.

(14) But tensions escalated after a group of 30 Chinese parents demanded that the principal, John Rodgers, increase security, and rumors spread that "gangs of blacks" were attacking Chinese. Both incidents, however, were one-on-one conflicts and neither attacker was black. In some cases, Mr. Rodgers said, Chinese students say they are attacked by blacks but that they cannot identify their attackers because all blacks look alike to them.

(15) In response to the parents' concerns, Mr. Rodgers said, he increased security and brought in a speaker on cross-cultural conflict.

(16) Traditionally, Asian parents have not been that outspoken, educators say. While they often place enormous pressures on their children to do well, most Asian parents tend not to get involved with the schools.

(17) Lisa Chang, a 17-year-old senior at Seward Park—which is 48 percent Asian—recalled being one of six Asians at a predominantly black intermediate school.

(18) "Inside the school was no big deal," she said. "I was in special classes and everyone was smart. Then I remember one day being outside in the snow and this big black boy pushed me. He called me Chink.

(19) "Then, at home, my parents didn't want me to dress a certain way, to listen to heavy metal music," Ms. Chang said. When she told her dermatologist that she liked rock and roll, the doctor accused her of "acting like a Caucasian."

(20) Ms. Chang and other students say there are two routes some Asian students take: they form cliques with other Asians or they play down their culture and even their intelligence in hopes of fitting in.

(21) **Wedged Between Two Cultures** Most Asian students are acutely aware of being wedged between two cultures. They say their parents want them to compete successfully with Americans but not become too American—they frown on dating and hard-rock music. There is also peer pressure not to completely assimilate. A traitor is a "banana"—yellow on the outside, white on the inside.

(22) There is anger, too, over the perception that they are nerdy bookworms and easy targets for bullies.

(23) "A lot of kids are average; they are not what the myth says," said Doris Liang, 17, a junior at Seward Park. "In math, I'm only an average student and I have to work really hard."

(24) Ms. Liang said she sometimes envies the school's Hispanic students.

(25) **"Not Make Any Mistakes"** "The Hispanic kids, in a way they are more open," she said. "They're not afraid to bring their dates home. If you're Chinese and you bring your date home they ask a lot of questions. My parents only went to junior high school in China, so when we got here they wanted us to do well in school."

(26) Nicole Tran, a 15-year-old senior who spent the early part of her life in Oregon, said she believes her generation will be far more assertive.

(27) "We are the minority minority," said Ms. Tran. "We are moving too fast for them," she said of the dominant white culture.

(28) Dr. Jerry Chin-Li Huang, a Seward Park guidance counselor, said he believes that Asians in New York are in part experiencing the cultural transformations common to all immigrants.

(29) He notes that more of the new Asian immigrants—whose numbers in New York have swelled 35 to 50 percent in the past five years to about 400,000—are coming from smaller towns and poorer, less educated families.

(30) It was the early waves of educated, middle-class Asian immigrants whose children became the model minority, Dr. Huang said. Many of the students he sees have problems.

(31) For one thing, Dr. Huang said many Asian parents are reluctant to admit that their children need help, even in severe cases. He said he had a schizophrenic Chinese student who began constantly wearing a coat, even on the hottest summer days. The parents were of little help.

(32) "I have other children who run away from home because of the pressures," said Dr. Huang. "I had two sisters who had to go to school, then work in the factories, sewing. Their parents could not speak English so they were helping them with the bills. The girls said they barely had time to sleep."

(33) Dr. Huang said many non-Asian teachers come to him for his insights because they have few Asian co-workers. Asians are 1.4 percent of all school

counselors; 0.8 percent of all principals, and 1.4 percent of all teachers in New York City.

(34) Among its recommendations, the task force called for more Asian counselors and teachers.

(35) People like Ms. Hsu, of Asian-American Communications, are optimistic that the situation for Asian students will improve as students and educators talk openly about it.

(36) "I gave a workshop and I talked about the quotas, the Chinese exclusion act," said Ms. Hsu. "Two black girls came up to me. One said: 'You know, I always thought the Chinese kids were snooty. Now after hearing what you went through I feel you're my brothers and sisters.'"

(1491 words)

Vocabulary List

Here are some of the more difficult words in "Model Minority."

advocacy
(paragraph 10)

ad·vo·ca·cy (ad'və kə sē) *n.* [ME & OFr *advocacie* < ML *advocatia* < L *advocatus*: see fol.] the act of advocating, or speaking or writing in support (*of* something)
ad·vo·cate (ad'və kit; *for v.,* -kāt') *n.* [ME *advocat, avocat* < L *advocatus*, a counselor < *advocare*, to summon (for aid) < *ad-*, to + *vocare*, to call] 1 a person who pleads another's cause; specif., a lawyer 2 a person who speaks or writes in support of something [an *advocate* of lower taxes] —*vt.* -cat'ed, -cat'ing [< the *n.*] to speak or write in support of; be in favor of —*SYN.* SUPPORT —ad'·vo·ca'tor *n.*

assimilate
(paragraph 21)

as·sim·i·late (ə sim'ə lāt') *vt.* -lat'ed, -lat'ing [ME *assimilaten* < L *assimilatus*, pp. of *assimilare* < *ad-*, to + *similare*, make similar < *similis*, like: see SAME] 1 to change (food) into a form that can be taken up by, and made part of, the body tissues; absorb into the body 2 to absorb and incorporate into one's thinking 3 to absorb (groups of different cultures) into the main cultural body 4 to make like or alike; cause to resemble: with *to* 5 [Now Rare] to compare or liken 6 *Linguis.* to cause to undergo assimilation —*vi.* 1 to become like or alike 2 to be absorbed and incorporated 3 *Linguis.* to undergo assimilation —as·sim'i·la·ble (-ə lə bəl) *adj.*

Caucasian
(paragraph 19)

Cau·ca·sian (kô kā'zhən) *adj.* 1 of the Caucasus, its people, or their culture 2 CAUCASOID 3 designating or of the two independent families of languages spoken in the area of the Caucasus: North Caucasian includes Circassian, and South Caucasian includes Georgian Also Cau·cas'ic (-kas'ik) —*n.* 1 a native of the Caucasus 2 CAUCASOID 3 the Caucasian languages; Circassian, Georgian, etc.

Cau·ca·sus (kô'kə səs) 1 border region between SE Europe and W Asia, between the Black and Caspian seas: often called the Caucasus 2 mountain range in the Caucasus, running northwest to southeast between the Black and Caspian seas: highest peak, Mt. Elbrus: in full Caucasus Mountains

clique
(paragraph 20)

clique (klēk; *also* klik) *n.* [Fr < OFr *cliquer*, to make a noise: of echoic orig.] a small, exclusive circle of people; snobbish or narrow coterie —*SYN.* COTERIE —cliqu'ish (-ish), cliqu'ey, or cliqu'y (-ē) *adj.* —cliqu'ish·ly *adv.*

dermatologist
(paragraph 19)

der·ma·tol·o·gy (dur'mə täl'ə jē) *n.* [DERMATO- + -LOGY] the branch of medicine dealing with the skin and its diseases —der'ma·to·log'ic (-tə läj'ik) or der'ma·to·log'i·cal (-läj'i kəl) *adj.* —der·ma·tol'o·gist *n.*

docile
(paragraph 4)

doc·ile (däs'əl; *Cdn & Brit, usually* dō'sīl') **adj.** [Fr < L *docilis,* easily taught < *docere,* to teach: see DECENT] **1** [Now Rare] easy to teach; teachable **2** easy to manage or discipline; submissive —*SYN.* OBEDIENT —**doc'ilely adv. —do·cil·ity** (dō sil'ə tē; *often* dä-) *n.*

emigré
(paragraph 4)

em·i·grant (em'i grənt) **adj.** [L *emigrans,* prp. of *emigrare*] **1** emigrating **2** of emigrants or emigration —*n.* a person who emigrates
em·i·grate (em'i grāt') **vt.** -**grat'ed, -grat'ing** [< L *emigratus,* pp. of *emigrare,* to move away < *e-,* out + *migrare,* to move, MIGRATE] to leave one country or region to settle in another: opposed to IMMIGRATE —*SYN.* MIGRATE
é·mi·gré or **e·mi·gré** (em'i grā', em'i grā') *n.* [Fr < pp. of *émigrer* < L *emigrare:* see EMIGRATE] **1** an emigrant **2** a person forced to flee his country for political reasons, as a Royalist during the French Revolution —*SYN.* ALIEN

escalated
(paragraph 14)

☆**es·ca·late** (es'kə lāt') **vi.** -**lat'ed, -lat'ing** [back-form. < fol.] **1** to rise on or as on an escalator **2** to expand step by step, as from a limited or local conflict into a general, esp. nuclear, war **3** to grow or increase rapidly, often to the point of becoming unmanageable, as prices or wages —*vt.* to cause to escalate —**es'ca·la'tion** *n.*

Hispanic
(paragraph 24)

His·pan·ic (hi span'ik) **adj.** [L *Hispanicus*] **1** Spanish or Spanish-and-Portuguese **2** of or relating to Hispanics —*n.* a usually Spanish-speaking person of Latin American origin who lives in the U.S. —**His·pan'i·cism** (-i siz'əm) *n.* —**His·pan'i·cist** *n.*

nerdy
(paragraph 22)

☆**nerd** (nurd) *n.* [? rhyming slang for TURD] [Slang] a person regarded as dull, unsophisticated, ineffective, etc. —**nerd'y** (-ē) **adj.**

peer
(paragraph 21)

peer¹ (pir) *n.* [ME *peir* < OFr *per* < L *par,* an equal: see PAR] **1** a person or thing of the same rank, value, quality, ability, etc.; equal; specif., an equal before the law **2** a noble; esp., a British duke, marquess, earl, viscount, or baron —*vt.* [Archaic] to match or equal —**peer of the realm** any of the British peers entitled to a seat in the House of Lords

schizophrenic
(paragraph 31)

schizo·phre·nia (skit'se frē'nē ə, skiz'ə-; *also,* -frā'-; *occas.,* -fren'ē ə) *n.* [ModL < SCHIZO- + Gr *phrēn,* the mind + -IA] a major mental disorder of unknown cause typically characterized by a separation between the thought processes and the emotions, a distortion of reality accompanied by delusions and hallucinations, a fragmentation of the personality, motor disturbances, bizarre behavior, etc., often with no loss of basic intellectual functions: this term has largely replaced *dementia praecox,* since it does not always result in deterioration (*dementia*) or always develop in adolescence or before maturity (*praecox*)
schizo·phren·ic (-fren'ik, -frē'nik; *occas.,* -frā'nik) **adj.** of or having schizophrenia —*n.* a person having schizophrenia: also **schiz'o·phrene'** (-frēn')

stoicism
(paragraph 11)

Sto·ic (stō'ik) *n.* [ME *Stoycis* (pl.) < L *stoicus* < Gr *stōikos* < *stoa,* porch, colonnade (see STOA): because Zeno taught under a colonnade at Athens] **1** a member of a Greek school of philosophy founded by Zeno about 308 B.C., holding that all things, properties, relations, etc. are governed by unvarying natural laws, and that the wise man should follow virtue alone, obtained through reason, remaining indifferent to the external world and to passion or emotion **2** [s-] a stoical person —**adj. 1** of the Stoics or their philosophy **2** [s-] STOICAL —*SYN.* IMPASSIVE
sto·i·cal (stō'i kəl) **adj.** [ME: see prec. & -AL] **1** showing austere indifference to joy, grief, pleasure, or pain; calm and unflinching under suffering, bad fortune, etc. **2** [S-] STOIC —**sto'i·cally adv.**

Sto·i·cism (stō'i siz'əm) *n.* **1** the philosophical system of the Stoics **2** [s-] indifference to pleasure or pain; stoical behavior; impassivity —*SYN.* PATIENCE

usurping
(paragraph 9)

u·surp (yōō zurp', -surp') **vt.** [ME *usurpen* < MFr *usurper* < L *usurpare* < *usus,* a USE + *rapere,* to seize: see RAPE¹] to take or assume (power, a position, property, rights, etc.) and hold in possession by force or without right —*vi.* to practice or commit usurpation (*on* or *upon*) —**u·surp'er** *n.* —**u·surp'ingly adv.**

16A VOCABULARY

Using the vocabulary words listed on pages 182–183, fill in the blanks.

1. His _____ in the face of so much pain was surprising.

2. Teenagers often give in to _____ pressure in deciding right from wrong.

3. _____ in this country often experience difficulties as

   they try to _____ into a new culture.

4. I would like to _____ for lower taxes on your behalf.

5. A severe skin rash should be treated only by a licensed

   _____ .

6. _____ is a slang expression for an unsophisticated person.

7. The younger prince was arrested for _____ power from his father, the king.

8. A large _____ population lives in the southwestern United States.

9. The puppy from the dog pound was a very _____ animal even though he had been mistreated.

10. A _____ usually has skin color varying from very light to brown.

11. The feud between the two nations finally _____ into all-out war.

12. Jane's bizarre behavior and hallucinations led the doctor to diagnose

    her as _____ .

13. The students from an exclusive part of town formed a

    _____ that excluded the majority of their classmates.

Name   Date

16B CENTRAL THEME AND MAIN IDEAS
Follow the directions for each item below.

_____ 1. The central theme of "Model Minority" might be stated as follows:
   a. The ability of Asian-American students in math and science causes resentment among other students.
   b. Recent Asian immigrants are not as skilled in math and science as their predecessors were.
   c. A harmful myth exists regarding the educational ability of Asian-American students.
   d. Asian-American students are harassed by youthful gang members in New York City because of their science and math ability.

   2. In your own words, what is the main idea of paragraph 7?

   _____

   _____

   _____

_____ 3. What is the main idea of paragraph 21?
   a. Asian children are discontented with their parents' values and teachings.
   b. Asian-American parents do not want their children to date non-Asians.
   c. Asian-American parents feel that rock music is ruining the climate of the traditional household and their children's attitudes.
   d. Asian-American students recognize the problem of holding steadfast to tradition while competing in the American education system.

16C MAJOR DETAILS
Decide whether each detail is true (T), false (F), or not discussed (ND).

_____ 1. Asian immigrants excel in math and science.

_____ 2. Asian-American students who drop out of school are not able to obtain jobs that pay more than minimum wage.

_____ 3. The dropout rate among Asian-American students is rising.

_____ 4. Asian-American students seldom face open hostility from their American counterparts.

185

| Name | Date |

_____ 5. Asian-American students sometimes go to school full-time while working full-time.

_____ 6. Asian-American parents often do not recognize the problems their children face in trying to survive in two cultures.

16D INFERENCES

Decide whether each statement below can be inferred (YES) or cannot be inferred (NO) from the reading selection.

_____ 1. The U.S. education system is sensitive to the plight of immigrant children in American schools.

_____ 2. Asian-American students would benefit from an increase of Asian counselors, teachers, and principals in their schools.

_____ 3. Asian-American students spend more time with other students of their own racial background than they do with non-Asian students.

_____ 4. In this era of multicultural awareness, Asian-American students are being accepted into mainstream American education by their peers.

_____ 5. Asian-American students are the objects of envy and discrimination more frequently than are other immigrant groups to the United States.

_____ 6. Asian-American students often carry a greater family burden than do their American counterparts.

_____ 7. Asian-American students are not comfortable with the myth of their academic success but fail to verbalize their discomfort.

_____ 8. Chinese-American students are frequently preyed upon by black students.

_____ 9. Recent Asian immigrants are as mathematically inclined as previous immigrants but do not study as diligently.

16E CRITICAL READING: FACT OR OPINION

Decide whether each statement, even if it quotes someone, contains a FACT or OPINION.

_____ 1. *From paragraph 1:* Zhe Zeng insists that his life is no model.

_____ 2. *From paragraph 3:* "They work hard for me," he said, "so I have to work hard for them."

Name   Date

_____ 3. *From paragraph 5:* Some students do not fit the academic stereotype.

_____ 4. *From paragraph 6:* Dr. Sun Yat Sen Junior High School is 83 percent Chinese.

_____ 5. *From paragraph 9:* . . . Asian students are easy targets for harassment.

_____ 6. *From paragraph 15:* Mr. Rodgers increased security and brought in a speaker on cross-cultural conflict.

_____ 7. *From paragraph 18:* "He called me Chink."

_____ 8. *From paragraph 24:* Ms. Liang said she sometimes envies the school's Hispanic students.

_____ 9. *From paragraph 27:* "We are moving too fast for them."

_____ 10. *From paragraph 25:* "They're not afraid to bring their dates home."

_____ 11. *From paragraph 35:* ". . . the situation for Asian students will improve as students and educators talk."

16F   CRITICAL READING: THE WRITER'S CRAFT
Choose the best answer.

_____ 1. To capture the reader's interest, the author starts by
   a. comparing the ability of Asian students with that of American students.
   b. quoting an expert in the field of Asian-American relations.
   c. focusing on the dilemma of a single Asian student.
   d. sympathizing with the plight of Asian immigrants.

_____ 2. The author attempts to balance facts and statistics with students' comments and experts' remarks. Her purpose in doing this is to
   a. sway the reader with a somewhat emotional appeal.
   b. demonstrate her ability to explain adequately two sides of a dispute.
   c. present both the analytical and the subjective aspects of the issue.
   d. prevent the reader from basing an opinion solely on student sentiment.

187

_____ 3. The author quotes very few non-Asians in "Model Minority." She does this in order to
   a. prevent the reader from being misled by the non-Asian population.
   b. concentrate on the problem as interpreted by the members of the Asian community.
   c. illustrate that only Asian-American students are experiencing this problem.
   d. explain a problem that non-immigrant students are incapable of comprehending.

_____ 4. *Read paragraph 36 again.* The essay ends on a note of
   a. hope.
   b. happiness.
   c. desperation.
   d. panic.

16G   INFORMED OPINION

1. Do you think that immigrant children who are competing successfully in the American education system should be forced by their parents to adhere to the customs and traditions of the "old country"? Why or why not?

2. In your opinion, is it easier for immigrant children or adults to adjust to life in the United States? Using specific examples, explain your answer.

How Did You Do?   16 Model Minority

SKILL (number of items)	Number Correct		Points for Each	Score
Vocabulary* (14)	_____	×	2	= _____
Central Theme and Main Ideas (3)	_____	×	4	= _____
Major Details (6)	_____	×	2	= _____
Inferences (9)	_____	×	2	= _____
Critical Reading: Fact or Opinion (11)	_____	×	2	= _____
Critical Reading: The Writer's Craft (4)	_____	×	2	= _____

(Possible Total: 100) *Total* _____

SPEED

Reading Time: _____ Reading Rate (page 350): _____ Words Per Minute

*Question 3 in this exercise calls for two separate answers. In computing your score, count each separate answer toward your total score.

Name   Date

Selection 17

A New Dawn

Sam Moses

(1) In the annals of great escapes, the flight by 17-year-old Lester Moreno Perez from Cuba to the U.S. surely must rank as one of the most imaginative. At 8:30 on the night of Thursday, March 1, Lester crept along the beach at Varadero, a resort town on the north coast of Cuba, and launched his sailboard into the shark-haunted waters of the Straits of Florida. Guided first by the stars and then by the hazy glow from concentrations of electric lights in towns beyond the horizon, Lester sailed with 20-knot winds, heading for the Florida Keys, 90 miles away.

(2) Two hours past daybreak on Friday, Lester was sighted by the Korean crew of the *Tina D,* a Bahamian-registered freighter. The boom on his craft was broken, and he was just barely making headway, 30 miles south of Key West. The astonished crew pulled Lester aboard, fed him spicy chicken with white rice, and then radioed the U.S. Coast Guard, which sent the patrol boat *Fitkinak* to take him into custody. After five days in the Krome Detention Center in Miami while paper-work was being processed, he was issued a visa by U.S. immigration officials and released into the welcoming arms of his relatives.

(3) Except for his rich imagination and broad streak of courage, Lester could be any 17-year-old who decides to leave home. He was raised in the shoreside town of Varadero, the second-oldest of five chil-dren in his family. "As soon as I started thinking a little bit—when I was seven or eight years old—I wanted to come to America," he says. Independent thinking ran in the family; his grandfather, Urbino, had been imprisoned for attending a counterrevolutionary meeting early in Fidel Castro's regime and spent nearly five years in jail. Furthermore, Lester's sister Leslie, who had been on the national swim team and had traveled to several foreign countries, had told intriguing tales of life outside Cuba. Lester also did not like the idea of serving three years in the Cuban army and then facing the possibility of having his career chosen for him by the Communist Party. There was also trouble at home; he and his stepfather, Roberto, were at odds, mostly over poli-tics. So Lester decided he wanted to go to America, not Angola.

(4) When he was 10 years old, Lester taught himself to windsurf by hanging around the European and Canadian tourists who rented boards on the beach at Varadero. "If you made friends with them, they would sometimes let you use their equipment," he says. As he grew

older and got better at the sport, he found he liked the isolation and freedom of the sea. "Sometimes I would sail for eight hours without stopping, and go very far out," he says. His windsurfing to freedom seemed destined.

(5) Recently, Lester sat in a big easy-chair in the Hialeah, Fla., apartment of Ana and Isidro Perez, the great-aunt and great-uncle who took him in. Lester is so skinny—5'6", 130 pounds—that it seems there is room for two or three more of him in the chair. On his head he wears Walkman earphones, which he politely removes when a visitor enters the room. He has been in America only a few weeks, but he has already been interviewed several times and has been chauffeured all over Miami in a limo on a radio station-sponsored shopping spree. The tops of his feet are still covered with scabs, the result of the hours he spent in the sailboard's footstraps; but his hands show no blisters, only hard, white calluses.

(6) As he waits for a translator to arrive, Lester rocks back and forth in the chair like a hyperactive child. He clicks the television on with the remote control, passes a Spanish-language station and stops at a morning show on which a man is explaining, in English, how to prevent snoring by placing a Ping-Pong ball between your shoulder blades, a move that forces one to sleep face-down. When a visitor demonstrates this to Lester through gestures and snores, the young man rolls his dark eyes, smiles and says in perfect English, "People are all crazy here."

(7) A few minutes later, the translator, who owns a windsurfing shop in Miami, arrives, and Lester begins to tell his story through him.

(8) "I had only been thinking of making the trip on a sailboard for about a month," he says. "Before then, I'd been thinking of leaving the country by marrying a Canadian girl—every couple of months a few would come that were pretty nice-looking. But I decided to sail because I was training hard and was confident I would be able to make the trip easily. I had windsurfed in bad weather, and even surfed during Hurricane Gilbert, so I was already out in really rough conditions and wasn't worried about it.

(9) "Right before I left, I was watching the wind patterns. A cold front had passed by and it was pretty strong, so I waited until it subsided a little. Usually after a cold front passes, the wind shifts to the east, and it's just a straight reach to the U.S., so I waited for that. Then I told two of my friends, who said they would help me. I wasn't hungry, but I ate a lot—three or four fried eggs, some rice and half a liter of milk—so I would be strong for the journey." His friends also persuaded him to take along some water, a can of condensed milk and a knife.

(10) At 7:00 on the evening of March 1, Lester, who had said nothing to his family, slipped out of his house and went down to the

Varadero beach, where he worked at a windsurfing rental booth by day, while attending high school at night. Earlier that day, he had carefully rigged the best mast and strongest boom he could find with a big 5.0-square-meter sail. Then he had lashed the sail rig in the sand with the rental boards. Under cover of darkness, he unlocked the shed where the privately owned boards were kept and removed his sleek and durable Alpha model. It had been a gift to him from a man who sympathized with his plight—a generous East German whom Lester called Rambo for the camouflage hat he always wore. Lester fastened the sail rig to the board and carried it to the water. He waded into the ocean until he was knee-deep, glanced over his shoulder to make sure he hadn't been seen, and stepped onto the board. His ride on the wind to freedom had begun.

(11) "I wasn't nervous," he says. "I had to be very clear minded once I decided to go; otherwise they would catch me and I would be in a lot of trouble. It would have meant three or four years in prison if I had been caught. No lie about what I was doing was possible."

(12) About one and a half blocks away from the beach was a tower usually manned by guards with infrared binoculars. Lester, who was sailing without lights, also had to keep an eye out for freighters and pleasure boats that would be cruising in the busy Straits of Florida.

(13) "At first I wasn't able to get my feet in the footstraps," he says, "because there wasn't enough wind for my sail. But as I got farther out and was able to get fully powered up, I began feeling more confident. The swells were very steep, maybe four or five meters, and I was going so fast I had no choice but to jump them."

(14) As he recalls the moment, Lester rises from his chair, plants his bare feet on the tile floor and extends his thin arms, grasping an imaginary boom. He begins in English, "Wind coming, coming, coming . . . out, out, out . . . is very strong." He's hanging in his invisible harness now, arms stretched wide, eyes lit up, flying over the waves. "Whoosh!" he cries. "Is good!"

(15) For 10 hours he rode the wind, never once fearing failure, or drowning. He thought of his family and how worried they would be when they discovered he was missing. But he wasn't alone out there. "Ever since I left, I could see the sharks coming out and in, coming up on the board. I was hoping and thinking they were dolphins, but when the sun came up, I would see there was no way they were dolphins.

(16) Around daybreak, the aluminum boom broke, separating the connection to the mast like pieces of a wishbone. He tried fixing the boom with his knife but couldn't, so he sailed on, clutching the pieces of the broken wishbone. This made control of the board extremely difficult, and he couldn't rest in the harness he had rigged. "My arms and hands were getting really tired, but by then I could already see the big

kites of the fishermen, so I wasn't really worried. When I saw the freighter, I tried to point [into the wind] as much as I could and sail toward it."

(17) A similar crossing was made in January 1984, by Arnaud de Rosnay, a Frenchman who boardsailed from Key West to Cuba as a personal challenge and a publicity stunt. De Rosnay, one of the best board-sailors in the world, had sailed in daylight with a chase boat. His trip included two stops for repairs and two stops to rest, and he completed the crossing in about seven hours. (In November of the same year, de Rosnay vanished while trying to cross the Straits of Formosa.) But only a month before Lester's odyssey, another young Cuban had perished attempting to reach the Keys in a raft.

(18) Not surprisingly, Hollywood has come knocking at Lester's door. "The story is a natural," says Paul Madden, the president of Madden Movies. "It's *Rocky* and *The Old Man and the Sea* in one. If this picture is done right, by the end of it the audience will be standing up in the theater and cheering." Madden might not be one of those doing the cheering; he was outbid for the rights to Lester's story by Ron Howard's Imagine Films.

(19) Lester has handled the movie offers—assumed to have reached six figures—and the media blitz with uncommon courtesy and self-assurance. A new acquaintance has even invited him to spend the summer at Hood River, Ore., where he will be able to jump the formidable swells of the Columbia River. This sounds good to Lester. But right now, one of his teenage friends has invited him to go sailing off Miami Beach. That sounds like the most fun of all.

(1792 words)

Here are some of the more difficult words in "A New Dawn."

Angola
(paragraph 3)

An·go·la (aŋ gō′lə, an-) country on the SW coast of Africa: formerly a Portuguese territory, it became independent (1975): 481,351 sq. mi. (1,246,700 sq. km); pop. 8,164,000; cap. Luanda —**An·go′lan** *adj.*, *n.*

annals
(paragraph 1)

an·nals (an′əlz) *n.pl.* ⟦L *annalis*, pl. *annales* < *annus*, year: see ANNUAL⟧ **1** a written account of events year by year in chronological order **2** historical records or chronicles; history **3** any journal containing reports of discoveries in some field, meetings of a society, etc.

blitz
(paragraph 19)

blitz (blits) *n.* ⟦< fol.⟧ **1** a sudden, destructive attack, as by aircraft or tanks **2** *a*) any sudden, overwhelming attack *b*) a concentrated effort, intensive campaign, etc. ☆**3** *Football* a sudden charge by a defensive backfield player through a gap in the line in an effort to tackle the opposing quarterback —*vt.* **1** to subject to a blitz; overwhelm and destroy ☆**2** *Football* to charge (the quarterback) in a blitz —☆*vi.* *Football* to make a blitz

calluses
(paragraph 5)

cal·lus (kal′əs) *n.*, *pl.* **-lus·es** ⟦L, var. of *callum*, hard skin⟧ **1** a hardened, thickened place on the skin **2** the hard substance that forms at the break in a fractured bone and serves to reunite the parts **3** a disorganized mass of cells that develops over cuts or wounds on plants, as at the ends of stem or leaf cuttings —*vi.*, *vt.* to develop or cause to develop a callus

camouflage
(paragraph 10)

cam·ou·flage (kam′ə fläzh′, -fläj′) *n.* ⟦Fr < *camoufler*, to disguise; prob. altered (infl. by *camouflet*, puff of smoke) < It *camuffare*, to disguise⟧ **1** the disguising of troops, ships, guns, etc. to conceal them from the enemy, as by the use of paint, nets, or leaves in patterns merging with the background **2** a disguise or concealment of this kind **3** any device or action used to conceal or mislead; deception —*vt.*, *vi.* **-flaged′**, **-flag′ing** to disguise (a thing or person) in order to conceal —**cam′ou·flag′er** *n.*

chauffeured
(paragraph 5)

chauf·feur (shō′fər, shō fur′) *n.* ⟦Fr, lit., stoker (operator of a steam-driven car) < *chauffer*, to heat: see CHAFE⟧ a person hired to drive a private automobile for someone else —*vt.*, *vi.* to act as chauffeur to (someone)

counterrevolutionary
(paragraph 3)

coun·ter·rev·o·lu·tion (-rev′ə lōō′shən) *n.* **1** a political movement or revolution against a government or social system set up by a previous revolution **2** a movement to combat revolutionary tendencies —**coun′ter·rev′o·lu′tion·ar·y**, *pl.* **-aries**, *n.*, *adj.* —**coun′ter·rev′o·lu′tion·ist** *n.*

immigration
(paragraph 2)

im·mi·grate (im′ə grāt′) *vi.* **-grat′ed**, **-grat′ing** ⟦< L *immigratus*, pp. of *immigrare*, to go or remove into: see IN-¹ & MIGRATE⟧ to come into a new country, region, or environment, esp. in order to settle there: opposed to EMIGRATE —*vt.* to bring in as an immigrant —*SYN.* MIGRATE
im·mi·gra·tion (im′ə grā′shən) *n.* **1** an act or instance of immigrating **2** the number of immigrants entering a country or region during a specified period

Vocabulary List

intriguing
(paragraph 3)

in·trigue (in trēg'; *for n., also* in'trēg) *vi.* -trigued', -trigu'ing [Fr *intriguer* < It *intrigare* < L *intricare:* see INTRICATE] 1 to carry on a secret love affair 2 to plot or scheme secretly or underhandedly — *vt.* 1 to bring on or get by secret or underhanded plotting 2 to excite the interest or curiosity of; fascinate [the puzzle *intrigued* her] 3 [Archaic] to trick or perplex 4 [Obs.] to entangle —*n.* 1 an intriguing; secret or underhanded plotting 2 a secret or underhanded plot or scheme; machination 3 a secret love affair —*SYN.* PLOT —in·trigu'er *n.*

odyssey
(paragraph 17)

Odys·sey (äd'i sē) [L *Odyssea* < Gr *Odysseia*] an ancient Greek epic poem, ascribed to Homer, about the wanderings of Odysseus during the ten years after the fall of Troy —*n., pl.* -seys [o-] any extended wandering or journey —Od'ys·se'an *adj.*

straits
(paragraph 1)

strait (strāt) *adj.* [ME *streit* < OFr *estreit* < L *strictus:* see STRICT] 1 [Archaic] restricted or constricted; narrow; tight; confined 2 [Archaic] strict; rigid; exacting 3 [Now Rare] straitened; difficult; distressing —*n.* 1 [Rare] a narrow passage 2 [*often pl.*] a narrow waterway connecting two large bodies of water 3 [*usually pl.*] difficulty; distress 4 [Rare] an isthmus —*SYN.* EMERGENCY

17A   VOCABULARY

Choose the best answer.

_____ 1. A **chauffeured** car is driven
   a. on Sunday mornings.
   b. by the owner of the car.
   c. by a hired individual.
   d. to work and home daily.

_____ 2. A **counterrevolutionary** movement will
   a. cause an outbreak of global warfare.
   b. occur in the regions that make up the former Yugoslavia.
   c. be unsuccessful in the twentieth century.
   d. overthrow the government of a previous revolution.

_____ 3. A **callus** can best be described as
   a. someone emotionally hardened.
   b. a patch of hard, thick skin.
   c. a rock between two hard places.
   d. a tender red spot on the elbow.

_____ 4. An **odyssey** is a
   a. wandering journey.
   b. visit to one's parents.
   c. fictional voyage.
   d. short cruise.

Name   Date

_____ 5. **Angola** is a country
   a. east of South Africa
   b. that is larger than Canada.
   c. known for its frigid temperatures.
   d. on the southwest coast of Africa.

_____ 6. **Immigration** laws regulate
   a. birds flying south each November.
   b. foreigners entering the United States.
   c. produce leaving the United States.
   d. citizens leaving the United States.

_____ 7. The town's **annals** revealed its unique
   a. geography.
   b. annual list of politicians.
   c. stories of famous mayors.
   d. history.

_____ 8. A **strait** joins
   a. two large bodies of water.
   b. a city with its suburbs.
   c. two large bodies of land.
   d. a town with its closest body of water.

_____ 9. An **intriguing** secret
   a. is against the law.
   b. is seldom revealed.
   c. pokes fun at politicians.
   d. excites or fascinates.

_____ 10. To **camouflage** is to
   a. assign to a military unit.
   b. hide illegal weapons.
   c. disguise any device or action.
   d. wear army-issue clothes.

_____ 11. A **blitz** is
   a. a Sunday afternoon journey.
   b. a creamy pastry.
   c. a sudden, overpowering attack.
   d. repeatedly used during war games.

Name   Date

17B CENTRAL THEME AND MAIN IDEAS
Follow the directions for each item below.

1. In your own words, give the central theme of "A New Dawn."

   _____

   _____

   _____

_____ 2. Choose the best answer. What is the main idea of paragraph 2?
   a. Lester was rescued and fed spicy food because he was starving.
   b. The Coast Guard detained Lester in Miami for five days.
   c. After five days in the Krome Detention Center, Lester was given naturalization papers.
   d. Lester was rescued, processed in Miami, and given a temporary visa.

_____ 3. Choose the best answer. What is the main idea of paragraph 3?
   a. Lester's grandfather, Urbino, encouraged Lester to leave home so that Lester wouldn't be imprisoned.
   b. Leslie, Lester's sister, told Lester about her wonderful life in the United States.
   c. Lester is no different from many 17-year-olds except that he had the courage and imagination to leave home for a new country.
   d. Lester was afraid that after he spent three years in the Cuban army, the Communist party would choose his career for him.

_____ 4. Choose the best answer. What is the main idea of paragraphs 18–19?
   a. Madden Movies wants to remake *Rocky* using a Cuban youth in the lead.
   b. Hollywood is interested in stories of bravery and survival.
   c. Lester would rather spend time with his new friends than make his movie.
   d. Audiences will cheer at the end of Lester's movie.

Name   Date

17C   MAJOR DETAILS

Decide whether each detail is true (T), false (F), or not discussed (ND).

_____ 1. Lester used a compass to guide him from his Cuban homeland to the Florida shore.

_____ 2. The United States immigration's decision to allow Lester to remain was based on whether his relatives would take him in.

_____ 3. The courage Lester inherited from his grandfather enabled him to leave Cuba.

_____ 4. The stories Leslie told of living in America made Lester decide to go there instead of to Angola.

_____ 5. The European and Canadian tourists taught Lester to windsurf.

_____ 6. Lester knew his family would be worried about him.

_____ 7. De Rosnay, the famous French boardsailor, made his trip in the shortest amount of time ever recorded.

_____ 8. Sharks closely accompanied Lester throughout the night.

_____ 9. The boom on the board's sailing rig broke as one swell after another washed over Lester.

17D   INFERENCES

Choose the best answer.

_____ 1. *Read the title again.* It describes Lester's
   a. seeing the sun rise over Miami soon after his rescue.
   b. seeing the United States in a new light.
   c. awakening the first day back on dry land.
   d. new beginning in a new country.

_____ 2. *Read paragraph 4 again.* Lester found he liked the remoteness and isolation of windsurfing when
   a. tourists loaned him equipment but largely ignored him otherwise.
   b. he thought of spending hours alone sailing from Cuba to the United States.
   c. he spent hours alone on the open sea and liked it.
   d. his younger brothers and sisters no longer needed his help.

Name   Date

_____ 3. *Read paragraph 8 again.* Lester decided not to marry a Canadian tourist because
  a. he knew he was in good enough condition to escape Cuba by sailing to the U.S.
  b. he couldn't find a Canadian girl who would agree to marry him.
  c. if a hurricane killed him while he was windsurfing, she would be a widow.
  d. his parents did not approve of marrying foreigners.

_____ 4. *Read paragraph 17 again.* Arnaud de Rosnay's trip from Key West to Cuba was not as daring as Lester's because
  a. de Rosnay was quite a bit older than Lester.
  b. de Rosnay was making the trip only as a publicity stunt.
  c. it was made during the day with friends in a chase boat.
  d. failure to reach his destination would not have resulted in a prison sentence for de Rosnay.

17E CRITICAL READING: FACT OR OPINION

Decide whether each statement, even if it quotes someone, contains a FACT or OPINION.

_____ 1. *From paragraph 3:* Except for his rich imagination and broad streak of courage, Lester could be any 17-year-old who decides to leave home.

_____ 2. *From paragraph 9:* His friends also persuaded him to take along some water, a can of condensed milk and a knife.

_____ 3. *From paragraph 16:* Around daybreak, the aluminum boom broke, separating the connection to the mast like pieces of a wishbone.

_____ 4. *From paragraph 18:* Not surprisingly, Hollywood has come knocking on Lester's door.

_____ 5. *From paragraph 19:* That sounds like the most fun of all.

Name   Date

17F CRITICAL READING: THE WRITER'S CRAFT

Choose the best answer.

_____ 1. To get the reader's interest, the author begins by
   a. briefly summarizing Lester's odyssey.
   b. defining windsurfing for the novice.
   c. building sympathy for Lester's family life.
   d. describing Lester's famous ancestors.

_____ 2. *Read paragraph 5 again.* The last sentence describes the results of Lester's trip in order to
   a. illustrate the dangers of windsurfing.
   b. highlight Lester's carelessness during his voyage.
   c. dramatize the physical aspects of Lester's ordeal.
   d. demonstrate inappropriate windsurfing techniques.

_____ 3. *Read paragraphs 8 and 9 again.* The author uses dialogue here
   a. to show he remembers exact details.
   b. so that the reader will be impressed with Lester's planning.
   c. because dialogue is an impressive technique.
   d. to highlight the most important part of the conversation.

17G INFORMED OPINION

1. From your own knowledge and experience, under what circumstance(s) would it be valid for a person to abandon family and country forever? Be specific in explaining your point of view.

2. In your own words, what effects do you think sudden fame might have on the person it happens to? Use specific examples to explain your answer.

199

Name   Date

How Did You Do?   **17** A New Dawn

SKILL (number of items)	Number Correct		Points for Each		Score
Vocabulary (11)	_____	×	3	=	_____
Central Theme and Main Ideas (4)	_____	×	4	=	_____
Major Details (9)	_____	×	3	=	_____
Inferences (4)	_____	×	2	=	_____
Critical Reading: Fact or Opinion (5)	_____	×	2	=	_____
Critical Reading: The Writer's Craft (3)	_____	×	2	=	_____
	(Possible Total: 100) *Total*				_____

SPEED

Reading Time: _____ Reading Rate (page 350): _____ Words Per Minute

Name   Date

5. Imagine your feelings upon discovering that a member of your family has mysteriously disappeared. Describe how you would feel. What, if anything, would you try to do about it?

IDEAS FOR ESSAYS

1. People have long been interested in having one language that could be spoken throughout the world. Some people feel that such a language would promote understanding and better feeling among nations and it would increase cultural and economic ties among various countries. The English language is used by more than 450 million people in almost every part of the world. Do you think English should be made the universal language? State your opinion and then give specific advantages or disadvantages to support your point of view.

2. An organization named U.S. English wants to amend the constitution so that it names English the official language of the United States. Write a research report about the effort of this special interest group to make English the only official language. How would an official language affect employment? National unity? Give specific reasons for this movement.

3. Twin studies are providing evidence that our natures are at least partially determined by our genes. Still, many scientists believe that environment shapes our natures. What do you believe: is it "nature or nurture"? Using specific examples, discuss your point of view fully.

4. What is the current suicide rate in America among different age groups and within different job categories? Write a research report about suicide statistics and about what psychologists think are the major reasons for suicide today.

5. In order to meet their financial obligations, in many families both the husband and the wife often work outside the home and leave their child(ren) in day care centers. What effects do you think this has on the children—emotionally, educationally, and socially? Use specific examples to support your point of view.

6. Interview a classmate from another country. Ask the student about the country's climate, geography, political situation, food, transportation, housing conditions, and pace of life. Then write the findings of your interview.

7. The United States is really a country of immigrants. Europeans began to arrive in the United States in the seventeenth century. Immigrants are still coming to the United States. Why do many people resent the recent influx of immigrants to the United States? Be specific with your reasons.

What are *your* ideas on the subjects that you have read about in Part 3 of this book? Now is *your* chance to express your ideas in writing.

Below are some topics to write about. You are not expected to write on all of them, of course. Just select what appeals to you. Or feel free to make up your own topics. Most important, try to find a subject that moves you to want to express yourself in writing.

All of the topics below relate in some way to the reading selections in Part 3 of this book. Some of the topics have been touched on already in the opening section of Part 3, "Thinking: Getting Started," page 139, or in the Informed Opinion questions that followed each of the reading selections in Part 3. Others of these topics are introduced here for the first time.

The topics below give you a choice among various kinds of writing. You can write a **narrative** that will tell your reader an interesting story. You can write a **description** that will give your reader a vivid picture of the image you have in mind. You can write a **report** that will give your reader important information about a subject, process, or event. You can write an **argument** to try to persuade your reader to agree with you. Differences among these kinds of writing are not always clear-cut, and so you can feel free to use any **combination** that works for you. As you write, try to use the new vocabulary words you have been studying in Part 3.

IDEAS FOR PAR

1. Have you ever been in a situation, such as in a restaurant or market-place, where you needed to communicate with someone who spoke another language that you didn't speak? If so, give the background for the situation and the way you solved the problem.

2. What would be the effect on society if everyone started to carry guns or other lethal weapons? Using specific examples, explain your point of view fully.

3. Do you believe that rearing a child can be as fulfilling an occupation as a traditional career? Explain your reasons fully.

4. If you had a choice of having a college or job roommate of your nation-ality or of another nationality, which would you choose? Using specific examples of the advantages or disadvantages of either, explain your choice.

PART

4

Thinking:
Getting Started

As you read the selections in Part 4, keep in mind that reading takes place at three levels: *on the line, between the lines, and beyond the lines.* The reading selections in Part 4 particularly challenge you to move with more confidence into reading *between the lines and beyond the lines.* As you attend to the stated material (what is *on the line*) also be alert for the logical conclusions that can be drawn from the material (what is *between the lines*). What is not stated is often as important as what is stated.

When you read *between the lines and beyond the lines,* you experience most dramatically the interplay between what your eyes see and your mind thinks about. First, use the visuals and accompanying questions on the next three pages to access your prior knowledge. Next, survey and ask questions. Then as you read, be aware that the material *between the lines and beyond the lines* will round out your understanding of a reading selection. Work particularly closely with the exercises on inferences, critical reading, and informed opinion that follow each reading selection.

Photo by Richard Stacks, San Francisco.

Why is it that sometimes animals get along with each other, and sometimes they fight to the death?
(See "Terror at Tinker Creek.")

"He likes to say we're a team, but really he's the coach and *I'm* the team."

Drawing by Weber; © 1977 The New Yorker Magazine, Inc.

Why do many married women today keep their unmarried name or hyphenate their unmarried name with their husband's last name?
(See "Should a Wife Keep Her Name?")

David Berg. © 1987 by E. C. Publications, Inc.

What reasons, other than worry about damage to the car, do parents have for not wanting their older teenage children to drive? (See "License to Drive.")

More on next page . . .

Under what circumstances,
if any, should the babies of
single mothers be separated
from those mothers?
(See "The Babies of Bedford.")

© Paul Fusco/Magnum Photos.

Copyright by © Dale Stephanos.

In addition to nuclear pollution, what other kinds of pollution can harm people?
(See "Noise: It Can Kill You.")

Terror at Tinker Creek

Annie Dillard

(1) A couple of summers ago I was walking along the edge of the island to see what I could see in the water, and mainly to scare frogs. Frogs have an inelegant way of taking off from invisible positions on the bank just ahead of your feet, in dire panic, emitting a froggy "Yike!" and splashing into the water. Incredibly, this amused me, and incredibly, it amuses me still. As I walked along the grassy edge of the island, I got better and better at seeing frogs both in and out of the water. I learned to recognize, slowing down, the difference in texture of the light reflected from mudbank, water, grass, or frog. Frogs were flying all around me. At the end of the island I noticed a small green frog. He was exactly half in and half out of the water, looking like a schematic diagram of an amphibian, and he didn't jump.

(2) He didn't jump; I crept closer. At last I knelt on the island's winterkilled grass, lost, dumbstruck, staring at the frog in the creek just four feet away. He was a very small frog with wide, dull eyes. And just as I looked at him, he slowly crumpled and began to sag. The spirit vanished from his eyes as if snuffed. His skin emptied and drooped; his very skull seemed to collapse and settle like a kicked tent. He was shrinking before my eyes like a deflating football. I watched the taut, glistening skin on his shoulders ruck, and rumple, and fall. Soon, part of his skin, formless as a pricked balloon, lay in floating folds like bright scum on top of the water: It was a monstrous and terrifying thing. I gaped bewildered, appalled. An oval shadow hung in the water behind the drained frog; then the shadow slided away. The frog skin bag started to sink.

(3) I had read about the giant water bug, but never seen one. "Giant water bug" is really the name of the creature, which is an enormous, heavy-bodied brown beetle. It eats insects, tadpoles, fish, and frogs. Its grasping forelegs are mighty and hooked inward. It seizes a victim with these legs, hugs it tight, and paralyzes it with enzymes injected during a vicious bite. That one bite is the only bite it ever takes. Through the puncture shoot the poisons that dissolve the victim's muscles and bones and organs—all but the skin—and through it the giant water bug sucks out the victim's body, reduced to a juice. This event is

quite common in warm fresh water. The frog I saw was being sucked by a giant water bug. I had been kneeling on the island grass; when the unrecognizable flap of frog skin settled on the creek bottom, swaying, I stood up and brushed the knees of my pants. I couldn't catch my breath.

490 words

Vocabulary List

Here are some of the more difficult words in "Terror at Tinker Creek."

amphibian
(paragraph 1)

am·phib·i·an (am fib′ē ən) *n.* [< ModL *Amphibia* < Gr *amphibia*, neut. pl. of *amphibios*: see AMPHIBIOUS] **1** any of a class (Amphibia) of coldblooded, scaleless vertebrates, consisting of frogs, toads, newts, salamanders, and caecilians, that usually begin life in the water as tadpoles with gills and later develop lungs **2** any amphibious animal or plant **3** any aircraft that can take off from and come down on either land or water **4** a tank or other vehicle that can travel on either land or water —*adj.* **1** of amphibians **2** AMPHIBIOUS

appalled
(paragraph 2)

ap·pall (ə pôl′) *vt.* [ME *apallen* < OFr *apalir* < *a-*, to + *palir*, to grow pale < L *palescere* < *pallere*, to be pale: see PALE¹] to fill with horror or dismay; shock —*SYN.* DISMAY

drooped
(paragraph 2)

droop (drōōp) *vi.* [ME *droupen* < ON *drūpa*: for IE base see DRIP] **1** to sink down; hang or bend down **2** to lose vitality or strength; become weakened; languish **3** to become dejected or dispirited —*vt.* to let sink or hang down —*n.* an act or instance of drooping

gaped
(paragraph 2)

gape (gāp; *occas.* gap) *vi.* **gaped, gap′ing** [ME *gapen* < ON *gapa* < IE *ghēp-* < IE *ghēp-* < base *ghe-*, to yawn, gape > GAB, Gr *chasma*, abyss, L *hiatus*] **1** to open the mouth wide, as in yawning or hunger **2** to stare with the mouth open, as in wonder or surprise **3** to open or be opened wide, as a chasm —*n.* **1** the act of gaping; specif., *a)* an open-mouthed stare *b)* a yawn **2** a wide gap or opening **3** *Zool.* the measure of the widest possible opening of a mouth or beak —**the gapes 1** a disease of young poultry and birds, characterized by gasping and choking and caused by gapeworms **2** a fit of yawning —gap′er or gap′ingly *adv.*

inelegant
(paragraph 1)

in·el·e·gant (in el′ə gənt) *adj.* [Fr *inélégant* < L *inelegans*] not elegant; lacking refinement, good taste, grace, etc.; coarse; crude —in·el′e·gant·ly *adv.*

ruck
(paragraph 2)

ruck² (ruk) *n., vt., vi.* ⟦prob. via dial. < ON *hrukka*⟧ crease, fold, wrinkle, or pucker

rumple
(paragraph 2)

rum·ple (rum′pəl) *n.* ⟦MDu *rompel* < *rompe*, a wrinkle, akin to OE *hrympel*, a wrinkle < IE *(s)kremb-*, to twist: see SHRIMP⟧ an uneven fold or crease; wrinkle —*vt., vi.* -**pled**, -**pling** **1** to make rumples (in); crumple **2** to make or become disheveled or tousled —**rum′ply** *adv.*

schematic
(paragraph 1)

sche·mat·ic (skē mat′ik, skə-) *adj.* ⟦ModL *schematicus*⟧ of, or having the nature of, a scheme, schema, plan, diagram, etc. —*n.* a schematic diagram, as of electrical wiring in a circuit —**sche·mat′i·cal·ly** *adv.*

scum
(paragraph 2)

scum (skum) *n.* ⟦ME < MDu *schum*, akin to Ger *schaum*, foam, scum, prob. < IE base *(s)keu-*, to cover > SKY⟧ **1** a thin layer of impurities which forms on the top of liquids or bodies of water, often as the result of boiling or fermentation **2** the dross or refuse on top of molten metals **3** worthless parts or things; refuse **4** [Colloq.] a low, despicable person, or such people collectively; lowlife —*vt.* **scummed**, **scum′ming** to remove scum from; skim —*vi.* to form scum; become covered with scum

snuffed
(paragraph 2)

snuff¹ (snuf) *n.* ⟦ME < ?⟧ the charred end of a candlewick —*vt.* ⟦ME *snuffen* < the *n.*⟧ **1** to trim off the charred end of (a candlewick) **2** to put out (a candle) with snuffers or by pinching **3** [Slang] to kill; murder —*adj.* designating or of a kind of pornographic film that shows someone being murdered as the climax of sexual activity —**snuff out** **1** to put out (a candle, etc.); extinguish **2** to bring to an end suddenly; destroy

taut
(paragraph 2)

taut (tôt) *adj.* ⟦ME *toght*, tight, firm, prob. < pp. of *togen* (< OE *togian*), to pull, TOW¹⟧ **1** tightly stretched, as a rope **2** showing strain; tense *[a taut smile]* **3** trim, tidy, well-disciplined, efficient, etc. *[a taut ship]* —**SYN.** TIGHT —**taut′ly** *adv.* —**taut′ness** *n.*

vicious
(paragraph 3)

vi·cious (vish′əs) *adj.* ⟦ME < OFr *vicieus* < L *vitiosus*, full of faults, corrupt, vicious < *vitium*, VICE¹⟧ **1** *a)* given to or characterized by vice; evil, corrupt, or depraved *b)* tending to deprave or corrupt; pernicious *[vicious interests]* *c)* harmful, unwholesome, or noxious *[a vicious concoction]* **2** ruined by defects, flaws, or errors; full of faults *[a vicious argument]* **3** having bad or harmful habits; unruly *[a vicious horse]* **4** malicious; spiteful; mean *[a vicious rumor]* **5** very intense, forceful, sharp, etc. *[a vicious blow]* —**vi′cious·ly** *adv.* —**vi′cious·ness** *n.*

18A VOCABULARY

Using the vocabulary words on pages 208–209, fill in this crossword puzzle.

Across

5. a frog, toad, newt, etc.
6. The architect made a _____ diagram of the house.
8. His new jacket has a deep _____ down the back.
9. become crumpled and disheveled
10. tight
11. hung down

Down

1. stared in wonder
2. She was _____ when he was very cruel to his best friend.
3. The angry bear killed the helpless camper with a _____ swat of its paw.
4. lacking good grace; crude
6. The candles were _____ out before we left the room.
7. A layer of _____ covered the still pond.

Name _____   Date _____

18B   CENTRAL THEME AND MAIN IDEAS

Choose the best answer.

_____ 1. What is the central theme of "Terror at Tinker Creek"?
   a. Frogs are easy to observe in nature once a person learns what to look for.
   b. People are better off if they stay away from waters that frogs live in.
   c. Nature can be joyful one moment and terribly brutal the next.
   d. Man has to find a way to exterminate all giant water bugs.

_____ 2. What is the main idea of paragraph 1?
   a. As the author was enjoying the jumping frogs, she suddenly saw a frog that did not jump.
   b. Tinker Creek is one of the best places in America to observe frogs in their natural setting.
   c. Frogs are usually invisible on land, except to a person trained to recognize how frogs reflect light from the mudbank.
   d. In zoology diagrams, amphibians are usually shown sitting half in and half out of the water.

_____ 3. What is the main idea of paragraph 3?
   a. The author had never seen a giant water bug.
   b. The giant water bug is an enormous, heavy-bodied beetle with mighty grasping forelegs.
   c. After the giant water bug finished sucking out the frog's insides, the frog's skin settled to the bottom of the creek.
   d. The giant water bug seizes its victim, injects it with enzymes that dissolve its internal organs to a juice, and sucks it dry.

18C   MAJOR DETAILS

Decide whether each detail is true (T), false (F), or not discussed (ND).

_____ 1. While walking along the water's edge one summer, the author was enjoying her ability to get frogs on land to jump into the water.

_____ 2. Frogs spend much more time on land than they do in the water.

_____ 3. One small green frog caught the author's attention because of its particularly bright colors.

Name   Date

_____ 4. The small green frog was reduced to only a bag of skin right before the author's eyes.

_____ 5. The frog had been eaten by a giant water bug.

_____ 6. Before it had been attacked, the small green frog had been sickly, which made it easy prey for the giant water bug.

_____ 7. Giant water bugs do not eat anything but frogs.

_____ 8. It is common in fresh water for giant water bugs to attack frogs.

_____ 9. The author tried to rescue the small green frog, but it was too late.

_____ 10. The author killed the giant water bug after it had sucked out the small green frog's internal organs.

18D INFERENCES

Decide whether each statement below can be inferred (YES) or cannot be inferred (NO) from the reading selection.

_____ 1. The author enjoys torturing frogs.

_____ 2. The author felt "lost, dumbstruck" because it was a rare event for her to see an animal die right before her eyes.

_____ 3. At first, the author thought that her coming near the frog caused it to die of fright.

_____ 4. The "giant water bug" has no natural enemies.

_____ 5. Once a frog is grasped by the giant water bug, it is almost never able to escape.

_____ 6. The author's knowledge about frogs and water bugs indicates that she majored in zoology in college.

_____ 7. The fact that the author could not catch her breath reveals that she has respiratory problems.

_____ 8. The author's reaction to the events she describes suggests that she is fascinated, yet horrified by the cruelty of nature.

_____ 9. The title of the reading selection indicates that the author was terrified of being bitten by the giant water bug.

Name   Date

18E   CRITICAL READING: THE WRITER'S CRAFT

Choose the best answer.

1. The author ends paragraph 1 and starts paragraph 2 with the same three words. What are they?

   _____

   _____

   _____

_____ 2. The author repeats these words to emphasize
   a. her knowledge of zoology.
   b. the drama of the event.
   c. the comedy of the event.
   d. her understanding of schematic diagrams.

_____ 3. In paragraph 2 the author compares the sight of the dying frog to all of these *except*
   a. a pricked balloon.
   b. a flat tire.
   c. a deflating football.
   d. a kicked tent.

_____ 4. All of the words listed below are used in paragraph 2. By studying the context in which each word is used, decide which *one* word is *not* used to describe the frog's being sucked to death by the giant water bug.
   a. crumpled   g. shrinking
   b. sag   h. ruck
   c. vanished   i. rumple
   d. snuffed   j. fall
   e. emptied   k. hung
   f. drooped   l. drained

18F   INFORMED OPINION

1. How would you have reacted if you had witnessed what the author did? Explain.

2. Why does nature sometimes have to be what humans call "cruel"? Explain.

Name   Date

How Did You Do?   **18** Terror at Tinker Creek

SKILL (number of items)	Number Correct		Points for Each		Score
Vocabulary (12)	_____	×	3	=	_____
Central Theme and Main Ideas (3)	_____	×	6	=	_____
Major Details (10)	_____	×	2	=	_____
Inferences (9)	_____	×	2	=	_____
Critical Reading: The Writer's Craft (4)	_____	×	2	=	_____

(Possible Total: 100) *Total* _____

SPEED

Reading Time: _____ Reading Rate (page 350): _____ Words Per Minute

Name   Date

Should a Wife Keep Her Name?

Norman Lobsenz

(1) Encouraged by feminism to maintain their separate identities, many brides have chosen to keep their maiden name* or to combine it somehow with their husband's name. Yet the emotional and technical problems that arise from this decision have made some women think twice.

(2) "I felt an obligation to carry on the family name and heritage," says Catherine Bergstrom-Katz, an actress. "But I also believed that combining our names was the fair thing to do; if I was going to take my husband's name, the least he could do was take mine." Her husband's legal name now is also Bergstrom-Katz. Though he does not use it at work, it is on all the couple's legal documents—mortgage, house deed, insurance and credit cards. Mail comes addressed to both spouses under their own names, their hyphenated name and, says Catherine, "sometimes to 'Allan Bergstrom.'" The couple's first child was named Sasha Bergstrom-Katz.

(3) Not all wives are so adamant. Some use their maiden name in business and their husband's name socially. And a growing number of women who once insisted on hyphenating maiden and married names have dropped the hyphen and are using the maiden name as a middle name.

(4) Despite the popular use of linked, merged or shared names, "there is still a surprising amount of opposition to the idea," says Terri Tepper, who for many years ran an information center in Barrington, Illinois, advising women who wished to retain their maiden names. Family counselors point out that it triggers highly emotional reactions, not only between the couple but also among parents and in-laws. "What about your silver and linens?" one woman asked her daughter. "How can I have them monogrammed if you and Bill have different names?"

(5) While such concerns may seem relatively trivial, there are others that raise significant issues.

*Alternate terms for "maiden name" are often preferred because they are considered less demeaning to women; such terms include "given name," "family name," and "pre-marriage name," although these alternatives are only beginning to come into widespread use.

- *Control and commitment.* "Names have always been symbols of power," says Constance Ahrons, a therapist at the University of Southern California. "To a modern woman, keeping her name is a symbol of her independence. But a man may feel that implies a lack of commitment to him and to the marriage." Thus when a San Diego woman told her fiancé she had decided to keep her name, he was hurt. "Aren't you proud to be my wife?" he asked. Most men are more understanding. When Maureen Poon, a publicist, married Russell Fear, her English-Irish husband sympathized with his wife's desire to preserve her Chinese-Japanese heritage, especially since she was an only child. "We began married life as Poon-Fear," says Maureen. "I've since dropped the hyphen—it just confuses too many people—but Russell continues to use it when we're out together. He feels that we are 'Poon-Fear,' that we are one."

- *Cultural differences.* "Men raised in a macho society find it hard to accept a wife who goes by her own name," says Dr. Judith Davenport, a clinical social worker. For example, New York-born Jennifer Selvy, now a riding instructor in Denver, says her Western-rancher fiancé was horrified that she wanted to keep her name. "What will my friends say?" he protested. "Nobody will believe we're married!" His distress was so real that Selvy reluctantly yielded.

- *What to name the children.* When couples began hyphenating surnames, it was amusing to consider the tongue-twisters that might plague the next generation. But psychologists point out that youngsters with complex names are often teased by classmates or embarrassed if their parents have different names. And how does one explain to grandparents that their grandchild, apple of their eye, will not be carrying on the family name?

- *Technical troubles.* While there are no legal barriers in any state to a woman's keeping her maiden name—or resuming it in mid-marriage—technology can cause complications. Hyphenated names are often too long for computers to handle; others are likely to be filed incorrectly. One reason Maureen Poon-Fear dropped the hyphen in her name was "it created a problem in consistency." She explains: "The Department of Motor Vehicles lists me as POONFEAR. Some of my charge accounts are listed under 'P' and others under 'F,' and I was concerned about the effect on my credit rating if my payments were not properly credited."

(6) Given the difficulties of keeping one's maiden name in a society that has not yet fully adjusted to the idea, should a woman make the effort to do so?

(7) "Clearly, yes, if the name has value to her in terms of personal, family or professional identity," says Alan Loy McGinnis, co-director of the Valley Counseling Center in Glendale, California. "But if keeping one's maiden name makes either spouse feel less secure about the relationship, perhaps the couple needs to find another way to symbolize mutual commitment. After all, marriage today needs all the reinforcement it can get."

792 words

Vocabulary List

Here are some of the more difficult words in "Should a Wife Keep Her Name?"

adamant
(paragraph 3)

ad|a·mant (ad′ə mənt, -mant′) *n.* ⟦ME & OFr < L *adamas* (gen. *adamantis*), the hardest metal < Gr *adamas* (gen. *adamantos*) < *a-*, not + *daman*, to subdue: see TAME⟧ **1** in ancient times, a hard stone or substance that was supposedly unbreakable **2** [Old Poet.] unbreakable hardness —*adj.* **1** too hard to be broken **2** not giving in or relenting; unyielding —*SYN.* INFLEXIBLE —ad′|a·mant|ly *adv.*

commitment
(paragraph 5)

com·mit (kə mit′) *vt.* -mit′ted, -mit′ting ⟦ME *committen* < L *committere*, to bring together, commit < *com-*, together + *mittere*, to send: see MISSION⟧ **1** to give in charge or trust; deliver for safekeeping; entrust; consign *[we commit his fame to posterity]* **2** to put officially in custody or confinement *[committed to prison]* **3** to hand over or set apart to be disposed of or put to some purpose *[to commit something to the trash heap]* **4** to do or perpetrate (an offense or crime) **5** to bind as by a promise; pledge; engage *[committed to the struggle]* **6** to make known the opinions or views of *[to commit oneself on an issue]* **7** to refer (a bill, etc.) to a committee to be considered —**commit to memory** to learn by heart; memorize —**commit to paper** (or **writing**) to write down; record —com·mit′ta·ble *adj.*
SYN.—**commit**, the basic term here, implies the delivery of a person or thing into the charge or keeping of another; **entrust** implies committal based on trust and confidence; **confide** stresses the private nature of information entrusted to another and usually connotes intimacy of relationship; **consign** suggests formal action in transferring something to another's possession or control; **relegate** implies a consigning to a specific class, sphere, place, etc., esp. one of inferiority, and usually suggests the literal or figurative removal of something undesirable

com·mit·ment (-mənt) *n.* **1** a committing or being committed **2** official consignment by court order of a person as to prison or a mental hospital **3** a pledge or promise to do something **4** dedication to a long-term course of action; engagement; involvement **5** a financial liability undertaken, as an agreement to buy or sell securities **6** the act of sending proposed legislation to a committee

feminism
(paragraph 1)

fem|i·nism (fem′ə niz′əm) *n.* ⟦< L *femina*, woman + -ISM⟧ **1** [Rare] feminine qualities **2** *a)* the principle that woman should have political, economic, and social rights equal to those of men *b)* the movement to win such rights for women —fem′|i·nist *n., adj.* —fem′|i·nis′-tic *adj.*

heritage
(paragraph 5)

her·it·age (her′i tij′) *n.* ⟦ME < OFr < *heriter* < LL(Ec) *hereditare*, to inherit < L *hereditas*: see HEREDITY⟧ **1** property that is or can be inherited **2** *a)* something handed down from one's ancestors or the past, as a characteristic, a culture, tradition, etc. *b)* the rights, burdens, or status resulting from being born in a certain time or place; birthright
SYN.—**heritage**, the most general of these words, applies either to property passed on to an heir, or to a tradition, culture, etc. passed on to a later generation *[our heritage of freedom]*; **inheritance** applies to property, a characteristic, etc. passed on to an heir; **patrimony** strictly refers to an estate inherited from one's father, but it is also used of anything passed on from an ancestor; **birthright**, in its stricter sense, applies to the property rights of a first-born son

macho
(paragraph 5)

ma·cho (mä′chō; *Sp* mä′chô̱) *n.*, *pl.* -**chos** (-chō̱z; *Sp*, -chô̱s) [*Sp* < Port, ult. < L *masculus*, MASCULINE] **1** an overly assertive, virile, and domineering man **2** MACHISMO —*adj.* exhibiting or characterized by machismo; overly aggressive, virile, domineering, etc.

mutual
(paragraph 7)

mu·tu·al (myōō′chōō əl) *adj.* [LME *mutuall* < MFr *mutuel* < L *mutuus*, mutual, reciprocal < *mutare*, to change, exchange: see MISS¹] **1** *a*) done, felt, etc. by each of two or more for or toward the other or others; reciprocal [*mutual* admiration] *b*) of, or having the same relationship toward, each other or one another [*mutual* enemies] **2** shared in common; joint [our *mutual* friend] **3** designating or of a type of insurance in which the policyholders elect the directors, share in the profits, and agree to indemnify one another against loss —**mu′tu·al′i·ty** (-al′ə tē), *pl.* -**ties**, *n.* —**mu′tu·al·ly** *adv.*
SYN.—**mutual** may be used for an interchange of feeling between two persons [John and Joe are *mutual* enemies] or may imply a sharing jointly with others [the *mutual* efforts of a group]; **reciprocal** implies a return in kind or degree by each of two sides of what is given or demonstrated by the other [a *reciprocal* trade agreement], or it may refer to any inversely corresponding relationship [the *reciprocal* functions of two machine parts]; **common** simply implies a being shared by others or by all the members of a group [our *common* interests]

plague
(paragraph 5)

plague (plāg) *n.* [ME *plage* < MFr < L *plaga*, a blow, misfortune, in LL(Ec), plague < Gr *plēgē*, *plaga* < IE *plaga*, a blow < base *plag-*, to strike > FLAW²] **1** anything that afflicts or troubles; calamity; scourge **2** any contagious epidemic disease that is deadly; esp., bubonic plague **3** [Colloq.] a nuisance; annoyance **4** *Bible* any of various calamities sent down as divine punishment: Ex. 9:14, Num. 16:46 —*vt.* **plagued, plagu′ing 1** to afflict with a plague **2** to vex; harass; trouble; torment —**SYN.** ANNOY —**plagu′er** *n.*

resuming
(paragraph 5)

re·sume (ri zōōm′, -zyōōm′) *vt.* -**sumed′**, -**sum′ing** [ME *resumen*, to assume < MFr *resumer* < L *resumere* < *re-*, again + *sumere*, to take: see CONSUME] **1** *a*) to take, get, or occupy again [to *resume* one's seat] *b*) to take back or take on again [to *resume* a former name] **2** to begin again or go on with again after interruption [to *resume* a conversation] **3** to summarize or make a résumé of —*vi.* to begin again or go on again after interruption —**re·sum′a·ble** *adj.*

surnames
(paragraph 5)

sur·name (sʉr′nām′; *for v.*, *also* sʉr·nām′) *n.* [ME < *sur-* (see SUR-¹) + *name*, infl. by earlier *surnoun* < OFr *surnom* < *sur-* + *nom* < L *nomen*, NAME] **1** the family name, or last name, as distinguished from a given name **2** a name or epithet added to a person's given name (Ex.: Ivan *the Terrible*) —*vt.* -**named′**, -**nam′ing** to give a surname to

symbolize
(paragraph 7)

sym·bol (sim′bəl) *n.* [< Fr & L: Fr *symbole* < L *symbolus*, *symbolum* < Gr *symbolon*, token, pledge, sign by which one infers a thing < *symballein*, to throw together, compare < *syn-*, together + *ballein*, to throw: see BALL²] **1** something that stands for, represents, or suggests another thing; esp., an object used to represent something abstract; emblem [the dove is a *symbol* of peace] **2** a written or printed mark, letter, abbreviation, etc. standing for an object, quality, process, quantity, etc., as in music, mathematics, or chemistry **3** *Psychoanalysis* an act or object representing an unconscious desire that has been repressed —*vt.* -**boled** or -**bolled**, -**bol·ing** or -**bol·ling** SYMBOLIZE

sym·bol·ize (-īz′) *vt.* -**ized′**, -**iz′ing** [Fr *symboliser* < ML *symbolizare*] **1** to be a symbol of; typify; stand for **2** to represent by a symbol or symbols —*vi.* to use symbols —**sym′bol·i·za′tion** *n.* —**sym′bol·iz′er** *n.*

19A   VOCABULARY

Using the vocabulary words listed on pages 218–219, fill in the blanks.

1. Adopting a child demands a tremendous emotional

   _____ .

2. To succeed in getting into better physical shape, amateur athletes

   must be _____ about exercising regularly, no matter
   how tempted they may be to skip a workout.

3. In successful marriages, the partners realize that they share

   _____ rights as well as responsibilities.

4. The new owners of the house did not know that mosquitoes would

   _____ them each summer.

5. After working as a clown in a circus for six months, my neighbor

   recently returned home and is now _____ his career as a
   stockbroker.

6. Many forms, including employment applications, require people to

   give their _____ before their first names.

7. Instead of the groom giving the bride a ring, many couples now
   prefer double-ring ceremonies because they want the exchange of

   rings to _____ their equality of partnership.

8. In recent years many people are choosing to study a foreign language, and many select the language of their grandparents as a way

   of preserving their _____ .

9. Little boys raised in a _____ culture may grow up to
   feel they are superior to women, but such an attitude is resented by
   many women today.

10. Over the last quarter century, the principles of _____
    have encouraged many women to pursue careers that their mothers
    often did not have the chance to consider.

19B   CENTRAL THEME AND MAIN IDEAS
Choose the best answer.

_____ 1. What is the central theme of "Should a Wife Keep Her Name?"
a. The use of hyphenated surnames causes confusion because the wife may seem not to be committed to the marriage, the children face ridicule, and computer errors are likely to occur.
b. Some men are horrified by their fiancées' wish to keep their maiden names, in part because these men feel their friends will not believe a couple is married unless the woman adopts the man's name.
c. Technical and emotional problems that sometimes arise when a woman does not take her husband's name are causing some women to think through the issues before they make a decision about their married surnames.
d. Feminism is seen as the force behind the modern phenomenon of women keeping their maiden names after they get married.

_____ 2. What is the main idea of paragraph 5?
a. Many concerns about women's married surnames often seem relatively trivial.
b. The important issues about women's surnames after marriage are control and commitment, cultural differences, and what to name the children.
c. Most men are understanding about their wives' desire to keep their maiden names or to hyphenate their maiden and married names.
d. Some concerns about women's married surnames have raised a number of significant issues.

3. In your own words, give the main idea of paragraph 4.

_____

_____

_____

Name   Date

19C   MAJOR DETAILS
Decide whether each detail is MAJOR or MINOR.

_____ 1. Many brides have chosen to keep their maiden names.

_____ 2. Catherine Bergstrom-Katz is an actress.

_____ 3. Even though her husband does not use their hyphenated name at work, Bergstrom-Katz appears on all the family's legal documents.

_____ 4. Some women have decided to use their maiden names as middle names.

_____ 5. The issue of linked names can trigger highly emotional reactions.

_____ 6. One woman is worried about what monograms to put on silver and linens that she wants to give her daughter who is keeping her maiden name.

_____ 7. Maureen Poon-Fear's husband is of English-Irish descent.

_____ 8. Russell Poon-Fear feels he and his wife are one, so he continues to use their hyphenated surnames.

_____ 9. Jennifer Selvy is now a riding instructor in Denver.

_____ 10. Psychologists point out that youngsters with complex names are often teased by classmates.

_____ 11. Jennifer Selvy's fiancé worried about what his friends would think if his wife kept her name.

_____ 12. Hyphenated surnames sometimes create problems in keeping official government and financial records consistent.

Name   Date

19D INFERENCES

Choose the best answer.

_____ 1. *Read paragraph 5 again.* Why have names always been symbols of power?
a. Traditionally, when a woman married and took her husband's name, he gained complete legal and financial control of her life.
b. Many primitive tribes used to name people after animals, hoping the animals' powers would transfer to their name-sakes.
c. Traditionally, when a husband's surname is associated with great political and financial power, the man feels he is sharing that power with his wife by giving her his name.
d. Knowing someone's name can enable anyone to look up that person's records and thereby pry into his or her life.

_____ 2. *Read paragraph 5 again.* What does Russell Poon-Fear think of his marriage?
a. Because of his own background, he is glad that he has married someone of mixed heritage.
b. He considers that through marriage his wife has become his partner in all aspects of life.
c. He feels protective of his wife because she has no other family.
d. He feels that without his wife he had no identity.

_____ 3. *Read paragraph 7 again.* Alan Loy McGinnis says "marriage today needs all the reinforcement it can get." He is implying that
a. people often marry for the wrong reasons, so many marriages are very fragile.
b. divorce has become too easy, so a couple has to avoid all causes for disagreements if they want their marriage to last.
c. modern marriages face many pressures from within and from outside sources.
d. married couples have to resist the influence of people who want to encourage the couple to get divorced.

Name   Date

19E   CRITICAL READING: THE WRITER'S CRAFT

Choose the best answer.

_____ 1. In order to illustrate his point, the author does all of the following *except*
   a. give examples.
   b. quote women who have used shared names.
   c. give statistics.
   d. quote authorities on family counseling.

_____ 2. *Read paragraph 5 again.* The author presents the information in the form of a list for all these reasons *except* to
   a. emphasize main points.
   b. achieve conciseness.
   c. make reading easier.
   d. write sentence fragments.

_____ 3. The author uses all of the following verbs to connect speakers' names to their quotations *except*
   a. protested.
   b. says.
   c. explains.
   d. stated.

19F   INFORMED OPINION

1. Do you think married women should keep their maiden names? If so, in what form: the maiden name alone or hyphenated with the husband's name? Using examples of specific situations, explain your point of view.

2. Do you think that husbands of women who hyphenate their names should also hyphenate their names, as Maureen Poon-Fear's did? Why or why not?

3. What influence do you think feminism has had on women? On men? On children? Using specific examples, explain your point of view.

Name   Date

How Did You Do?   19 Should a Wife Keep Her Name?

SKILL (number of items)	Number Correct		Points for Each		Score
Vocabulary (10)	_____	×	4	=	_____
Central Theme and Main Ideas (3)	_____	×	8	=	_____
Major Details (12)	_____	×	2	=	_____
Inferences (3)	_____	×	2	=	_____
Critical Reading: The Writer's Craft (3)	_____	×	2	=	_____

(Possible Total: 100) *Total* _____

SPEED

Reading Time: _____ Reading Rate (page 350): _____ Words Per Minute

Name   Date

Restored to the Sea

Robin Micheli

(1) In the soft orange-and-pink light of dawn, the scene at Seal Rocks on Australia's eastern coast looked like an all-night beach party. People in wet suits warmed themselves before bonfires, as families with small children carried buckets of water from shore to sand, where they worked diligently on what might have been huge sand castles.

(2) But it was rescue, not revelry, on the minds of the hardy souls who had braved the night's 43°F temperatures. An eerie black row of stranded false killer whales (so named because the creatures, though gentle, resemble real killer whales) lay helpless on the sand while beyond them, in the frigid surf, 16 others were held and rocked by shivering divers. The morning before, 49 of the whales had run ashore in New South Wales, and three had died by dusk. The survival of the pod now depended on the ministrations of the residents of the tiny hamlet of Seal Rocks, aided by hundreds of volunteers who had traveled as far as 500 miles.

(3) Why the whales ran aground is a mystery. Experts can only speculate why the creatures, which can grow up to 20' long, sometimes find themselves stranded. "Along shallow beaches, it may be that their sonar doesn't work properly," says Kerrie Haynes-Lovell, a marine-mammal trainer at Sea World in Queensland, who drove 10 hours to assist in the rescue. With no echoes bouncing back from sloping shores to guide it away, a whale may mistakenly head toward land and become disoriented. Disaster may follow. "If one whale gives out distress signals," Haynes-Lovell says, "they may all come in to help."

(4) Humans were quick to answer signals for help after the whales were discovered early on Tuesday morning, July 14, by a visitor walking on the beach. Wayne Kelly, keeper of the Sugarloaf Point Lighthouse, which sits above the rocks and sand where they foundered, says the sight of the bloodied, wailing animals was "pretty distressing. They were writhing around, obviously very uncomfortable." The 200 or so volunteers kept the whales' delicate skin moist in the sun by dousing them continuously with seawater and draping them with soaked towels. Some rescuers, like Susan Clarke, a former registered nurse from nearby Bulahdelah, "adopted" individual whales and became their protectors. "You're a really good boy," Clarke cooed, gently stroking the whale she named Hope as it took a gasping breath from its blowhole. "Hang in there. You'll be in the water soon."

(5) Rescue leaders eventually decided to transport the whales from the rough, open beach to a sheltered cove on the other side of Sugarloaf Point.

From *People Weekly*, August 3, 1992. © 1992 Time Inc. Reprinted by permission of *People Weekly*.

Teams of 10 to 20 volunteers began hoisting the whales, which weighed as much as 750 lbs., by hand into a trailer. During Tuesday night, 150 volunteers took turns calming the whales in the cove and making sure their blowholes stayed above water. Four people were treated for hypothermia and many others for exhaustion. Kelly Gray, 17, broke her wrist on Tuesday when a whale rolled over on it. But as soon as it was wrapped, she was back at the beach, in the water. "I couldn't leave him," she said. "How could you, when they're so reliant on you and need you so much?"

(6) Volunteers watched helplessly as two of the whales died on Tuesday night. The spent and emotionally drained crowd of volunteers finally had cause for rejoicing late Wednesday afternoon, when 15 of the stranded whales were led out to sea. Three of the largest, dominant bulls were towed in a wire cage a quarter mile from shore, and surfers shepherded the rest after them. Within 24 hours, they had joined another pod of whales and were spotted heading north. In the end, a total of 37 whales were saved.

(7) Their ordeal over, the whales headed east and by midday were swimming freely 12 miles from shore. Homemaker Jenny Mervyn-Jones, who was awake for 36 hours caring for one whale, watched wistfully as they prepared her whale to head out. "You almost don't want to see it go, but you'll do anything you can to save it," she said. "I really can't wait to wave goodbye to the last one and wish it the best of luck."

(697 words)

Vocabulary List

Here are some of the more difficult words in "Restored to the Sea."

blowhole
(paragraph 4)

blow·hole (-hōl') *n.* **1** a nostril in the top of the head of whales and certain other cetaceans, through which they breathe **2** a hole through which gas or air can escape, esp. in lava **3** a hole in the ice to which seals, whales, etc. come to get air **4** a fissure in a cliff face along a shore through which water spouts up by the action of the waves **5** a flaw in cast metal caused by an air or gas bubble

diligently
(paragraph 1)

dili·gent (dil'ə jənt) *adj.* ⟦ME < OFr < L *diligens*: see DILIGENCE¹⟧ **1** persevering and careful in work; industrious **2** done with careful, steady effort; painstaking —*SYN.* BUSY —**dil'i·gently** *adv.*

disoriented
(paragraph 3)

dis·o·ri·ent (dis ôr'ē ent') *vt.* ⟦Fr *désorienter*: see DIS- & ORIENT, *v.*⟧ **1** orig., to turn away from the east **2** to cause to lose one's bearings **3** to confuse mentally, esp. with respect to time, place, and the identity of persons and objects Also **dis·o'ri·en·tate'** (-ən tāt') **-tat'-ed, -tat'ing** —**dis·o'ri·en·ta'tion** *n.*

dousing
(paragraph 4)

douse² (dous) *vt.* **doused, dous'ing** ⟦< ? prec.⟧ **1** to plunge or thrust suddenly into liquid **2** to drench; pour liquid over —*vi.* to get immersed or drenched —*n.* a drenching

eerie
(paragraph 2)

ee·rie or **ee·ry** (ir'ē, ē'rē) *adj.* **-ri·er, -ri·est** ⟦N Eng dial & Scot < ME *eri*, filled with dread, prob. var. of *erg*, cowardly, timid < OE *earg*, akin to Ger *arg*, bad, wicked: for IE base see ORCHESTRA⟧ **1** orig., timid or frightened; uneasy because of superstitious fear **2** mysterious, uncanny, or weird, esp. in such a way as to frighten or disturb —*SYN.* WEIRD —**ee'ri·ly** *adv.* —**ee'ri·ness** *n.*

foundered
(paragraph 4)

foun·der[1] (foun'dər) *vi.* ⟦ME *foundren* < OFr *fondrer*, to fall in, sink < *fond*, bottom < L *fundus*, bottom: see FOUND[2]⟧ **1** to stumble, fall, or go lame **2** to become stuck as in soft ground; bog down **3** to fill with water, as during a storm, and sink: said of a ship or boat **4** to become sick from overeating: used esp. of livestock **5** to break down; collapse; fail —*vt.* to cause to founder —*n.* ⟦< the *vi.*, 1⟧ LAMINITIS

hypothermia
(paragraph 5)

hy·po·ther·mi·a (-thur'mē ə) *n.* ⟦ModL < HYPO- + Gr *thermē*, heat: see WARM⟧ a subnormal body temperature

mammal
(paragraph 4)

mam·mal (mam'əl) *n.* ⟦< ModL *Mammalia* < LL *mammalis*, of the breasts < L *mamma*: see prec.⟧ any of a large class (Mammalia) of warmblooded, usually hairy vertebrates whose offspring are fed with milk secreted by the female mammary glands —**mam·ma·li·an** (mə mā'lē ən, ma-) *adj., n.*

ministrations
(paragraph 2)

min·is·tra·tion (min'is trā'shən) *n.* ⟦ME *ministracion* < L *ministra-tio* < pp. of *ministrare*, to MINISTER⟧ **1** MINISTRY (sense 2a) **2** administration, as of a sacrament **3** the act or an instance of giving help or care; service —**min'is·tra'tive** *adj.*

pod
(paragraph 2)

☆**pod**[2] (päd) *n.* ⟦? special use of prec.⟧ a small group of animals, esp. of seals or whales —*vt.* **pod'ded, pod'ding** to herd (animals) together

revelry
(paragraph 2)

rev·el·ry (rev'əl rē) *n., pl.* **-ries** ⟦ME *revelrie*⟧ reveling; noisy merry-making; boisterous festivity

sonar
(paragraph 3)

so·nar (sō'när') *n.* ⟦*so(und) n(avigation) a(nd) r(anging)*⟧ an appara-tus that transmits high-frequency sound waves through water and registers the vibrations reflected from an object, used in finding submarines, depths, etc.

speculate
(paragraph 3)

spec·u·late (spek'yŏŏ lāt') *vi.* **-lat'ed, -lat'ing** ⟦< L *speculatus*, pp. of *speculari*, to view < *specula*, watchtower < *specere*, to see: see SPY⟧ **1** to think about the various aspects of a given subject; meditate; ponder; esp., to conjecture **2** to buy or sell stocks, commodities, land, etc., usually in the face of higher than ordinary risk, hoping to take advantage of an expected rise or fall in price; also, to take part in any risky venture on the chance of making huge profits —*SYN.* THINK[1] —**spec'u·la'tor** *n.*

writhing
(paragraph 4)

writhe (rīth) *vt.* **writhed, writh'ing** ⟦ME *writhen* < OE *writhan*, to twist, wind about, akin to ON *rītha* < IE base *wer-, to bend, twist > WREATH, WRY⟧ to cause to twist or turn; contort —*vi.* **1** to make twisting or turning movements; contort the body, as in agony; squirm **2** to suffer great emotional distress, as from embarrassment, revulsion, etc. —*n.* a writhing movement; contortion —**writh'er** *n.*

20A   VOCABULARY

Choose the best answer.

_____ 1. **Dousing** as used in "Restored to the Sea" means to
   a. drown out.
   b. keep moist.
   c. pour water over.
   d. splash playfully.

_____ 2. A **diligent** person would be considered
   a. hard working.
   b. lacking in reserve.
   c. energetic.
   d. restless.

_____ 3. An **eerie** feeling would best be described as
   a. extremely funny.
   b. heart warming.
   c. suspicious.
   d. frightening or disturbing.

_____ 4. If the whale **foundered,** it
   a. sank in deep waters.
   b. became stuck or grounded.
   c. traveled in small groups.
   d. rolled all the way over.

_____ 5. A person suffering from **hypothermia** has
   a. a serious lung disease.
   b. a high fever.
   c. extremely low body temperature.
   d. a cold or allergy.

_____ 6. The whale's **blowhole** can best be described as
   a. its dorsal fin.
   b. an opening for taking in water.
   c. a nostril through which it breathes.
   d. an organ used for swimming and balancing.

_____ 7. A **disoriented** person is likely to be
   a. unaccustomed to confusion.
   b. mentally confused.
   c. helplessly nervous.
   d. unfamiliar with directions.

Name   Date

_____ 8. If the editorial writer **speculated** on the senator's problem, she
     a. engaged in a risky business venture with him.
     b. turned all of her information over to the press.
     c. disregarded the likely outcome.
     d. reflected on its various aspects.

_____ 9. **Revelry** at a funeral could best be described as
     a. a violation of the law.
     b. showing respect.
     c. inappropriate.
     d. suspicious behavior.

_____ 10. A **pod** of whales is usually considered to
     a. have identical features.
     b. swim only with their mates.
     c. be dangerous to outsiders.
     d. be a small group.

_____ 11. A **mammal** is a (n)
     a. warmblooded vertebrate.
     b. animal with fins.
     c. ocean-faring fish.
     d. member of the whale family.

_____ 12. A person who is **writhing** in pain
     a. should go to a hospital.
     b. has tremendous will power.
     c. is suffering great distress.
     d. needs to lie down.

_____ 13. **Ministrations,** as used in "Restored to the Sea," means to
     a. conduct religious services.
     b. give directions or verbal assistance.
     c. administer help or give care.
     d. cure one's illness.

_____ 14. **Sonar** would most probably be used to
     a. count the number of whales in a pod.
     b. track submarines through the ocean.
     c. calculate ocean depths.
     d. all of the above.

Name   Date

20B CENTRAL THEME AND MAIN IDEAS
Follow the directions for each item below.

_____ 1. The story is mainly about
   a. volunteers who have traveled from all over Australia to help.
   b. the rescue of stranded whales by concerned citizens.
   c. the hardships many volunteers endured.
   d. a malfunction in the whales' sonar.

_____ 2. The underlying central theme of "Restored to the Sea" is that
   a. rescuing stranded false killer whales is dangerous work.
   b. volunteers became attached to the whales and even named them.
   c. caring for creatures in distress can be a rewarding experience.
   d. most of the whales were eventually saved by the volunteers.

3. In your own words, give the main idea of paragraph 3.

   _____

   _____

_____ 4. What is the main idea of paragraph 5?
   a. The whales were moved from the open beach to a sheltered cove.
   b. Whales weigh as much as 750 lbs. each and were difficult for the volunteers to move.
   c. The volunteers battled exhaustion and cold but were devoted.
   d. Faithful volunteers who were injured returned to the rescue again.

20C MAJOR DETAILS
Decide whether each detail is true (T), false (F), or not discussed (ND).

_____ 1. Stranded false killer whales are known to attack humans.

_____ 2. Volunteers from Seal Rocks rescued 37 of the whales.

_____ 3. One whale was the cause of the stranding of 49 others.

_____ 4. Some volunteers traveled great distances to help.

_____ 5. The whales' malfunctioning sonar may have led them astray.

_____ 6. Humans are quick to answer calls to help any animal in distress.

Name   Date

_____ 7. The volunteers' previous training prepared them for the rescue attempt.

_____ 8. Whales are by nature nervous creatures.

20D INFERENCES

Decide whether each statement below can be inferred (YES) or cannot be inferred (NO) from the reading selection.

_____ 1. In paragraph 1 the volunteers were celebrating with a beach party because the work had not yet begun.

_____ 2. Scientific studies proved why the whales became stranded.

_____ 3. Like humans, whales can become excited and distressed.

_____ 4. If a whale's blowhole remains underwater indefinitely, the animal will drown.

_____ 5. Watching helpless whales die was an event the volunteers were prepared for when they began the mission.

_____ 6. It is common for whales to become stranded.

_____ 7. The size of the whales hampered the volunteers' attempts to rescue them.

_____ 8. False killer whales become stranded more often than gray whales.

_____ 9. The volunteers felt a sense of accomplishment after saving 37 of the whales.

_____ 10. Kerrie Haynes-Lovell had worked with whales before.

20E CRITICAL READING: THE WRITER'S CRAFT

Choose the best answer.

_____ 1. *Read paragraph 4 again.* What would be missing if the description "bloodied, wailing animals" were replaced by the phrase "beached whales"?
   a. the drama of the event
   b. the visual and auditory impact
   c. a sense of desperation
   d. all of the above

Name   Date

_____ 2. *Read paragraph 4 again.* The tone of the "conversation" between Susan Clarke and her whale Hope is
   a. pessimistic and sorrowful.
   b. impatient yet hopeful.
   c. sad but promising.
   d. reassuring and optimistic.

_____ 3. To get the reader's attention, the author starts by
   a. contrasting the party atmosphere in paragraph 1 with the somber reality in paragraph 2.
   b. explaining the behavior of the people on the beach before introducing the whales to the scene.
   c. encouraging the reader to visualize the row of stranded false killer whales.
   d. comparing the beach before and after the whales became stranded.

20F INFORMED OPINION

1. Volunteerism plays an important role in our American culture, whether it pertains to animal rights, senior citizens, hospital organizations, or children's protection. Being specific, what benefits or rewards do you believe arise from donating time to any worthwhile charity, organization, or belief?

2. Some researchers contend that the "survival of the fittest" principle should take precedence over attempts to rescue animals in peril. Do you believe this much human energy should be exerted on a project to rescue animals such as that described in "Restored to the Sea"? Explain your answer.

How Did You Do?   20 Restored to the Sea

SKILL (number of items)	Number Correct	Points for Each	Score
Vocabulary (14)	_____ ×	3	= _____
Central Theme and Main Ideas (4)	_____ ×	4	= _____
Major Details (8)	_____ ×	2	= _____
Inferences (10)	_____ ×	2	= _____
Critical Reading: The Writer's Craft (3)	_____ ×	2	= _____

(Possible Total: 100) *Total* _____

SPEED

Reading Time: _____ Reading Rate (page 350): _____ Words Per Minute

Name   Date

A License to Drive

Jerrold Mundis

(1) I was speaking with my son Jesse over the telephone. He's 15 and lives with his mother and her new husband 120 miles north, in the Catskills. It was Friday evening. I asked him what he'd done that afternoon.

(2) Gone into Kingston, he told me, to see a movie. Gone with his friend Eric.

(3) Kingston is 25 miles away.

(4) I was startled: he had never before left his home in a car driven by one of his own friends.

(5) I was also frightened.

(6) I have a photograph somewhere of Jesse and me when he was 2 or 3 months old. I haven't looked at it in years and don't need to. The image, and the tactile memory, are both graven into my mind. His head rests in my hand, he lies on my forearm and his feet barely touch against my inner elbow.

(7) Eric, 16, had just received his license, the pointman among Jesse's contemporaries. I listened only partly while Jesse talked about the movie.

(8) I was thinking about Jennie, an 18-year-old up there who was killed in a car driven by one of her friends. And Mike, 19, who went off the same road that Jesse took into Kingston and hit a tree. His body is still alive, but nothing else is; he neither functions nor responds. And Penny, a girl in my own high school graduating class, whose date drove into the rear of a tractor trailer. She was decapitated.

(9) If I close my eyes I can still see clearly the wooded mountains where I used to live with my wife and children, and those narrow, winding back-country roads with their hidden dips and blind curves.

(10) I remember when Jesse's head reached my belt line. He was about 5 then.

(11) And I remember the day I got my own driver's license. That license is more truly a rite of passage in this culture than confirmation or a bar mitzvah. Its significance, on a personal level, is of dizzying sweep. It is a stunning leap into freedom and it more radically alters a young man's life than perhaps any other event ever will. In one stroke, the shackles that bind a boy physically to home are struck off, the lifelong hourly supervision of parents falls away and the world opens, in all its possibilities.

(12) Baby Doll was a car I owned when I was 17, a 1950 Ford convertible. It was stripped of all chrome but a single lateral line on each side, had louvered fender skirts, and was painted a dull primer gray. The headlights and hood were "Frenched"—hooded with fiberglass—and there were no exterior handles, neither on the doors nor the trunk. The doors opened by electric solenoid buttons, one set mounted on a panel below the dashboard, the other hidden in the well beneath the gas-tank flap. The seats were plush, rolled black-and-white leather. There were dual exhausts with steel-pack mufflers, which could produce a thunderous roar. That car was more important to me, more a source of joy, and more integrated into my being than any object ever was or has been since.

(13) It was emancipation, responsibility, identity, pride of ownership and claim upon adulthood. With all that came an occasional wild, celebratory recklessness, a bloodsong of youth. It also meant mortal danger—I sensed it even then and with dread know it for certain now. Intoxicated with life, I roared down moonlit highways at 80, 90, and 100 miles an hour shouting at the top of my lungs. I was in drag races. I played one, maybe two games of chicken. I raced into the parking lots of forest preserves, empty in winter, and stomped on the brake pedal, sending my car spinning round and round across the ice.

(14) Jesse grew. He fit just precisely under my arm when I extended it straight out. We laughed about that. Then, shortly afterward, I didn't live with him in that house any more.

(15) We each made the adjustment, at our own cost. By the end of our first year in this new mode, he stood as tall as my shoulder. He's grown a lot over the last three years. Last weekend, we noted that his eyes are nearly on a level with mine. I was conscious from the beginning that our weekends together were finite, that they would become largely a thing of the past when he went to college. While I'm grateful there are still two more years until then, I have prepared. I was ready to start letting go when he went to college.

(16) But I wasn't ready for him to slip into a car next to his friend, for his own imminent license, for the gut-wrenching images of blood and twisted metal that came to me when he told me he'd gone into Kingston with Eric. He is moving down those tricky mountain roads and traveling highways at high speeds in the hands of another boy, and shortly, he, my youngest son, will himself be behind the wheel of two tons of hurtling automobile.

(17) I have to swallow my fear. It is a crystalline time for him. I won't allow my own apprehensions to mar it for him. The best I can do is to tell him, honestly, how it was for me and to rejoice with him.

(18) By the end of the year, he'll be taller than I. That pleases him. He likes the idea of his own height. As he should, as is fitting.

907 words

Here are some of the more difficult words in "A License to Drive."

apprehensions
(paragraph 17)

ap·pre·hen·sion (-hen'shən) *n.* [ME *apprehencioun* < LL *apprehensio*: see APPREHEND] **1** capture or arrest **2** mental grasp; perception or understanding **3** a judgment or opinion **4** an anxious feeling of foreboding; dread

crystalline
(paragraph 17)

crys·tal (kris'təl) *n.* [altered (modeled on L) < ME & OFr *cristal*, OE *cristalla* < L *crystallum*, crystal, ice < Gr *krystallos* < *kryos*: see CRUDE] **1** *a*) a clear, transparent quartz *b*) a piece of this cut in the form of an ornament **2** *a*) a very clear, brilliant glass *b*) an article or articles made of this glass, such as goblets, bowls, or other ware ☆**3** the transparent protective covering over the face of a watch **4** anything clear and transparent like crystal **5** a solidified form of a substance in which the atoms or molecules are arranged in a definite pattern that is repeated regularly in three dimensions: crystals tend to develop forms bounded by definitely oriented plane surfaces that are harmonious with their internal structures: see CRYSTAL SYSTEM **6** *Radio, Elec.* a piezoelectric body or plate, as of quartz, used to control very precisely the frequency of an oscillator or as a circuit element in a crystal filter or a body, often of Rochelle salt, used in a transducer, as in a crystal pickup or microphone —*adj.* **1** of or composed of crystal **2** like crystal; clear and transparent **3** *Radio* of or using a crystal

crys·tal·line (kris'təl in, -ın', -ēn') *adj.* [ME < OFr & L; OFr *crystalin* < L *crystallinus* < Gr *krystallinos*: see CRYSTAL] **1** consisting or made of crystal or crystals **2** like crystal; clear and transparent **3** having the structure of a crystal

emancipation
(paragraph 13)

e|man·ci·pate (ē man'sə pāt', i-) *vt.* -pat|ed, -pat'ing [< L *emancipatus*, pp. of *emancipare* < *e-*, out + *mancipare*, to deliver up or make over as property < *manceps*, purchaser < *manus*, the hand (see MANUAL) + *capere*, to take (see HAVE)] **1** to set free (a slave, etc.); release from bondage, servitude, or serfdom **2** to free from restraint or control, as of social convention **3** *Law* to release (a child) from parental control and supervision —*SYN.* FREE —e|man'ci·pa'tion *n.* —e|man'ci·pa'tive or e|man'ci·pa·to'|ry (-pe tôr'ē) *adj.* —e|man'ci·pa'tor *n.*

finite
(paragraph 15)

fi·nite (fī'nīt') *adj.* [ME *finit* < L *finitus*, pp. of *finire*, FINISH] **1** having measurable or definable limits; not infinite **2** *Gram.* having limits of person, number, and tense: said of a verb that can be used in a predicate **3** *Math. a*) capable of being reached, completed, or surpassed by counting (said of numbers or sets) *b*) neither infinite nor infinitesimal (said of a magnitude) —*n.* anything that has measurable limits; finite thing —fi'nite|ly *adv.* —fi'nite'ness *n.*

fitting
(paragraph 18)

fit·ting (fit'iŋ) *adj.* suitable; proper; appropriate —*n.* **1** an adjustment or trying on of clothes, etc. for fit **2** a small part used to join, adjust, or adapt other parts, as in a system of pipes **3** [*pl.*] the fixtures, furnishings, or decorations of a house, office, automobile, etc. —fit'ting|ly *adv.*

graven
(paragraph 6)

grave (grāv) *n.* [ME < OE *græf* (akin to OFris *gref*, Ger *grab*) < base of *grafan*, to dig: see the *vt.*] **1** *a*) a hole in the ground in which to bury a dead body *b*) any place of burial **2** final end or death; extinction —*vt.* graved, grav'|en or graved, grav'ing [ME *graven* < OE *grafan*; akin to Ger *graben* < IE base *ghrebh-*, to scratch, scrape] **1** [Obs.] *a*) to dig *b*) to bury **2** [Archaic] *a*) to shape by carving; sculpture *b*) to engrave; incise **3** to impress sharply and clearly; fix permanently —**have one foot in the grave** to be very ill, old, or infirm; be near death —**make one turn (over) in one's grave** to be or do something that would have shocked or distressed one now dead

imminent
(paragraph 16)

im·mi·nent (im'ə nənt) *adj.* [L *imminens*, prp. of *imminere*, to project over, threaten < *in-*, on + *minere*, to project: see MENACE] likely to happen without delay; impending; threatening: said of danger, evil, misfortune —im'mi·nent|ly *adv.*

Vocabulary List

Integrated
(paragraph 12)

in·te·grate (in'tə grāt') vt. -grat'ed, -grat'ing [[< L integratus, pp. of integrare, to make whole, renew < integer: see INTEGER]] 1 to make whole or complete by adding or bringing together parts 2 to put or bring (parts) together into a whole; unify 3 to give or indicate the whole, sum, or total of ☆4 a) to remove the legal and social barriers imposing segregation upon (racial groups) so as to permit free and equal association b) to abolish segregation in; desegregate (a school, neighborhood, etc.) 5 Math. a) to calculate the integral or integrals of (a function, equation, etc.) b) to perform the process of integration upon 6 Psychol. to cause to undergo integration —vi. to become integrated —in'te·gra'tive adj.

mar
(paragraph 17)

mar (mär) vt. marred, mar'ring [[ME marren < OE mierran, to hinder, spoil, akin to Goth marzjan, to offend < IE base *mer-, to disturb, anger > Sans mṛṣyate, (he) forgets, neglects]] to injure or damage so as to make imperfect, less attractive, etc.; spoil; impair; disfigure —n. [Rare] something that mars; an injury or blemish

mortal
(paragraph 13)

mor·tal (môr'təl, môrt''l) adj. [[OFr < L mortalis < mors (gen. mortis), death, akin to mori, to die < IE base *mer-, to die, be worn out > MURDER, Sans marati, (he) dies]] 1 that must eventually die [all mortal beings] 2 of man as a being who must eventually die 3 of this world 4 of death 5 causing death; deadly; fatal 6 to the death [mortal combat] 7 not to be pacified [a mortal enemy] 8 very intense; grievous [mortal terror] 9 [Colloq.] a) extreme; very great b) very long and tedious c) conceivable; possible [of no mortal good to anyone] 10 Theol. causing spiritual death: said of a sin serious in itself, adequately recognized as such, and committed with full consent of one's will: compare VENIAL —n. a being who must eventually die; esp., a human being; person —adv. [Dial.] extremely —SYN. FATAL —mor'tal·ly adv.

radically
(paragraph 11)

rad·i·cal (rad'i kəl) adj. [[ME < LL radicalis < L radix (gen. radicis), ROOT¹]] 1 a) of or from the root or roots; going to the foundation or source of something; fundamental; basic [a radical principle] b) extreme; thorough [a radical change in one's life] 2 a) favoring fundamental or extreme change; specif., favoring basic change in the social or economic structure b) [R-] designating or of any of various modern political parties, esp. in Europe, ranging from moderate to conservative in program 3 Bot. of or coming from the root 4 Math. having to do with the root or roots of a number or quantity —n. 1 a) a basic or root part of something b) a fundamental 2 a) a person holding radical views, esp. one favoring fundamental social or economic change b) [R-] a member or adherent of a Radical party 3 Chem. a group of two or more atoms that acts as a single atom and goes through a reaction unchanged, or is replaced by a single atom: it is normally incapable of separate existence 4 Math. a) the indicated root of a quantity or quantities, shown by an expression written under the radical sign b) RADICAL SIGN —SYN. LIBERAL —rad'i·cal·ness n.

rad·i·cal·ly (rad'i kəl ē, -klē) adv. 1 a) as regards root or origin b) fundamentally; basically; completely 2 in a manner characterized by radicalism

rite of passage
(paragraph 11)

rite of passage 1 a ceremony, often religious, marking the significant transitions in one's life, as birth, puberty, marriage, or death 2 an event, achievement, etc. in a person's life regarded as having great significance Also [Fr.] rite de pas·sage (rēt də pä sázh')

shackles
(paragraph 11)

shack·le (shak'əl) n. [[ME schakel < OE sceacel, akin to MDu schakel, chain link < ? IE base *(s)kenk-, to gird, bind]] 1 a metal fastening, usually one of a linked pair, for the wrist or ankle of a prisoner; fetter; manacle 2 anything that restrains freedom of expression or action [the shackles of ignorance] 3 any of several devices used in fastening or coupling —vt. -led, -ling 1 to put shackles on; fetter 2 to fasten or connect with a shackle or shackles 3 to restrain in freedom of expression or action —shack'ler n.

tactile
(paragraph 6)

tac·tile (tak'təl; chiefly Brit, -til') adj. [[Fr < L tactilis < tangere, to touch: see TACT]] 1 that can be perceived by the touch; tangible 2 of, having, or related to the sense of touch —tac·til'i·ty (-til'ə tē) n.

21A VOCABULARY

Using the vocabulary words listed on pages 235–236, fill in this crossword puzzle.

Across

2. an event in a person's life having ceremonial significance
7. to injure or damage
9. The townspeople hurried to prepare themselves for the _____ hurricane.
10. having measurable limits
13. unified
14. related to the sense of touch

Down

1. like clear, brilliant glass
3. freedom from restraint or influence
4. anxious feelings of foreboding
5. impressed sharply and permanently
6. restrains freedom of expression or reaction
8. appropriate or suitable
11. deadly
12. fundamentally and completely

237

21B CENTRAL THEME AND MAIN IDEAS

Choose the best answer.

_____ 1. What is the central theme of "A License to Drive"?
- a. After divorce, parents who do not live with their children worry more about their young adult children than do the parents who live with the children.
- b. Mountain roads are especially dangerous for new, young drivers.
- c. The author is having a difficult time with the realization that his son is growing up and will soon be on his own.
- d. The author likes to recall his teenage adventures with his car and is happy that his son is starting to have the same pleasures.

_____ 2. What is the main idea of paragraph 11?
- a. Getting a driver's license is a stunning leap into freedom that radically alters a young man's life.
- b. Getting a driver's license enables teenagers to get away from parental supervision.
- c. Only male teenagers find their lives radically changed when they get their driver's licenses.
- d. When the author got his own driver's license, it was like a time of confirmation or bar mitzvah.

_____ 3. What is the main idea of paragraph 16?
- a. The author does not like his son to accept rides into town from teenage drivers.
- b. The author is not ready for the news that his son was in a car driven by a teenager on dangerous mountain roads—or that soon the son would be driving them.
- c. The mountain roads near Kingston are especially dangerous at night for new drivers, such as Jesse's friend Eric.
- d. The author was upset by the images of blood and twisted metal that came to his mind.

21C MAJOR DETAILS

Decide whether each detail is MAJOR or MINOR.

_____ 1. Jesse is 15.

_____ 2. Jesse does not live with his father.

_____ 3. Kingston is 25 miles away from Jesse's home.

Name   Date

_____ 4. Jesse went to Kingston to see a movie.

_____ 5. Eric's driver's license is new.

_____ 6. Jesse was five years old when his head reached his father's belt line.

_____ 7. The car the author owned when he was seventeen years old was named Baby Doll.

_____ 8. Baby Doll was a 1950 Ford convertible.

_____ 9. The author used to make his car skid on the ice on forest preserve parking lots that were empty in winter.

_____ 10. The author was prepared to let his son go when the boy reached college age.

21D INFERENCES

Choose the best answer.

_____ 1. *Read paragraph 8 again.* Why does the author remember these car accident victims so vividly?
   a. Tragic news about other people's children increases the author's fear for his own child's safety.
   b. Some of the victims were his best friends, and others were the children of his best friends.
   c. Eric is related to all of the victims, so he is probably a wild driver who races down mountain roads.
   d. A memorial statue to these accident victims stands in front of the Kingston movie theater.

_____ 2. *Read paragraph 14 again.* Why was the author not living in the house with his son anymore?
   a. The author decided he did not like living in the Catskill Mountains.
   b. The author took a job in another state, but Jesse and his mother decided to stay in Kingston.
   c. Because of his allergies, the author was ordered to leave the mountains by his doctor.
   d. The author and Jesse's mother had separated or divorced.

_____ 3. *Read paragraph 18 again.* Why is it "fitting" that Jesse "likes the idea of his own height"?
   a. As a short person, the author has always been teased, so he is glad that Jesse will not have to have the same experience.
   b. Getting taller is a symbol of adulthood, and Jesse deserves to enjoy his growth and new sense of freedom.
   c. If Jesse is growing, it will be easier for him to see over the steering wheel when he starts to drive, so he will be a safer driver.
   d. When Jesse becomes taller than his father, his father will be able to stop worrying about him because Jesse will be an adult.

21E   CRITICAL READING: FACT OR OPINION

Decide whether each statement contains a FACT or an OPINION.

_____ 1. *From paragraph 1:* I was speaking with my son Jesse over the telephone.

_____ 2. *From paragraph 4:* I was startled: he had never before left his home in a car driven by one of his own friends.

_____ 3. *From paragraph 9:* If I close my eyes I can still see clearly the wooded mountains where I used to live.

_____ 4. *From paragraph 11:* That license is more truly a rite of passage in this culture than confirmation or a bar mitzvah.

_____ 5. *From paragraph 12:* The seats were plush, rolled black-and-white leather.

_____ 6. *From paragraph 13:* It was emancipation, responsibility, identity, pride of ownership and claim upon adulthood.

_____ 7. *From paragraph 13:* I roared down moonlit highways at 80, 90 and 100 miles an hour shouting at the top of my lungs.

_____ 8. *From paragraph 15:* Last weekend, we noted that his eyes are nearly on a level with mine.

_____ 9. *From paragraph 17:* The best I can do is to tell him, honestly, how it was for me and to rejoice with him.

_____ 10. *From paragraph 18:* As he should, as is fitting.

Name   Date

21F CRITICAL READING: THE WRITER'S CRAFT

Choose the best answer.

_____ 1. The author begins "A License to Drive" with
   a. an anecdote.
   b. an indirect quotation.
   c. a comparison.
   d. a definition.

_____ 2. *Read paragraph 2 again.* The author writes this paragraph in the form of two sentence fragments for all these reasons *except*
   a. he wants to interest his reader.
   b. he wants to use a variety of sentence types to demonstrate his skill as a writer.
   c. he is reporting what Jesse told him, and Jesse spoke in fragments.
   d. he is trying to create a dramatic effect, to show that only the key words stood out when he heard them.

_____ 3. Why does the author include so many references to Jesse's physical growth?
   a. He wants readers to see that he is sorry that his son is growing up.
   b. He uses physical growth as a symbol of mental and emotional growth.
   c. He wants his readers to know he feels physically threatened by his son's increasing size.
   d. He wants his readers to understand that he feels that he does not get to see Jesse enough.

_____ 4. *Read paragraph 12 again.* By describing Baby Doll in such detail, the author communicates that he wants his readers
   a. to picture what the car looked like because a 1950 Ford convertible is a valuable car today.
   b. to know that he assumes most readers are males who like detailed descriptions of cars.
   c. to recognize that he treasured the car a great deal.
   d. to know that he realizes that his reckless behavior endangered an expensive car.

21G INFORMED OPINION

1. What advice would you give to a teenage beginning driver? Using specific examples, explain your answer.

2. Parents are often torn between letting go of their young adult children and keeping them protected and dependent. What message did your parents' behavior send you as you were assuming greater independence in life? Using specific examples, explain your answer.

Name   Date

How Did You Do?   **21** A License to Drive

SKILL (number of items)	Number Correct		Points for Each		Score
Vocabulary (14)	_____	×	2	=	_____
Central Theme and Main Ideas (3)	_____	×	6	=	_____
Major Details (10)	_____	×	3	=	_____
Inferences (3)	_____	×	2	=	_____
Critical Reading: Fact or Opinion (10)	_____	×	1	=	_____
Critical Reading: The Writer's Craft (4)	_____	×	2	=	_____

(Possible Total: 100) *Total* _____

SPEED

Reading Time: _____ Reading Rate (page 350): _____ Words Per Minute

Name   Date

The Babies of Bedford

Jean Harris

(1) The babies are the infants born to incarcerated women. The place is Bedford Hills Correctional Facility, the only maximum-security prison for women in New York State. It is a place where I spent 12 years as an inmate, from February 1981 to January 1993. During 11 of those years, I worked in the Parenting Center with inmate mothers and their children, much of the time teaching parenting classes to young mothers and pregnant women.

(2) When I entered prison, there were approximately 600 women incarcerated in New York State; when I left there were more than 3500. Women made up about 3 percent of the total national prison population in 1981. Today they make up 6 percent of it. They are coming to prison faster than men are.

(3) On any given day, 75 to 80 percent of incarcerated women are mothers. The percentage of those who give birth in prison has been estimated nationally at 9 percent, but that's closer to a guess than a fact. The thousands of statistics published by the United States Department of Justice still don't include the words "prison births."

(4) America doesn't keep track of how many babies are born to incarcerated women. I think this reflects the fact that while we profess to love babies, manufacture billions of plastic diapers and $100 teddy bears for them, we essentially take them for granted rather than take good care of them. We worry far more about their high-school curriculum than whether they enter kindergarten prepared to learn. Many enter malnourished, not knowing their full name, where they live or that a pencil is not to eat. Education and attitudes begin in the crib, and so does crime.

(5) New York is the only state where infants can stay with their incarcerated mothers in a prison nursery until their first birthdays, or for 18 months if the mother will be paroled within that time. Bedford sets an important example, but in the other 49 states the impulse to punish the mother takes precedence over the good that can be done to both mother and infant if they can be together.

(6) At Bedford, if a mother is deemed physically and emotionally fit to care for her baby, has lived with her other children and will probably be the principal care giver of the child when she leaves prison, she is allowed to keep the baby with her. Approximately two-thirds of the women who apply are approved. The nursery averaged five babies a month in 1981; last year, it averaged 28 infants, and sometimes there were as many as 33. Since many of the young mothers are serving sentences of one-to-three or

two-to-four years, for drug possession, more than half are paroled in time to go home with the child.

(7) Babies of the rejected one-third go directly from the hospital to relatives (usually grandmothers), neighbors, foster care or anyone who will take them. I know of cases in which placing a baby has taken more than 50 calls by a counselor or Sister Elaine Roulet, founder and head of the prison's Parenting Center. Twice that I know of, Sister Elaine bundled up a baby and took it home with her until placement could be made.

(8) It is hard to imagine how a young woman, even one with a bad track record, must feel when she can't keep her baby and no one else wants it. I will always remember the letter a mother received from her 8-year-old daughter: "Dear Mama, come home—don't nobody else want Jamel and me."

(9) Babies have lived on the Bedford property since 1901, when a reformatory for young women was established there. In 1930 a section of the facility was designated a prison. Today it is entirely a prison. In 1931 a law was passed permitting prison women to keep their babies in the nursery, with the added provision that babies be born in neighborhood hospitals and have nothing about the mother's incarceration on the birth certificates. This is still on the books as Statute 611 of the State Correction Law. Some other states with reformatory nurseries did away with them after the reformatories reverted to prisons. Their arguments for doing so went something like this: "The baby didn't commit a crime so it shouldn't be in prison," "Why coddle prisoners by letting them keep their babies?" and, a favorite one of the Florida Assembly when it voted in 1981 to forbid prisoners to keep their babies with them, "A baby born in prison will never smile." The infants in Bedford have no awareness of prison and know only feeling comfortable, safe and wanted, feelings that can be the beginning of healthy social adjustment.

(10) A prison nursery cannot save every infant from the toll of a mother's excesses in drugs, alcohol and promiscuous sex, but it can help to cut those losses. Having adequate medical care and having the mother near while she takes required parenting lessons and furthers her education not only help save babies, but also cost taxpayers less than foster care or the ravages of premature births and untrained mothers would. Furthermore, closeness between mother and child is especially important to Bedford babies since fathers usually play a minor role in their lives. Until the 1970s, felon mothers at Bedford could visit their babies only on Tuesdays. The rest of the week the babies were cared for by a constantly changing parade of other inmates. As the concept of mother-infant bonding grew more widely accepted, mothers and babies were put together on the same floor and eventually in the same cell.

(11) If you know a woman is going to be a child's main care giver, and you know she may not have experienced much mothering during her own

childhood, it is logical to take advantage of the time she is required to be in prison to help develop parenting skills along with job skills to enable her to support the child. The mother, the baby and society are all the better for it.

(12) Many public parenting classes are taught with dolls. But baby dolls don't have colic, or throw up or wake you in the middle of the night. Yet those are the times that babies are bruised or beaten or even killed—the times that put parenting to the test. At Bedford, the subject is taught while mother and baby live closely together, in a relatively safe, supervised area.

(13) Each pregnant woman at Bedford takes a three-month parenting course, five afternoons a week from 1 to 3:30, whether this is her first child or her 14th. It is far easier to teach the new mother than the one with seven children who has long since fallen into the customs of her own childhood—frequent smacks to the head and shouted expletives. Allison is deaf in one ear and partly deaf in the other from smacks to her head by her alcoholic mother. But who is taking care of her two children while Allison is in prison? Her mother.

(14) In addition to taking parenting class, a mother must, six weeks after the baby's birth, return to her prison job or prison classes if she hasn't earned her high-school diploma. More than half haven't. Trained inmates and an outside volunteer run a prison day-care center for prison babies. A working mother can still be a good mother.

(15) When I taught parenting classes at Bedford I always asked, "Do you hope to be as good a mother as your mother was, or a better one?" The answer, 95 percent of the time, was "I want to be as good as my mother was," no matter how grim their childhoods were. Their logic was simple. "She done the best she could," and the added clincher, "She's the only one stuck by me." Their expectations for themselves are about the same. They'll do the best they can, with no promises about how good that best will be.

(16) It's hard for a young prison mother to learn that she is the most important person in her child's life and that how she holds, touches, feeds and speaks to the child, even in the first year, can play a role in the quality of the child's future, can be the beginning of hope for a better future than she had. Hopelessness is rampant in prison. It's contagious and dangerous.

(17) Telling the women they were important was often received with patent disdain. "Me? An important person? Come off it, old lady." They have spent their lifetimes being put down, often used as a sexual object, and tragically, many have accepted the role. When Mary wrote down the ages of her children as 3, 3 1/2, 3 1/2, 6 and 7, I said, "Oh, you had triplets?" "Naw," she said, "Only twins and another one. I'm a fast breeder like my mother." Charmaine had her first baby at age 10. Corine celebrated her 21st birthday three days before the birth of her seventh child. Rhonda told me her 10-year-old sister "can't wait to have sex." When I explained to

them that doctors recommend that a woman not resume intercourse until six weeks after her baby's birth, the class response was a loud guffaw. "Hell, we done it in the *hospital*," one woman said.

(18) It's difficult for people on the outside, especially those who have been victims of crime, to care for people in prison, or even to accept the fact that many of them are victims of crime, too. But babies have hurt no one. It should be easier to look upon them with concern for their future, for their future is ours. As long as women are incarcerated anywhere in America, their babies should have the same chance for a decent beginning as the babies of Bedford have.

(1611 words)

Vocabulary List

Here are some of the more difficult words in "The Babies of Bedford."

clincher
(paragraph 15)

clinch|er (-ər) *n.* a person or thing that clinches; specif., a conclusive or decisive point, argument, act, etc.

coddle
(paragraph 9)

cod·dle (käd″l) *vt.* -dled, -dling ⟦prob. < CAUDLE⟧ 1 to cook (esp. eggs in the shell) gently by heating in water not quite at boiling temperature 2 to treat (an invalid, baby, etc.) tenderly

colic
(paragraph 12)

col|ic (käl′ik) *n.* ⟦ME colik < OFr colique < LL colicus, pertaining to colic, sick with colic < Gr kōlikos < kōlon, incorrect form for kolon, colon: from being seated in the colon and parts adjacent⟧ 1 acute abdominal pain caused by various abnormal conditions in the bowels 2 a condition of infants characterized by frequent crying due to various discomforts —*adj.* 1 of colic 2 of or near the colon —**col′·ick|y** (-ik ē) *adj.*

contagious
(paragraph 16)

con·ta·gious (-jəs) *adj.* ⟦OFr contagieus < LL contagiosus⟧ 1 spread by direct or indirect contact; communicable: said of diseases 2 carrying, or liable to transmit, the causative agent of a contagious disease 3 for the care of contagious patients 4 spreading or tending to spread from person to person *[contagious laughter]* —**con·ta′·giously** *adv.* —**con·ta′gious·ness** *n.*

designated
(paragraph 9)

des·ig·nate (dez′ig nāt′; *for adj.,* -nit, -nāt′) *adj.* ⟦ME < L designatus, pp. of designare: see prec.⟧ named for an office, etc. but not yet in it *[ambassador designate]* —*vt.* -nat′ed, -nat′ing 1 to point out; mark out; indicate; specify 2 to refer to by a distinguishing name, title, etc.; name 3 to name for an office or duty; appoint —**des′ig·na′tive** *adj.* —**des′ig·na′tor** *n.*

expletives
(paragraph 13)

ex·ple|tive (eks′plə tiv) *n.* ⟦LL expletivus, serving to fill < L expletus, pp. of explere, to fill < ex-, out, up + plere, to fill: see FULL¹⟧ 1 an oath or exclamation, esp. an obscenity 2 a word, phrase, etc. not needed for the sense but used merely to fill out a sentence or metrical line, for grammar, rhythm, balance, etc. *[there in "there is nothing left" is an expletive]* 3 [Rare] anything serving as a filler —*adj.* used to fill out a sentence, line, etc. Also **ex′ple·to′·ry** (-tôr′ē)

felon
(paragraph 10)

fel|on¹ (fel′ən) *n.* ⟦ME < OFr < ML felo, earlier fello < ?⟧ 1 [Obs.] a villain 2 *Law* a person guilty of a major crime; criminal —*adj.* [Old Poet.] wicked; base; criminal

guffaw
(paragraph 17)

guf·faw (gu fô′, gə-) *n.* ⟦echoic⟧ a loud, coarse burst of laughter —*vi.* to laugh in this way —**SYN.** LAUGH

incarcerated
(paragraph 1)

in·car·cer·ate (in kär′sər āt′) *vt.* **-at′ed, -at′ing** ⟦< ML *incarceratus*, pp. of *incarcerare*, to imprison < L *in*, in + *carcer*, prison⟧ **1** to imprison; jail **2** to shut up; confine —**in·car·cer′a′tion** *n.* —**in·car′cer′a′tor** *n.*

malnourished
(paragraph 4)

mal·nour·ished (mal nur′isht) *adj.* improperly nourished

nour·ish (nur′ish) *vt.* ⟦ME *norischen* < OFr extended stem of *norrir* < L *nutrire*: see NURSE⟧ **1** to feed or sustain (any plant or animal) with substances necessary to life and growth **2** to foster; develop; promote (a feeling, attitude, habit, etc.) —**nour′ish·er** *n.*

paroled
(paragraph 5)

pa·role (pə rōl′) *n.* ⟦Fr, a word, formal promise < OFr < LL(Ec) *parabola*, a speech, PARABLE⟧ **1** orig., word of honor; promise; esp., the promise of a prisoner of war to abide by certain conditions, often specif. to take no further part in the fighting, in exchange for full or partial freedom **2** the condition of being on parole ☆**3** *a)* the release of a prisoner whose sentence has not expired, on condition of future good behavior: the sentence is not set aside and the individual remains under the supervision of a parole board *b)* the conditional freedom granted by such release, or the period of it **4** [Obs.] *Mil.* a special password used only by certain authorized persons —*vt.* **-roled′, -rol′ing** ☆to grant parole to (a prisoner) —**on parole** at liberty under conditions of parole

precedence
(paragraph 5)

prec·e·dence (pres′ə dəns; prē sēd′′ns, pri-) *n.* ⟦< fol.⟧ **1** the act, right, or fact of preceding in time, order, rank, etc. **2** priority as because of superiority in rank **3** an official or conventional ranking of dignitaries in order of importance Also **prec′e·den·cy**

promiscuous
(paragraph 10)

pro·mis·cu·ous (prō mis′kyōō əs, prə-) *adj.* ⟦L *promiscuus* < *pro-*, forth (see PRO-²) + *miscere*, to MIX⟧ **1** consisting of different elements mixed together or mingled without sorting or discrimination **2** characterized by a lack of discrimination; specif., engaging in sexual intercourse indiscriminately or with many persons **3** without plan or purpose; casual —**pro·mis′cu·ous·ly** *adv.* —**pro·mis′cu·ous·ness** *n.*

rampant
(paragraph 16)

ramp·ant (ram′pənt) *adj.* ⟦ME < OFr, prp. of *ramper*: see RAMP²⟧ **1** growing luxuriantly; flourishing *[rampant* plants] **2** spreading unchecked; widespread; rife **3** violent and uncontrollable in action, manner, speech, etc. **4** *Archit.* having one abutment higher than the other: said of an arch **5** *a)* rearing up on the hind legs *b) Heraldry* depicted thus in profile, with one forepaw raised above the other *[a* lion *rampant]* —**ramp′an·cy** *n.* —**ramp′ant·ly** *adv.*

ravages
(paragraph 10)

rav·age (rav′ij) *n.* ⟦Fr < OFr *ravir*: see RAVISH⟧ **1** the act or practice of violently destroying; destruction **2** ruin; devastating damage *[the ravages* of time] —*vt.* **-aged, -ag·ing** ⟦Fr *ravager* < the *n.*⟧ to destroy violently; ruin —*vi.* to commit ravages —**rav′ag·er** *n.*
SYN.—**ravage** implies violent destruction, usually in a series of depredations or over an extended period of time, as by an army or a plague; **devastate** stresses the total ruin and desolation resulting from a ravaging; **plunder** refers to the forcible taking of loot by an invading or conquering army; **sack** and **pillage** both specifically suggest violent destruction and plunder by an invading or conquering army, **sack** implying the total stripping of all valuables in a city or town; **despoil** is equivalent to **sack** but is usually used with reference to buildings, institutions, etc.

reformatory
(paragraph 9)

☆**re·form·a·to·ry** (ri fôr′mə tôr′ē) *adj.* reforming or aiming at reform —*n., pl.* **-ries 1** an institution to which young offenders convicted of lesser crimes are sent for training and discipline intended to reform rather than punish them **2** a penitentiary for women

reverted
(paragraph 9)

re·vert (ri vurt′) *vi.* ⟦ME *reverten* < OFr *revertir* < VL *revertire*, for L *revertere* < *re-*, back + *vertere*, to turn: see VERSE⟧ **1** to go back in action, thought, speech, etc.; return, as to a former practice, opinion, state, or subject **2** *Biol.* to return to a former or primitive type; show ancestral characteristics normally no longer present in the species **3** *Law* to go back to a former owner or the heirs of such owner —*n.* a person or thing that reverts; esp., one who returns to a previous faith —**re·vert′i·ble** *adj.*

statute
(paragraph 9)

stat·ute (stach′ōōt) *n.* ⟦ME < OFr *statut* < LL *statutum*, neut. of L *statutus*, pp. of *statuere*: see STATUE⟧ **1** an established rule; formal regulation **2** *a)* a law passed by a legislative body and set forth in a formal document *b)* such a document —*SYN.* LAW

22A   VOCABULARY

Using the vocabulary words listed on pages 246–247, fill in this crossword puzzle.

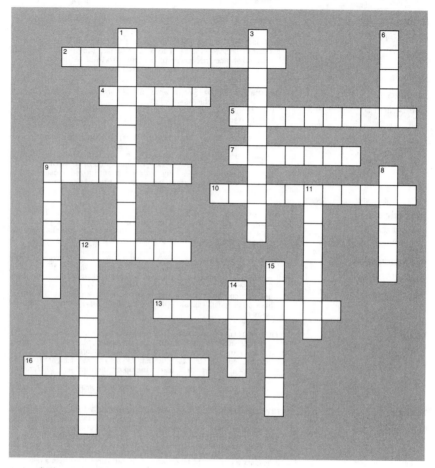

ACROSS

2. improperly fed
4. freedom granted a prisoner on condition of good behavior
5. the act of preceding in rank
7. ruin or destruction
9. returned to former practice
10. engaging in sex with many persons
12. to treat tenderly
13. obscenities
16. indicated or specified

DOWN

1. imprisoned
3. an institution for offenders of lesser crimes
6. a condition of infants marked by frequent crying
8. a laugh
9. widespread
11. laws
12. spread by direct or indirect contact
14. criminal
15. the deciding factor

Name   Date

22B CENTRAL THEME AND MAIN IDEAS

Choose the best answer.

_____ 1. What is the central theme of "The Babies of Bedford"?
  a. The Bedford plan should be used as a model for other states.
  b. Jean Harris is a renowned leader in the prison reform movement.
  c. If adopted by other states, the Bedford plan would help lower the number of births to incarcerated women.
  d. It is surprising how many babies are born to incarcerated mothers each year.

_____ 2. What is the main idea of paragraph 4?
  a. America should keep track of the number of babies born in prison.
  b. Children born in prison are not being counted, implying that they don't count.
  c. Education at the elementary level is more important than education at the high school level.
  d. Babies born in prison should be better educated than those born elsewhere.

_____ 3. What is the main idea of paragraph 6?
  a. Young mothers serve shorter sentences than other offenders.
  b. The number of women having babies in prison has greatly increased.
  c. A majority of the women who apply are allowed to keep their babies.
  d. If a woman has other children, she will be allowed to keep the baby with her in prison.

_____ 4. What is the main idea of paragraph 9?
  a. Politicians feel that allowing mothers to keep their babies would be special treatment.
  b. Statute 611 is the backbone of the Bedford Hills Correctional Facility plan.
  c. A prison is not a safe, healthy environment for a baby.
  d. Allowing incarcerated women to keep their newborn babies with them has been a successful policy at Bedford since the early 1900s.

_____ 5. What is the main idea of paragraph 15?
  a. Inmates tend to forget how grim their childhoods were.
  b. Inmates do not try to be as good as their own mothers.
  c. Inmates believe their own mothers did a good job raising them.
  d. Inmates model their parenting ambitions on their own mothers' behavior.

22C MAJOR DETAILS

Decide whether each detail is true (T), false (F), or not discussed (ND).

_____ 1. Jean Harris spent twelve years in prison for committing a murder.

_____ 2. Women are entering the prison system at about the same rate as men are entering.

Name   Date

_____ 3. Women make up less than 10 percent of the total national prison population.

_____ 4. Only one state allows babies to stay with their incarcerated mothers in a prison nursery.

_____ 5. More than half of the women who apply to keep their babies with them are approved.

_____ 6. Women serving sentences for drug possession are paroled earlier than those serving time for other crimes.

_____ 7. Babies who are not allowed to stay with their mothers go immediately to their next of kin.

_____ 8. Jean Harris is an authority on the Parenting Center because she spent all of her incarceration working with inmate mothers.

_____ 9. Because of the author's campaign, mothers and babies at Bedford now share the same cell.

_____ 10. It is easier to train a mother who has several children than to train a new mother in parenting skills.

_____ 11. Fewer than 50 percent of the mothers at Bedford have earned their high school diplomas.

_____ 12. Many of the mothers interviewed by the author are bitter over being used as sexual objects.

_____ 13. It is difficult for most of these young mothers to plan a better life for their children than they had.

22D INFERENCES
Choose the best answer.

_____ 1. *Read paragraph 3 again.* The Department of Justice statistics don't include the words "prison births" probably because
   a. it's impossible to keep track of these births in all fifty states.
   b. recognizing these births would call for guidelines concerning them.
   c. the numbers are constantly changing.
   d. the Department of Justice doesn't see the need to track these births.

_____ 2. *Read paragraph 9 again.* Statute 611 provides that prisoners' babies be born in local hospitals and that their birth certificates contain no mention of the mother's incarceration
   a. so that the babies will not grow up with this label attached to them.
   b. so that there is no information that would be damaging to the mother's reputation.
   c. because neighborhood hospitals do not want it known that the babies were born there.
   d. so that the babies will not know that their mothers were incarcerated.

Name   Date

_____ 3. *Read paragraph 12 again.* Babies are most often bruised, beaten, or even killed during times when they are being especially demanding. Such mistreatment probably occurs when
  a. the baby is very young.
  b. there is no one available to supervise the mother and baby.
  c. the parents are most likely to be tired, overworked, or unhappy.
  d. the baby is an only child.

22E CRITICAL READING: FACT OR OPINION
Decide if each statement, even if it quotes someone, contains a FACT or OPINION.

_____ 1. *From paragraph 2:* They [the women] are coming to prison faster than men are.

_____ 2. *From paragraph 4:* We essentially take them [babies] for granted rather than take good care of them.

_____ 3. *From paragraph 5:* New York is the only state where infants can stay with their mothers in a prison nursery.

_____ 4. *From paragraph 9:* A baby born in prison will never smile.

_____ 5. *From paragraph 10:* Closeness between mother and child is especially important to Bedford babies because fathers usually play a minor role in their lives.

_____ 6. *From paragraph 11:* The mother, the baby and society are all the better for it.

_____ 7. *From paragraph 15:* She done the best she could.

22F CRITICAL READING: THE WRITER'S CRAFT
Choose the best answer.

_____ 1. *Read paragraphs 2, 3, and 6 again.* The author quotes a number of statistics in order to
  a. build support for her position to allow inmate mothers to keep their newborn babies with them.
  b. impress the reader with her knowledge of the prison system.
  c. criticize other states' prison programs.
  d. emphasize the number of women who benefit from the program.

_____ 2. *Read paragraph 9 again.* The author provides historical information about Bedford Hills Correctional Facility in order to
  a. demonstrate how women's reformatories were maintained in the early 1900s.
  b. prove that any program that has been in effect since 1901 must be good.
  c. emphasize how the infant care program has evolved.
  d. verify that, contrary to popular belief, babies born in prison are happy and secure.

_____ 3. The author ends this selection with
    a. a lecture on prison reform measures.
    b. a summary of the Bedford Hills Correctional Facility program.
    c. a rationale for continuing the program.
    d. a plea for prison reform.

_____ 4. The author's tone throughout this selection is
    a. excitable but informative.
    b. measured and even.
    c. angry yet reasonable.
    d. calm and somewhat vague.

22G   INFORMED OPINION

1. Is it surprising to you that women make up approximately 6 percent of the total national prison population? Why or why not?

2. Do you think it is in an infant's best interest to spend up to the first eighteen months of life with its mother in a prison or prison nursery? Explain your point of view fully.

3. Read paragraphs 3 and 4 again. If the Department of Justice began keeping track of "prison births," what changes (both positive and negative) might occur in the prison system?

How Did You Do?   22 The Babies of Bedford

SKILL (number of items)	Number Correct	Points for Each	Score
Vocabulary (18)	_____ ×	1	= _____
Central Theme and Main Ideas (5)	_____ ×	5	= _____
Major Details (13)	_____ ×	2	= _____
Inferences (3)	_____ ×	3	= _____
Critical Reading: Fact or Opinion (7)	_____ ×	2	= _____
Critical Reading: The Writer's Craft (4)	_____ ×	2	= _____

(Possible Total: 100) *Total* _____

SPEED

Reading Time: _____ Reading Rate (page 351): _____ Words Per Minute

Name   Date

Selection 23

Noise: It Can Kill You

Sylvia Resnick

(1) QUIET (kwi'et): free from disturbance. That's how the dictionary defines this fast disappearing aspect of our everyday life.

(2) When was the last time you experienced the luxury of peace and tranquility in your environment? When did you last listen to the quiet? Or hear the undisturbed song of a bird?

(3) NOISE (noiz): clamor. NOISOME (noi'sum): injurious to health; noxious, disgusting.

(4) America is fast becoming the most noise-infiltrated country on this planet. While we protest (and make some effort to control) the pollution of our environment by noxious gases, industrial wastes, and warn against cigarette smoking, etc., most people in this country go blithely about their business unaware of the vicious killer that is slowly robbing them of their precious gift of hearing.

(5) *Noise. It'll get you if you don't watch out!* Sound like some cute chant a kid might repeat? Think again. The Environmental Protection Agency reports that noise is becoming one of our nation's most serious health hazards. It is one with which every person should and must seriously concern himself. We have become so immune to the extraneous sounds that daily assault our hearing and create havoc with our nerves that most people have developed a kind of elephant's hide where noise is concerned. In many instances being deprived of excessive noise that has become a part of our lives can (and often does) create anxieties. I learned this from personal experience recently.

(6) While visiting relatives on their small farm in a rural area of Wisconsin this past spring, I suddenly found myself overcome by a bad case of the jitters. We were sitting quietly on the porch of the old farmhouse that first night. It was a beautiful night; the sky was clear enough to count each star. I was doing just that, enjoying the stillness that was interrupted only by the chirping of crickets and an occasional croak of a bullfrog from the nearby pond. No airplanes or helicopters buzzed overhead; no motorcycles zoomed by with their engines roaring; there wasn't a stereo being played anywhere within earshot.

(7) After a while I felt myself growing restless and jumping to my feet; I suggested that we take a ride into town. I grew more fidgety by the minute and inside of me was this terrible feeling that something was wrong. Something was *different* all right. It was too quiet for my noise-polluted system.

253

(8) It took me three days to unwind. By that time I realized that I had become so used to the assault on my nerves by a constant barrage of noises that my system simply couldn't adjust to the wonderful stillness of the country. Statistics on what noise can and does do to us, both physically and mentally, explain my case of the jitters.

(9) The World Health Organization defines health as freedom from disease and a state of well-being. One of the prerequisites to the latter is a good night's sleep. Each time your sleep is disturbed or interrupted by noise you experience stress. Stress has been proven in experimental laboratories to raise the cholesterol levels in the blood. Stress is a factor in heart disease and high blood pressure. The correlation of noise to a rise in blood pressure has been documented. Since hypertension is the forerunner to cardio-vascular disease and noise can raise the blood pressure it is vital to the well-being of every person in this country that he be able to sleep through the night undisturbed by unnecessary noise. The more times you are awakened the worse it is.

(10) How often are your nerves jangled throughout the normal course of the day by the sounds of our technological world? Sirens, jets, amplifiers, refuse collectors banging garbage cans, revved up motors, jackhammers on construction sites all contribute to the assault generated by noise.

(11) Scientifically, levels of sound are measured by decibels. Starting with zero, decibels reach a very loud 150 for a jet on takeoff. The degree and constancy of exposure to high decibels of noise can be the difference between good and poor health. Repeated exposure to sound levels of 85 or more decibels can cause permanent hearing loss. In the case of our young people who frequent discotheques where the decibels level usually exceeds 115, and who at home have stereo units that play to a damaging 90 decibels, the warning is out. Leading otologists throughout the country have predicted that today's teenagers and those in their early twenties face a grim future with impaired hearing—the price they will pay for their rash disregard of medically proven evidence that music that blares hath no charm whatsoever.

(12) Is there anything you can do to protect your environment against the lethal menace of noise pollution?

(13) The People's Lobby, a branch of Ralph Nader's Raiders in Los Angeles, suggests the following methods to try.

1. Talk to the person making the noise. In the case of a neighbor playing his stereo too loud or letting a noisy air conditioner run all night, a friendly request to consider your need for rest should bring cooperation.

2. In the case of a neighborhood situation such as a machine that is used to clean a nearby shopping center or anything of that nature, ask the police to take a decibel count. Get a copy of your local noise ordinance and, if the decibel count exceeds the limits set by the law, file a petition with the city attorney. You'll need at least ten signatures and will be assigned a date and time for a hearing on your complaint.

In New York City where a yearly average on construction is around 12,000 and there are some 75–80,000 street repairs, an ordinance has been set limiting decibels for certain types of machinery with fines being imposed of $1,000 per day on convicted offenders.

The townspeople of Mahopac Point, New York went right to the source to create peaceful sleep-in Sunday mornings. A rule incorporated in the community handbook forbids the operation of all machinery until after 10 A.M. This means no lawn mowers, electric saws or drills, or motorbikes to mar the morning hours.

3. Seek the assistance of your local councilman. He can attempt to exert pressure on the person or persons creating the disturbance.

4. Finally, if all else fails to bring some measure of cooperation, seek an all-out publicity campaign. No one likes to be labeled a bad guy publicly. Alert your local newspapers of the situation; contact your local television station. Ask for assistance in publicizing this infringement upon your right to live in a healthful environment. Attend city council meetings and make yourself heard.

How many of these noise pollutants are you falling victim to?

Window Air Conditioner	60 decibels
Electric Typewriter	85 decibels
Vacuum Cleaner	75 decibels
Restaurant at Peak Hour	70 + decibels
Power Lawn Mower	100 decibels
Heavy Traffic	100 decibels
Music Amplified	95 decibels
Helicopter Overhead	100 decibels
Motorcycle	100 + decibels
Garbage Trucks	100 decibels
Jackhammers	105 decibels
Rock Band Concert	130 decibels
Automatic Dishwasher	70 decibels

(14) Form a Citizen's Action Committee in your area. Last year 1,000 residents in the area of Universal Amphitheater on the grounds of Universal Studios met with management of the studio and city and county officials to expound on the very important issue of noise from the Amphitheater during the late spring and summer months when the outdoor facilities provide entertainment, with resulting complaints of excessive and annoying noise that lasts far into the night.

(15) The meeting resulted in the promise of a noise level reading and plans to bring in consultants who would attempt to reduce the noise level of summer concerts by 15 decibels.

(16) Ralph Nader suggests that you urge your congressman to vote for federal funds to research the noise situation in this country and to support legislation directed to control present sources of noise.

(17) If you own a noisy piece of household machinery, write to the manufacturer. Demand action on his part to eliminate noisy parts from household appliances. There is no reason to submit to having your hearing blasted while you are vacuuming. A little money invested by manufacturers of washing machines, vacuum cleaners, air conditioners, and refrigerators can result in lowering the decibel count on these things that make modern day living easier. Machinery can be efficient *and noiseless*.

(18) We have passed our bicentennial year. Our progress has been recorded in the annals of history. Most of it is good. Medical advances have eliminated and found cures for many dread diseases of the past. Transportation has gone from the horse and buggy to jumbo jets that fly across the continent in six hours. Communication is possible to anywhere in the world with the lifting of a telephone receiver. Yet despite our technical advancement made over the past two hundred years we are facing a time when, unless both government and industry take immediate action, we will have to pay dearly for our progress.

(19) The price is unreasonable and unnecessary. Noise is not a fact we should accept and try to ignore. It is an insidious killer—all the more vicious because it robs us of the right to hear the beauty in the world. Since 1940, noise pollution has more than doubled. If *you* sit back and do nothing about this growing menace, we face a bleak future where the sweet sounds of nature will be lost to us in the roar of machinery.

(20) Don't let it happen to you! Activate your own noise pollution prevention program today.

1680 words

Here are some of the more difficult words in "Noise: It Can Kill You."

assault
(paragraph 5)

as·sault (ə sôlt') *n.* ⟦ME *assaut* < OFr *assaut, assalt* < VL **assaltus* < **assalire*: see ASSAIL⟧ **1** a violent attack, either physical or verbal **2** *euphemism for* RAPE¹ **3** *Law* an unlawful threat or unsuccessful attempt to do physical harm to another, causing a present fear of immediate harm **4** *Mil. a)* a sudden attack upon a fortified place *b)* the close-combat phase of an attack —*vt., vi.* to make an assault (upon) —*SYN.* ATTACK —**as·saul'tive** *adj.*

blithely
(paragraph 4)

blithe (blī*th*, blī*th*) *adj.* ⟦ME < OE; ult. < ᴵE base **bhlei-*, to shine, gleam⟧ showing a gay, cheerful disposition; carefree —**blithe'ly** *adv.* —**blithe'ness** *n.*

decibels
(paragraph 11)

dec·i·bel (des'ə bəl', -bel') *n.* ⟦DECI- + BEL⟧ **1** *Acoustics* a numerical expression of the relative loudness of a sound: the difference in decibels between two sounds is ten times the common logarithm of the ratio of their power levels **2** *Electronics, Radio* a numerical expression of the relative differences in power levels of electrical signals equal to ten times the common logarithm of the ratio of the two signal powers Sometimes an absolute reference is used in the power ratio (10^{-16} watt per sq. cm in acoustics, one milliwatt in electronics and radio)

extraneous
(paragraph 5)

ex·tra·ne·ous (eks trā'nē əs, ik strā'-) *adj.* ⟦L *extraneus*, external, foreign < *extra*: see EXTRA-⟧ **1** coming from outside; foreign *[an extraneous substance]* **2** not truly or properly belonging; not essential **3** not pertinent; irrelevant —*SYN.* EXTRINSIC —**ex·tra'ne·ous·ly** *adv.* —**ex·tra'ne·ous·ness** *n.*

fidgety
(paragraph 7)

fidg·et (fij'it) *n.* ⟦< obs. *fidge*, to fidget < ME *fichen* < ? or akin to ON *fikja*, to fidget⟧ **1** the state of being restless, nervous, or uneasy **2** a fidgety person —*vi.* to move about in a restless, nervous, or uneasy way —*vt.* to make restless or uneasy —**the fidgets** restless, uneasy feelings or movements

fidg·et·y (-it ē) *adj.* nervous; uneasy —**fidg'et·i·ness** *n.*

havoc
(paragraph 5)

hav·oc (hav'ek; *also* hav'äk') *n.* ⟦earlier esp. in phrase CRY HAVOC (see below) < ME & Anglo-Fr *havok* < OFr *havot*, prob. < *haver*, to hook, take, *hef*, a hook < Frank **haf-*, to seize: for IE base see HAVE⟧ great destruction and devastation, as that resulting from hurricanes, wars, etc. —*vt.* **-ocked, -ock·ing** [Obs.] to lay waste; devastate —*SYN.* RUIN —**cry havoc 1** orig., to give (an army) the signal for pillaging **2** to warn of great, impending danger —**play havoc with** to devastate; destroy; ruin

infiltrated
(paragraph 4)

in·fil·trate (in fil'trāt, in'fil trāt') *vi., vt.* **-trat·ed, -trat·ing** ⟦IN-¹ + FILTRATE⟧ **1** to pass, or cause (a fluid, cell, etc.) to pass, through small gaps or openings; filter **2** to pass through, as in filtering **3** to pass, or cause (individual troops) to pass, through weak places in the enemy's lines in order to attack the enemy's flanks or rear **4** to penetrate, or cause to penetrate (a region or group) gradually or stealthily, so as to attack or to seize control from within —*n.* something that infiltrates —**in'fil·tra'tion** *n.* —**in'fil·tra'tive** *adj.* —**in'fil'·tra·tor** *n.*

infringement
(paragraph 13)

in·fringe (in frinj') *vt.* **-fringed', -fring'ing** ⟦L *infringere*, to break off, break, impair, violate < *in-*, in + *frangere*, to BREAK⟧ to break (a law or agreement); fail to observe the terms of; violate —*SYN.* TRESPASS —**infringe on** (or **upon**) to break in on; encroach or trespass on (the rights, patents, etc. of others) —**in·fringe'ment** *n.*

insidious
(paragraph 19)

in·sid·i·ous (in sid'ē əs) *adj.* ⟦L *insidiosus* < *insidiae*, an ambush, plot < *insidere*, to sit in or on, lie in wait for < *in-*, in + *sedere*, to SIT⟧ **1** characterized by treachery or slyness; crafty; wily **2** operating in a slow or not easily apparent manner; more dangerous than seems evident *[an insidious disease]* —**in·sid'i·ous·ly** *adv.* —**in·sid'i·ous·ness** *n.*

menace
(paragraph 19)

men·ace (men'əs) *n.* ⟦OFr < L *minacia* < *minax* (gen. *minacis*), projecting, threatening < *minari*, to threaten < *minae*, threats, orig. projecting points of walls < IE base **men-*, to project > Cornish *meneth*, mountain⟧ **1** a threat or the act of threatening **2** anything threatening harm or evil **3** [Colloq.] a person who is a nuisance —*vt., vi.* **-aced, -ac·ing** to threaten or be a danger (to) —*SYN.* THREATEN —**men'ac·ing·ly** *adv.*

Vocabulary List

257

23A   VOCABULARY

From the context of "Noise: It Can Kill You," explain the meaning of each of the vocabulary words shown in boldface below.

1. *From paragraph 4:* America is fast becoming the most noise-**infiltrated** country on this planet.

   _____

   _____

2. *From paragraph 4:* Most people in this country go **blithely** about their business unaware of the vicious killer that is slowly robbing them of their precious gift of hearing.

   _____

   _____

3. *From paragraph 5:* We have become so immune to the **extraneous** sounds that daily **assault** our hearing and create **havoc** with our nerves that most people have developed a kind of elephant's hide where noise is concerned.

   _____

   _____

   _____

   _____

   _____

4. *From paragraph 7:* I grew more **fidgety** by the minute and inside of me was this terrible feeling that something was wrong.

   _____

   _____

5. *From paragraph 11:* Scientifically, levels of sound are measured by **decibels**.

   _____

   _____

6. *From paragraph 13:* Ask for assistance in publicizing this **infringement** upon your right to live in a healthful environment.

   _____

   _____

Name   Date

7. *From paragraph 19:* [Noise] is an **insidious** killer.

_____

_____

_____

8. *From paragraph 19:* If *you* sit back and do nothing about this growing **menace,** we face a bleak future.

_____

_____

_____

23B   CENTRAL THEME AND MAIN IDEAS
Follow the directions for each item below.

_____ 1. *Choose the best answer.* What is the central theme of "Noise: It Can Kill You"?
   a. Noise is harmless if taken in small doses.
   b. People can fight noise pollution in many ways.
   c. Noise is becoming one of the nation's most serious health problems.
   d. We are all going to become deaf if something isn't done about noise pollution.

2. *In your own words, give the main idea of paragraph 9.*

_____

_____

_____

_____ 3. *Choose the best answer.* What is the main idea in paragraph 11?
   a. Leading otologists predict that today's teenagers who listen to loud music face a grim future with impaired hearing.
   b. Repeated exposure to sound decibels of 85 or more can cause permanent hearing loss.
   c. Jet takeoff noise levels reach 150 decibels.
   d. Scientifically, levels of sound are measured by decibels.

Name   Date

23C MAJOR DETAILS
Fill in the word or words that correctly complete each statement.

1. Most people are unaware that noise is a vicious killer that is slowly

   robbing them of their precious gift of _____ .

2. The degree and constancy of exposure to high decibels of noise can be

   the difference between good and poor _____ .

3. Repeated exposure to sound levels of _____ or more
   decibels can cause permanent hearing loss.

4. _____ _____ suggests that you urge your
   congressman to vote for federal funds to research the noise situation

   in this country and to support _____ directed to control
   present sources of noise.

5. The table on page 255 lists _____ major sources of noise
   in our lives.

6. Of the noise pollutants listed in the table on page 255, a

   _____ _____ is the loudest at 130 decibels,

   jackhammers produce _____ decibels, and a

   total of _____ other things create 100 or more decibels.

23D INFERENCES
Choose the best answer.

_____ 1. *Read paragraph 11 again.* Why do teenagers still go to discotheques in the face of these facts?
   a. Most teenagers do not believe health warnings.
   b. Teenagers' need to be part of the "in" group frequently makes
      them disregard health warnings.
   c. Many teenagers feel that medical science will be able to cure
      any hearing impairment they might suffer.
   d. Many teenagers think that the local authorities would not
      permit discotheques to stay in business if they created a hear-
      ing hazard.

_____ 2. *Read paragraph 13 again.* Why are Ralph Nader's investigators called "Raiders"?
a. The group has a reputation of soliciting stockholders' votes to gain control of corporations.
b. The group seeks out and exposes corrupt public officials.
c. The group attacks businesses that create environmental pollution and unsafe products.
d. The group often raids the staffs of other consumer groups to persuade them to join Nader.

23E   CRITICAL READING: FACT OR OPINION
Decide whether each statement contains a FACT or OPINION.

_____ 1. *From paragraph 5:* The Environmental Protection Agency reports that noise is becoming one of our nation's most serious health hazards.

_____ 2. *From paragraph 5:* [Noise] is [a problem] with which every person should and must seriously concern himself.

_____ 3. *From paragraph 9:* The World Health Organization defines health as freedom from disease and a state of well-being.

_____ 4. *From paragraph 11:* Scientifically, levels of sound are measured by decibels.

_____ 5. *From paragraph 19:* If *you* sit back and do nothing about this growing menace, we face a bleak future where the sweet sounds of nature will be lost to us in the roar of machinery.

23F   CRITICAL READING: THE WRITER'S CRAFT
Choose the best answer.

_____ 1. *Read paragraph 17 again.* The topic sentence is
a. at the beginning of the paragraph.
b. in the middle of the paragraph.
c. not stated in the paragraph.
d. at the end of the paragraph.

_____ 2. To add interest to her conclusion, the author
a. tells an amusing anecdote.
b. urges people to action.
c. asks a send-off question.
d. makes a forecast for the future.

261

Name   Date

_____ 3. The table on page 255 does *not*
   a. summarize information.
   b. dramatize information.
   c. debate information.
   d. display information.

23G   INFORMED OPINION

1. After reading "Noise: It Can Kill You," has your attitude toward noise changed at all? Explain.

2. Do you think that if people knew about the danger of noise levels at rock concerts, they would stop attending? Explain.

How Did You Do?   **23** Noise: It Can Kill You

SKILL (number of items)	Number Correct		Points for Each		Score
Vocabulary (8)	_____	×	2	=	_____
Central Theme and Main Ideas (3)	_____	×	5	=	_____
Major Details* (6)	_____	×	4	=	_____
Inferences (2)	_____	×	4	=	_____
Critical Reading: Fact or Opinion (5)	_____	×	3	=	_____
Critical Reading: The Writer's Craft (3)	_____	×	2	=	_____

(Possible Total: 100) *Total* _____

SPEED

Reading Time: _____ Reading Rate (page 351): _____ Words Per Minute

*Question 4 in this exercise calls for two separate answers. Question 6 calls for three separate answers. In computing your score, count each separate answer toward your total score.

Name   Date

Writing: Expressing Yourself

What are *your* ideas on the subjects that you have read about in Part 4 of this book? Now is *your* chance to express your ideas in writing.

Below are some topics to write about. You are not expected to write on all of them, of course. Just select what appeals to you. Or, feel free to make up your own topics. Most important, try to find a subject that moves you to want to express yourself in writing.

All of the topics below relate in some way to the reading selections in Part 4 of this book. Some of the topics have been touched on already in the opening section of Part 4, "Thinking: Getting Started," page 203, or in the Informed Opinion questions that followed each of the reading selections in Part 4. Others of these topics are introduced here for the first time.

The topics below give you a choice among various kinds of writing. You can write a **narrative** that will tell your reader an interesting story. You can write a **description** that will give your reader a vivid picture of the image you have in mind. You can write a **report** that will give your reader important information about a subject, process, or event. You can write an **argument** to try to persuade your reader to agree with you. Differences among these kinds of writing are not always clear-cut, and so you can feel free to use any **combination** that works for you. As you write, see if you can make use of the new vocabulary words that you have been studying in Part 4.

IDEAS FOR PARAGRAPHS

1. Do you enjoy observing nature closely? Being as specific as possible, explain your answer.

2. What is the difference between being called equal and being treated as equal? Using a specific example, describe the difference.

3. Often you read in the newspaper about people who participate in efforts to rescue an animal, such as a cat in a tree or a duckling in a sewer drain. Why do you think people willingly give of their time and effort to rescue stranded animals?

4. Have you ever worked as a volunteer after a natural disaster, such as a floor or tornado? Why did you do this? What were the benefits? Would you do it again? Be specific with your reasons.

5. Imagine your feelings on the day your own son or daughter gets his/her driver's license. What would probably go through your mind? Why?

6. Is the child care "crisis" a real one? Explain in detail why you do or do not think so.

7. Many people have been affected by pollution of one or more sorts—air, water, land, noise, etc. Using specific examples, discuss how pollution has affected you personally.

IDEAS FOR ESSAYS

1. If you have ever been tremendously impressed by something that you have observed in nature, describe what you saw and how it made you feel. Write about the experience so that your readers will be able to imagine that they were there.

2. Can people learn truths about human life from observing animals in their natural settings? Using specific examples, explain your point of view.

3. In 1985 a humpback whale, later affectionately called Humphrey, made an unprecedented visit to San Francisco Bay, and from there to the Sacramento River Delta region, where he remained for twenty-four days. It took $50,000 and the combined efforts of many individuals to persuade him to return from the water of the Delta to the safety of his natural ocean habitat. Do you think the money and man-hours spent in rescuing this whale were justified? Defend your position with specific reasons.

4. If you drive, describe how your life would change if you no longer could. If you do not drive, describe how your life would change if you did. Using specific examples, consider many aspects of the impact, practical as well as intangible matters. Also, try to tie your speculations into your attitude toward issues such as cultural attitudes toward cars and time pressures in modern life.

5. Explain the following statement: "Education and attitudes begin in the crib, and so does crime" ("The Babies of Bedford," paragraph 4).

6. How do you react to loud noise that goes for a long time? Using a specific example, describe how you feel and what, if anything, you try to do about it.

Thinking:
Getting Started

In Part 5, you will encounter a wider variety of types of reading than before in this book. Try to use these selections to the fullest: they are challenging so that you can stretch. You may find that your comprehension, your exercise scores, your reading rate, or other areas slip back somewhat at first. Do not be discouraged. Some kinds of reading are supposed to be slower than other kinds. Also, mistaken answers give you a chance to learn and to catch on to the more subtle aspects of reading. If you have worked through most of Parts 1–4 in this book, you are ready to dig into material that will help you grow stronger as a reader.

Selection 24 will particularly engage you—and your sense of humor—on, between, and beyond the lines. Selection 25 will demand close reading, probably at a somewhat slower pace, and particular attention to vocabulary and to understanding the author's attitude. Selection 26 provides much material to construct in your mind. Selections 27, 28, and 29, taken from textbooks used in college courses, offer you opportunities to practice and reinforce your knowledge of the SQ3R technique, as discussed and illustrated in the opening chapter of this book. Selection 30 has many unspoken subtexts only hinted at by the story, so it allows you, the reader, one of the special joys of reading: the chance to compose a world in the privacy of your mind.

A blood clot the size of this dot can cause a Heart Attack.

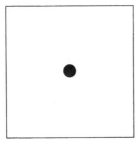

Or a stroke.

Every year, thousands die because of a blood clot. Thousands more become disabled, some permanently.

What's being done to stop it.

Plenty.

We're the American Heart Association. We're giving scientists the chance to find out more about blood clots.

How to detect them. How to treat them. How to keep them from happening.

We're fighting hard. With new drugs. New kinds of treatment. Better ways to help heart attack and stroke victims return to a normal life.

And it's only a part of the total war we're waging against the number one cause of death in this country: heart disease and stroke.

But we can't fight without your money. When the Heart Association volunteer asks for your dollars, be generous.

The blood clot is small, the problem is enormous.

Please give generously to the American Heart Association ♥

WE'RE FIGHTING FOR <u>YOUR</u> LIFE

How does this ad make you feel? How far are you willing to go in order to protect your health? (See "How to Stay Alive.")

What do you know about the workings of the heart? (See "The Heart Beat.")

In what ways does "thinking that you can" help you succeed?

How can parents help their children believe in themselves—even, for example, in the face of prejudice? (See "My Father's Funeral.")

In what ways are people's characters revealed when they have to face prejudice? (See "On Campus: New Interest in Prejudice.")

If they think they can, they can.

© Tom Stack & Associates/Dick Pietrzyk.

Reprinted with permission. © 1982 American Greetings Corp.

Why is it important for people to understand their relation to the forces of nature? (See "Magnetism.")

More on next page . . .

Phyllis Jean Pittman and Mary Cooly Craddock. Eye Talk of Texas.

How do pictographs such as these serve as a "universal language"? (See "How Many Languages?")

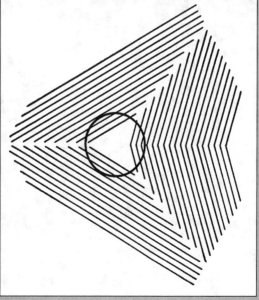

Copyright © 1965 by Dover Publications, Inc.

In this optical illusion, the circle looks distorted because of the superimposed lines. In what ways can you (or can't you) trust what you see and feel? (See "The Chaser.")

How to Stay Alive

Art Hoppe

Once upon a time there was a man named Snadley Klabberhorn who was the healthiest man in the whole wide world.

Snadley wasn't always the healthiest man in the whole wide world. When he was young, Snadley smoked what he wanted, drank what he wanted, ate what he wanted, and exercised only with young ladies in bed. 5

He thought he was happy. "Life is absolutely peachy," he was fond of saying. "Nothing beats being alive."

Then along came the Surgeon General's Report linking smoking to lung cancer, heart disease, emphysema, and tertiary coreopsis. 10

Snadley read about The Great Tobacco Scare with a frown. "Life is so peachy," he said, "that there's no sense taking any risks." So he gave up smoking.

Like most people who went through the hell of giving up smoking, Snadley became more interested in his own health. In fact, he became fas- 15 cinated. And when he read a WCTU tract which pointed out that alcohol caused liver damage, brain damage, and acute *weltanschauung*, he gave up alcohol and drank dietary colas instead.

At least he did until The Great Cyclamate Scare.

"There's no sense in taking any risks," he said. And he switched to 20 sugar-sweetened colas, which made him fat and caused dental caries. On realizing this he renounced colas in favor of milk and took up jogging, which was an awful bore.

That was about the time of The Great Cholesterol Scare.

Snadley gave up milk. To avoid cholesterol, which caused athero- 25 sclerosis, coronary infarcts, and chronic chryselephantinism, he also gave up meat, fats, and dairy products, subsisting on a diet of raw fish.

Then came the Great DDT Scare.

"The presence of large amounts of DDT in fish . . ." Snadley read with anguish. But fortunately that's when he met Ernestine. They were 30 made for each other. Ernestine introduced him to home-ground wheat germ, macrobiotic yogurt, and organic succotash.

They were very happy eating this dish twice daily, watching six hours of color television together, and spending the rest of their time in bed.

They were, that is, until The Great Color Television Scare. 35

"If color tee-vee does give off radiations," said Snadley, "there's no sense taking risks. After all, we still have each other."

And that's about all they had. Until The Great Pill Scare.

On hearing that The Pill might cause carcinoma, thromboses, and lingering stichometry, Ernestine promptly gave up The Pill—and Snadley. "There's no sense taking any risks," she said. 40

Snadley was left with jogging. He was, that is, until he read somewhere that 1.3 percent of joggers are eventually run over by a truck or bitten by rabid dogs.

He then retired to a bomb shelter in his back yard (to avoid being hit 45
by a meteor), installed an air purifier (after The Great Smog Scare) and spent the next 63 years doing Royal Canadian Air Force exercises and poring over back issues of The Reader's Digest.

"Nothing's more important than being alive," he said proudly on reaching 102. But he never did say anymore that life was absolutely 50
peachy.

* * *

CAUTION: Being alive may be hazardous to your health.

520 words

Vocabulary List

Here are some of the more difficult words in "How to Stay Alive."

carcinoma
(line 39)

car·ci·no|ma (kär′sə nō′mə) *n., pl.* **-mas** or **-ma|ta** (-mə tə) [L < Gr *karkinōma*, cancer < *karkinoun*, affect with a cancer < *karkinos*, crab: see CANCER] any of several kinds of cancerous growths deriving from epithelial cells: see SARCOMA —**car′ci·nom′a·tous** (-näm′ə təs, -nō′mə-) *adj.*

chronic
(line 26)

chron|ic (krän′ik) *adj.* [Fr *cronique* < L *chronicus* < Gr *chronikos*, of time < *chronos*, time] **1** lasting a long time or recurring often: said of a disease, and distinguished from ACUTE **2** having had an ailment for a long time [a *chronic* patient] **3** continuing indefinitely; perpetual; constant [a *chronic* worry] **4** by habit, custom, etc.; habitual; inveterate [a *chronic* complainer] —*n.* a chronic patient —**chron′i·cal|ly** *adv.* —**chro·nic·i|ty** (krə nis′ə tē) *n.*
SYN.—**chronic** suggests long duration or frequent recurrence and is used especially of diseases or habits that resist all efforts to eradicate them [*chronic* sinusitis]; **inveterate** implies firm establishment as a result of continued indulgence over a long period of time [an *inveterate* liar]; **confirmed** suggests fixedness in some condition or practice, often from a deep-seated aversion to change [a *confirmed* bachelor]; **hardened** implies fixed tendencies and a callous indifference to emotional or moral considerations [a *hardened* criminal]

coronary
(line 26)

cor|o·nar|y (kôr′ə ner′ē, kär′-) *adj.* [L *coronarius:* see CROWN] **1** of, or in the form of, a crown **2** *Anat. a)* like a crown; encircling *b)* designating or relating to either of two arteries, or their branches, coming from the aorta and supplying blood directly to the heart muscle —☆*n., pl.* **-nar|ies** CORONARY THROMBOSIS

DDT
(line 29)

DDT (dē′dē′tē′) *n.* [*d(ichloro)d(iphenyl)t(richloroethane)*] a powerful insecticide $(ClC_6H_4)_2CHCCl_3$, effective upon contact: its use is restricted by law due to damaging environmental effects

emphysema
(line 10)

em·phy·se|ma (em'fə sē'mə; -zē'-) *n.* [ModL < Gr *emphysēma*, infla-
tion < *emphysaein*, to inflate, blow in < *en-*, in + *physaein*, to blow
< IE **phus-* < base **pu-*, **phu-*, echoic of blowing with puffed
cheeks] **1** an abnormal swelling of body tissues caused by the accumulation of air; esp., such a swelling of the lung tissue, due to the
permanent loss of elasticity, or the destruction, of the alveoli, which
seriously impairs respiration **2** HEAVES —em'phy·se'|ma·tous (-sē'
mə təs, -sem'-) *adj.*

macrobiotic
(line 32)

mac|ro·bi·ot·ics (mak'rō bi ät'iks) *n.pl.* [see MACRO- & -BIOTIC] [*with
sing. v.*] the study of prolonging life, as by special diets, etc. —
mac'ro·bi·ot'|ic *adj.*

weltanschauung
(line 17)

Welt·an·schau·ung (velt'än shou'ooŋ) *n.* [Ger, world view] a comprehensive, esp. personal, philosophy or conception of the universe
and of human life

"How to Stay Alive" has many unusual words in it. To help you read the
essay easily, here are some quick definitions.

tertiary	(line 10)	third
coreopsis	(line 10)	tickseed plant
WCTU	(line 16)	Women's Christian Temperance Union
cholesterol	(line 24)	fatty substances in the blood
atherosclerosis	(line 25–26)	hardening of the arteries
infarcts	(line 26)	obstruction of blood vessels
chryselephantinism	(line 26)	being overlaid with gold and ivory
yogurt	(line 32)	a fermented milk food
succotash	(line 32)	lima beans and corn cooked together
thromboses	(line 39)	blood clots
stichometry	(line 40)	practice of writing prose

24A VOCABULARY

Choose the best answer.

_____ 1. If you had **emphysema** you would
a. be breaking the law.
b. have trouble breathing.
c. get frequent headaches.
d. be unable to digest food.

_____ 2. The word **weltanschauung** is closest in meaning to
a. peptic ulcers.
b. a passion for German opera.
c. cruelty to children.
d. a personal philosophy of life.

Name   Date

_____ 3. The word **coronary** refers to
    a. the arteries leading to the heart.
    b. a medical examiner.
    c. kidney disease.
    d. the arteries leading to the brain.

_____ 4. A **chronic** illness is best described as
    a. painful.
    b. extremely expensive to treat.
    c. continuing indefinitely.
    d. likely to result in death.

_____ 5. **DDT** is best known as
    a. the FBI's list of "most wanted" criminals.
    b. a deadly insecticide.
    c. the cause of high blood pressure.
    d. a foreign sports car.

_____ 6. Anything that is **macrobiotic** is
    a. believed to prolong life.
    b. hazardous to your health.
    c. very delicious.
    d. pornographic.

_____ 7. **Carcinoma** is a medical term for
    a. tuberculosis.
    b. cancer.
    c. heart disease.
    d. measles.

24B CENTRAL THEME

Choose the best answer.

_____ 1. What is the central theme of "How to Stay Alive"?
    a. The secret of living to a ripe old age is avoiding indulgences that are hazardous to your health.
    b. Snadley Klabberhorn enjoyed life until he changed his habits in reaction to every health scare.
    c. Snadley Klabberhorn's main goal was to live to 102 without giving up smoking, drinking, sweets, and color television.
    d. Everyone should disregard health scares and live life to its fullest.

            Name   Date

24C MAJOR DETAILS

Decide whether each detail is true (T), false (F), or not discussed (ND).

_____ 1. Snadley liked to say, "Nothing beats being alive."

_____ 2. With each new health scare, Snadley altered his life to avoid the danger.

_____ 3. The Great Noise Scare led Snadley to wear ear plugs all the time.

_____ 4. Snadley's wife Ernestine refused to give up The Pill even after hearing about its health hazards.

_____ 5. Snadley liked to say, "Nothing beats being healthy."

_____ 6. Snadley finally retired to his bomb shelter to avoid all hazards.

_____ 7. By the time Snadley reached the age of 102, he no longer said that life was absolutely peachy.

24D INFERENCES

Choose the best answer.

_____ 1. "How to Stay Alive" implies that people
   a. should avoid anything that might cause disease.
   b. should live recklessly.
   c. cannot expect to avoid all health hazards.
   d. cannot live long in today's world.

_____ 2. *Read lines 10, 26, and 40 again.* The author uses the words "tertiary coreopsis," "chronic chryselephantinism," and "stichometry," which are not medical terms. Why does he use them?
   a. He thinks big words will impress the reader.
   b. He likes to teach his readers difficult words.
   c. He thinks that they are connected with good health and staying alive.
   d. He is poking fun at the use of big technical words to name well-known diseases.

Name   Date

24E   CRITICAL READING: THE WRITER'S CRAFT

Choose the best answer.

_____ 1. The author starts with the words "once upon a time" because he is writing
   a. a story for young children.
   b. in the style of a fable.
   c. a story for adults.
   d. in the style of a short story.

_____ 2. The author ends with a "caution" which is
   a. a call for government regulations.
   b. a humorous summary.
   c. a key question.
   d. a forecast of the future.

24F   INFORMED OPINION

1. Have you ever changed your habits because of health warnings? Using a specific example of a health warning, explain why you did or did not change your habits.

2. Do you think that health hazards are an avoidable or unavoidable by-product of modern progress? Using specific examples, explain your answer.

How Did You Do?   **24** How to Stay Alive

SKILL (number of items)	Number Correct	Points for Each	Score
Vocabulary (7)	_____ ×	5	= _____
Central Theme (1)	_____ ×	7	= _____
Major Details (7)	_____ ×	6	= _____
Inferences (2)	_____ ×	4	= _____
Critical Reading: The Writer's Craft (2)	_____ ×	4	= _____

(Possible Total: 100) *Total* _____

SPEED

Reading Time: _____ Reading Rate (page 351): _____ Words Per Minute

Name   Date

Selection 25

My Father's Funeral

James Baldwin

It seemed to me, of course, that it was a very long funeral. But it was,
if anything, a rather shorter funeral than most, nor, since there were no
overwhelming, uncontrollable expressions of grief, could it be called—if
I dare to use the word—successful. The minister who preached my
father's funeral sermon was one of the few my father had still been see-   5
ing as he neared his end. He presented to us in his sermon a man whom
none of us had ever seen—a man thoughtful, patient, and forbearing, a
Christian inspiration to all who knew him, and a model for his children.
And no doubt the children, in their disturbed and guilty state, were
almost ready to believe this; he had been remote enough to be anything   10
and, anyway, the shock of the incontrovertible, that it was really our
father lying up there in that casket, prepared the mind for anything. His
sister moaned and this grief-stricken moaning was taken as corroboration. The other faces held a dark, noncommittal thoughtfulness. This was
not the man they had known, but they had scarcely expected to be con-   15
fronted with *him;* this was, in a sense deeper than questions of fact, the
man they had not known, and the man they had not known may have
been the real one. The real man, whoever he had been, had suffered and
now he was dead: this was all that was sure and all that mattered now.
Every man in the chapel hoped that when his hour came he, too, would   20
be eulogized, which is to say forgiven, and that all of his lapses, greeds,
errors, and strayings from the truth would be invested with coherence
and looked upon with charity. This was perhaps the last thing human
beings could give each other and it was what they demanded, after all, of
the Lord. Only the Lord saw the midnight tears, only He was present   25
when one of His children, moaning and wringing hands, paced up and
down the room. When one slapped one's child in anger the recoil in the
heart reverberated through heaven and became part of the pain of the
universe. And when the children were hungry and sullen and distrustful
and one watched them, daily, growing wilder, and further away, and run-   30
ning headlong into danger, it was the Lord who knew what the charged
heart endured as the strap was laid to the backside; the Lord alone who
knew what one *would* have said if one had had, like the Lord, the gift of
the living word. It was the Lord who knew of the impossibility every parent in that room faced: how to prepare the child for the day when the   35
child would be despised and how to *create* in the child—by what
means?—a stronger antidote to this poison than one had found for one-

self. The avenues, side streets, bars, billiard halls, hospitals, police stations, and even the playgrounds of Harlem—not to mention the houses of correction, the jails, and the morgue— 40 testified to the potency of the poison while remaining silent as to the efficacy of whatever antidote, irresistibly raising the question of whether or not such an antidote existed; raising, which was worse, the question of whether or not an antidote was desirable; perhaps poison should be fought with poison. 45 With these several schisms in the mind and with more terrors in the heart than could be named, it was better not to judge the man who had gone down under an impossible burden. It was better to remember: *Thou knowest this man's fall; but thou knowest not his wrassling.* 50

630 words

Here are some of the more difficult words in "My Father's Funeral."

Vocabulary List

antidote
(line 37)

an|ti·dote (ant'ə dōt') *n.* [ME & OFr *antidote* < L *antidotum* < Gr *antidoton* < *anti-*, against + *dotos*, given < *didonai*, to give: see DATE¹] **1** a remedy to counteract a poison **2** anything that works against an evil or unwanted condition —**an'ti·dot'al** *adj.*

coherence
(line 22)

co·her·ence (kō hir'əns; *also*, -her'-) *n.* [Fr < L *cohaerentia* < *cohaerens*, prp. of COHERE] **1** the act or condition of cohering; cohesion **2** the quality of being logically integrated, consistent, and intelligible; congruity [his story lacked *coherence*] **3** *Physics* that property of a set of waves or sources of waves in which the oscillations maintain a fixed relationship to each other Also **co·her'en|cy**

corroboration
(lines 13–14)

cor·rob|o·rate (kə räb'ə rāt') *vt.* -rat|ed, -rat'ing [< L *corroboratus*, pp. of *corroborare*, to strengthen < *com-*, intens. + *roborare* < *robur*, strength: see ROBUST] **1** *orig.*, to strengthen **2** to make more certain the validity of; confirm; bolster; support [evidence to *corroborate* his testimony] —**SYN.** CONFIRM —**cor·rob'o·ra'tion** *n.* —**cor·rob'o·ra'-tor** *n.*

efficacy
(line 42)

ef·fi·ca·cy (ef'i kə sē) *n., pl.* **-cies** [ME & OFr *efficace* < L *efficacia* < *efficax*: see EFFICACIOUS] power to produce effects or intended results; effectiveness

eulogized
(line 21)

eu·lo·gize (yōō'lə jīz') *vt.* **-gized', -giz'ing** to praise highly; compose a eulogy about; extol —*SYN.* PRAISE —eu'lo·gist or eu'lo·giz'er *n.*

eu·lo·gy (yōō'lə jē) *n., pl.* **-gies** [ME *euloge* < ML *eulogia* < Gr, praise, lit., fine language (in LXX & N.T., blessing) < *eulegein*, to speak well of, bless: see EU- & -LOGY] **1** speech or writing in praise of a person, event, or thing; esp., a formal speech praising a person who has recently died **2** high praise; commendation —*SYN.* TRIBUTE

forbearing
(line 7)

for·bear¹ (fôr ber') *vt.* **-bore'** or **-bare', -borne', -bear'ing** [ME *forberen* < OE *forberan*: see FOR- & BEAR¹] **1** to refrain from; avoid or cease (doing, saying, etc.) **2** [Now Chiefly Dial.] to endure; tolerate —*vi.* **1** to refrain or abstain **2** to keep oneself in check; control oneself under provocation —*SYN.* REFRAIN¹ —for·bear'er *n.* —for·bear'ing·ly *adv.*

incontrovertible
(line 11)

in·con·tro·vert·i·ble (in' kän'trə vurt'ə bəl) *adj.* that cannot be controverted; not disputable or debatable; undeniable —in'con'tro·vert'·i·bil'i·ty *n.* —in'con'tro·vert'i·bly *adv.*

reverberated
(line 28)

re·ver·ber·ate (-bə rāt'; *for adj.,* -bə rit) *vt.* **-at'ed, -at'ing** [< L *reverberatus,* pp. of *reverberare,* to beat back, repel < *re-*, again + *verberare,* to beat < *verber,* a lash, whip, akin to VERBENA] **1** to cause (a sound) to reecho **2** *a)* to reflect (light, etc.) *b)* to deflect (heat, flame, etc.), as in a reverberatory furnace **3** to subject to treatment in a reverberatory furnace or the like —*vi.* **1** to reecho or resound **2** *a)* to be reflected, as light or sound waves *b)* to be deflected, as heat or flame in a reverberatory furnace **3** to recoil; rebound **4** to have repercussions, as an event or action [a governmental decision *reverberating* throughout the entire economy] —*adj.* [Rare] reverberated

schisms
(line 46)

schism (siz'əm; *occas.* skiz'əm) *n.* [ME *scisme* < OFr *cisme* < LL(Ec) *schisma* < Gr < *schizein,* to cleave, cut: see SCHIZO-] **1 a** split or division in an organized group or society, esp. a church, as the result of difference of opinion, of doctrine, etc. **2** the act of causing or trying to cause a split or division in a church **3** any of the sects, parties, etc. formed by such a split

sullen
(line 29)

sul·len (sul'ən) *adj.* [ME *solein,* alone, solitary < VL *solanus,* alone < L *solus,* alone, SOLE²] **1** showing resentment and ill humor by morose, unsociable withdrawal **2** gloomy; dismal; sad; depressing **3** somber; dull [*sullen* colors] **4** slow-moving; sluggish **5** [Obs.] baleful; threatening —sul'len·ly *adv.* —sul'len·ness *n.*

25A VOCABULARY

Using the vocabulary words listed on pages 276–277, fill in the blanks.

1. The shock of the assassination of Martin Luther King

   _____ throughout the free world.

2. James Baldwin suffered several _____ in the mind
   when thinking about his father.

3. At least one witness was needed for _____ of the criminal charges against Mr. Simmons.

4. Some writing is difficult to read because it lacks

   _____ .

5. The doctor carried an _____ for snakebite.

6. The _____ of the new treatment for cancer will not be
   fully known for years.

7. His _____ nature helped him abstain from punishing
   his son too severely.

8. It is an _____ fact that Robert is brilliant.

9. Upon his death, Franklin D. Roosevelt was _____ in
   every church throughout the United States.

10. After being accused of a crime he did not commit, the young student

    became _____ .

25B CENTRAL THEME

Choose the best answer.

_____ 1. What is the central theme of "My Father's Funeral"?
   a. It was a very long funeral.
   b. The eulogy of the author's father revealed a kind and inspir-
      ing man.
   c. The author's father had a hard life.
   d. Everyone knew of the sins of the author's father but not of his
      agony.

Name   Date

25C MAJOR DETAILS

Write YES if the statement is made in "My Father's Funeral," and write NO if it is not.

_____ 1. It seemed to be a long funeral.

_____ 2. No one could quite recognize the author's deceased father from the way the minister described him.

_____ 3. No one mourned out loud at the funeral.

_____ 4. Each person in the chapel hoped he would be forgiven for his errors when his time came.

_____ 5. The author's father never slapped or used a strap on his children.

25D INFERENCES

Choose the best answer.

_____ 1. Why were the children at the funeral in a "guilty state" (line 9)?
   a. They had not visited their father even once while he was on his deathbed.
   b. They had purchased a very inexpensive casket for their father.
   c. They felt guilty for being bored at their father's funeral.
   d. They could not remember their father in the way the minister was eulogizing him.

_____ 2. What does the author mean by "perhaps poison should be fought with poison" (line 46)?
   a. Discrimination is a type of poison that sometimes must be resisted with similar antisocial action.
   b. The use of poisonous substances may be a way of fighting those who try to hurt us.
   c. The father's death was caused by a poison for which the only antidote was another poison.
   d. The father had thought of killing his children to keep them from growing up in such a poisonous society.

25E CRITICAL READING: THE WRITER'S CRAFT

Choose the best answer.

_____ 1. The author starts his description with a
   a. portrait.
   b. definition.
   c. fact.
   d. contrast.

Name   Date

_____ 2. If the word "wrassling" (line 50) were replaced by the word "suffering," what tone would be missing?
   a. informality
   b. anger
   c. fear
   d. seriousness

25F INFORMED OPINION

1. Do you think people should say only good things about a loved one who has died? Explain your point of view, being as specific as possible.

2. *Read lines 35–36 again.* If you had a child and had "to prepare the child for the day when the child would be despised," what kind of training and preparation would you provide? Using specific examples, explain your answer.

How Did You Do?   **25** My Father's Funeral

SKILL (number of items)	Number Correct	Points for Each		Score
Vocabulary (10)	_____	×	4	= _____
Central Theme (1)	_____	×	9	= _____
Major Details (5)	_____	×	7	= _____
Inferences (2)	_____	×	4	= _____
Critical Reading: The Writer's Craft (2)	_____	×	4	= _____

(Possible Total: 100) *Total* _____

SPEED

Reading Time: _____ Reading Rate (page 351): _____ Words Per Minute

Name   Date

On Campus: New Interest in Prejudice

Jamie Talan

(1) Jack Levin—sociologist, writer and teacher of a course on the nature of prejudice—tries not to offend any one group of people. When he talks about prejudice and discrimination, he includes people of all ages, colors, heights, weights and sexes. "I have to be careful," Levin said. "I talk about all kinds of prejudice. If I were to talk about racial prejudice exclusively, I'd have seven people in my class." Indeed, Levin turned away students last semester, and still 180 students packed his twice-weekly class at Northeastern University in Boston.

(2) There were years when Levin's class—and similar courses taught nationwide—had dwindling enrollments. However, over the last few years student interest has increased. Researchers aren't sure why. Levin suspects that there is a relationship between higher enrollments and an unexplained increase in the number of racial incidents occurring around the country.

(3) Researchers define prejudice as an opinion formed before the facts are known. Discrimination would be acting on such beliefs. During the 1960s, the heyday of the civil rights movement, courses in race and prejudice were jammed with young adults eager to learn about the issues that divided people by color, age, and sex. At the same time, sociologists and psychologists had high hopes of explaining why people discriminated against certain groups. What was at the heart of prejudice? Was it a personality flaw or an attitude reinforced by mainstream society? Decades of study have not brought any concrete answers. Researchers who analyze trends say behavior toward minority groups has changed for the better, but they admit that underlying attitudes—the feelings that can lead to certain behavior—may be as they were decades, perhaps centuries, ago.

(4) Some of Levin's students say they are taking the course to understand the role prejudice plays in their lives. For example, there is Mary Rogers. A 23-year-old with blonde hair, hazel eyes and freckles, she has taken this course, she said, because she comes from an interracial family. Three of her six brothers and sisters are adopted; two are mulatto and one is half white, half Vietnamese. In a soft, shy voice, she added, "If I hated everyone who was prejudiced, I would have no friends."

(5) And there is Victor Rivera who left Puerto Rico to attend college in America. His chiseled features, friendly smile and open eyes invite many people into his world. But once they learn he is not French or Italian but Puerto Rican, the friendships are over. "I lost my human privileges in America," he said. "I have had people literally stop talking in mid-sentence when they learn where I come from."

(6) Students in Levin's class didn't have to think too long about discrimination. Some are overweight. Others are in their 50s—considered "old" among college students. Some are light-skinned, others dark. Some are foreigners on American soil, some are Americans on what feels like foreign soil. And they all share stories that make prejudice more than an abstract notion of somebody else's problem. One black student recalled a white teacher's telling him that his lips were too thick to play the trumpet. A slim woman described what it had felt like being a 165-pound 12-year-old.

(7) Levin, concerned about the recent number of racial attacks around the country, said courses on prejudice may help quell such attacks. He added that talking about age and sex discrimination helps pave the way for discussions of racial discrimination. During the 1986–87 school year, there were racial fights at such top schools as Columbia University, the University of Massachusetts and the University of Michigan. The brutal attack on black teenagers by whites in Howard Beach continues to draw national public attention. The incident led to the death of one black teenager, who was killed by a car while fleeing the attackers. "It's very disturbing. You have violent incidents occurring everywhere," said Gary Rubin of the American Jewish Committee.

(8) Such incidents confuse researchers in the field who have been documenting a positive change in racial attitudes over the last three decades. Polls conducted yearly to measure changes in racial attitudes suggest that the distinctions between the races have narrowed, Rubin said. But he and others wonder whether the decline in negative attitudes towards minorities is real or whether the polls are not telling the whole story.

(9) Tom W. Smith, a senior study director of the National Opinion Research Center at the University of Chicago, is in charge of annual surveys of 1,300 whites. The organization asks a series of questions to judge racial attitudes and behaviors. Recently, similar groups of blacks have been polled. The findings suggest that attitudes are moving in a positive direction. For example, in 1942, 70 percent of whites surveyed favored separate schools for blacks and whites. In 1976, 17.4 percent were still in favor of separation. Almost a decade later, in 1985, the number fell to 8.5 percent, low enough for the survey team to delete the question in future polls. Another question that was dropped: Should whites be hired before blacks for a job? In 1944, 58 percent said yes. In 1963, 17 percent agreed.

And in 1972, the number dropped to 4 percent. In 1958, only 37 percent of whites said they would be willing to vote for a black presidential candidate. This increased to 75 percent in 1977. In 1986, it was 84 percent.

(10) Researchers admit that such trends could indicate that people are less willing to tell the truth and that the underlying feelings of discrimination remain deeply ingrained in society. Sociologist Howard Schuman, program director of the Survey Research Center at the University of Michigan, suspects that people interviewed feel pressured to answer in specific ways that conform with the general norms and values of contemporary society: "Nobody knows what their underlying feelings are. We measure what people think they should feel."

(11) Regarding the increase in racial incidents around the nation, Schuman, co-author of "Racial Attitudes in America: Trends and Interpretations" (Harvard University Press), said: "We won't know for several years if there has been a step backwards in racial attitudes."

(12) Back in the 1950s, researchers supported the notion that prejudice, particularly racially motivated, was a personality trait describing an authoritarian personality. Today, there is more emphasis on a behavioral view. According to Norval Glenn, Ashbel Smith professor of sociology at the University of Texas, Austin, "We don't have the cognitive or perceptual ability to see people as individuals. Instead, we see them in groups, stereotypes. It serves a psychological purpose." Bernard Kramer, a sociologist at the University of Massachusetts, added, "There are so many stimuli impinging on the mind that humans need rough and ready ideas—stereotypes—to cope with the information overload."

(13) Kramer has spent three decades studying racial prejudice. Unfortunately, he said, little has *really* changed in that time. Despite the civil rights movement and laws making job discrimination illegal, "The gap between whites and blacks remains quite substantial: income, education, housing. Discrimination is not legal but is still practiced," he said. "I think that the white population in general has moved away from its genuine support for the black community. If I were black, I'd say these were bad times. In the 1960s, at least there was a light at the end of the tunnel."

(14) Modern research on prejudice suggests he may be right. A classic example is the following experiment: White subjects receive a telephone call. The person calling is frantic. His car broke down and he is calling Joe's Garage. The subject tells the caller he has the wrong number, but the caller must get through to Joe's Garage and doesn't have another dime. Might the subject place the call? Half the callers were black, half white. In one experiment, about 80 percent of people who got "white" voices made a call to Joe's Garage, but only 20 percent responded in kind to the "black" voices.

(15) Sociologists and psychologists continue to hope that change may come from the students who are willing to look at their own ideas about prejudice. They are happy with the increased enrollments.

(16) "It never fails," said Kramer, who teaches a course on the nature of prejudice. "A number of students come up and say they never knew these things happen. I talk about slavery and the Holocaust and they are tremendously moved. Maybe they will act and think differently."

1396 words

Vocabulary List

Here are some of the more difficult words in "On Campus: New Interest in Prejudice."

cognitive
(paragraph 12)

cog·ni·tion (käg nish'ən) *n.* ⟦ME *cognicioun* < L *cognitio*, knowledge < *cognitus*, pp. of *cognoscere*, to know < *co-*, together + *gnoscere*, KNOW⟧ 1 the process of knowing in the broadest sense, including perception, memory, and judgment 2 the result of such a process; perception, conception, etc. —**cog·ni'tion|al** *adj.* —**cog'ni·tive** (-nə tiv) *adj.*

conform
(paragraph 10)

con·form (kən fôrm') *vt.* ⟦ME *conformen* < OFr *conformer* < L *conformare*, to fashion, form < *com-*, together + *formare*, to FORM⟧ 1 to make the same or similar /to *conform* one's idea to another's/ 2 to bring into harmony or agreement; adapt: often used reflexively — *vi.* 1 to be or become the same or similar 2 to be in accord or agreement /the house *conforms* to specifications/ 3 to behave in a conventional way, esp. in accepting without question customs, traditions, prevailing opinion, etc. 4 *Eng. History* to adhere to the practices of the Anglican Church —*SYN.* ADAPT, AGREE —**con·form'|er** *n.* —**con·form'ism** *n.* —**con·form'ist** *n.*

documenting
(paragraph 8)

doc|u·ment (däk'yo͞o mənt, -yə-; *for v.,* -ment') *n.* ⟦ME & OFr < L *documentum*, lesson, example, proof < *docere*, to teach: see DECENT⟧ 1 anything printed, written, etc., relied upon to record or prove something 2 anything serving as proof —*vt.* 1 to provide with a document or documents 2 to provide (a book, pamphlet, etc.) with documents or supporting references 3 to prove, as by reference to documents —**doc'|u·men'tal** (-ment''l) *adj.*

dwindling
(paragraph 2)

dwin·dle (dwin'dəl) *vi.*, *vt.* **-dled, -dling** ⟦freq. of obs. *dwine*, to languish, fade < ME *dwinen* < OE *dwinan*, akin to ON *dvína* < IE base *dheu-*: see DIE¹⟧ to keep on becoming or making smaller or less; diminish; shrink —*SYN.* DECREASE

heyday
(paragraph 3)

hey·day (hā'dā') *n.* ⟦ME *hei dai*, full daylight, well on in the day < *hei*, HIGH + *dai*, DAY⟧ the time of greatest health, vigor, success, prosperity, etc.; prime —*interj.* ⟦earlier *heyda* prob. < (or akin to) Ger & Dan *heida*, Du *heidaar*, hey there!: see HEY⟧ [Archaic] an exclamation of surprise, joy, or wonder

Holocaust
(paragraph 16)

hol·o·caust (häl′ə kôst′, hō′lə-; *also* hô′lə-, hul′ə-) *n.* ⟦ME < OFr *holocauste* < LL(Ec) *holocaustum*, a whole burnt offering < Gr *holokauston* (neut. of *holokaustos*), burnt whole < *holos*, whole (see HOLO-) + *kaustos*, burnt: see CAUSTIC⟧ **1** an offering the whole of which is burned; burnt offering **2** great or total destruction of life, esp. by fire [*nuclear holocaust*] —☆**the Holocaust** [*also* h-] the systematic destruction of over six million European Jews by the Nazis before and during World War II

Impinging
(paragraph 12)

im·pinge (im pinj′) *vi.* -pinged′, -ping′ing ⟦L *impingere* < *in-*, in + *pangere*, to strike: see FANG⟧ **1** *a)* to strike, hit, or dash (*on, upon,* or *against* something) *b)* to touch (*on* or *upon*); have an effect [an idea that *impinges* on one's mind] **2** to make inroads or encroach (*on* or *upon* the property or rights of another) —im·pinge′ment *n.* —im·ping′er *n.*

Ingrained
(paragraph 10)

in·grained (in′grānd′, -grānd′) *adj.* **1** *a)* worked into the fiber *b)* firmly fixed or established [*ingrained* principles] **2** inveterate; thoroughgoing [an *ingrained* liar]

mulatto
(paragraph 4)

mu·lat·to (mə lät′ō, -lat′ō; myoo͞-) *n., pl.* -toes *or* -tos ⟦Sp & Port *mulato*, mulatto, of mixed breed, orig. young mule < *mulo*, mule < L *mulus*⟧ **1** a person who has one black parent and one white parent **2** technically, any person with mixed black and Caucasoid ancestry —*adj.* **1** of a mulatto **2** of the light-brown color of a mulatto's skin

norms
(paragraph 10)

norm (nôrm) *n.* ⟦L *norma*, carpenter's square, rule, prob. via Etr < Gr *gnōmōn*, carpenter's square, lit., one that knows: see GNOMON⟧ a standard, model or pattern for a group; esp., *a)* such a standard of achievement as represented by the median or average achievement of a large group *b)* a standard of conduct that should or must be followed *c)* a way of behaving typical of a certain group —*SYN.* AVERAGE

perceptual
(paragraph 12)

per·cep·tion (pər sep′shən) *n.* ⟦L *perceptio* < pp. of *percipere:* see PERCEIVE⟧ **1** *a)* the act of perceiving or the ability to perceive; mental grasp of objects, qualities, etc. by means of the senses; awareness; comprehension *b)* insight or intuition, or the faculty for these **2** the understanding, knowledge, etc. gotten by perceiving, or a specific idea, concept, impression, etc. so formed —per·cep′tion·al *adj.*

quell
(paragraph 7)

quell (kwel) *vt.* ⟦ME *quellen* < OE *cwellan*, to kill, akin to *qwalu*, death, Ger *quälen*, torment, afflict < IE base *gwel-*, to stab, pain, death > OIr *at-baill*, (he) dies⟧ **1** to crush; subdue; put an end to **2** to quiet; allay —*n.* [Obs.] a killing; murder —quell′er *n.*

stereotypes
(paragraph 12)

ster·e·o·type (ster′ē ə tip′, stir′-) *n.* ⟦Fr *stéréotype*, adj.: see STEREO- & -TYPE⟧ **1** a one-piece printing plate cast in type metal from a mold (*matrix*) taken of a printing surface, as a page of set type **2** STEREOTYPY **3** an unvarying form or pattern; specif., a fixed or conventional notion or conception, as of a person, group, idea, etc., held by a number of people, and allowing for no individuality, critical judgment, etc. —*vt.* -typed′, -typ′ing **1** to make a stereotype of **2** to print from stereotype plates —ster′e·o·typ′er *or* ster′e·o·typ′ist *n.*

285

26A VOCABULARY

From the context of "On Campus: New Interest in Prejudice," explain the meaning of each of the vocabulary words shown in boldface below.

1. *From paragraph 2:* There were years when Levin's class . . . had **dwindling** enrollments.

   _____

   _____

2. *From paragraph 3:* During the 1960s, the **heyday** of the civil rights movement, courses in race and prejudice were jammed with young adults.

   _____

   _____

3. *From paragraph 4:* Three of her six brothers and sisters are adopted; two are **mulatto** and one is half white, half Vietnamese.

   _____

   _____

4. *From paragraph 7:* Levin, concerned about the recent number of racial attacks around the country, said courses on prejudice may help **quell** such attacks.

   _____

   _____

5. *From paragraph 8:* Such incidents confuse researchers in the field who have been **documenting** a positive change in racial attitudes.

   _____

   _____

6. *From paragraph 10:* Researchers admit that such trends could indicate that people are less willing to tell the truth and that the underlying feelings of discrimination remain deeply *ingrained* in society.

   _____

   _____

Name   Date

7. *From paragraph 10:* Sociologist Howard Schuman . . . suspects that people interviewed feel pressured to answer in specific ways that **conform** with the general **norms** and values of contemporary society.

_____

_____

_____

_____

8. *From paragraph 12:* We don't have the **cognitive** or **perceptual** ability to see people as individuals. Instead, we see them in groups, **stereotypes**.

_____

_____

_____

_____

_____

_____

9. *From paragraph 12:* There are so many stimuli **impinging** on the mind that humans need rough and ready ideas . . . to cope with the information overload.

_____

_____

_____

_____

10. *From paragraph 16:* I talk about slavery and the **Holocaust** and they are tremendously moved.

_____

_____

_____

_____

| Name | Date |

26B CENTRAL THEME AND MAIN IDEAS
Follow the directions for each item below.

_____ 1. *Choose the best answer.* What is the central theme of "On Campus: New Interest in Prejudice"?
   a. Enrollment is at an all-time high in college courses about prejudice, and many students have to be turned away because of filled classes.
   b. Sociologists hope that the popularity of college classes about prejudice will lead students who take the courses to be less prejudiced in their thoughts and actions.
   c. In spite of polls showing the decline of prejudice, negative attitudes towards minorities, particularly racial minorities, are still common.
   d. Prejudice based on age, sex, or weight is as common and destructive as is racial prejudice.

2. *In your own words, give the main idea of paragraph 3.*

_____

_____

_____

_____ 3. *Choose the best answer.* What is the main idea of paragraph 12?
   a. Since the 1950s, researchers have known that prejudiced people have overly authoritarian personalities.
   b. People who are comfortable only when they are with groups of people like themselves tend to be prejudiced against anyone outside their group.
   c. People who rely on stereotypes have psychological problems caused by weak cognitive and perceptual skills.
   d. Many people rely on stereotypes as a way of coping with information overload.

4. *In your own words, give the main idea of paragraph 14.*

_____

_____

_____

Name   Date

26C MAJOR DETAILS

Fill in the word or words that correctly complete each statement.

1. Student interest in _____ has increased over the last few years.

2. In his course on prejudice, Jack Levin discusses the problems of people of all _____ , _____ , _____ , _____ , and _____ .

3. Prejudice is an _____ formed before the facts are known.

4. _____ is the result of acting on beliefs based on prejudiced opinions.

5. During the 1960s, _____ and _____ wanted to find out why people discriminate against one another.

6. _____ of study have not brought any concrete answers.

7. Behavior toward minority groups has changed for the _____ .

8. However, underlying _____ may not have changed.

9. Levin's students sometimes share their experiences; Mary Rogers spoke of the difficulties of coming from an _____ family, and Victor Rivera said that he feels he has lost his human _____ when people find out he comes from _____ .

10. Annual polls to measure racial attitudes indicate that race relations are _____ ; for example, the percentage of whites who want separate schools for blacks and whites fell from _____ percent in 1942 to _____ percent in 1985.

11. The National Opinion Research Center surveys _____

    whites annually; recently _____ have also been

    _____ .

12. People interviewed might feel _____ to answer in specific ways.

13. Many people use _____ in their thinking to help them
    cope with the information overload.

14. Discrimination is often still practiced, even though it is

    _____ .

15. Sociologists and psychologists hope that change may come from

    the _____ who are willing to look at their own ideas
    about prejudice.

16. Many of the students in today's classes on prejudice are shocked to

    learn about _____ and the _____ .

26D INFERENCES
Choose the best answer.

_____ 1. *Read paragraph 1 again.* Why does Jack Levin feel fewer students
    would take his class if only racial prejudice were discussed?
    a. People think they already know all they need to about racial
       prejudice from reading newspapers and watching television
       news and documentaries.
    b. He thinks that racial prejudice is a problem that interests only
       members of minority groups, and even many people who are
       minorities do not want to discuss their situation publicly.
    c. Most people feel racial prejudice is not their problem; by
       broadening the definition of prejudice to include all types,
       Levin enables more students to identify and become interested in the topic before he focuses on racial prejudice.
    d. He believes that students would fear that class would become
       a series of political debates between the teacher and radical
       students from the minority and majority groups.

Name   Date

_____ 2. *Read paragraph 2 again.* What might be the connection between rising enrollment in classes about prejudice and the increased number of racial incidents?

   a. People who learn about these incidents are shocked and want to understand what motivates such behavior.

   b. When the media heavily publicize problems in race relations, students become more interested in studying the history of prejudice.

   c. As people realize that racial prejudice takes many forms, the victims are coming to college seeking explanations for what has happened to them and gathering information for lawsuits.

   d. The students at Northeastern University are eager to avoid racial incidents, so they hope to learn what to do to prevent prejudiced behavior.

_____ 3. *Read paragraph 6 again.* Why do some Americans in these classes feel as if they are on foreign soil?

   a. They grew up in homes where English was not spoken, so that they do not speak English fluently and without an accent.

   b. The college has many rules that the students are not used to, and so they feel they are living in a strange country that almost seems like a dictatorship.

   c. They feel isolated because they often hear people on campus speaking languages other than English, and they think that they are not in the United States.

   d. They are not comfortable in college yet because the academic world is very different from any other situation they have ever been in.

_____ 4. *Read paragraphs 10 and 11 again.* Why might people be less willing to tell the truth and more likely to feel pressured to answer in specific ways?

   a. They want to convince themselves that they are not prejudiced, so they answer to please themselves, not to be truthful.

   b. The researchers are members of minority groups, and the people answering questions do not want to hurt the researchers' feelings.

   c. The people being polled want the researchers to stop bothering them, so they give the researchers the answers they seem to want to hear.

   d. Because we live in a computerized age, some respondents know that the government will find out how they answered and will investigate them.

Name   Date

26E CRITICAL READING: FACT OR OPINION

Decide whether each statement, even if it quotes someone, contains a FACT or OPINION.

_____ 1. *From paragraph 1:* Levin turned away students last semester, and still 180 students packed his twice-weekly class at Northeastern University in Boston.

_____ 2. *From paragraph 3:* Researchers who analyze trends say behavior toward minority groups has changed for the better.

_____ 3. *From paragraph 4:* "If I hated everyone who was prejudiced, I would have no friends."

_____ 4. *From paragraph 5:* "I have had people literally stop talking in mid-sentence when they learn where I come from."

_____ 5. *From paragraph 6:* Students in Levin's class didn't have to think too long about discrimination.

_____ 6. *From paragraph 6:* Others are in their 50s—considered "old" among college students.

_____ 7. *From paragraph 6:* A slim woman described what it had felt like being a 165-pound 12-year-old.

_____ 8. *From paragraph 7:* Courses on prejudice may help quell such attacks.

_____ 9. *From paragraph 8:* The distinctions between the races have narrowed.

_____10. *From paragraph 10:* Such trends could indicate that people are less willing to tell the truth and that the underlying feelings of discrimination remain deeply ingrained in society.

26F CRITICAL READING: THE WRITER'S CRAFT

Choose the best answer.

_____ 1. To get the reader's interest, the author starts by
   a. introducing an authority on the subject.
   b. giving a specific example.
   c. giving a definition.
   d. telling an amusing anecdote.

_____ 2. To support her argument, the author uses all of the following *except*
   a. statistics.
   b. quotations from scholars and average people.
   c. summaries of legal actions.
   d. comparisons of legal actions.

_____ 3. The author shows connections between her ideas with all of these words *except:*
   a. indeed   (paragraph 1)
   b. however   (2)
   c. at the same time   (3)
   d. but   (3)
   e. for example   (4)
   f. because   (4)
   g. and there is   (5)
   h. but once   (5)
   i. and   (6)
   j. recently   (9)
   k. almost a decade later (9)
   l. another   (9)
   m. today   (12)
   n. according to   (12)
   o. instead   (12)
   p. unfortunately   (13)

_____ 4. In the final two paragraphs, the author concludes her essay by
   a. summarizing her main points.
   b. pointing to the future with hope.
   c. quoting a student.
   d. pointing to the future with despair.

26G   INFORMED OPINION

1. Why do you think people enroll in college classes on prejudice? Using specific examples, explain your answer.

2. Do you think prejudice of all the types discussed in the essay is lessening? Using specific examples, explain your answer.

Name   Date

How Did You Do?

26 On Campus: New Interest in Prejudice

SKILL (number of items)	Number Correct		Points for Each		Score
Vocabulary (10)	_____	×	2	=	_____
Central Theme and Main Ideas (4)	_____	×	4	=	_____
Major Details* (28)	_____	×	1	=	_____
Inferences (4)	_____	×	3	=	_____
Critical Reading: Fact or Opinion (10)	_____	×	1	=	_____
Critical Reading: The Writer's Craft (4)	_____	×	2	=	_____

(Possible Total: 100) *Total* _____

SPEED

Reading Time: _____ Reading Rate (page 351): _____ Words Per Minute

*Question 2 in this exercise calls for five separate answers. Questions 5 and 16 call for two separate answers. Questions 9, 10, and 11 call for three separate answers. In computing your score, count each separate answer toward your total score.

Name   Date

The Heart Beat

from "Circulation" in Human Physiology

Robert I. Macey

(1) Like any muscle, the heart can be stimulated, and it will conduct action potentials. In many ways, it behaves like a skeletal muscle, but there are some exceptions. Skeletal muscles contract only if they receive some external stimulus. Ordinarily, the stimulus is a nerve impulse leading to the muscle. This is not true of heart muscle, which seems to be capable of exciting itself. Even if we cut all the nerves leading to the heart, it will continue to beat. This capacity for self-excitation is common to all heart tissue.

(2) If we remove the heart of a cold-blooded animal (a frog, say), place it in a dish, and cover it with Ringer's solution, the heart continues to beat—even when it is completely disconnected from the body. If we now cut the heart into pieces, even the pieces continue to beat. However, some pieces beat faster than others. Those from the upper parts of the heart (the **atrium**) beat faster than those from further down (the **ventricle**).

(3) We do not know what causes this built-in rhythm of the heart. In a normal heart, the various parts do not beat at different times and with independent rhythms. This is because there is an excellent conduction system in the heart. The first piece of tissue that becomes excited generates an action potential. The action potential is then quickly transmitted to all parts of the heart, exciting the entire tissue. As a result, the entire heart beat is coordinated, pumping with maximum force, and sending the blood surging into the arteries.

(4) Figure 1 shows the heart in more detail. In addition to being divided into a right and left side, each side is subdivided into two chambers—the atrium and the ventricle. At rest, the atrium serves as a storage depot for blood returning from the veins toward the heart. When the heart begins its beat, the atrium contracts first. Although it may help fill the ventricles with blood, it plays a very minor role in the pumping of blood. A moment later the ventricles contract, sending the blood into the arteries. The ventricles contribute most of the pumping action of the heart. The right ventricle is responsible for pumping blood through the lungs; the left ventricle is responsible for pumping blood through the rest of the body.

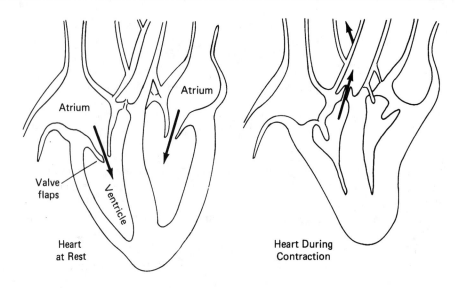

Figure 1. Blood flows into the heart from the veins when the heart is at rest. When the heart contracts, blood is forced into the arteries. Valves in the heart prevent blood from flowing in the reverse direction.

ONE-WAY FLOW

(5) When the heart muscles contract, why isn't blood squirted backward into the veins as well as forward into the arteries? And when the heart relaxes, why doesn't blood flow into it from the veins and arteries?

(6) Imagine that the heart is transparent and that we can watch the action of blood flowing in and out of it (Figure 1). First we see the heart at rest and notice **valve flaps** between the atrium and ventricle (the **A-V** valves) on each side of the heart. Blood is pushing down on them from above. Below the flap there is very little pressure, because the heart is relaxed. This means that the pressure of the blood from above pushes the flaps open and fills the ventricle.

(7) Now the muscles in the walls of the heart start pumping. They begin contracting and squeezing the blood in the ventricles. This is the time when we might expect blood to flow back into the veins through which it entered, but as we watch we notice something happening to the valve flaps. The pressure below the flaps is now much greater than that above. This forces the flaps of the valve toward one another until they close up tight. Blood cannot push its way back into the atria. Instead, it is forced into the arteries. The opening into the arteries is guarded by two other sets of valves, located between the ventricles and their arteries. When the heart was at rest, these valves were closed tight. The pressure in

the arteries was greater than the pressure in the ventricles; this kept the valves shut and prevented blood backing up from the arteries into the ventricles. (Notice that the flaps of these valves do not hang down into the ventricle like the A-V valves. Instead, they point upward into the arteries.) When the heart makes its pumping stroke, the high pressure of the blood in the ventricle pushes on the flaps of the valves guarding the arteries and forces them open. Blood now flows through the open valves, because the pressure of blood in the ventricle is now greater than the pressure in the artery. Each time the valves open and close they produce a sound. If you listen closely to your heart beat, you hear two distinct sounds: "lub-dup." The first sound corresponds to closure of the A-V valves, the second to snapping shut of the valves between the ventricles and arteries. When these valves are damaged, the sounds change. For example, damaged valves between the left ventricle and aorta convert the sound to "lub-shh."

CARDIAC OUTPUT

(8) The amount of blood pumped by the heart is staggering. When you are at complete rest, your heart pumps enough blood to fill four automobile gasoline tanks each hour. Let's break this down into more precise figures. During rest, the heart beats about 70 times per minute. During each beat, each side of the heart pumps roughly 70 ml of blood. The amount of blood pumped during each minute would then equal 70 ml per beat × 70 beats per minute, or 4,900 ml per minute (almost 5 liters, or 5¼ quarts, per minute).

(9) The amount of blood pumped by each side of the heart during each minute is called the **cardiac output.** During activity, the cardiac output changes. When you exercise strenuously, your cardiac output may rise to as much as 25 liters per minute. When a trained athlete exercises, his output may go as high as 40 liters per minute.

(10) The cardiac output is controlled in part by nerves of the autonomic nervous system. Impulses carried by sympathetic nerves to the heart tend to increase cardiac output by increasing both the rate of the heart beat and the strength of each beat. Impulses carried by the parasympathetic nerves to the heart tend to decrease cardiac output by slowing the rate of heart beat.

CORONARY CIRCULATION

(11) Blood leaving the heart enters the aorta en route to the organs of the body. The heart itself is one of these organs and its thick muscular walls must be supplied with fresh blood. This is accomplished through the **coronary circulation.** You can see from Figure 2 that **coronary arteries** arise from the base of the aorta and conduct blood back into the walls of the heart. These vessels branch into smaller arteries and capillaries which

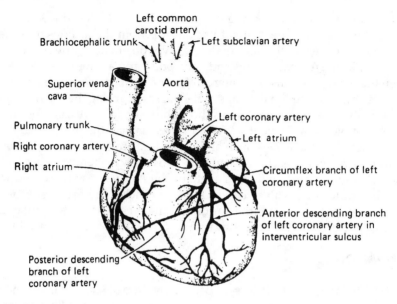

Figure 2. The coronary arteries.

are imbedded in the heart muscle and, finally, blood is conveyed into the right atrium primarily through a large vein called the **coronary sinus.**

(12) When one of the coronary vessels becomes occluded, the portion of the heart supplied by that vessel is deprived of oxygen and energy sources and it stops contracting. This is what we call a heart attack. When a large portion of the heart is involved it will no longer pump enough blood for survival. Coronary occlusion is responsible for about 30 percent of all deaths.

(13) Coronary occlusion often results from a disease called **athero-sclerosis** in which fatty substances containing large amounts of choles-terol are deposited in the walls of arteries. In later stages of atherosclerosis, fibrous tissue and calcium compounds intermingle with the fatty deposit so that the vessel walls become more rigid; this is called **arteriosclerosis (hardening of the arteries).**

(14) If the fatty deposits break through the inside lining of a blood vessel, they form a surface on which blood can clot. The vessel may become occluded at the site where the clot has formed or the clot may break loose only to occlude another vessel downstream. Death occurs if a coronary occlusion is severe. If only a small coronary vessel is involved, the heart is weakened but may improve with time as connections with neighboring blood vessels enlarge to supply new blood.

1530 words

Here are some of the more difficult words in "The Heart Beat."

cardiac
(heading at paragraph 8)

car·di·ac (kär'dē ak') *adj.* ⟦Fr *cardiaque* < L *cardiacus* < Gr *kardiakos* < *kardia*, HEART⟧ **1** of, near, or affecting the heart **2** relating to the part of the stomach connected with the esophagus — *n.* **1** a medicine that stimulates cardiac action **2** a person with a heart disorder

conduction
(paragraph 3)

con·duc·tion (kən duk'shən) *n.* ⟦L *conductio*: see CONDUCT⟧ **1** a conveying, as of liquid through a channel, esp. in plants **2** *Physics a)* transmission of electricity, heat, etc. through a material *b)* CONDUC-TIVITY (see also CONVECTION, RADIATION) **3** *Physiol.* the transmission of nerve impulses

contraction
(Figure 1)

con·trac·tion (kən trak'shən) *n.* ⟦ME *contraccioun* < OFr *contrac-tion* < L *contractio*⟧ **1** a contracting or being contracted **2** the shortening and thickening of a muscle fiber or a muscle in action, esp. of the uterus during labor **3** *Gram. a)* the shortening of a word or phrase by the omission of one or more sounds or letters *b)* a word form resulting from this (Ex.: *she's* for *she is*, *aren't* for *are not*) **4** *Econ.* a period of decrease in business activity —**con·trac'tion·al** *adj.*

en route
(paragraph 11)

en route (en rōōt', än-, ôn-; *also*, -rout'; *Fr* än rōōt') ⟦Fr⟧ on the way; along the way

occlusion
(paragraph 12)

oc·clude (ə klōōd', ä-) *vt.* **-clud'ed, -clud'ing** ⟦L *occludere* < *ob-* (see OB-) + *claudere*, to CLOSE[2]⟧ **1** to close, shut, or block (a passage) **2** to prevent the passage of; shut in or out **3** to conceal, hide, or obscure **4** *Chem.* to retain or absorb (a gas, liquid, or solid) —*vi.* *Dentistry* to meet with the cusps fitting close together: said of the upper and lower teeth —**oc·clud'ent** *adj.*

oc·clu·sion (ə klōō'zhən) *n.* **1** an occluding or being occluded **2** *Dentistry* the fitting together of the upper and lower teeth, or the way in which these fit together when the jaws are closed **3** *Meteorol.* OCCLUDED FRONT **4** *Phonet.* the complete closing of the air passages in pronunciation, as of a stop —**oc·clu'sive** *adj.*

stimulus
(paragraph 1)

stim|u·lus (-ləs) *n.*, *pl.* **-|u·li'** (-lī') ⟦L, a goad, sting, torment, pang, spur, incentive: see STYLE⟧ **1** something that rouses or incites to action or increased action; incentive **2** *Physiol., Psychol.* any action or agent that causes or changes an activity in an organism, organ, or part, as something that excites an end organ, starts a nerve impulse, activates a muscle, etc.

strenuously
(paragraph 9)

stren|u·ous (stren'yōō əs) *adj.* ⟦L *strenuus*, vigorous, active < IE base *(s)ter-*, rigid > STARE, Gr *strēnēs*, strong⟧ **1** requiring or char-acterized by great effort or energy [a *strenuous* game of handball] **2** vigorous, arduous, zealous, etc. [*strenuous* efforts] —*SYN.* ACTIVE — **stren'|u·ous|ly** *adv.* —**stren'|u·ous·ness** *n.*

Vocabulary List

valves
(Figure 1)

valve (valv) *n.* [ME, a door leaf < L *valva*, leaf of a folding door, akin to *volvere*, to roll: see WALK; senses 3, 4, 8 < ModL *valva* < L] **1** orig., either of the halves of a double door or any of the leaves of a folding door **2** a gate regulating the flow of water in a sluice, channel, etc. **3** *Anat.* a membranous fold or structure which permits body fluids to flow in one direction only, or opens and closes a tube, chamber, etc. **4** *Bot. a)* any of the segments into which a pod or capsule separates when it bursts open *b)* a lidlike part in some anthers, through which pollen is discharged *c)* either of the boxlike halves forming the cell walls of a diatom **5** *Elec., Radio a)* a device consisting of a metal in contact with a solution or compound across the boundary of which current flows in one direction only *b)* *Brit., etc.* term for ELECTRON TUBE **6** *Mech. a)* any device in a pipe or tube that permits a flow in one direction only, or regulates the flow of whatever is in the pipe, by means of a flap, lid, plug, etc. acting to open or block passage *b)* the flap, lid, plug, etc. **7** *Music* a device in certain brass instruments, as the trumpet, that opens (or closes) an auxiliary to the main tube, lengthening (or shortening) the air column and lowering (or raising) the pitch **8** *Zool. a)* each separate part making up the shell of a mollusk, barnacle, etc. *b)* any of the parts forming the sheath of an ovipositor in certain insects —*vt., vi.* **valved, valv'ing** **1** to fit with or make use of a valve or valves **2** to regulate the flow of (a fluid) by means of a valve or valves —**valve'less** *adj.*

VALVE

27A1 VOCABULARY

From the context of "The Heart Beat," explain the meaning of each of the vocabulary words shown in boldface below.

1. *From paragraph 1:* Skeletal muscles contract only if they receive some external **stimulus.**

   _____

   _____

2. *From paragraph 3:* This is because there is an excellent **conduction** system in the heart.

   _____

   _____

3. *From Figure 1:* Heart during **contraction**

   _____

   _____

Name   Date

4. *From Figure 1:* **Valves** in the heart prevent blood from flowing in the reverse direction.

   _____

   _____

5. *Heading at paragraph 8:* **Cardiac** Output

   _____

   _____

6. *From paragraph 9:* When you exercise **strenuously,** your cardiac output may rise to as much as 25 liters per minute.

   _____

   _____

7. *From paragraph 11:* Blood leaving the heart enters the aorta **en route** to the organs of the body.

   _____

   _____

8. *From paragraph 13:* Coronary **occlusion** often results from a disease called atherosclerosis.

   _____

   _____

27A2 SPECIAL TEXTBOOK VOCABULARY

Key terms in this textbook selection are explained as they are discussed. Referring to "The Heart Beat," fill in the blanks.

1. According to paragraph 2, the chamber found in each side of the

   upper part of the heart is called the _____ , and the chamber found in each side of the lower part of the heart is called the

   _____ .

2. According to paragraph 6 and Figure 1, _____ can be seen between the atrium and the ventricle on each side of the heart.

Name   Date

3. According to paragraph 9, _____ _____ is the amount of blood pumped by each side of the heart during one minute.

4. According to paragraph 11, blood is sent to the walls of the heart by

_____ _____ .The blood is carried by the

_____ _____ from the base of the aorta back to the walls of the heart.

The _____ _____ , which is a vein, then carries the blood to the right atrium.

5. According to paragraph 13, _____ is a disease in

which fatty substances containing _____ are deposited on the walls of the arteries. A later stage of this disease

is called _____ , or _____ of the

_____ , which is caused by the intermingling of fatty

deposits, _____ tissue, and _____ compounds.

27B   CENTRAL THEME AND MAIN IDEAS
Choose the best answer.

_____ 1. The textbook section called "The Heart Beat" could be part of a course in
   a. health.
   b. psychology.
   c. biology.
   d. human sexuality.

_____ 2. The main purpose of paragraphs 1 through 4 is to describe
   a. how the heart pumps blood.
   b. the action potentials of the heart.
   c. the different parts of the heart.
   d. self-excitation of heart tissue.

Name   Date

_____ 3. *Read paragraphs 5 through 7 again.* What keeps the blood flowing in one direction only?
  a. "One-way" heart valves prevent blood backflow as contractions pump the blood.
  b. The force of gravity keeps the blood from flowing in the "wrong" direction.
  c. The pumping action of the heart keeps the blood flowing in one direction.
  d. The contractions of the muscles in the ventricles steer the blood toward the arteries and away from the atria.

_____ 4. *Read paragraphs 8 through 10 again.* What is cardiac output?
  a. the amount of gasoline it takes to fill a car's tank
  b. 5¼ quarts of blood each minute
  c. the reaction of the autonomic nervous system to the body's need for blood
  d. the amount of blood pumped each minute according to the body's needs at the time

_____ 5. *Read paragraphs 11 through 13 again.* What does coronary circulation do?
  a. It carries blood to all the organs of the body.
  b. It carries blood to the walls of the heart itself.
  c. It prevents coronary occlusions.
  d. It carries fatty substances which are deposited on the walls of the arteries.

27C   MAJOR DETAILS
Decide whether each detail is true (T), false (F), or not discussed (ND).

_____ 1. According to Figure 1, blood flows into the heart from the arteries.

_____ 2. According to Figure 1, heart contractions force blood from the ventricles into the arteries.

_____ 3. The cardiac output is controlled entirely by the autonomic nervous system.

_____ 4. According to Figure 2, the aorta leads to major coronary arteries.

_____ 5. When a portion of the heart is deprived of oxygen and energy sources, that portion stops contracting.

_____ 6. Exercise helps prevent heart attacks.

_____ 7. All coronary occlusions cause death.

Name   Date

27D INFERENCES

Choose the best answer.

_____ 1. *Read paragraph 2 again.* To illustrate his point, why does the author use a cold-blooded animal (for example, a frog) rather than a warm-blooded animal (for example, a hamster, guinea pig, or any mammal) for dissection?
   a. Cold-blooded animals feel no pain.
   b. A frog's heart is the only animal's heart that is the perfect size for study in a laboratory.
   c. People do not mind killing cold-blooded animals as much as they do warm-blooded animals.
   d. The heart of a cold-blooded animal can be kept alive outside its host longer than can that of a warm-blooded animal.

_____ 2. *Read paragraphs 6 and 7 again.* The author assumes that the reader understands all of the following *except*
   a. "atria" is the plural of "atrium."
   b. the definition of a valve.
   c. that "one-way" blood flow is crucial to the circulation process.
   d. that the heart is transparent.

_____ 3. *Read paragraph 9 again.* During strenuous exercise the heart beats at a faster rate because
   a. the blood must quickly replenish spent oxygen and other nourishment needed by the body's tissues.
   b. this is the only time that the heart can exercise itself.
   c. it is nature's way of warning a person to slow down.
   d. a fast heartbeat feels very exciting, and so it is nature's way of encouraging people to exercise.

_____ 4. In referring in paragraph 11 to Figure 2, the author assumes that the reader will be able to do all of the following *except*
   a. use the drawing to get a *general* idea of the coronary arteries.
   b. use the drawing to follow the exact path of blood flow.
   c. understand why the "coronary sinus" cannot be found in the drawing.
   d. understand why all the labels in the drawing are not explained in the text.

Name   Date

27E   CRITICAL READING: THE WRITER'S CRAFT

Choose the best answer.

_____ 1. *Read these three sentences again: paragraph 3, last sentence; paragraph 5, first sentence; paragraph 8, first sentence.* What feeling do these words convey: "surging," "squirted," "staggering"?
   a. indirect humor
   b. gentle harmony
   c. urgent danger
   d. dramatic strength

_____ 2. *Read paragraph 5 again.* It consists of two questions, and it is the only time that the author uses questions. He does this for all of these reasons *except*
   a. to stimulate the reader's thinking.
   b. to change the reading pace a little.
   c. to reveal two of science's unanswered questions about the heart.
   d. to give the readers a sense of the drama and miracle of nature.

_____ 3. *Read paragraph 8 again.* By using the familiar gasoline tank to describe the unfamiliar heart, the author hopes that the reader will be able to
   a. picture cardiac output more clearly.
   b. understand that the supply of blood is as plentiful as the supply of gasoline.
   c. picture the capacity of gasoline tanks more clearly.
   d. understand that the heart functions exactly as a gasoline tank does.

_____ 4. The author uses figures in his textbook for all of these reasons *except*
   a. they help to reduce the need for overly lengthy verbal material.
   b. they provide help to readers who learn better with visual illustrations than they do with words.
   c. they illustrate the author's artistic ability.
   d. they help to illustrate and clarify the author's verbal explanations.

Name   Date

27F INFORMED OPINION

1. Some people become uncomfortable when they read technical information about how the human body functions. Why do you think this happens?

2. *Read paragraphs 12 and 13 again.* Does the information given influence you not to eat foods with high cholesterol content? Why or why not?

How Did You Do?   27 The Heart Beat

SKILL (number of items)	Number Correct		Points for Each		Score
Vocabulary (8)	_____	×	3	=	_____
Spacial Textbook Vocabulary* (14)	_____	×	1	=	_____
Central Theme and Main Ideas (5)	_____	×	5	=	_____
Major Details (7)	_____	×	3	=	_____
Inferences (4)	_____	×	2	=	_____
Critical Reading: The Writer's Craft (4)	_____	×	2	=	_____

(Possible Total: 100) *Total* _____

SPEED

Reading Time: _____ Reading Rate (page 351): _____ Words Per Minute

*Question 1 in this exercise calls for two separate answers. Question 4 calls for three separate answers. Question 5 calls for seven separate answers. In computing your score, count each separate answer toward your number correct.

Name   Date

Selection 28

How Many Languages?

in *The Cambridge Encyclopedia of Language*

David Crystal

(1) There is no agreed total for the number of languages spoken in the world today. Most reference books give a figure of 4,000 to 5,000, but estimates have varied from 3,000 to 10,000. To see why there is such uncertainty, we need to consider the many problems facing those who wish to obtain accurate information, and also the reasons (linguistic, historical and cultural) which preclude a simple answer to the question "What counts as a language?"

DISCOVERIES

(2) An obvious reason for the uncertainty over numbers is that even today new peoples, and therefore languages, continue to be discovered in the unexplored regions of the world—especially in the Amazon basin (as the Transamazonica road system is extended), Central Africa, and New Guinea. However, only a few languages are likely to be encountered in this way; and it is much more usual to find parts of the world where the people are known, but the languages spoken in their area are not. There are in fact many countries where linguistic surveys are incomplete or have not even begun. It is often assumed that the people speak one of the known languages in their area; or that they speak a dialect of one of these languages; but upon investigation their speech is found to be so different that it has to be recognized as a separate language.

ALIVE OR DEAD?

(3) Against this steady increase in the world language total, there is a major factor which decreases it. For a language to count as "living," there obviously have to be native speakers alive who use it. But in many parts of the world, it is by no means an easy matter to determine whether native speakers are still living—or, if they are, whether they still use their mother tongue regularly.

(4) The speed with which a language can die in the smaller communities of the world is truly remarkable. The Amazonian explorations led to the discovery of many new languages, but they also led to their rapid death, as the Indians became swallowed up by the dominant western culture. Within a generation, all traces of a language can disappear. Political

From *The Cambridge Encyclopedia of Language*, pp. 284–285. Reprinted by permission of Cambridge University Press.

decisions force tribes to move or be split up. Economic prospects attract younger members away from the villages. New diseases take their toll. In 1962, Trumai, spoken in a single village on the lower Culuene River in Venezuela, was reduced by an influenza epidemic to a population of fewer than 10 speakers. In the 19th century, there were thought to be over 1,000 Indian languages in Brazil; today, there are fewer than 200.

LANGUAGE—OR DIALECT?

(5) For most languages, the distinction between language and dialect is fairly clear-cut. In the case of English, for example, even though regional vocabulary and local differences of pronunciation can make communication difficult at times, no one disputes the existence of an underlying linguistic unity that all speakers identify as English, and which is confirmed by the use of a standard written language and a common literary heritage. But in hundreds of cases, considerations of this kind are in conflict with each other, or do not clearly apply.

(6) The best-known conflicts occur when the criteria of national identity and mutual intelligibility do not coincide. The most common situation is one where two spoken varieties are mutually intelligible, but for political and historical reasons, they are referred to as different languages. For example, using just the intelligibility criterion, there are really only two Scandinavian languages: Continental (Swedish, Danish, and two standard varieties of Norwegian) and Insular (Icelandic, Faeroese). Swedes, Danes, and Norwegians can understand each other's speech, to a greater or lesser extent. But as soon as non-linguistic criteria are taken into account, we have to recognize at least five languages. To be Norwegian is to speak Norwegian; to be Danish is to speak Danish; and so on. In such cases, political and linguistic identity merge. And there are many other similar cases where political, ethnic, religious, literary, or other identities force a division where linguistically there is little difference—Hindi vs. Urdu, Bengali vs. Assamese, Flemish vs. Dutch, Serbian vs. Croatian, Twi vs. Fante, Xhosa vs. Zulu.

(7) The opposite situation is also quite common. Here we find cases where spoken varieties are mutually unintelligible, but for political, historical or cultural reasons they are nonetheless called varieties of the same language. The three main "dialects" of Lapp fall into this category, for example. Chinese is a case where linguistic criteria alone are in conflict with each other. From the viewpoint of the spoken language, the many hundreds of dialects in China can be grouped into eight main types, which are mutually *unintelligible* to various degrees. But speakers of all these dialects share the same written language tradition, and those who have learned the system of Chinese characters are able to commu-

nicate with each other. Despite the linguistic differences, therefore, Chinese is considered by its speakers to be a single language.

(8) In the above cases, the languages in question have been well studied, and many speakers are involved. When languages have been little studied, or have very few speakers, it is much more difficult for linguists to interpret all the factors correctly. For example, when two languages are in close proximity, they often borrow words from each other—sometimes even sounds and grammar. On first acquaintance, therefore, the languages may seem more alike than they really are, and analysts may believe them to be dialects of the same language. This has proved to be a real problem in such parts of the world as South America, Africa, and Southeast Asia, where whole groups of languages may be affected in this way. Similarly, decisions about how to analyze all cases of dialect continua will affect our final total of languages.

LANGUAGE NAMES

(9) A big problem, in working on lesser-known areas, is deciding what credence to give to a language name. This issue does not arise when discussing the main languages of the world, which are usually known by a single name that translates neatly into other languages—as in the case of *Deutsch, German, Tedesco, Nemetskiy,* and *Allemand,* for instance. But in many cases the situation is not so straight-forward.

(10) At one extreme, many communities have no specific name for their language. The name they use is the same as a common word or phrase in the language, such as the word for "our language" or "our people." This is often so in Africa (where the name *Bantu,* which is given to a whole family of languages, means simply "people"), and also in Meso- and South America. In the latter areas, we find such examples as *Carib* = "people," *Tapuya* = "enemy," and *Macu* = "forest tribes." Some tribes were called *chichimecatl* (= "lineage of dogs"), *chontalli* (= "foreigners") or *popoloca* (= "barbarians"), and these labels led to the modern language names Chichimeca, Chontal, and Popoloca. Frequently, the name is the same as a river on which a tribe has been observed to live, as with the many groups of Land Dayak, in the West Indonesian family. In several Australian aboriginal languages, the name for the language is the word for "this": for example, the nine languages within the Yuulngu family are known as *Dhuwala, Dhuwal, Dhiyakuy, Dhangu, Dhay'yi, Djangu, Djinang, Djining,* and *Nhangu.* Asking native speakers what language they speak is of little practical help, in such circumstances, if they only answer "this"!

(11) At the other extreme, it is quite common to find a community whose language has too many names. A South American Indian tribe, for instance, may have several names. A tribe, first of all, will have a

name for itself (see above). But adjacent tribes may give the people a different name (e.g., Puelche means "people from the east" in Araucanian). The Spanish or Portuguese explorers may have given them a third name—perhaps a characteristic of their appearance (e.g., *Coroado* means "crowned" in Portuguese). More recently, anthropologists and other investigators may have used another name, often based on the geographical location of the tribe (e.g., "up-river" vs. "down-river"). And lastly, the same language may be spelled differently in Spanish, Portuguese, English, or in its own writing system (if one has been devised). For example, Machacali, spoken in Minas Gerais, Brazil, is sometimes spelled Maxakali, sometimes Maxakari. When the initial letters vary (as when the Peruvian language Candoshi is spelled Kandoshi), indexing is especially awkward.

(12) There are further complications. Sometimes, the same name is applied to two different languages, as when *mexicano* is used in Mexico to refer to Spanish (otherwise known as *español* or *castellano*) and to the main Indian language (*nahuatl*). Sometimes, speakers from different backgrounds may disagree about whether their ways of speaking should be related at all. Speakers of Luri, spoken in south-west Iran, say that their speech is a dialect of Persian; speakers of Persian disagree. Asking the native speakers is evidently no solution, for their perceptions will be governed by non-linguistic considerations, especially of a religious, nationalistic, or socioeconomic kind.

TO CONCLUDE

(13) When all these factors are taken into account, it is plain that there will be no single answer to the question "How many languages?" In some parts of the world, there has been a tendency to over-estimate, by taking names too literally and not grouping dialects together sufficiently— the Malayo-Polynesian languages are often cited in this connection. In other places, the totals are likely to have been underestimated— Indonesian languages, for example. There are over 20,000 language or dialect names listed in the Voegelins' great *Classification and Index of the World's Languages* (1977), and these have been grouped into around 4,500 living languages. Since the publication of that work, the total must have become somewhat less, in view of the trend indicated in the table of population estimates on the next page; but it seems unlikely that it should be less than 4,000.

Table 28–1. Number of speakers of the world's languages, based on Voegelin and Voegelin's *Classification and Index of the World's Languages.* Languages which they classify as of uncertain existence (marked by a question mark in their book) have been excluded. In about three-quarters of the cases where no numerical estimates are available, the numbers of speakers are extremely small. The total number of languages (excluding extinct ones) is 4,522.

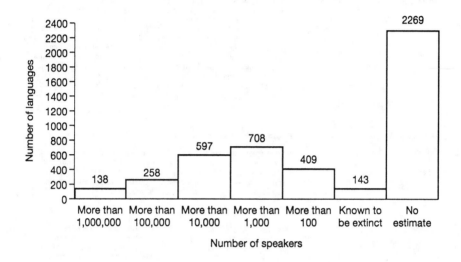

(1734 words)

Vocabulary List

Here are some of the more difficult words in "How Many Languages?"

aboriginal
(paragraph 10)

ab·o·rig·i·nal (ab'ə rij'ə nəl) **adj.** ⟦< fol. + -AL⟧ **1** existing (in a place) from the beginning or from earliest days; first; indigenous **2** of or characteristic of aborigines —**n.** an aboriginal animal or plant —**SYN.** NATIVE —ab·o·rig'i·nal·ly **adv.**

Amazonian
(paragraph 4)

Am·a·zon (am'ə zän', -zən) ⟦so named by Spaniards, who believed its shores inhabited by female warriors: see the **n.**⟧ river in South America, flowing from the Andes in Peru across N Brazil into the Atlantic: c. 4,000 mi. (6,400 km) —**n.** ⟦L < Gr Amazōn, of unknown orig., but deriv. by folk etym. < a-, without + mazos, breast, hence the story that the Amazons cut off one breast to facilitate archery⟧ **1** Gr. Myth. any of a race of female warriors supposed to have lived in Scythia, near the Black Sea **2** [a-] a tall, strong, aggressive woman **3** a small, greenish parrot (genus Amazona) of Central and South America, often kept as a pet **4** any of a genus (Polyergus) of ants that makes slaves of other ants: also **Amazon ant**
Am·a·zo·ni·an (am'ə zō'nē ən) **adj.** **1** of, like, or characteristic of an Amazon **2** [often a-] warlike and masculine: said of a woman **3** of the Amazon River or the country around it

anthropologists
(paragraph 11)

an·thro·pol·o·gist (an'thrō päl'ə jist, -thrə-) **n.** a person who specializes in anthropology
an·thro·pol·o·gy (an'thrō päl'ə jē, -thrə-) **n.** ⟦ANTHROPO- + -LOGY⟧ the study of humans, esp. of the variety, physical and cultural characteristics, distribution, customs, social relationships, etc. of humanity —an'thro·po·log'i·cal (-pō läj'i kəl, -pə-) or an'thro·po·log'ic **adj.** —an'thro·po·log'i·cal·ly **adv.**

credence
(paragraph 9)

cre·dence (krēd''ns) **n.** ⟦OFr < ML credentia < L credens, prp. of credere: see CREED⟧ **1** belief, esp. in the reports or testimony of another [to give credence to rumors] **2** credentials: now only in the phrase LETTERS OF CREDENCE —**SYN.** BELIEF

criteria
(paragraph 6)

cri·te·ri·on (krī tir'ē ən) **n.,** pl. -ri·a (-ē ə) or -ri·ons ⟦< Gr kritērion, means of judging < kritēs, judge; akin to kritikos: see fol.⟧ a standard, rule, or test by which something can be judged; measure of value —**SYN.** STANDARD

dialect
(paragraph 2)

di·a·lect (dī'ə lekt') **n.** ⟦L dialectus < Gr dialektos, discourse, discussion, dialect < dialegesthai, to discourse, talk < dia-, between (see DIA-) + legein, to choose, talk (see LOGIC)⟧ **1** the sum total of local characteristics of speech **2** [Rare] the sum total of an individual's characteristics of speech; idiolect **3** popularly, any form of speech considered as deviating from a real or imaginary standard speech **4** Linguis. a) the form or variety of a spoken language peculiar to a region, community, social group, occupational group, etc. (in this sense, dialects are regarded as being, to some degree, mutually intelligible while languages are not mutually intelligible) b) any language as a member of a group or family of languages [English is a West Germanic dialect] —**adj.** of or in a dialect [dialect ballads] —di·a·lec'tal **adj.** —di'a·lec'tal·ly **adv.**
SYN.—**dialect**, in this comparison, refers to a form of a language peculiar to a locality or group and differing from the standard language in matters of pronunciation, syntax, etc.; **vernacular** today commonly refers to the informal or colloquial variety of a language as distinguished from the formal or literary variety; **cant**, in this connection, refers to the distinctive stock words and phrases used by a particular sect, class, etc. [clergymen's cant]; **jargon** is used of the special vocabulary and idioms of a particular class, occupational group, etc., esp. by one who is unfamiliar with these; **argot** refers esp. to the secret jargon of thieves and tramps; **lingo** is a humorous or mildly contemptuous term applied to any language, dialect, or jargon by one to whom it is unintelligible

intelligibility
(paragraph 6)

in·tel·li·gi·ble (in tel'i jə bəl) **adj.** ⟦ME < L intelligibilis < intelligere: see INTELLECT⟧ **1** that can be understood; clear; comprehensible **2** understandable by the intellect only, not by the senses —in·tel'li·gi·bil'i·ty **n.** —in·tel'li·gi·bly **adv.**

lInguistic
(paragraph 1)

lin·guis·tic (lin gwis′tik) *adj.* 1 of language 2 of linguistics —**lin·guis′ti·cal**l**y** *adv.*

lin·guis·tics (lin gwis′tiks) *n.pl.* ⟦ < LINGUISTIC ⟧ [*with sing. v.*] 1 the science of language, including phonetics, phonology, morphology, syntax, and semantics: sometimes subdivided into *descriptive, historical, comparative, theoretical,* and *geographical linguistics*: often **general linguistics** 2 the study of the structure, development, etc. of a particular language and its relationship to other languages [English *linguistics*]

nationalistic
(paragraph 12)

na·tion·al·ism (nash′ə nəl iz′əm) *n.* 1 *a*) devotion to one's nation; patriotism *b*) excessive, narrow, or jingoist patriotism; chauvinism 2 the doctrine that national interest, security, etc. are more important than international considerations 3 the desire for or advocacy of national independence
na·tion·al·ist (-nəl ist) *n.* a person who believes in or advocates nationalism —*adj.* of nationalism or nationalists: also **na′tion·al·is′tic** —**na′tion·al·is′ti·cal**l**y** *adv.*

preclude
(paragraph 1)

pre·clude (prē kl o͞o d′, pri-) *vt.* -**clud′**ed, -**clud′ing** ⟦ L *praecludere,* to shut off < *prae-,* before (see PRE-) + *claudere,* to CLOSE² ⟧ to make impossible, esp. in advance; shut out; prevent —*SYN.* PREVENT — **pre·clu′sion** (-kl o͞o ′zhən) *n.* —**pre·clu′sive** (-siv) *adj.* —**pre·clu′sive**l**y** *adv.*

socioeconomic
(paragraph 12)

☆**so·ci**l**o·e**l**co·nom**l**ic** (-ē′kə näm′ik, -ek′ə-) *adj.* of or involving both social and economic factors

28A VOCABULARY

From the context of "How Many Languages?" explain the meaning of each of the vocabulary words shown in boldface below.

1. *From paragraph 1:* To see why there is such uncertainty, we need to consider the many problems . . . , and also the reasons (**linguistic,** historical and cultural) which **preclude** a simple answer . . .

   _____

   _____

   _____

   _____

2. *From paragraph 2:* . . . or that they speak a **dialect** of one of these languages.

   _____

   _____

3. *From paragraph 4:* The **Amazonian** explorations led to the discovery of many new languages . . .

   _____

   _____

313

4. *From paragraph 6:* The best-known conflicts occur when the **criteria** of national identity and mutual **intelligibility** do not coincide.

_____

_____

_____

_____

5. *From paragraph 9:* A big problem, in working on lesser-known language areas, is deciding what **credence** to give to a language name.

_____

_____

6. *From paragraph 10:* In several Australian **aboriginal** languages . . .

_____

_____

7. *From paragraph 11:* More recently, **anthropologists** and other investigators may have used another name . . .

_____

_____

8. *From paragraph 12:* . . . their perceptions will be governed by non-linguistic considerations, especially of a religious **nationalistic,** or **socio-economic** kind.

_____

_____

_____

_____

28B CENTRAL THEME AND MAIN IDEAS
Follow the directions for each item below.

1. In your own words, state the central theme of "How Many Languages?"

   _____

   _____

   _____

_____ 2. What is the main idea of paragraph 2?
   a. Surveys are difficult to carry out in the Amazon.
   b. There are parts of the world where new people and/or new languages are still being discovered.
   c. Languages and dialects are often confused.
   d. Scientists should work harder to uncover new peoples and languages.

_____ 3. Read paragraphs 9–12 again. List the three reasons that working on language names in lesser-known areas of the world is a big problem.

   a. _____

   b. _____

   c. _____

28C MAJOR DETAILS
Fill in the word or words that correctly complete each statement.

1. The reasons specialists have such a difficult time agreeing on the number of languages spoken in the world may be _____ ,

   _____ , or _____ .

2. Even today, new peoples and/or new languages are being discovered in _____ regions of the world.

3. However, it is likely that more new languages will be discovered in regions already explored because _____ .

4. Languages may also die. For instance, there were thought to be over _____ Indian languages in Brazil in the nineteenth century. Today, there are fewer than _____ .

Name   Date

5. _____ , _____ , or _____ may
   lead to the rapid death of a language.

6. It is often difficult to distinguish between two languages as opposed

   to a language and a _____ .

7. The eight main types of Chinese dialects are mutually

   _____ in varying degrees.

8. Even though there are many dialects, Chinese is considered a single
   language because the people share a common _____ .

9. Often languages that are in close proximity to each other

   _____ words, sounds, or even grammar and thus appear
   to be dialects of the same language.

28D FACT OR OPINION

Decide whether each statement contains a FACT or an OPINION.

_____ 1. *From paragraph 4:* The speed with which a language can die in the
smaller communities of the world is truly remarkable.

_____ 2. *From paragraph 6:* To be Norwegian is to speak Norwegian.

_____ 3. *From paragraph 10:* At one extreme, many communities have no
specific name for their language.

_____ 4. *From paragraph 11:* At the other extreme, it is quite common to
find a community whose language has too many names.

_____ 5. *From paragraph 13:* It seems unlikely that it should be less than
4,000.

_____ 6. *From the graph:* There is no estimate of the number of speakers of
over fifty percent of the world's languages.

Name   Date

28E CRITICAL READING: THE WRITER'S CRAFT

Choose the best answer.

_____ 1. Expressions that show connections may contain one word or several words. There is an abundance of such connectors in the last paragraphs of this selection. Which of the following is *not* used to show connections?

a. in the above cases	(paragraph 8)
b. similarly	(paragraph 8)
c. At one extreme	(paragraph 10)
d. for example	(paragraph 10)
e. At the other extreme	(paragraph 11)
f. for instance	(paragraph 11)
g. more recently	(paragraph 11)
h. lastly	(paragraph 11)
i. In some parts of the world	(paragraph 12)
j. There are further complications	(paragraph 12)

_____ 2. The purpose of the graph on page 311 is to
   a. display and debate the information.
   b. dramatize and evaluate the information.
   c. summarize and display the information.
   d. communicate and translate the information.

_____ 3. Read paragraphs 9–12 again. The author shows many individual words in italics in order to
   a. explain unusually spelled words to the reader.
   b. assist the student in identifying any unfamiliar words.
   c. indicate those words that are of central importance to the selection.
   d. highlight those words that are foreign to the English language.

_____ 4. The author's goal in this selection is to
   a. persuade readers of the need to study the world's languages.
   b. convey a sense of the range of the world's languages and complex issues of studying them.
   c. communicate factual information about the world's languages.
   d. narrate a story about the study of language and its development.

Name	Date

28F   INFORMED OPINION

1. Do you agree with the idea that all people within a certain country should speak the same language or dialect? Explain your point of view, being as specific as possible.

2. Assume that you work for a corporation that will soon send you to a foreign country where three languages are spoken. How would you decide which language is the appropriate one for you to learn? Be specific in explaining the reasons for your choice.

How Did You Do?   **28** How Many Languages?

SKILL (number of items)	Number Correct		Points for Each		Score
Vocabulary* (11)	_____	×	3	=	_____
Central Theme and Main Ideas (3)	_____	×	5	=	_____
Major Details* (14)	_____	×	2	=	_____
Critical Reading: Fact or Opinion (6)	_____	×	2	=	_____
Critical Reading: The Writer's Craft (4)	_____	×	3	=	_____

(Possible Total: 100) *Total* _____

SPEED

Reading Time: _____ Reading Rate (page 351): _____ Words Per Minute

*Questions in these exercises may call for multiple answers. In computing your score, count each separate answer toward your number correct.

Name   Date

Selection 29

Magnetism

in *Electricity for Technicians*

Abraham Marcus and Charles M. Thomson

(1) The ancient people knew about that mysterious, heavy black stone (which we now know is a mineral containing iron) called a **magnet,** which could attract pieces of iron. They also knew that if a bar of iron were stroked with this stone, the iron, too, would be able to attract other pieces of iron. (We know today that a magnet can attract not only pieces of iron, but certain other metals, such as nickel and cobalt, although with less force. We call substances that can be attracted by a magnet **magnetic,** and the ability of a magnet to attract magnetic substances we call **magnetism.**)

(2) Further, legend has it that thousands of years ago, the Chinese discovered that if a magnet were suspended so that it could swing freely, one end would always point in the general direction of north and the other end in the general direction of south. The north-seeking end is called a **north pole** (N) and the south-seeking end a **south pole** (S). Such a device is called a **compass,** and for centuries navigators have used the compass to guide their ships. It is for this reason that the magnet was also known as **lodestone** (leading stone). In addition, it was found that if the north-seeking end of the magnet were brought near the north-seeking end of another, the two magnets would be repelled. Similarly, if two south-seeking ends were brought together, they also would repel each other. On the other hand, if a north-seeking end were brought near a south-seeking end, they would attract each other.

(3) About 1600 A.D. William Gilbert, the same man who investigated the properties of amber, undertook the first serious study of magnets. He found, among other things, that the attractive property of the magnet was concentrated at its two opposite ends, called **poles,** with very little attractive force between the poles. He theorized that the earth is a huge magnet with its magnetic north pole near its geographic north pole and its magnetic south pole near its geographic south pole. It is the attraction between the north-seeking pole of the compass (which is, in reality, a south pole) and the north pole of the earth that causes the compass to act as it does.

From Abraham Marcus and Charles M. Thomson, "Magnetism" in *Electricity for Technicians,* 3rd ed., © 1982, pp. 33–40. Reprinted by permission of Prentice-Hall, Inc., Englewood Cliffs, N.J.

A. THE MAGNETIC FIELD

(4) This matter of attraction and repulsion between poles of magnets warrants close attention. It was found that the poles need not touch each other. Even if they are a distance apart, like poles will repel each other and unlike poles will attract each other. If a nonmagnetic substance is placed between the poles, their attraction or repulsion is unchanged. Thus, if a sheet of glass or copper is placed between two unlike magnetic poles, they continue to attract each other as though the glass or copper were not there.

(5) We may understand this phenomenon a little more clearly if we consider the electric field existing between charged bodies (see Chapter 1, subdivision C). Here, under the influence of the field of force existing between them, bodies containing similar charges repel each other. If the bodies have unlike charges they attract each other. It would appear, then, that a **magnetic force,** or **field,** exists between the two opposite poles of a magnet. We may find out more about this magnetic field by means of a simple experiment. Place a magnet on a wooden table. Over it, place a sheet of glass. Sprinkle iron filings on the glass and tap the glass lightly. The iron filings will assume a definite pattern on the glass sheet (see Figure 3–1). The iron filings are attracted to the magnet through the glass sheet. Although the glass prevents these iron filings from touching the magnet, nevertheless the filings will form a pattern which will show the form of the magnetic field. Note that the iron filings arrange themselves outside the magnet in a series of closed loops that extend from pole to pole.

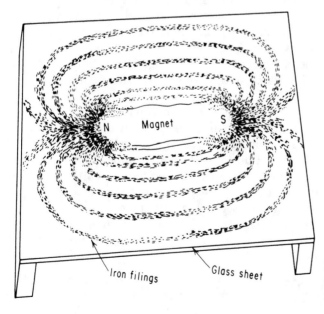

Figure 3–1. How iron filings show the form of the magnetic field around a magnet.

(6) It is in this way that we visualize the magnetic field around a magnet. We say that the magnet acts as though **magnetic lines of force** surround it in the pattern formed by the iron filings. Of course, the pattern formed in Figure 3–1 represents the magnetic field only in the horizontal plane. To obtain a true picture, we should consider the magnetic field surrounding the magnet as existing in three dimensions—that is, over and under the magnet as well as on either side of it.

(7) Note that the magnetic lines of force, like the electric lines of force discussed in Chapter 1, are imaginary. Nevertheless, the field acts as though the lines of force were present. It would seem that these lines try to follow the shortest distance from pole to pole, at the same time repelling each other. As with the electric lines of force, it might help if we think of the magnetic lines of force as a bundle of stretched rubber bands that tend to shorten and, simultaneously, push each other away sidewise.

(8) We arbitrarily assume the force acts from the north pole to the south pole. It is as if lines of force "flowed" from the north pole to the south pole. If, theoretically, we were to place a small north pole in the magnetic field, it would be repelled from the north pole of the magnet and move along the path of a line of force until it reached the south pole. We can see now why like poles repel and unlike poles attract. If we place two unlike poles near each other, as in Figure 3–2A, the lines of force flow from the north pole to the south pole. Since these lines of force tend to shorten, the two magnets are pulled to each other. If, on the other hand, we place two like poles near each other, as in Figure 3–2B, the lines of force tend to repel each other and the two magnets are pushed apart.

(9) The magnetic lines of force are known as the **magnetic flux,** which is considered to flow in closed loops. This is illustrated in Figure

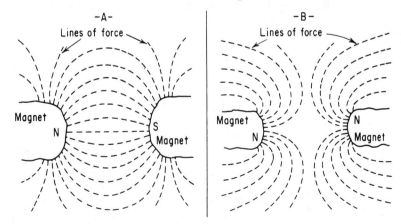

Figure 3–2. A. Pattern of the resulting magnetic field when two unlike poles are placed near each other.
B. Pattern of the resulting magnetic field when two like poles are placed near each other.

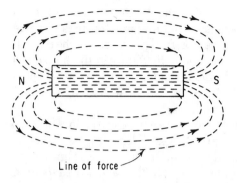

Figure 3–3. Magnetic flux around and through a magnet.

Line of force

3–3, which shows the flux around and through a magnet. The lines of force flow out of the north pole, through the air, and back into the south pole of the magnet. Within the magnet, they flow back to the north pole, thus completing the loop. (In the previous figures the flow of flux within the magnets was omitted for the sake of simplicity.) We find that the magnetic flux encounters less opposition flowing through magnetic substances, such as iron, than through nonmagnetic substances, such as air, glass, or copper. We call the opposition to the flow of magnetic flux, **reluctance.** The reluctances of all nonmagnetic substances are the same. Thus the flux will flow with the same ease (or difficulty) through air, glass, copper, and so on.

(10) On the other hand, it will flow much more readily through a piece of iron placed in its path. Thus, if a piece of iron is placed within the magnetic field, the lines of force will distort their pattern to take the easier path through the iron, as shown in Figure 3–4A. If, as in Figure 3–4B, an iron washer is placed within the magnetic field, the flux will flow through the iron of the washer, and no lines of force will be found in the air space within the washer.

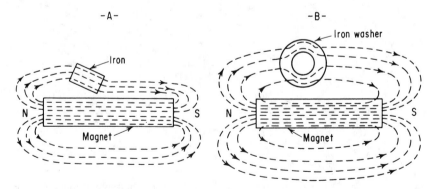

Figure 3–4. A. Distortion of the magnetic field around a magnet by a piece of iron.
B. Distortion of the magnetic field around a magnet by an iron washer. Note that there are no lines of force in the air space within the washer.

B. THE MOLECULAR THEORY OF MAGNETISM

(11) A nineteenth-century German physicist, Wilhelm Weber, proposed a molecular theory of magnetism. According to this theory, the molecules of magnetic material, such as iron, are tiny magnets, each with a north and south magnetic pole and with a surrounding magnetic field. In the unmagnetized piece of iron these magnetic molecules are arranged helter-skelter (see Figure 3–5A). As a result of this arrangement, the magnetic fields around the molecules cancel each other out and there is no external magnetic field. But if the iron is magnetized, the molecules line up in an orderly array, with the north pole of one molecule facing the south pole of another (see Figure 3–5B). The result, then, is that all the magnetic fields aid each other and we have a magnet with an external magnetic field.

(12) This theory explains a number of things we know about magnets. For example, note that in the magnetized iron all the north poles of the molecules are facing one way and all the south poles are facing the opposite way. The result, then, is that we have a magnet whose magnetism is concentrated at the two opposite poles. Further, it was found that if you break a magnet in two, you obtain two magnets, each with a set of poles, as illustrated in Figure 3–6. Also, you can destroy the magnetism of a magnet by any means that will disarrange the orderly array of the molecules, such as by heating or jarring the magnet.

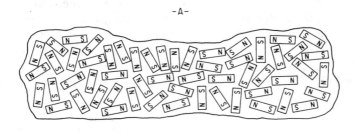

-A-

-B-

Figure 3–5. Arrangements of molecules in a piece of magnetic material.
      A. Unmagnetized.
      B. Magnetized.

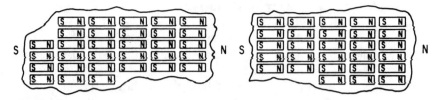

Figure 3–6. Arrangement of molecules showing why two magnets are formed when a magnet is broken in two.

(13) If a piece of unmagnetized magnetic material is placed in the magnetic field of a magnet (as, for example, a bar of iron is stroked by a magnet), the attraction between the external magnet and the molecules of the magnetic substance causes these molecules to line up in the necessary orderly array (see Figure 3–7). Magnetism produced in this way is called **induced magnetism.**

(14) We now can explain why a magnet can attract an unmagnetized piece of iron. Under the influence of the magnetic field of the magnet, the piece of iron becomes magnetized by induction, two poles being produced at the ends of the iron. The end nearest the magnet is an unlike pole. The attraction between unlike poles draws the piece of iron to the magnet. A nonmagnetic substance, such as glass or copper, resists all attempts to align its molecules in orderly fashion. Nor do all magnetic substances submit to this lining-up process to the same degree. In some substances, such as soft iron, the molecules are easily moved and will line up readily under the influence of the magnetic field of another magnet. However, once the external magnetic field is removed, the molecules of the soft iron revert to their original, disorderly condition. The soft iron forms a **temporary magnet,** which is magnetized only so long as it is acted on by an external magnetic field.

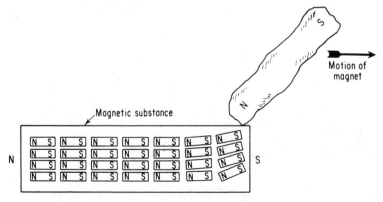

Figure 3–7. How a piece of magnetic material may be magnetized by stroking with a magnet.

(15) On the other hand, the molecules of some substances, such as steel, require a much greater magnetic force to produce an orderly arrangement. However, when the external magnetic field is removed, these molecules will retain their positions, and consequently these substances form **permanent magnets.** As we have seen, however, heating or jarring the magnet will disarrange its molecules and thus destroy its magnetic properties. The greater the number of aligned molecules of a magnetic substance, the stronger will be its magnetic field. When all the molecules are aligned, the substance is said to be **saturated.** Then, increasing the strength of the aligning force will produce no increase in the magnetic field of the substance.

1890 words

Here are some of the more difficult words in "Magnetism."

align
(paragraph 14)

a‖lign (ə lin′) *vt.* 〚Fr *aligner* < *a-*, to + *ligner* < *ligne*, LINE[1]〛 1 to bring into a straight line; adjust by line 2 to bring (parts or components, as the wheels of a car) into proper coordination 3 to bring into agreement, close cooperation, etc. /he *aligned* himself with the liberals/ —*vi.* to come or fall into line; line up

arbitrarily
(paragraph 8)

ar·bi·trar·ly (är′bə trer′ē) *adj.* 〚L *arbitrarius* < *arbiter*, prec.〛 1 not fixed by rules but left to one's judgment or choice; discretionary /arbitrary decision, *arbitrary* judgment/ 2 based on one's preference, notion, whim, etc.; capricious 3 absolute; despotic —*SYN.* DICTATORIAL —**ar′bi·trar′i‖ly** *adv.* —**ar′bi·trar‖i·ness** *n.*

array
(paragraph 12)

ar·ray (ə rā′) *vt.* 〚ME *arraien* < OFr *areer* < ML *arredare*, to put in order < L *ad-*, to + Gmc *raid-*: for IE base see RIDE 〛 1 to place in order; marshal (troops for battle, etc.) 2 to dress in fine or showy attire; deck out —*n.* 1 an orderly grouping or arrangement, esp. of troops 2 troops in order; military force 3 an impressive display of assembled persons or things 4 fine clothes; finery 5 *Comput.* a group of two or more logically related elements, identified by a single name and usually stored in consecutive storage locations in main memory 6 *Math., Statistics* a systematic arrangement of numbers or symbols in rows and columns

horizontal
(paragraph 6)

hor‖i·zon·tal (hôr′i zänt″l) *adj.* 〚ModL *horizontalis* < L *horizon* (gen. *horizontis*): see HORIZON 〛 1 of or near the horizon 2 *a*) parallel to the plane of the horizon; not vertical *b*) placed, operating, or acting chiefly in a horizontal direction 3 flat and even; level 4 at, or made up of elements at, the same levels of industrial production and distri-

repel
(paragraph 2)

re·pel (ri pel′) *vt.* -**pelled′**, -**pel′ling** 〚ME *repellen* < L *repellere*, to drive back < *re-*, back + *pellere*, to drive: see PULSE[1]〛 1 to drive or force back; hold or ward off /to *repel* an attack/ 2 to refuse to accept, agree to, or submit to; reject /to *repel* advances/ 3 to refuse to accept (a person); spurn /to *repel* a suitor/ 4 *a*) to cause distaste or dislike in; disgust /the odor *repelled* him/ *b*) to cause (insects, etc.) to react by staying away 5 *a*) to be resistant to, or present an opposing force to /a coating that *repels* moisture/ *b*) to fail to mix with or adhere to /water *repels* oil/ —*vi.* 1 to drive off, or offer an opposing force to, something 2 to cause distaste, dislike, or aversion —**re·pel′ler** *n.*

repulsion
(paragraph 4)

re·pul·sion (ri pul'shən) *n.* ⟦LL *repulsio*⟧ **1** a repelling or being repelled **2** strong dislike, distaste, or aversion; repugnance **3** *Physics* the mutual action by which bodies or particles of matter tend to repel each other: opposed to ATTRACTION

simultaneously
(paragraph 7)

si·mul·ta·ne·ous (sī'məl tā'nē əs, -tān'yəs; *chiefly Brit & Cdn*, sim'əl-) *adj.* ⟦ML *simultaneus* < *simultas*, simultaneity < L, competition, rivalry < *simul*: see SAME⟧ occurring, done, existing, etc. together or at the same time —*SYN.* CONTEMPORARY —**si'mul·ta·ne'i·ty** (-tə nē'ə tē) or **si'mul·ta'ne·ous·ness** *n.* —**si'mul·ta'ne·ous·ly** *adv.*

theoretically
(paragraph 8)

the·o·ret·i·cal (thē'ə ret'i kəl) *adj.* ⟦< LL *theoreticus* < Gr *theōrētikos* < -AL⟧ **1** of or constituting theory **2** limited to or based on theory; not practical or applied; hypothetical **3** tending to theorize; speculative Also **the'o·ret'ic** —**the'o·ret'i·cal·ly** *adv.*

theorized
(paragraph 3)

the·o·rize (thē'ə rīz') *vi.* **-rized'**, **-riz'ing** to form a theory or theories; speculate —**the'o·riz'er** *n.* —**the'o·ri·za'tion** *n.*

theory
(paragraph 11)

the·o·ry (thē'ə rē; thē'rē, thir'ē) *n., pl.* **-ries** ⟦< Fr or LL: Fr *théorie* < LL *theoria* < Gr *theōria*, a looking at, contemplation, speculation, theory < *theōrein*: see THEOREM⟧ **1** orig., a mental viewing; contemplation **2** a speculative idea or plan as to how something might be done **3** a systematic statement of principles involved [the *theory* of equations in mathematics] **4** a formulation of apparent relationships or underlying principles of certain observed phenomena which has been verified to some degree **5** that branch of an art or science consisting in a knowledge of its principles and methods rather than in its practice; pure, as opposed to applied, science, etc. **6** popularly, a mere conjecture, or guess
SYN.—**theory**, as compared here, implies considerable evidence in support of a formulated general principle explaining the operation of certain phenomena [the *theory* of evolution]; **hypothesis** implies an inadequacy of evidence in support of an explanation that is tentatively inferred, often as a basis for further experimentation [the nebular *hypothesis*]; **law** implies an exact formulation of the principle operating in a sequence of events in nature, observed to occur with unvarying uniformity under the same conditions [the *law* of the conservation of energy]

warrants
(paragraph 4)

war·rant (wôr'ənt, wär'-) *n.* ⟦ME *warant* < NormFr (OFr *garant*), a warrant < Frank *warand* < prp. of *warjan*; akin to OE *werian*, to guard, defend: see WEIR⟧ **1** *a)* authorization or sanction, as by a superior or the law *b)* justification or reasonable grounds for some act, course, statement, or belief **2** something that serves as an assurance, or guarantee, of some event or result **3** a writing serving as authorization or certification for something; specif., *a)* authorization in writing for the payment or receipt of money *b)* a short-term note issued by a municipality or other governmental agency, usually in anticipation of tax revenues *c)* an option issued by a company granting the holder the right to buy certain securities, generally common stock, at a specified price and usually for a limited time *d)* *Law* a writ or order authorizing an officer to make an arrest, seizure, or search, or perform some other designated act *e)* *Mil.* the certificate of appointment to the grade of warrant officer (cf. WARRANT OFFICER) —*vt.* **1** *a)* to give (someone) authorization or sanction to do something *b)* to authorize (the doing of something) **2** to serve as justification or reasonable grounds for (an act, belief, etc.) [a remark that did not *warrant* such anger] **3** to give formal assurance, or guarantee, to (someone) or for (something); specif., *a)* to guarantee the quality, quantity, condition, etc. of (goods) to the purchaser *b)* to guarantee to (the purchaser) that goods sold are as represented *c)* to guarantee to (the purchaser) the title of goods purchased; assure of indemnification against loss *d)* *Law* to guarantee the title of granted property to (the grantee) **4** [Colloq.] to state with confidence; affirm emphatically [I *warrant* they'll be late] —*SYN.* ASSERT —**war'rant·a·ble** *adj.*

29A1 VOCABULARY

From the context of "Magnetism," explain the meaning of each of the vocabulary words shown in boldface below.

1. *From paragraph 2:* Similarly, if two south-seeking ends were brought together, they would also **repel** each other.

   _____

   _____

2. *From paragraph 3:* He **theorized** that the earth is a huge magnet with its magnetic north pole near its geographic north pole.

   _____

   _____

3. *From paragraph 4:* This matter of attraction and **repulsion** between poles of magnets **warrants** close attention.

   _____

   _____

   _____

   _____

4. *From paragraph 6:* Of course, the pattern formed in Figure 3–1 represents the magnetic field only in the **horizontal** plane.

   _____

   _____

5. *From paragraph 7:* Think of the magnetic lines of force as a bundle of stretched rubber bands that tend to shorten and, **simultaneously,** push each other away sidewise.

   _____

   _____

6. *From paragraph 8:* We **arbitrarily** assume the force acts from the north pole to the south pole.

   _____

   _____

7. *From paragraph 8:* If, **theoretically,** we were to place a small north pole in the magnetic field. . . .

   _____

   _____

Name   Date

8. *From paragraph 11:* A nineteenth-century German physicist, Wilhelm Weber, proposed a molecular **theory** of magnetism.

_____

_____

9. *From paragraph 12:* . . . by any means that will disarrange the orderly **array** of molecules.

_____

_____

10. *From paragraph 14:* A nonmagnetic substance . . . resists all attempts to **align** its molecules in orderly fashion.

_____

_____

29A2   SPECIAL TEXTBOOK VOCABULARY

Key terms in this textbook selection are explained as they are discussed. Referring to "Magnetism," fill in the blanks.

1. A _____ can attract pieces of iron.

2. _____ is known as the ability of a magnet to attract

   _____ substances.

3. In a _____ , a magnet swings freely.

4. In a free-swinging magnet, the end that points in the general

   direction of the north is called its _____

   _____ , and the end that points in the general direction of the south is called its

   _____ .

5. Because the magnet is so important to navigators at sea, it is known

   as a _____ , which means "stone that leads."

6. Magnets attract at their _____ and not in between.

7. Between the two opposite poles of a magnet, there is an invisible

   _____ _____ which is also known as a

   _____ _____ .

Name   Date

8. Surrounding a magnet are _____ _____

   _____ along all three dimensions. These lines are called

   _____ _____ . Opposition to these lines is

   called _____ .

9. _____ _____ is created when an unmagne-
   tized material is made magnetic by being placed in the magnetic
   field of a magnet. Some materials lose their magnetism as soon as
   they are removed from the magnetic field; they are called

   _____ _____ . Other materials keep their
   magnetism even after they are removed from the magnetic field; they

   are called _____ _____ .

10. When all the molecules in a substance are lined up north and south,
    the substance cannot be made into a stronger magnet than it is, and it

    is therefore said to be _____ .

29B   CENTRAL THEME AND MAIN IDEAS
Choose the best answer.

_____ 1. The textbook selection called "Magnetism" could be part of a
          course in
          a. biology.
          b. physical science.
          c. algebra.
          d. chemistry.

_____ 2. The main purpose of paragraphs 1 through 3 is to give
          a. historical information.
          b. mathematical information.
          c. navigational information.
          d. geographical information.

_____ 3. The main purpose of paragraphs 4 through 10 is to describe
          a. attraction and repulsion.
          b. iron filings.
          c. lines of force.
          d. the magnetic field.

Name   Date

_____ 4. *Read Section A again.* A magnetic field is
   a. the force between the two opposite ends of a magnet.
   b. a pattern created by iron filings.
   c. the attraction between iron and glass.
   d. created by a stretched rubber band.

_____ 5. The main purpose of paragraphs 11 through 15 is to explain
   a. the process of magnetizing unmagnetized substances.
   b. the molecular theory of magnetism.
   c. nineteenth-century physics.
   d. magnetic molecule alignment to the point of saturation.

_____ 6. *Read Section B again.* The central idea of the "molecular theory of magnetism" is that
   a. molecules are arranged helter-skelter in a magnet.
   b. iron can be easily magnetized.
   c. every molecule in a magnet is a tiny magnet.
   d. in magnetized iron all north poles of the molecules are facing one way, and all south poles are facing the other way.

29C MAJOR DETAILS
Decide whether each detail is true (T), false (F), or not discussed (ND).

_____ 1. According to Figure 3–1, iron filings can be used to demonstrate a magnetic field.

_____ 2. According to Figure 3–2, lines of force in a magnetic field move toward like poles (north to north; south to south).

_____ 3. The concept of magnetic flux is important for our understanding of how electricity works.

_____ 4. According to Figure 3–4, a magnetic field flows so much more easily through iron that the force will actually go out of its way to flow through iron when it is available.

_____ 5. According to Figure 3–5, molecules in magnetized material are arranged in a helter-skelter fashion.

_____ 6. According to Figure 3–6, two magnets are formed when a magnet is broken in two because the break is very clean.

_____ 7. According to Figure 3–7, magnets are like humans in that they like to stroke each other.

29D INFERENCES

Choose the best answer.

_____ 1. *Read paragraph 1 again.* In ancient times, why did the people think that the "heavy black stone" was "mysterious"?
   a. It was very difficult to find and, therefore, was rare.
   b. The source of its force was unseen and, therefore, seemed magical.
   c. It was important in ceremonies of religious worship.
   d. It was pleasant to stroke even though it was a hard stone.

_____ 2. "Magnetism" is part of Chapter 3 in a textbook called *Electricity for Technicians.* Read paragraphs 5 and 7 again. The authors refer to Chapter 1 for all of these reasons *except*
   a. to indicate what the authors assume the students know as the authors move ahead.
   b. to tell students where to look to refresh their memories.
   c. to give students practice in looking up information.
   d. to avoid having to repeat information already given.

29E CRITICAL READING: THE WRITER'S CRAFT

Choose the best answer.

_____ 1. Why do the authors begin by giving the historical development of our knowledge about magnetism?
   a. to show that the evolution of scientific knowledge is a slow, painstaking process
   b. to give the reader confidence that the authors know their subject well
   c. to illustrate the contribution made to science by the ancient Chinese
   d. to be able to include the contribution that William Gilbert made to science

_____ 2. The authors show certain words in boldface print. They do this for all of these reasons *except*
   a. to indicate that these words relate to the figures in the text.
   b. to indicate that these are the key words in the text.
   c. to help students who might want to outline the text.
   d. to aid students who preview their material before going back and reading it slowly and carefully.

Name   Date

29F INFORMED OPINION

1. When you first learn about a technical subject, do you prefer to read about it or to see it demonstrated, if at all possible? Using specific examples, explain your answer.

2. The material explained in "Magnetism" falls into the category of "pure science." Why is it important for all educated people, even if they are not science majors, to understand the basics of "pure science"? Use specific examples to support your answer.

How Did You Do?   29 Magnetism

SKILL (number of items)	Number Correct		Points for Each		Score
Vocabulary (10)	_____	×	2	=	_____
Special Textbook Vocabulary* (17)	_____	×	2	=	_____
Central Theme and Main Ideas (6)	_____	×	4	=	_____
Major Details (7)	_____	×	2	=	_____
Inferences (2)	_____	×	2	=	_____
Critical Reading: The Writer's Craft (2)	_____	×	1	=	_____

(Possible Total: 100) *Total* _____

SPEED

Reading Time: _____ Reading Rate (page 352): _____ Words Per Minute

*Questions 2, 4, and 7 call for two separate answers each. Questions 8 and 9 call for three separate answers each. In computing your score, count each separate answer toward your number correct.

Name   Date

The Chaser*

John Collier

(1) Alan Austen, as nervous as a kitten, went up certain dark and creaky stairs in the neighborhood of Pell Street, and peered about for a long time on the dim landing before he found the name he wanted written obscurely on one of the doors.

(2) He pushed open this door, as he had been told to do, and found himself in a tiny room, which contained no furniture but a plain kitchen table, a rocking-chair, and an ordinary chair. On one of the dirty buff-colored walls were a couple of shelves, containing in all perhaps a dozen bottles and jars.

(3) An old man sat in the rocking-chair, reading a newspaper. Alan, without a word, handed him the card he had been given. "Sit down, Mr. Austen," said the man very politely. "I am glad to make your acquaintance."

(4) "Is it true," asked Alan, "that you have a certain mixture that has—er—quite extraordinary effects?"

(5) "My dear sir," replied the old man, "my stock in trade is not very large—I don't deal in laxatives and teething mixtures—but such as it is, it is varied. I think nothing I sell has effects which could be precisely described as ordinary."

(6) "Well, the fact is—" began Alan.

(7) "Here, for example," interrupted the old man, reaching for a bottle from the shelf. "Here is a liquid as colorless as water, almost tasteless, quite imperceptible in coffee, milk, wine, or any other beverage. It is also quite imperceptible to any known method of autopsy."

(8) "Do you mean it is a poison?" cried Alan, very much horrified.

(9) "Call it a glove-cleaner if you like," said the old man indifferently. "Maybe it will clean gloves. I have never tried. One might call it a life-cleaner. Lives need cleaning sometimes."

(10) "I want nothing of that sort," said Alan.

(11) "Probably it is just as well," said the old man. "Do you know the price of this? For one teaspoonful, which is sufficient, I ask five thousand dollars. Never less. Not a penny less."

(12) "I hope all your mixtures are not as expensive," said Alan apprehensively.

(13) "Oh dear, no," said the old man. "It would be no good charging that sort of price for a love potion, for example. Young people who need a love potion very seldom have five thousand dollars. Otherwise they would not need a love potion."

(14) "I am glad to hear that," said Alan.

(15) "I look at it like this," said the old man. "Please a customer with one article, and he will come back when he needs another. Even if it is more costly. He will save up for it, if necessary."

(16) "So," said Alan, "you really do sell love potions?"

(17) "If I did not sell love potions," said the old man, reaching for another bottle, "I should not have mentioned the other matter to you. It is only when one is in a position to oblige that one can afford to be so confidential."

(18) "And these potions," said Alan. "They are not just—just—er—"

(19) "Oh, no," said the old man. "Their effects are permanent, and extend far beyond casual impulse. But they include it. Bountifully, insistently. Everlastingly."

(20) "Dear me!" said Alan, attempting a look of scientific detachment. "How very interesting!"

(21) "But consider the spiritual side," said the old man.

(22) "I do, indeed," said Alan.

(23) "For indifference," said the old man, "they substitute devotion. For scorn, adoration. Give one tiny measure of this to the young lady—its flavor is imperceptible in orange juice, soup, or cocktails—and however gay and giddy she is, she will change altogether. She will want nothing but solitude, and you."

(24) "I can hardly believe it" said Alan. "She is so fond of parties."

(25) "She will not like them any more," said the old man. "She will be afraid of the pretty girls you may meet."

(26) "She will actually be jealous?" cried Alan in rapture. "Of me?"

(27) "Yes, she will want to be everything to you."

(28) "She is, already. Only she doesn't care about it."

(29) "She will, when she has taken this. She will care intensely. You will be her sole interest in life."

(30) "Wonderful!" cried Alan.

(31) "She will want to know all you do," said the old man. "All that has happened to you during the day. Every word of it. She will want to know what you are thinking about, why you smile suddenly, why you are looking sad."

(32) "That is love!" cried Alan.

(33) "Yes," said the old man. "How carefully she will look after you! She will never allow you to be tired, to sit in a draught, to neglect your food. If you are an hour late, she will be terrified. She will think you are killed, or that some siren has caught you."

(34) "I can hardly imagine Diana like that!" cried Alan, overwhelmed with joy.

(35) "You will not have to use your imagination," said the old man. "And, by the way, since there are always sirens, if by any chance you should, later on, slip a little, you need not worry. She will forgive you, in the end. She will be terribly hurt, of course, but she will forgive you—in the end."

(36) "That will not happen," said Alan fervently.

(37) "Of course not," said the old man. "But, if it did, you need not worry.

She would never divorce you. Oh, no! And, of course, she herself will never give you the least, the very least, grounds for—uneasiness."

(38) "And how much," said Alan, "is this wonderful mixture?"

(39) "It is not as dear," said the old man, "as the glove-cleaner, or life-cleaner, as I sometimes call it. No. That is five thousand dollars, never a penny less. One has to be older than you are, to indulge in that sort of thing. One has to save up for it."

(40) "But the love potion?" said Alan.

(41) "Oh, that," said the old man, opening the drawer in the kitchen table, and taking out a tiny, rather dirty-looking phial. "That is just a dollar."

(42) "I can't tell you how grateful I am," said Alan, watching him fill it.

(43) "I like to oblige," said the old man. "Then customers come back, later in life, when they are rather better off, and want more expensive things. Here you are. You will find it very effective."

(44) "Thank you again," said Alan. "Good-by."

(45) "Au revoir," said the old man.

1075 words

Here are some of the more difficult words in "The Chaser."

au revoir (paragraph 45)	**au re·voir** (ō'rə vwär') ⟦Fr < *au*, to the + *revoir*, seeing again < L *revidere*, see again < *re-*, again + *videre*, see: see VISION⟧ until we meet again; goodbye: implies temporary parting
autopsy (paragraph 7)	**au·top·sy** (ô'täp'sē, ôt'əp sē) *n.*, *pl.* **-sies** ⟦ML & Gr *autopsia*, a seeing with one's own eyes < Gr *autos*, self + *opsis*, a sight < *ōps*, EYE⟧ **1** an examination and dissection of a dead body to discover the cause of death, damage done by disease, etc.; post-mortem **2** a detailed critical analysis of a book, play, etc., or of some event —*vt.* **-sied**, **-sy·ing** to examine (a body) in this manner
bountifully (paragraph 19)	**boun·ti·ful** (-tə fəl) *adj.* **1** giving freely and graciously; generous **2** provided in abundance; plentiful —**boun'ti·ful·ly** *adv.* —**boun'ti·ful·ness** *n.*
chaser (title)	**chas·er**[1] (chā'sər) *n.* ⟦CHASE[1] + -ER⟧ **1** a person or thing that chases or hunts; pursuer **2** a gun formerly placed on the stern (**stern chaser**) or bow (**bow chaser**) of a ship, used during pursuit by or of another ship ☆**3** a mild drink, as water, ginger ale, or beer, taken after or with whiskey, rum, etc.
confidential (paragraph 17)	**con·fi·den·tial** (kän'fə den'shəl) *adj.* **1** told in confidence; imparted in secret **2** of or showing trust in another; confiding **3** entrusted with private or secret matters [a *confidential* agent] —*SYN.* FAMILIAR —**con'fi·den'ti·al'i·ty** (-shē al'ə tē) or **con'fi·den'tial·ness** *n.* —**con'fi·den'tial·ly** *adv.*

Vocabulary List

draught
(paragraph 33)

draught (draft, dräft) *n.*, *vt.*, *adj.* now chiefly Brit. sp. of DRAFT

draft (draft, dräft) *n.* 〖ME *draught*, a drawing, pulling, stroke < base of OE *dragan*, DRAW〗 **1** *a*) a drawing or pulling, as of a vehicle or load *b*) the thing, quantity, or load pulled **2** *a*) a drawing in of a fish net *b*) the amount of fish caught in one draw **3** *a*) a taking of liquid into the mouth; drinking *b*) the amount taken at one drink **4** *a*) a portion of liquid for drinking; specif., a dose of medicine *b*) [Colloq.] a portion of beer, ale, etc. drawn from a cask **5** *a*) a drawing into the lungs, as of air or tobacco smoke *b*) the amount of air, smoke, etc., drawn in **6** a rough or preliminary sketch of a piece of writing **7** a plan or drawing of a work to be done **8** a current of air, as in a room, heating system, etc. **9** a device for regulating the current of air in a heating system **10** a written order issued by one person, bank, firm, etc., directing the payment of money to another; check **11** a demand or drain made on something **12** *a*) the choos-

imperceptible
(paragraph 7)

im·per·cep·ti·ble (im'pər sep'tə bəl) *adj.* 〖Fr < ML *imperceptibilis*: see IN-² & PERCEPTIBLE〗 not plain or distinct to the senses or the mind; esp., so slight, gradual, subtle, etc. as not to be easily perceived —im'per·cep·ti·bil'i·ty *n.* —im'per·cep'ti·bly *adv.*

obscurely
(paragraph 1)

ob·scure (əb skyoor', äb-) *adj.* 〖OFr *obscur* < L *obscurus*, lit., covered over < *ob-* (see OB-) + IE *skuro-* < base *(s)keu-*, to cover, conceal > HIDE¹, SKY〗 **1** lacking light; dim; dark; murky [the *obscure* night] **2** not easily perceived; specif., *a*) not clear or distinct; faint or undefined [an *obscure* figure or sound] *b*) not easily understood; vague; cryptic; ambiguous [an *obscure* explanation] *c*) in an inconspicuous position; hidden [an *obscure* village] **3** not well-known; not famous [an *obscure* scientist] **4** *Phonet.* pronounced as (ə) or (i) because it is not stressed; reduced; neutral: said of a vowel —*vt.* -scured', -scur'ing 〖L *obscurare* < the *adj.*〗 **1** to make obscure; specif., *a*) to darken; make dim *b*) to conceal from view; hide *c*) to make less conspicuous; overshadow [a success that *obscured* earlier failures] *d*) to make less intelligible; confuse [testimony that *obscures* the issue] **2** *Phonet.* to make (a vowel) obscure —*n.* [Rare] OBSCURITY —ob·scure'ly *adv.* —ob·scure'ness *n.*
SYN.—**obscure** applies to that which is perceived with difficulty either because it is concealed or veiled or because of obtuseness in the perceiver [their reasons remain *obscure*]; **vague** implies such a lack of precision or exactness as to be indistinct or unclear [a *vague* idea]; **enigmatic** and **cryptic** are used of that which baffles or perplexes, the latter word implying deliberate intention to puzzle [*enigmatic* behavior, a *cryptic* warning]; **ambiguous** applies to that which puzzles because it allows of more than one interpretation [an *ambiguous* title]; **equivocal** is used of something ambiguous that is deliberately used to mislead or confuse [an *equivocal* answer] —**ANT. clear, distinct, obvious**

phial
(paragraph 41)

phi·al (fī'əl) *n.* 〖ME *fiole* < OFr < Prov *fiola* < ML < L *phiala* < Gr *phialē*, broad, shallow drinking vessel〗 a small glass bottle; vial

rapture
(paragraph 26)

rap·ture (rap'chər) *n.* 〖ML *raptura*: see RAPT & -URE〗 **1** the state of being carried away with joy, love, etc.; ecstasy **2** an expression of great joy, pleasure, etc. **3** a carrying away or being carried away in body or spirit: now rare except in theological usage —*vt.* -tured, -tur·ing [Now Rare] to enrapture; fill with ecstasy —**SYN.** ECSTASY —**the rapture** [*often* **the R-**] in some Christian theologies, the bodily ascent into heaven just before Armageddon of those who are saved (see SAVE¹, *vt.* 7) —rap'tur·ous *adj.* —rap'tur·ous·ly *adv.*

siren
(paragraph 33)

si·ren (sī'rən) *n.* 〖ME *syrene* < OFr < LL *Sirena*, for L *Siren* < Gr *Seirēn* < ? *seira*, cord, rope (hence, orig. ? one who snares, entangles) < IE base *twer-*, to grasp〗 **1** *Gr. & Rom. Myth.* any of several sea nymphs, represented as part bird and part woman, who lure sailors to their death on rocky coasts by seductive singing **2** a woman who uses her sexual attractiveness to entice or allure men; a woman who is considered seductive **3** *a*) an acoustical device in which steam or air is driven against a rotating, perforated disk so as to produce sound; specif., such a device producing a loud, often wailing sound, used esp. as a warning signal *b*) an electronic device that produces a similar sound **4** any of a family (Sirenidae) of slender, eel-shaped salamanders without hind legs; esp., the mud eel —*adj.* of or like a siren; dangerously seductive [*siren* songs]

30A VOCABULARY

Using the vocabulary words for this selection, fill in the crossword puzzle.

ACROSS

1. an expression of great happiness and delight
3. told or divulged in secret
5. one drink
8. insignificant or not easily perceived
9. not distinctly or clearly
11. The _____ following his beer was simply a glass of water.

DOWN

2. given freely or graciously; abundantly
4. a small glass container
6. An _____ determined the cause of death.
7. the French expression for "farewell"
10. an enchantress or seductive woman

30B CENTRAL THEME AND MAIN IDEAS

Choose the best answer.

_____ 1. The central theme of "The Chaser" is that
   a. an old man sells only two types of potions.
   b. love potions may cause distinct personality changes.
   c. "true love" may also have a dark side.
   d. there are inherent dangers involved in using potions.

_____ 2. What is the underlying assumption of "The Chaser"?
   a. The effects of love potions are permanent and irreversible.
   b. People will resort to even more drastic measures to get out of a love relationship than to get into one.
   c. Young people have less money than older people to buy what they want.
   d. A love potion may cause unfounded jealousy and unsolicited adoration.

_____ 3. The unexpected main idea of paragraph 9 is
   a. the old man's cavalier attitude toward poisoning people.
   b. the unusual names the old man chooses to disguise his poison.
   c. the philosophy that lives sometimes need to be "cleaned out."
   d. that of the two potions the old man sells, one is poison.

_____ 4. The main idea of paragraph 43 is that
   a. the old man is pleased that his customers are happy with his potions.
   b. the old man is aware that he has a tremendous service to offer his customers.
   c. the old man is willing to give his customers what they think they want now, knowing that they'll be back later for a more expensive deadly potion.
   d. the old man is anxious for his customers to return so that he can sell them more of the same potion at a higher price.

30C MAJOR DETAILS

Decide whether each detail is MAJOR or MINOR.

_____ 1. The potion seller's tiny room was at the top of the dark and creaky stairs.

_____ 2. There was a tremendous difference in price between the two potions.

Name   Date

_____ 3. The old man refers to his poison as a "life-cleaner."

_____ 4. The effects of the love potion are permanent.

_____ 5. Diana will forgive Alan's indiscretions, "in the end."

_____ 6. The potion seller is an old man.

_____ 7. The old man sells only two potions.

_____ 8. The potion seller's room contained only the barest of furniture and shelves hung on dirty buff-colored walls.

_____ 9. The poison is imperceptible in any autopsy.

_____ 10. Of his two potions, the old man tells Alan about his "life-cleaner" first.

_____ 11. Diana is very fond of parties.

_____ 12. The old man hints that all customers who purchase the first potion return later in life for the second.

30D   INFERENCES
Choose the best answer.

_____ 1. The word "chaser" in the title refers to
   a. the orange juice, soup, or cocktail mixed with the love potion.
   b. the poisonous potion taken to counter the effects of the love potion.
   c. a mild drink taken following a stronger alcoholic drink.
   d. the love potion purchased from the old man by young customers.

_____ 2. *Read paragraph 13 again.* The author implies that
   a. young people seldom have a need for love potions.
   b. young people in love are generally poor but are mostly indifferent to their poverty.
   c. anyone with $5000 will have no need for a love potion because his money will make him desirable.
   d. expensive love potions would be wasted on young people, who rarely have much money anyway.

_____ 3. *Read paragraph 17 again.* The old man is implying that

    a. his potions can be very expensive and are a well-kept secret.

    b. if he did not sell love potions, Alan would not have come to see him in the first place.

    c. if he did not sell love potions, he would have no need to sell another potion to "cure" the effects of love potions.

    d. admitting to the need for a love potion is a very confidential matter.

_____ 4. *Read paragraphs 31–33 again.* Alan's exclamation of "That is love!" is answered with a flat "Yes." The old man's lack of enthusiasm is likely the result of

    a. his awareness that this love will eventually become clinging, possessive, and destructive.

    b. his belief that true love does not truly exist.

    c. his own experience with a past tragic love.

    d. his lack of interest in Alan's reaction to the potion's effects.

_____ 5. *Read paragraph 35 again.* The author uses the expression "in the end" twice, each time following the statement "She will forgive you." He does this because

    a. Alan must be persistent in asking Diana for forgiveness.

    b. Alan should be careful of these sirens and try to avoid them.

    c. Diana is likely to play the martyr first and inflict some guilt before granting forgiveness.

    d. Diana will be slow to forgive because of her confusion over Alan's unfaithfulness.

_____ 6. *Read paragraph 39 again.* The author implies that

    a. the poison is more expensive because people want it more badly than the love potion.

    b. young people have not lived long enough to have the problems associated with needing a "life-cleaner."

    c. older people can expect to need "life-cleaners" and are more willing to use poisons.

    d. the poison is a precious commodity because of its inherently expensive ingredients.

Name   Date

_____ 7. *Read paragraphs 44–45 again.* While Alan bids the old man "good-by," the old man responds with "au revoir," implying that

   a. he is more sophisticated than Alan.

   b. he has not been in the United States long enough yet to converse easily in English.

   c. Alan is also fluent in French and understands the exchange.

   d. the parting is not permanent and Alan will be coming back.

30E   CRITICAL READING: THE WRITER'S CRAFT

Choose the best answer.

_____ 1. Irony in fiction is the use of scenes, actions, or dialogue that convey to the reader the opposite of their literal meaning, often for comic effect. Which of the following statements by the two characters in "The Chaser" is best described as *ironic* in its effect?

   a. (paragraph 3) "Is it true," asked Alan, "that you have a certain mixture that has—er—quite extraordinary effects?"

   b. (paragraph 11) "For one teaspoonful, which is sufficient, I ask five thousand dollars. Never less. Not a penny less."

   c. (paragraph 32) "That is love!" cried Alan.

   d. (paragraph 39) "One has to be older than you are, to indulge in that sort of thing."

_____ 2. Fiction writers often create dramatic effects by giving the reader crucial pieces of knowledge that are not available to characters in the story. By the end of "The Chaser," who is meant to understand the full significance of the second potion?

   a. the old man and the reader

   b. Alan and the reader

   c. the old man, Alan, and the reader

   d. the reader and the author

30F   INFORMED OPINION

1. In your opinion, is it reasonable for the "glove-cleaner" to be so much more expensive than the love potion? Why or why not?

2. *(Read paragraphs 23–37 again.)* Would you purchase a love potion that promises the same permanent effects as those described in "The Chaser"? Using specific examples, explain your answer.

Name   Date

How Did You Do?   **30** The Chaser

SKILL *(number of items)*	Number Correct		Points for Each		Score
Vocabulary (11)	_____	×	2	=	_____
Central Theme and Main Ideas (4)	_____	×	5	=	_____
Major Details (12)	_____	×	2	=	_____
Inferences (7)	_____	×	4	=	_____
Critical Reading: The Writer's Craft (2)	_____	×	3	=	_____

(Possible Total: 100) *Total* _____

SPEED

Reading Time: _____ Reading Rate (page 352): _____ Words Per Minute

Name   Date

Writing:
Expressing Yourself

What are *your* ideas on the subjects that you have read about in Part 5 of this book? Now is *your* chance to express your ideas in writing.

Below are some topics to write about. You are not expected to write on all of them, of course. Just select what appeals to you. Or, feel free to make up your own topics. Most important, try to find a subject that moves you to want to express yourself in writing.

All the topics below relate in some way to the reading selections in Part 5 of this book. Some of the topics have been touched on already in the opening section of Part 5, "Thinking: Getting Started," page 265, or in the Informed Opinion questions that followed each of the reading selections in Part 5. Others of these topics are introduced here for the first time.

The topics below give you a choice among various kinds of writing. You can write a **narrative** that will tell your reader an interesting story. You can write a **description** that will give your reader a vivid picture of the image you have in mind. You can write a **report** that will give your reader important information about a subject, process, or event. You can write an **argument** to try to persuade your reader to agree with you. Differences among these kinds of writing are not always clear-cut, and so you can feel free to use any **combination** that works for you. As you write, see if you can make use of the new vocabulary words that you have been studying in Part 5.

IDEAS FOR PARAGRAPHS

1. Why do you think food additives are so common today? What steps, if any, can you take to avoid consuming the additives?

2. Do you prefer to ignore information about illnesses and health hazards? Using specific examples, explain your attitude.

3. Why after someone dies do people usually forget the person's faults and think mainly of the person's virtues? Using specific experiences you have heard about, explain why this is so.

4. Write a letter to a younger brother or sister who has just had his or her first experience confronting prejudice (of any of the many kinds discussed in "On Campus: New Interest in Prejudice").

5. What makes learning a foreign language difficult? Is it the vocabulary? The grammar? The pronunciation? Be specific as to your reasons.

6. Assume a friend came to you for advice about marriage. Would you encourage the person to marry for love, money, or some other factor? Explain fully.

IDEAS FOR ESSAYS

1. Make up a story about a typical hypochondriac. Describe the hypochondriac's habits and fears while you tell your story.

2. How can parents best help their children learn to believe in themselves—even, for example, in the face of prejudice? Be as specific as possible about what the children should be prepared to face in life; suggest steps parents might take to raise their children to have inner strength.

3. What is your opinion of preferential hiring practices to make up for past discrimination? Using specific examples, fully support your point of view.

4. What is the role of the lungs in the circulatory system? Write a research report about the lungs and their importance to the circulatory system of the human body.

5. Do you enjoy studying science? Being as specific as possible, explain your answer.

6. According to the Bible in Genesis 11, "the whole world had one language and a common speech." Noah's descendants, who were nomadic, decided to settle in Babylonia and build a tower in a city to honor themselves. God saw what they had accomplished by using one language and realized that nothing they would plan to do would be impossible for them, so their language was confused so that they would not understand each other. If the entire world spoke the same language today, how would it affect people? You might consider some of the following implications: social, educational, political, or economic.

7. Do you believe in the manufacture and distribution of a medication, such as a love potion, to affect a person's feelings for someone else? This medication might be prescribed in a situation of unrequited love. What are the advantages of such a medication? Are there any dangers? To whom would this be prescribed? Be specific with your paragraph development to persuade the reader to consider your point of view.

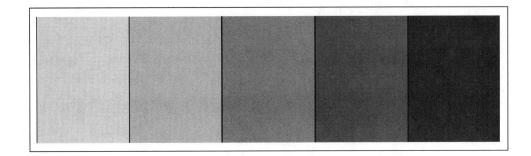

APPENDIX

Progress Charts

Total Score on Skill-Building Exercises Graph*

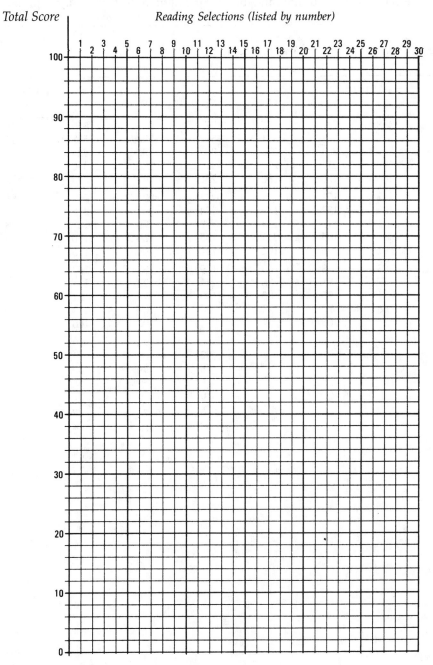

*Put a dot at your total score from the "How Did You Do?" box at the end of each reading selection. Connect the dots with a line to see your progress.

Reading Rate Table

Here's how to figure your reading rate. Time your reading to the nearest half-minute. Next, locate your time in the left column of this table. Then, stay on the line that lists your time and move to the right to locate the column for the

Time in half-minute intervals	Reading Selections (listed by number)						
	PART 1						PART 2
	1	2	3	4	5	6	7
1	498	527	557	775	800	850	215
1.5	332	351	371	517	533	567	143
2	249	264	279	388	400	425	108
2.5	199	211	223	310	320	340	86
3	166	176	186	258	267	283	72
3.5	142	151	159	221	229	243	61
4	125	132	139	194	200	213	54
4.5	111	117	124	172	178	189	48
5	97	105	111	155	160	170	
5.5	91	96	101	141	145	155	
6	83	88	93	129	133	162	
6.5	77	81	86	111	123	131	
7	71	75	80	103	114	121	
7.5	66	70	74	97	107	113	
8		66	70	91	100	106	
8.5			66	86	94	100	
9				82	89	94	
9.5				78	84	89	
10				74	80	85	
10.5				70	76	81	
11				67	73	77	
11.5				65	70	74	
12					67	71	
12.5						68	
13						65	
13.5							
14							
14.5							
15							
15.5							
16							
16.5							
17							
17.5							
18							
18.5							
19							
19.5							
20							

particular reading selection you have just completed. The number you meet is the number of words per minute you read in that reading selection. **This number of words per minute is your reading rate.** (If you would like to chart your reading rate, you can use the graph on page 353.)

Time in half-minute intervals	Reading Selections (listed by number)						
					PART 3		
	8	9	10	11	12	13	14
1	640	894	1004	1107	643	694	950
1.5	427	596	669	738	429	463	633
2	320	447	502	554	322	342	475
2.5	256	358	402	443	257	278	388
3	213	298	335	369	214	231	317
3.5	183	255	287	316	184	198	271
4	160	224	251	277	161	174	238
4.5	142	199	223	246	143	154	211
5	128	179	201	221	129	139	190
5.5	116	163	183	201	117	126	173
6	107	149	167	185	107	116	158
6.5	98	138	155	170	99	107	146
7	91	128	143	158	92	99	136
7.5	85	119	134	148	86	93	127
8	80	112	126	138	80	87	119
8.5	75	105	118	130	76	82	112
9	67	99	112	123	71	77	106
9.5	64	94	106	117	68	73	100
10		89	100	111	64	69	95
10.5		85	96	105	61	66	90
11		81	91	101		63	86
11.5		78	87	96			83
12		75	84	92			79
12.5		72	80	89			76
13		69	77	85			73
13.5			74	82			70
14			72	79			68
14.5			69	76			66
15			67	74			63
15.5			65	71			61
16				69			
16.5				67			
17				65			
17.5							
18							
18.5							
19							
19.5							
20							

Time in half-minute intervals	Reading Selections (listed by number)						
				PART 4			
	15	16	17	18	19	20	21
1	1197	1491	1792	409	792	697	907
1.5	798	994	1195	327	528	465	605
2	599	746	896	245	396	349	454
2.5	479	596	717	196	317	279	363
3	399	497	597	163	264	232	302
3.5	342	426	512	140	226	199	259
4	299	373	448	123	198	174	227
4.5	266	331	398	109	176	155	202
5	239	298	358	98	158	139	181
5.5	218	271	326	89	144	127	165
6	200	249	299	82	132	116	151
6.5	184	229	276	73	122	107	140
7	171	213	256	70	113	100	130
7.5	160	199	239	65	106	93	121
8	150	186	224		99	87	113
8.5	141	175	211		93	82	107
9	133	166	199		88	77	101
9.5	126	157	189		83	73	95
10	120	149	179		79	70	91
10.5	114	142	171		75	66	86
11	109	136	163		72	63	82
11.5	104	130	156		69	61	79
12	100	124	149				76
12.5	96	119	143				73
13	92	115	138				70
13.5	89	110	133				67
14	86	107	128				
14.5	83	103	124				
15	80	99	120				
15.5	77	96	116				
16	75	93	112				
16.5	73	90	109				
17	70	88	105				
17.5	68	85	102				
18	67	83	100				
18.5		81	97				
19		78	94				
19.5		76	92				
20		75	90				

Time in half-minute intervals	Reading Selections (listed by number)						
				PART 5			
	22	23	24	25	26	27	28
1	1611	1680	520	630	1396	1530	1734
1.5	1074	1120	346	420	931	1020	1156
2	806	840	260	315	698	765	867
2.5	644	672	208	252	558	612	694
3	537	560	173	210	465	510	578
3.5	460	480	149	180	399	437	495
4	403	420	130	158	349	383	434
4.5	358	373	116	140	310	340	385
5	322	336	104	126	279	306	347
5.5	292	305	95	115	254	278	315
6	269	280	87	105	233	255	289
6.5	248	258	80	97	215	235	267
7	230	240	74	90	199	219	248
7.5	215	224	69	84	186	204	231
8	201	210	65	79	175	191	217
8.5	190	198	61	74	164	180	204
9	179	187		70	155	170	193
9.5	170	177		66	147	161	183
10	161	168		63	140	153	173
10.5	153	160		60	133	146	165
11	146	153			127	139	158
11.5	140	146			121	133	151
12	134	140			116	128	145
12.5	129	134			112	122	139
13	124	129			107	118	133
13.5	119	124			103	113	128
14	115	120			100	109	124
14.5	111	116			96	106	120
15	107	112			93	102	116
15.5	103	108			90	99	112
16	101	105			87	96	108
16.5	98	102			85	93	105
17	95	99			82	90	102
17.5	92	96			80	87	99
18	90	93			78	85	96
18.5	87	91			75	83	94
19	85	88			73	81	91
19.5	83	86			72	78	89
20	81	84			70	77	87

Time in half-minute intervals	Reading Selections (listed by number)		continued	29	30
	29	30			
1	1890	1075	16	118	67
1.5	1260	717	16.5	115	65
2	945	538	17	111	63
2.5	756	430	17.5	108	61
3	630	358	18	105	60
3.5	540	307	18.5	102	
4	473	269	19	99	
4.5	420	239	19.5	97	
5	378	215	20	95	
5.5	344	196	20.5	92	
6	315	179	21	90	
6.5	291	165	21.5	88	
7	270	154	22	86	
7.5	252	143	22.5	84	
8	236	134	23	82	
8.5	222	127	23.5	80	
9	210	119	24	79	
9.5	199	113	24.5	77	
10	189	108	25	76	
10.5	180	102			
11	172	98			
11.5	164	94			
12	158	90			
12.5	151	86			
13	145	83			
13.5	140	80			
14	135	77			
14.5	130	74			
15	126	72			
15.5	122	69			

(continued at upper right)

Reading Rate Graph*

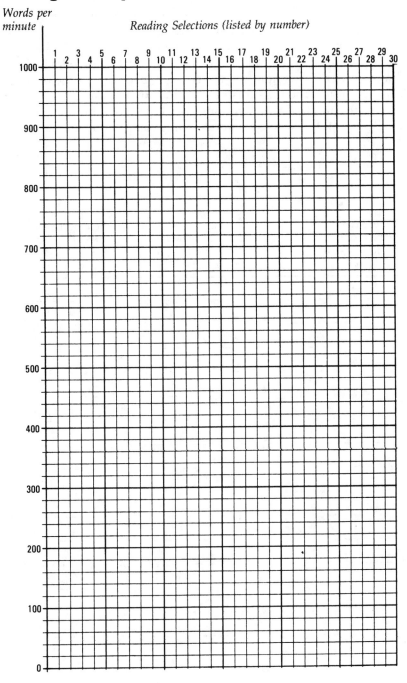

*Put a dot at the number of words you read per minute (reading rate) for each reading selection. Use pages 348–352 to compute your rate. Connect the dots with a line to see your progress.

353

Reading Competence Table

Here's how to figure one of the ways to measure your reading competence. For each reading selection you complete, fill in the number of words per minute you read (Reading Rate Table: pages 348–352). Next, fill in the total score you earned on the skill-building exercises following the reading selection. Then multiply the two numbers, taking the decimal points into consideration as explained in the column headings below. **The product of this multiplication, rounded off, is your reading competence score.** (If you would like to chart your reading competence, use the graph on page 356.)

Reading selection (listed by number)	Words per minute (Reading Rate: pages 348–352)		Total score on exercises (If less than 100, fill in to the right of the decimal point.)		Reading competence score (Round off to the nearest whole number.)
1	_____	×	_____ . _____	=	_____
2	_____	×	_____ . _____	=	_____
3	_____	×	_____ . _____	=	_____
4	_____	×	_____ . _____	=	_____
5	_____	×	_____ . _____	=	_____
6	_____	×	_____ . _____	=	_____
7	_____	×	_____ . _____	=	_____
8	_____	×	_____ . _____	=	_____
9	_____	×	_____ . _____	=	_____
10	_____	×	_____ . _____	=	_____
11	_____	×	_____ . _____	=	_____
12	_____	×	_____ . _____	=	_____
13	_____	×	_____ . _____	=	_____
14	_____	×	_____ . _____	=	_____
15	_____	×	_____ . _____	=	_____

Reading selection (listed by number)	Words per minute (Reading Rate: pages 348–352)	×	Total score on exercises (If less than 100, fill in to the right of the decimal point.)	=	Reading competence score (Round off to the nearest whole number.)
16	_____	×	_____ . _____	=	_____
17	_____	×	_____ . _____	=	_____
18	_____	x	_____ . _____	=	_____
19	_____	×	_____ . _____	=	_____
20	_____	×	_____ . _____	=	_____
21	_____	×	_____ . _____	=	_____
22	_____	×	_____ . _____	=	_____
23	_____	×	_____ . _____	=	_____
24	_____	×	_____ . _____	=	_____
25	_____	×	_____ . _____	=	_____
26	_____	×	_____ . _____	=	_____
27	_____	×	_____ . _____	=	_____
28	_____	×	_____ . _____	=	_____
29	_____	×	_____ . _____	=	_____
30	_____	×	_____ . _____	=	_____

Reading Competence Graph*

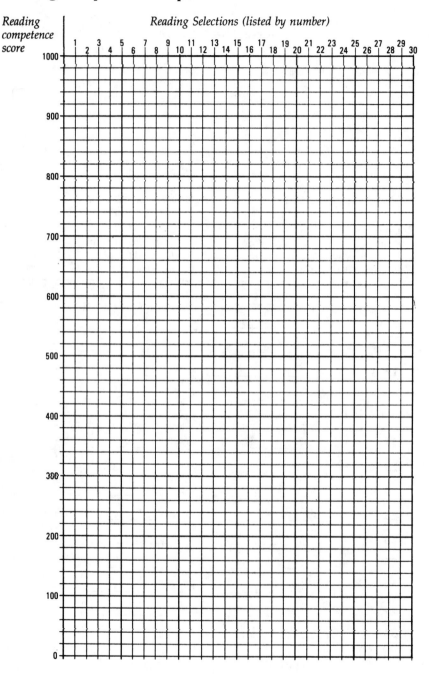

*Put a dot at the number of words you read per minute (reading rate) for each reading selection. Use pages 354–355 to compute your rate. Connect the dots with a line to see your progress.

Guide to Dictionary Use[*]

With a good dictionary you can do much more than check the meanings or spellings of words. The Third College Edition of *Webster's New World Dictionary of American English,* the dictionary featured in *Structured Reading,* is an example of a very good dictionary. The entries are clearly written, and they offer many resources of particular interest to students. This Guide to Dictionary Use can help you understand the basic features of the entries so that you can use them fully. For more details, consult the explanatory material in the front and back sections of the dictionary itself.

Main Entry Word

The technical term for each word included in the dictionary is **main entry word.** When you look up a word, the list of main entry words is what you consult. Listed alphabetically, they stand out because they are set in dark print (called *boldface*). If more than one spelling is given for a main entry word, the first spelling shown is the one more widely used. **Dictionary Entry** is the technical term for all the information given for a main entry word. This textbook contains 321 entries from the Third College Edition of *Webster's New World Dictionary of American English.*

Definitions

If a word has more than one meaning, its various **definitions** are listed in numerical order. The original meaning of the word (which is sometimes—but not always—outdated) comes first. The most recent meaning of the word appears last. There is one exception, however. Sometimes added information is given at the end of the entry, after the most recent meaning. You can tell this is happening because labels precede such information. The labels are explained here in the sections "Parts of Speech Labels," "Usage Labels," and "Field of Study Labels." For example, in the entry for *asset* (used with Selection 2 in this textbook), definition 2 gives the most recent meaning. The third definition gives a special meaning, as the label *Accounting* indicates; and the fourth definition gives a special meaning for the *Law.* Then verb definitions and a noun form are given.

---

*Based on "Guide to the Use of the Dictionary," *Webster's New World Dictionary of American English,* Third College Edition.

as·set (as'et) *n.* [earlier *assets* < Anglo-Fr *assetz* (in legal phrase *aver assetz*, to have enough) < OFr *assez*, enough < VL *ad satis*, sufficient < L *ad*, to + *satis*, enough: see SAD] **1** anything owned that has exchange value **2** a valuable or desirable thing to have [charm is your chief *asset*] **3** [*pl.*] *Accounting* all the entries on a balance sheet showing the entire resources of a person or business, tangible and intangible, including accounts and notes receivable, cash, inventory, equipment, real estate, goodwill, etc. **4** [*pl.*] *Law a)* property, as of a business, a bankrupt, etc. *b)* the property of a deceased person available to his or her estate for the payment of debts and legacies

To decide which meaning of a word fits your situation, review the context in which the word is being used. The context can tell you whether an older or recent meaning of a word applies. Ways to figure out a word's meaning from its context are discussed in this textbook on pages 6–8.

Americanisms

An open star (☆) in front of a word tells you that the word is an **Americanism.** This means that word has its origins in the United States. The entry for *chute* (used with Selection 2 in this textbook) shows that all the definitions are Americanisms.

☆**chute**[1] (sho͞ot) *n.* [Fr, a fall < OFr *cheute* < *cheoite*, pp. of *cheoir*, to fall < L *cadere*: see CASE[1]] **1** *a)* a waterfall *b)* rapids in a river **2** an inclined or vertical trough or passage down which something may be slid or dropped [laundry *chute*] **3** a steep slide, as for tobogganing

Syllabification

For pronunciation and writing purposes, words can be divided into syllables, unless a word is a single sound, such as *kiss.* Each syllable represents a single sound. **Syllabification,** also called **word division,** becomes important for writers when space runs out at the end of a line and a word has to be carried over onto the next line. Words can be divided only at breaks for syllables.

Two ways of showing a word's syllables are used in *Webster's New World Dictionary of American English.* A heavy dot centered between letters indicates a good place to divide a word. A hairline (|) between letters indicates that although a syllable is present, you should try to avoid dividing the word there if at all possible. The hairline indicator of an undesirable place for word division is a new feature that is of particular use to student writers. The entry for *deteriorate* (used with Selection 2 in this textbook) illustrates the two symbols for word division.

de·te·ri·o·rate (dē tir′ē ə rāt′, di-) *vt., vi.* -rat′ed, -rat′ing [< LL *deterioratus*, pp. of *deteriorare*, to make worse < L *deterior*, worse, inferior < *deter*, below < de-, from + -ter, compar. suffix] to make or become worse; lower in quality or value; depreciate —de·te′ri·o·ra′tion *n.*

Pronunciation

The symbols in parentheses immediately following the main entry word show **pronunciation.** You can figure out the sound indicated by each symbol by consulting a dictionary's key to pronunciation. A shortened version of the key appears at the bottom of every right-hand page in *Webster's New World Dictionary of American English.* A more complete "Key to Pronunciation" from that dictionary is shown here. To get used to the key, practice first with entries for words familiar to you. Then once you are comfortable with the key, practice with entries for words that are new to you. You can practice with the sample entries in this guide and with the entries with each selection in this textbook.

PRONUNCIATION KEY

Symbol	Key Words	Symbol	Key Words
a	asp, fat, parrot	b	bed, fable, dub, ebb
ā	ape, date, play, break, fail	d	dip, beadle, had, dodder
ä	ah, car, father, cot	f	fall, after, off, phone
		g	get, haggle, dog
e	elf, ten, berry	h	he, ahead, hotel
ē	even, meet, money, flea, grieve	j	joy, agile, badge
		k	kill, tackle, bake, coat, quick
i	is, hit, mirror	l	let, yellow, ball
ī	ice, bite, high, sky	m	met, camel, trim, summer
		n	not, flannel, ton
ō	open, tone, go, boat	p	put, apple, tap
ô	all, horn, law, oar	r	red, port, dear, purr
oo	look, pull, moor, wolf	s	sell, castle, pass, nice
o͞o	ooze, tool, crew, rule	t	top, cattle, hat
yo͞o	use, cute, few	v	vat, hovel, have
yoo	cure, globule	w	will, always, swear, quick
oi	oil, point, toy	y	yet, onion, yard
ou	out, crowd, plow	z	zebra, dazzle, haze, rise
u	up, cut, color, flood	ch	chin, catcher, arch, nature
ur	urn, fur, deter, irk	sh	she, cushion, dash, machine
		th	thin, nothing, truth
ə	a in ago	*th*	then, father, lathe
	e in agent	zh	azure, leisure, beige
	i in sanity	ŋ	ring, anger, drink
	o in comply	′	[indicates that a following l
	u in focus		or n is a syllabic consonant,
ər	perhaps, murder		as in *cattle* (kat′'l), *Latin*
			(lat′'n); see full explanation
			on p. xiii]

359

Parts of Speech Labels

The **part of speech** of a word is given after the pronunciation information in an entry. Parts of speech are abbreviated in the dictionary. They are shown in dark italic print. Here are major abbreviations and their meanings.

n.	noun
n. pl.	plural noun
vt.	transitive verb
vi.	intransitive verb
v. aux.	auxiliary verb
adj.	adjective
adv.	adverb
prep.	preposition
conj.	conjunction
pron.	pronoun
interj.	interjection

Some words are used as more than one part of speech. If you are unsure which part of speech applies to the word in the context you are dealing with, look at all the definitions in an entry to see what works for your context. To help you work with context, use the information about using context to figure out a word's meaning, discussed in this textbook on pages 6–8.

The entry for *harvest* (used with Selection 2 in this textbook) illustrates that one word can have multiple meanings. The meanings differ according to the part of speech (noun, verb) and within a part of speech.

> **har·vest** (här′vist) *n.* ⟦ME *hervest* < OE *hærfest*, akin to Ger *herbst* (OHG *herbist*) < IE *(s)kerp-* < base *(s)ker-*, to cut > SHEAR, SHORT, L *caro*, flesh, *cernere* & Gr *krinein*, to separate, *karpos*, fruit: basic sense "time of cutting"⟧ **1** the time of the year when matured grain, fruit, vegetables, etc. are reaped and gathered in **2** a season's yield of grain, fruit, etc. when gathered in or ready to be gathered in; crop **3** the gathering in of a crop **4** the outcome or consequence of any effort or series of events [the tyrant's *harvest* of hate] —*vt., vi.* **1** to gather in (a crop, etc.) **2** to gather the crop from (a field) **3** to catch, shoot, trap, etc. (fish or game), often for commercial purposes **4** to get (something) as the result of an action or effort —**har′vest·a·ble** *adj.*

Inflected Forms

The form of a word when it becomes plural or changes its tense is called its **inflected form**. Information about inflected forms comes after the part of speech label. Inflected forms are shown in small dark print.

Information for *heresy* (used with Selection 15 in this textbook) illustrates the plural noun form of the word; information for *repel* (used with Selection 29 in this textbook) illustrates letter doubling when -*ed* is added and when -*ing* is added.

> **her·e|sy** (her'i sē) *n., pl.* -|sies ⟦ME *heresie* < OFr < L *haeresis*, school of thought, sect, in LL(Ec), heresy < Gr *hairesis*, a taking, selection, school, sect, in LGr(Ec), heresy < *hairein*, to take ⟧ **1** *a)* a religious belief opposed to the orthodox doctrines of a church; esp., such a belief specifically denounced by the church *b)* the rejection of a belief that is a part of church dogma **2** any opinion (in philosophy, politics, etc.) opposed to official or established views or doctrines **3** the holding of any such belief or opinion

> **re·pel** (ri pel') *vt.* -**pelled'**, -**pel'ling** ⟦ME *repellen* < L *repellere*, to drive back < *re-*, back + *pellere*, to drive: see PULSE¹ ⟧ **1** to drive or force back; hold or ward off *[to repel* an attack*]* **2** to refuse to accept, agree to, or submit to; reject *[to repel* advances*]* **3** to refuse to accept (a person); spurn *[to repel* a suitor*]* **4** *a)* to cause distaste or dislike in; disgust *[the odor repelled* him*]* *b)* to cause (insects, etc.) to react by staying away **5** *a)* to be resistant to, or present an opposing force to *[a coating that repels* moisture*]* *b)* to fail to mix with or adhere to *[water repels* oil*]* —*vi.* **1** to drive off, or offer an opposing force to, something **2** to cause distaste, dislike, or aversion —**re·pel'ler** *n.*

Word History

For most main entry words, the **word history,** known as **etymology,** is given in brackets after the main entry word, its pronunciation, and any inflected forms. Abbreviations and symbols present information and origins, and words from languages other than English appear in italics. Etymology often suggests a word's flavor. The sample dictionary entries in this Guide use these frequently used symbols and abbreviations.

<	derived from
+	plus
Fr	French (MFr = Middle French; OFr = Old French)
Gr	Greek
IE	Indo-European
ME	Middle English
L	Latin (LL = Late Latin; VL = Vulgar Latin)
OE	Old English

Usage Labels

The customary way words are used—their **usage**—depends on many factors. The two major influences are the formality of occasion on which the word is used and the location where the word is used. Whenever the usage of a word differs from common practice in communication, the dictionary entry gives usage information. Usage labels, abbreviated, are shown in brackets immediately following a main entry word or one of its numbered definitions. Here are the most frequently seen usage labels and their meanings.

[Brit.]	*British:* Commonly accepted meaning in British English
[colloq.]	*colloquial:* used in conversation and informal writing
[dial.]	*dialect:* used in certain geographical areas of the United States
[obs.]	*obsolete:* no longer in use
[poet.]	*poetic:* used chiefly in poetry or for poetic meaning
[slang]	*slang:* highly informal and generally considered not standard; acceptable when used for effect or mood to convey a highly informal context.

The entry for *menace* (used with Selection 23 in this textbook) indicates that it is a colloquial word (definition 3). The entry for *deadeye* (used with Selection 5 in this textbook) says that its most recent meaning (definition 2) is a slang word.

men·ace (men′əs) *n.* ⟦OFr < L *minacia* < *minax* (gen. *minacis*), projecting, threatening < *minari*, to threaten < *minae*, threats, orig. projecting points of walls < IE base **men-*, to project > Cornish *meneth*, mountain⟧ **1** a threat or the act of threatening **2** anything threatening harm or evil **3** [Colloq.] a person who is a nuisance — *vt.*, *vi.* **-aced**, **-ac·ing** to threaten or be a danger (to) —**SYN.** THREATEN —**men′ac·ing·ly** *adv.*

dead·eye (-ī′) *n.* **1** a round, flat block of wood with three holes in it for a lanyard, used in pairs on a sailing ship to hold the shrouds and stays taut **2** [Slang] an accurate marksman

Field of Study Labels

Many words have special meanings when used in the context of various **fields of study**. For example, the entry for *derivative* (used in Selection 5 of this textbook) starts with its usual meanings as an adjective and then as a noun. Then come abbreviated labels that indicate special meanings from various fields of study: chemistry, linguistics, and math.

de·riv·a·tive (də riv′ə tiv) *adj.* ⟦ME *derivatif* < LL *derivativus* < L *derivatus*, pp. of *derivare*: see fol.⟧ **1** derived **2** using or taken from other sources; not original **3** of derivation —*n.* **1** something derived **2** *Chem.* a substance derived from, or of such composition and properties that it may be considered as derived from, another substance by chemical change, esp. by the substitution of one or more elements or radicals **3** *Linguis.* a word formed from another or others by derivation **4** *Math.* the limiting value of a rate of change of a function with respect to a variable; the instantaneous rate of change, or slope, of a function (Ex.: the derivative of y with respect to x, often written dy/dx, is 3 when $y = 3x$) —**de·riv′a·tive·ly** *adv.*

Synonyms

When a word has **synonyms** whose meanings cannot be interchanged with the main entry word, the dictionary entry ends with the symbol **SYN.** followed by a word in small capital letters. When you look up that word, you will find at the end of its entry a **synonymy**—a list of synonyms with definitions that explain slight differences in meaning among the words listed. The synonymy is signalled by the symbol *SYN.-*. To decide which synonym fits your situation, review the context in which the word appears and match it to the definitions in the synonym. The entry for *adapt* (used with Selection 12 in this textbook) offers a synonymy of four words.

a|dapt (ə dapt′) *vt.* ⟦Fr *adapter* < L *adaptare* < *ad-*, to + *aptare*, to fit: see APT⟧ **1** to make fit or suitable by changing or adjusting **2** to adjust (oneself) to new or changed circumstances —*vi.* to adjust oneself
SYN.—**adapt** implies a modifying so as to suit new conditions and suggests flexibility [to *adapt* oneself to a new environment]; **adjust** describes the bringing of things into proper relation through the use of skill or judgment [to *adjust* brakes, to *adjust* differences]; **accommodate** implies a subordinating of one thing to the needs of another and suggests concession or compromise [he *accommodated* his walk to the halting steps of his friend]; **conform** means to bring or act in harmony with some standard pattern, principle, etc. [to *conform* to specifications]

The following two pages show a sample dictionary page, with labels for your reference.

American place name with etymology

Idiomatic phrase

Synonymy

Part-of-speech labels

Derived entries

Americanism

Inflected forms

Usage label

Field label

Biographical entry

Cerritos / cevitamic açid 230

Cer·ri·tos (se rē'tōs) [Sp, little hills] city in SW Calif.: suburb of Los Angeles: pop. 53,000

Cerro de Pasco (ser'ō dä päs'kō) mining town in the mountains of WC Peru: alt. *c.* 14,000 ft. (4,250 m): pop. 72,000

cert 1 certificate 2 certified

cer·tain (surt'n) *adj.* [ME & OFr < VL *certanus* < L *certus*, determined, fixed, orig. pp. of *cernere*, to distinguish, decide, orig., to sift, separate: see HARVEST] 1 fixed, settled, or determined 2 sure (to happen, etc.); inevitable 3 not to be doubted; unquestionable /certain evidence/ 4 not failing; reliable; dependable /a certain cure/ 5 controlled; unerring /his certain aim/ 6 without any doubt; assured; sure; positive /certain of his innocence/ 7 not named or described, though definite and perhaps known /a certain person/ 8 some, but not very much; appreciable /to a certain extent/ —*pron.* [with pl. v.] a certain indefinite number; certain ones (of) —SYN. SURE —**for certain** as a certainty; without doubt

cer·tain·ly (-lē) *adv.* beyond a doubt; surely

cer·tain·ty (-tē) *n.* [ME *certeinte* < OFr *certaineté*] 1 the quality, state, or fact of being certain 2 *pl.* **-ties** anything certain; definite act —**of a certainty** [Archaic] without a doubt; certainly

SYN.—**certainty** suggests a firm, settled belief or positiveness in the truth of something; **certitude** is sometimes distinguished from the preceding as implying an absence of objective proof, hence suggesting unassailable blind faith; **assurance** suggests confidence, but not necessarily positiveness, usually in something that is yet to happen /I have assurance of his continuing support/; **conviction** suggests a being convinced because of satisfactory reasons or proof and sometimes implies earlier doubt —ANT. doubt, skepticism

cer·tes (sur'tēz') *adv.* [ME & OFr < VL *certas*, for L *certo*, surely < *certus*: see CERTAIN] [Archaic] certainly; verily

cer·ti·fi·able (surt'ə fī'ə bəl) *adj.* that can be certified —**cer'ti·fi'ably** (-blē) *adv.*

cer·tifi·cate (sər tif'i kit; *for v.*, -kāt') *n.* [ME & OFr *certificat* < ML *certificatum* < LL *certificatus*, pp. of *certificare*, CERTIFY] a written or printed statement by which a fact is formally or officially certified or attested; specif., *a)* a document certifying that one has met specified requirements, as for teaching *b)* a document certifying ownership, a promise to pay, etc. —*vt.* **-cat·ed, -cat·ing** to attest or authorize by a certificate: issue a certificate to —**cer·tif'i·ca·tor** *n.* —**cer·tif'i·ca·to·ry** (-kə tôr'ē) *adj.*

certificate of deposit a certificate issued by a bank or a savings and loan association acknowledging the receipt of a specified sum of money in a special kind of time deposit drawing interest and requiring written notice for withdrawal

certificate of incorporation a legal document stating the name and purpose of a proposed corporation, the names of its incorporators, its stock structure, etc.

certificate of origin a certificate submitted by an exporter to those countries requiring it, listing goods to be imported and stating their place of origin

cer·ti·fi·ca·tion (surt'ə fi kā'shən) *n.* [Fr] 1 a certifying or being certified 2 a certified statement

cer·ti·fied (surt'ə fīd') *adj.* 1 vouched for; guaranteed 2 having, or attested to by, a certificate

☆certified check a check for which a bank has guaranteed payment, certifying there is enough money on deposit to cover the check

☆certified mail 1 a postal service for recording the mailing and delivery of a piece of first-class mail 2 mail recorded by this service: it is not insurable

☆certified public accountant a public accountant certified by a State examining board as having met the requirements of State law

cer·tify (surt'ə fī') *vt.* **-fied', -fy'ing** [ME certifien < OFr certifier < LL certificare < L certus, CERTAIN + -FY] 1 to declare (a thing) true, accurate, certain, etc. by formal statement, often in writing; verify; attest 2 to declare officially insane and committable to a mental institution ☆3 to guarantee the quality or worth of (a check, document, etc.); vouch for 4 to issue a certificate or license to 5 [Archaic] to assure; make certain —*vi.* to testify (to) —SYN. APPROVE —**cer·ti·fi'er** *n.*

cer·ti·o·rari (sur'shē ə rer'ē) *n.* [ME < LL, lit., to be made more certain: a word in the writ] [Law] a discretionary writ from a higher court to a lower one, or to a board or official with some judicial power, requesting the record of a case for review

cer·ti·tude (surt'ə tōōd', -tyōōd') *n.* [OFr < LL(Ec) certitudo < L certus, CERTAIN] 1 a feeling of absolute sureness or conviction 2 sureness; inevitability —SYN. CERTAINTY

ce·ru·lean (sə rōō'lē ən) *adj.* [L caeruleus; prob. < caelulum, dim. of caelum, heaven: for IE base see CESIUM] sky-blue; azure

ce·ru·men (sə rōō'mən) *n.* [< L cera, wax; sp. infl. by ALBUMEN] EARWAX —**ce·ru'mi·nous** (-mə nəs) *adj.*

ce·ruse (sir'ōōs, sə rōōs') *n.* [OFr < L cerussa < ? Gr *kēroessa*, waxlike < kēros, wax] 1 WHITE LEAD 2 a former cosmetic containing white lead

ce·rus·site (sir'ə sīt', sə rus'īt') *n.* [< L cerussa (see prec.) + -ITE[1]] native lead carbonate, PbCO₃, widely distributed in crystalline or massive form

Cer·van·tes (Sə·al·ve·dra) (ther vän'tes sä'ä ved'rä; E sər van'tēz'), **Mi·guel de** (mē gel' *the*) 1547-1616; Sp. novelist, poet, & playwright; author of *Don Quixote*

cer·ve·lat (ser və lä', -lät') *n.* [Fr] a dry, smoked sausage of beef and pork Also sp. **cer·ve·las'** (-lä')

cer·vi·cal (sur'vi kəl) *adj.* [< L cervix (gen. cervicis), the neck + -AL] *Anat.* of the neck or cervix

cer·vi·ces (sər vī′sēz′, sur′və-) *n. alt. pl. of* CERVIX

cer·vi·ci·tis (sur′və sīt′is) *n.* [*see* -ITIS] inflammation of the cervix of the uterus

cervico- (sur′vi kō′, -kə) [< L *cervix*, neck] *combining form* cervical [*cervicitis*] Also, before a vowel, **cer′vic-**

cer·vid (sur′vid′) *adj.* [< ModL *Cervidae*, name of the family (< L *cervus*, stag, deer < IE **kerewos*, horned, a horned animal < base **ker-*, HORN) + -ID] of the deer family

Cer·vin (mōn ser van′), **Mont** *Fr. name of the* MATTERHORN

cer·vine (sur′vīn′, -vin) *adj.* [L *cervinus* < *cervus*: see CERVID] of or like a deer ——————— Main entry word

cer·vix (sur′viks) *n., pl.* **cer·vi·ces** (sər vī′sēz, sur′və-) or **-vixes** [L, the neck] 1 the neck, esp. the back of the neck 2 a necklike part, as of the uterus or urinary bladder

Ce·sar·e·an or **Ce·sar·i·an** (sə zer′ē ən) *adj., n.* CAESAREAN

ce·si·um (sē′zē əm) *n.* [ModL, orig. neut. of L *caesius*, bluish-gray (< IE base **(s)k̑ai-*, bright > -HOOD): so named (1860) by Robert Wilhelm BUNSEN because of the blue line seen in the spectroscope] ——————— Etymology
a soft, silver-white, ductile, metallic chemical element, the most electropositive of all the elements: it ignites in air, reacts vigorously with water, and is used in photoelectric cells: symbol, Cs; at. wt., 132.905; at. no., 55; sp. gr., 1.892; melt. pt., 28.64°C; boil. pt., 670°C: a radioactive isotope (**cesium-137**) with a half-life of 30.17 years is a fission product and is used in cancer research, radiation therapy, etc.

České Bu·dě·jo·vice (ches′ke bōō′de yō′vit sə) city in SW Czechoslovakia, on the Vltava River: pop. 93,000

Česko·slo·ven·sko (ches′kô slô ven′skô) Czech name of CZECHOSLOVAKIA

ces·pi·tose (ses′pə tōs′) *adj.* [ModL < L *caespes*, turf, grassy field + -OSE²] growing in dense, matlike clumps without creeping stems, as moss, grass, etc.

cess (ses) *n.* [prob. < ASSESS] in Ireland, an assessment; tax: now used only in **bad cess to bad luck** ——————— Pronunciation

ces·sa·tion (se sā′shən) *n.* [L *cessatio* < pp. of *cessare*, CEASE] a ceasing or stopping, either forever or for some time

ces·sion (sesh′ən) *n.* [OFr < L *cessio* < *cessus*, pp. of *cedere*, to yield: see CEDE] a ceding or giving up (of rights, property, territory, etc.) to another

ces·sion·ary (sesh′ə ner′ē) *n., pl.* **-aries** *Law* ASSIGNEE

cess·pit (ses′pit′) *n.* [< fol. + PIT²] a pit for garbage, excrement, etc.

cess·pool (-pōōl′) *n.* [< ? It *cesso*, privy < L *secessus*, place of retirement (in LL, privy, drain): see SECEDE] 1 a deep hole or pit in the ground, usually covered, to receive drainage or sewage from the sinks, toilets, etc. of a house 2 a center of moral filth and corruption ——————— Definitions

ces·ta (ses′tə) *n.* [Sp, basket < L *cista*: see CHEST] in jai alai, the narrow, curved, basketlike racket strapped to the forearm, in which the ball is caught and hurled against a wall

c'est la vie (se lä vē′) [Fr] that's life; such is life

ces·tode (ses′tōd′) *n.* [CEST(US)¹ + -ODE²] any of a class (Cestoda) ——————— Scientific name
of parasitic flatworms, with a ribbonlike body and no intestinal canal; tapeworm —*adj.* of such a worm

ces·toid (-toid′) *adj.* ribbonlike, as a tapeworm

ces·tus¹ (-təs) *n.* [L < Gr *kestos*, a girdle; akin to *kentein*, to stitch: see CENTER] in ancient times, a woman's belt or girdle

ces·tus² (-təs) *n.* [L *caestus* < *caedere*, to strike, cut down: see -CIDE] a contrivance of leather straps, often weighted with metal, worn on the hand by boxers in ancient Rome

ce·su·ra (si zyoor′ə, -zhoor′ə) *n., pl.* **-ras** or **-rae** (-ē) CAESURA

CETA Comprehensive Employment and Training Act

ce·ta·cean (sə tā′shən) *n.* [< ModL < L *cetus*, large sea animal, whale < Gr *kētos* + -ACE(A) + -AN] in some systems of classification, any of an order (Cetacea) of nearly hairless, fishlike water —————— Illustration with caption
mammals, lacking external hind limbs, but having paddlelike forelimbs, including whales, porpoises, and dolphins —*adj.* of the cetaceans Also **ce·ta′ceous** (-shəs)

ce·tane (sē′tān′) *n.* [< L *cetus* (see prec.) + -ANE] a colorless, liquid alkane, C₁₆H₃₄, found in petroleum and, sometimes, in vegetable matter, and used to test fuel oils

cetane number a number that increases with higher quality, representing the ignition properties of diesel engine fuel oils: it is determined by the percentage of cetane that must be mixed with a standard liquid to match the fuel oil's performance in a standard test engine: see OCTANE NUMBER

ce·te·ris pa·ri·bus (set′ər is par′ə bəs) [L, other things being equal] ——————— Foreign phrase
all else remaining the same

ce·tol·o·gy (sə täl′ə jē) *n.* [< L *cetus*, whale (see CETACEAN) + -OLOGY] the branch of zoology that deals with whales —**ce·to·log·i·cal** (sēt′ə läj′i kəl) *adj.* —**ce·tol′o·gist** *n.*

Ce·tus (sēt′əs) [L, whale] an equatorial constellation near Pisces

Ceu·ta (syoot′ə; Sp thā′ōō tä′) Spanish seaport in NW Africa, opposite Gibraltar: an enclave in Morocco: pop. 71,000

Cé·vennes (sā ven′) mountain range in S France, west of the Rhone: highest peak, 5,755 ft. (1,754 m)

ce·vi·che (sə vē′chä′, -chē′) *n.* [Sp SEVICHE ——————— Cross-reference

ce·vi·tam·ic acid (sē′vi tam′ik, -vi-) [< C + VITAM(IN) + -IC] ASCORBIC ACID

CESTUS

365

Vocabulary Index

General Index